CRASH OF THE TITANS

CRASH OF THE TITANS

THE EARLY YEARS
OF THE NEW YORK JETS
AND THE AFL

WILLIAM J. RYCZEK

Kingston, New York • • New York, New York

SPORTS ILLUSTRATED® and *Total*/SPORTS ILLUSTRATED are trademarks of Time Inc. Used under license.

For information about permission to reproduce selections from this book, please write to:

Total Sports Publishing
100 Enterprise Drive
Kingston, NY 12401

Back Cover Photo by Milardo Studio, provided courtesy of Liberty Bank
Cover Design: Todd Radom
Interior Design: Ann Sullivan

Library of Congress Cataloging-in-Publication Data
Ryczek, William J., 1953-
  Crash of the Titans : the early years of the New York Jets and the AFL
/ by William J. Ryczek.
    p. cm.
Includes index.
  ISBN 1-892129-27-2
  1. New York Titans (Football team)—History. 2. New York Jets
(Football team)—History. 3. American Football League—History. I.
Title.
  GV956.N42 R93 2000
  796.332'64'097471—dc21

                                            00-009464

Printed in Canada

www.totalsportspublishing.com

To Michael and Anne

TABLE OF CONTENTS

	Introduction	xv
1.	The Show Must Go On	1
2.	Oil and Rejection	7
3.	Congratulations	26
4.	Slingin' Sammy	35
5.	They'll Never Find Enough Good Players	51
6.	The Game They Played	68
7.	The First Training Camp	84
8.	We Don't Tote No Coloreds	103
9.	Opening Day	111
10.	The Punts	124
11.	Tragedy in Houston	135
12.	Out of Quarterbacks	145
13.	My Kingdom for a New Stadium	166
14.	A War at War Memorial	185
15.	7-7 Again	204
16.	Harry, Ernie, Joe, and the Bulldog	222
17.	The Quarterbacks	234
18.	Stroudsburg	247
19.	Victory in Oakland, Defeat in San Diego, and Where Is Samuel Gompers When You Really Need Him	257
20.	Out of Quarterbacks Again	270
21.	Crash of the Titans	281
	Epilogue: The Players	303
	Epilogue: The Team	320
Index		329

ACKNOWLEDGEMENTS

Crash of the Titans consists of two principal elements: first, the factual history of the New York Titans and the first three years of the American Football League, and second, the personal reminiscences of the players who were part of that experience. Gathering background information involved the assistance of many people, including John Hogrogian, an attorney, football historian, and Titan expert, especially regarding the legal aspects of the franchise. John was generous in sharing his own work, particularly in regard to the Polo Grounds and the eventual bankruptcy of the team. He also reviewed the manuscript in great detail and offered a number of helpful suggestions. Bob Golon kindly provided me with his research on the planning and construction of Shea Stadium.

As always, the staff of the hometown Wallingford Public Library was most accommodating, as were the employees of the New York Public Library, where I did much of my research. A number of librarians throughout the country were extremely helpful in tracking down obscure bits of data. The staff at the East Stroudsburg University library provided information about the Titans' final training camp, as did former ESU coach Jack Gregory and athletic director John Eilers.

The second part of my research involved interviewing a number of former players, principally by phone. While so many players were helpful, I owe a very special debt to Roger Ellis, who for three years played on the line for the Titans. During my first conversation with Roger, he stated defiantly, "If you're just going to make fun of us, I'm not going to help you." The last thing he wanted was another comical look at the Titans' descent into bankruptcy. Once Roger became convinced that I wanted to take a serious, balanced look at the team's history, there was no greater ally. He assisted me in locating other players and provided vast amounts of material from his collection and insightful feedback on the initial drafts. I cannot thank him enough for his support and friendship.

Big Jack Klotz, the offensive tackle, was another valuable aide. He, like Roger, provided me with items from his personal collection, read the manuscript, and introduced me to a number of former Titans and Jets.

Harold "Hayseed" Stephens, former quarterback and current minister and oilman, also dug up material from his scrapbook, mainly about his days playing for Sammy Baugh at Hardin-Simmons.

Don Maynard, whose memory for detail is astounding, gave two marvelous interviews and generously agreed to write the foreword. Another Hall of Famer, Sammy Baugh, spent an hour on the phone with this little-known writer and shared the experiences of 30 years of professional football in his unaffected, down-to-earth manner.

Bob Mischak and Larry McHugh, former Titan linemen, read a draft of the manuscript and offered helpful suggestions. Although both men have been successful in their post-football lives, they took time from their busy schedules to assist me.

Bill Wallace and Gordon White, former sports reporters for the *New York Herald Tribune* and *The New York Times*, shared their memories in lengthy interviews.

The following people also provided interviews. All were friendly, cooperative and, above all, fascinating subjects. I thank them and marvel at their memories, which remained intact over a span of nearly 40 years.

Don Allard	Pete Hart	Joe Pagliei
Ed Bell	Charley Hennigan	Dainard Paulson
Dewey Bohling	Mike Holovak	Art Powell
Gino Cappelletti	Mike Hudock	Bob Reifsnyder
Buddy Cockrell	Proverb Jacobs	Perry Richards
Thurlow Cooper	Dick Jamieson	Joe Ryan
Ted Daffer	Curley Johnson	Tom Rychlec
Cotton Davidson	Fred Julian	Rick Sapienza
Roger Donahoo	Karl Kaimer	Bob Scrabis
Al Dorow	Alex Kroll	Hank Soar
Dick Felt	Dean Look	Ed Sprinkle
Jerry Fields	Chris McMullan	George Strugar
Sid Gillman	Bob Marques	LaVerne Torczon
Larry Grantham	Blanche Martin	Frank Tripucka
Johnny Green	Bill Mathis	Mel West
Lee Grosscup	Nick Mumley	
Dick Guesman	Dr. James Nicholas	

I want to thank Ken Ilchuck of the New York Jets Public Relations Department. He and his staff were extremely helpful, allowed me access to their files, made many, many photocopies, and made me feel welcome at the Jets' alumni gatherings.

My friend Fred Dauch was kind enough to read the entire manuscript and honest enough to offer criticism where warranted. He improved the final product.

For my introduction to Total Sports Publishing, I am indebted to David Pietrusza. In March 1999, I attended the Casey Awards banquet in Cincinnati, a gourmet feast of hot dogs and peanuts established to honor the author of the best baseball book of the year. Dave won the award for *Judge and Jury*, his excellent biography of Kenesaw Mountain Landis. I placed second for my own work, *When Johnny Came Sliding Home*, but received a consolation prize much greater than I deserved. During the ride to the airport, which was fortunately extended by several wrong turns, Dave and I had a chance to discuss our writing projects. When I mentioned the Titans book, he said his associates at Total Sports might be interested. They were, and I thank David for the introduction. As he assured me, the staff at Total Sports has been more than supportive and helpful.

Finally, I would like to thank my wife, Susan, whose degree in English literature proved invaluable at those times I found myself befuddled by matters of style, grammar, and particularly punctuation. She read large portions of the manuscript, made many helpful suggestions, and listened patiently to numerous monologues about a football team she had never heard of.

Thank you all.

WILLIAM J. RYCZEK

FOREWORD

I still remember getting the call from the legendary Sammy Baugh, my fellow Texan and fellow Hall of Famer. There was a new professional football league starting and Sammy wanted me to come to New York, where he had been hired as the head coach of the New York Titans.

Now I had played in New York for the NFL Giants, and Sammy Baugh was one of my all-time heroes. When they talk about the greatest player ever, I'd argue for Baugh against any of them. Name me one other football player who could lead the league in passing and in interceptions besides being the best punter in NFL history.

Sammy had seen me play in college for Texas Western when he was coaching at Hardin-Simmons University in our home state. He chose me to play in the 1957 Blue-Gray Game (I was co-MVP), and the Giants selected me in the '58 draft. Ken Ford, the quarterback from Hardin-Simmons, with whom I shared the Blue-Gray award, was on the Giants' taxi squad that year, along with another young quarterback, Jack Kemp.

In 1958 we nearly went all the way, falling to the Colts in the famous overtime championship, which is often cited as the greatest game ever and also as the game that established pro football on TV. Soon there was obviously more fan interest—and more talent—than a 12-team league could provide. In 1959 Allie Sherman, the Giants' head coach, cut me, and I went to play for the Hamilton Tiger-Cats of the CFL. I played for Hamilton without an option because I believed that the AFL would be founded and would be a success.

The AFL was the brainchild of wealthy men—like Barron Hilton, Bud Adams, and Lamar Hunt—who were willing to spend the money to bring football to cities that were clamoring for teams but were locked out by the NFL. Lamar Hunt had a dream to own a football team, and when the NFL wouldn't let him, he started his own league. That's what America is all about, isn't it? Competition and free enterprise.

The Titans didn't have the financial clout that the oil barons' teams had. We couldn't even be sure of getting paid sometimes, but we were happy to play, just for "the love of the game." Of course, history shows how we persevered and how the Jets' Super Bowl III victory proved that the quality of AFL football was second to none. *Crash of the Titans* recaptures the struggle of an era that I am proud to have played a part in.

DON MAYNARD

INTRODUCTION

Why a book on the New York Titans? That was a question I often heard in the course of this project. Who, many asked, would care to read about a professional football franchise that lasted only three years, never achieved a record better than .500, and collapsed in bankruptcy almost 40 years ago? In March 1998, I interviewed Bill Wallace, retired reporter for *The New York Times*. As we began our conversation, he, like many others, questioned the wisdom of writing about the Titans. We then spent an animated hour discussing the likes of Harry Wismer, Sammy Baugh, Sid Youngelman, and the numerous tribulations of the team. "You know," Wallace said as we finished, "you just might have something here."

While recounting his experiences covering the team, Bill realized something I had discovered much earlier. A new football league, a wildly eccentric owner, and a coach who was a football legend are the beginnings of a great story. Add some unique personalities like Don Maynard, Lee Grosscup, Hubert Bobo, and Alex Kroll, and the result is a fascinating tale of a team often in chaos, a franchise that eventually self-destructed. The coach fought with the owner and the owner fought with the commissioner, while, in what sometimes seemed almost an afterthought, the players battled the Houston Oilers for supremacy in the AFL's Eastern Division.

My introduction to the Titans occurred in the fall of 1969, in the form of a *Sports Illustrated* article by former lineman Alex Kroll, entitled "Last of the Titans," a humorous tale of the hardship involved in playing for a team that was running out of money. I had some vague remembrances of seeing the club on television as a very young boy, but Kroll's article provided my first conscious impression of the old AFL team.

The memory of Kroll's article stayed with me, and, 23 years later, in 1992, I commenced a quest to learn more about the history of the New York Titans. I discovered it was much more than a story of chaotic decline into insolvency. Interviews with nearly 50 players provided a picture of the life of a professional athlete from a vastly different era, a time before multimillion-dollar contracts and endorsements. Each player had his own story, but there were many common themes. Foremost was the tremendous opportunity offered by the expansion of pro football. In 1959 there were only 12 professional teams in the United States, and many talented players were left unemployed. To Canada, to the coaching ranks, and to semipro ball they went, hoping for another shot in the National Football League. The formation of the AFL by Lamar Hunt gave these men a second chance. At a distance of nearly 40 years, they were able to view their careers in perspective and compare their own experiences with those of the game they see today.

The most enjoyable part of writing this book was meeting the men who played for or coached the Titans, and those who played against them. All of the old Titans were eager to see the forgotten story of their team told to a new generation of football fans, and were more than generous with their time and memories. "Finish it while we can still read it," urged Art Powell. I spoke with some players on several occasions, and developed friendships with a few. Their recollections were so vivid and engaging that eventually I felt as though I had lived through the Titans' experiences myself. Sammy Baugh, the Titans' first coach, said it best. "I enjoyed that bunch of boys," he said. "I really did." Well, Sam, so did I.

CHAPTER 1

THE SHOW MUST GO ON

On July 13, 1962, the New York Titans held the initial practice of their third preseason training camp. The location was East Stroudsburg State Teachers' College, nestled in the Pocono Mountains of eastern Pennsylvania, the third training site in the team's three-year history. Clyde "Bulldog" Turner, former star lineman of the Chicago Bears, was beginning his first year as head coach of the New York club. He replaced Sammy Baugh, who guided the Titans to 7–7 finishes in each of their first two seasons in the American Football League. Although he was no longer head coach, Baugh was also in East Stroudsburg, ostensibly to serve as kicking coach. In reality, he was in camp because in December 1959, he signed a three-year contract covering the 1960 through 1962 seasons. Titans owner Harry Wismer soured on Baugh after the 1961 season and decided to replace him with Turner. The financially strapped Wismer had no intention, however, of paying two coaches at the same time.

If he fired Baugh, Wismer would be obligated to pay him for the final year of his contract. On the other hand, if Baugh quit, or did not report for his assigned duties, he would breach the contract and the Titans would have no obligation to pay him. During the months separating the 1961 and 1962 seasons, Baugh heard nothing from the owner. Wismer didn't even tell him when and where training camp would be held. Baugh read in the newspapers that Turner had been hired as head coach, and that he had been demoted.

When the Titans reported to East Stroudsburg, Baugh was there. Several players had called to tell him where camp would be held. "I will be mighty happy teaching boys to kick for $20,000 a year," Baugh said. "I knew what Wismer was doing," he added later, "and didn't want him to get away with it."

Baugh's presence represented a difficult situation for Turner. The two men attended the same high school in Texas and, while not close friends, got along well. Baugh in no way resented Turner taking over, and, in fact, within days of Turner signing with the Titans, Baugh attended a luncheon to present him with a plaque marking Turner's induction into the Texas Hall of Fame. Before going to Stroudsburg, Baugh called Turner to let him know why he was planning to show up. Turner understood, but could not have welcomed the former coach's presence. Baugh had not gotten on particularly well with Wismer, but had been worshipped by the players. He was the ultimate players' coach, and, to a man, those Titans who played for Baugh expressed the greatest admiration and affection for him. Now, here was Turner, starting his first training camp as a head coach, with his predecessor lurking on the sidelines. Although Baugh was perhaps the greatest punter in the history of the game, he spent precious little time that summer teaching any of those skills to the Titans players. He stayed out of Turner's way and bided his time.

After watching Baugh linger on the periphery of the practice sessions for a few days, Wismer came to the reluctant conclusion that his old coach was not going to resign. He sent public relations director Murray Goodman to arrange a meeting between Wismer, Baugh, and their lawyers in New York. On July 17, Wismer agreed to pay Baugh his full 1962 salary in six monthly installments, commencing August 1, and to relieve him of his coaching duties. The two embraced for the cameras, and Wismer was moved to tears, indicating that he was considering making Baugh a director of the club. "You never know," he said, "Sam and I may be back in business again." Baugh said he was willing to scout players for the Titans and to help them in any way he could. With agreement in hand, he left Stroudsburg for his ranch in Rotan, Texas. Baugh indicated later, however, that he received only some of the payments.

Meanwhile, Turner busied himself trying to find 33 serviceable players with whom to start the season. Candidates came and went; every time another professional club cut its roster, the Titans scanned the lists of waived players and brought new bodies to Stroudsburg.

The turnover was tremendous. Guard Larry McHugh, a rookie from Southern Connecticut State College, remembered waking up nearly every morning with a different roommate. "The only people who made money that summer," he said, "were the ones running the buses between New York City and the Poconos. Almost every afternoon at four, a bus would come in with a new group and the next morning at ten, another bus would leave with the guys who had been cut the day before. It was incredible! They must have run two or three hundred people through camp that summer."

With so many players passing through camp, the competition for jobs was brutal. Every intrasquad scrimmage meant that a spot was earned and many were lost. In most professional training camps, scrimmages are rather pedestrian affairs, with marginal players battling for the final roster spots and regulars trying to avoid injury. That summer in East Stroudsburg, however, scrimmages were the setting for some unusual occurrences.

The first centered around fullback Curley Johnson, a loquacious, likable, free-spirited Texan who played the 1960 season with the AFL's Dallas Texans. Early in 1961, he ran afoul of disciplined coach Hank Stram. "He just didn't like me very much," Johnson recalled. He was released just before the start of that season and quickly signed by the Titans, against whom he had made a spectacular touchdown catch in an exhibition game. Johnson became the club's regular punter and filled in occasionally at fullback.

Prior to the start of training camp in 1962, Johnson signed a contract that called for a $1,500 bonus. When he went to cash the bonus check, it bounced, not an unusual event for a Wismer-issued negotiable instrument. Johnson contacted the Titans and asked them to make the check good, but, when he reported, he still did not have the money. He approached general manager George Sauer and asked him when he could expect a new check. Sauer hemmed and hawed, and another week went by. Finally, an exasperated Johnson went to Sauer and said, "Look, I want my damn money!"

Rather than pay Johnson his bonus, the Titans decided to release him. Word leaked out that he was to be held out of a Sunday morning scrimmage and then let go. On Saturday night, a number of the Titans were out having a few beers and griping about the unfair way in which Johnson was being treated. Wismer had gone after the wrong man, for Johnson was immensely popular with his teammates, a source of comic relief in an often-difficult situation. Led by linebacker Larry Grantham, the players hatched a scheme to save him.

When the Titans took the field the following day, Johnson was among them but, not expecting to play, was not in the best condition. Upset with his pending release, he had imbibed freely and was suffering from a monumental hangover. Shortly after the scrimmage began, starting fullback Bill Mathis feigned an injury and limped off the field. Although Turner was under orders not to play Johnson, he had no other fullback available and put him in. Whenever Johnson got the ball, he showed an amazing ability to elude tackles, break tackles, and run over defenders. The defensive players dove at his feet, let him slip from their grasp, and watched him pile up the yardage. The back who had only gained three yards rushing in 1961 looked like the second coming of Red Grange. There was no way Turner could release him. Johnson remained with New York through the 1968 season, taking part in their upset of the Baltimore Colts in Super Bowl III. He never did get his $1,500.

A second scrimmage episode occurred later in camp. Wismer had recently taken a new wife, the widow of reputed mobster Abner "Longy" Zwillman, who had hanged himself three years earlier in the basement of his New Jersey mansion. Mrs. Wismer was the former Mary de Groot Mendels Steinbach, granddaughter of one of the founders of the American Stock Exchange. Knowing of her monied background, many players thought Wismer's new wife would be the financial salvation of the sinking franchise, a hope apparently shared by the owner himself. At the wedding reception, a drunken Wismer announced to several guests that they had just witnessed a "merger." Mrs. Wismer's children prevented her new husband from getting his hands on any of their mother's fortune, but she did become an enthusiastic fan, and during training camp became particularly impressed with the potential of 5'7" scatback Jim "the Thriller" Tiller, a rookie from Purdue.

Throughout training camp, Tiller was hopefully compared to Buddy Young, who, at 5'4", had been a star halfback in the late 1940s and early

1950s. Tiller had a rather mediocre career at Purdue, although he was the Boilermakers' leading receiver in 1960 with 21 catches and also scored seven touchdowns that season. He played with Toledo of the United Football League in 1961 and came highly recommended by Bob Snyder, Toledo's coach and a former teammate of Turner. Tiller was fast (reported to have run 100 yards in 9.6 seconds) and elusive, but not necessarily effective. He had a disturbing tendency to maneuver east and west, creating numerous thrills but gaining precious little yardage. Lineman Alex Kroll described Tiller's running style as that of a bullfighter being chased by 11 bulls. He was also prone to fumbling, which led one of the assistant coaches to present him with a football that had several luggage handles taped to it. Finally, at 165 pounds, Tiller was not big enough to block blitzing linebackers, a shortcoming that would eventually cost the Titans their starting quarterback.

Wismer was willing to overlook Tiller's numerous liabilities in order to please his new bride. If Mary Wismer thought she had discovered a star in Tiller, he would be a star. At halftime of one scrimmage, Turner, undoubtedly on orders from Wismer, told his players that they needed to generate some excitement. When the code words "the show must go on" were sent into the offensive and defensive huddles, the ball was to go to Tiller, the offense was to block, but the defense was not to tackle. "It was like a Broadway play," remembered guard Bob Mischak. "We were trying to convince the audience that this was sensational." Defensive back Dainard Paulson thought, "What am I doing out here? This is like the movies."

Sure enough, the signal came in, and away they went. Tiller touched the ball only twice during the scrimmage, carrying for 47 yards on a running play and catching a 72-yard pass on his other opportunity. Mrs. Wismer was duly impressed. Unfortunately, when the regular season started, Turner could not send instructions to the opponents' defensive huddle. The show did not go on.

The incidents in Stroudsburg were a prelude to one of the most bizarre seasons in the history of pro football. Quarterback Lee Grosscup, who chronicled the events of 1962 in a diary-style book entitled *Fourth and One*, observed later, "It was truly an unusual season."

"You never knew what was going to happen from day to day," added defensive back Paul Hynes. "You never knew if you had a football field to play on. You never knew if Harry Wismer had been repossessed." By November, the Titans would be bankrupt, their expenses paid by the league. Players would come and go through a revolving door, stage a brief strike, and learn to sprint to the bank with their paychecks before the money ran out.

The most enduring memory of the Titans is of that disastrous final season, the alcoholic ravings of Harry Wismer and the eventual bankruptcy of the franchise. Yet, there was much more. Despite their reputation, sullied by the collapse of 1962, the Titans were not a bad team. In their first two years, under Baugh, they had an exciting offense, produced a number of all-stars, and challenged Houston for the division title.

The club, and the AFL as a whole, represented an opportunity for hundreds of football players, shut out by the 12-team NFL, to play professionally in the United States. For Don Maynard, who but for the advent of the AFL might have been relegated to permanent obscurity, it meant a place in the Pro Football Hall of Fame. For Art Powell, Larry Grantham, Bill Mathis, and others who would have had difficulty cracking NFL rosters, it was an opportunity to show that the old league's obstinate refusal to expand was a mistake.

Given the unfortunate stigma that adhered to the Titans after the 1962 season, with the bounced paychecks and the difficult playing conditions, one might think that those who played under such circumstances would be bitter. Not so. Roger Ellis, who played with all three Titans clubs, said, "Those were the happiest three years of my life." Thurlow Cooper, a three-year starter at tight end, added, "It was the greatest experience of my life. We were one big happy family. We laughed things off when the checks were bouncing."

No story of the Titans would be complete without an understanding of the men beneath the blue and gold helmets. In the days before big salaries and bonuses, these men played a simpler game and experienced a camaraderie that seems to have gone the way of the straight-on field-goal kicker. They represented a new league in a city where the Giants ruled supreme. They played in the rundown Polo Grounds and sometimes went without pay. Yet, they played well, with the fierce pride of underdogs, and established a new franchise in a new league. This is the story of the men who were the Titans.

CHAPTER 2

OIL AND REJECTION

The American Football League was born of oil and rejection. Oil was the seed that produced the capital with which a pair of young Texans, Lamar Hunt and Kenneth "Bud" Adams, were able to finance two of the strongest teams in the new league. Their rejection by the NFL drove them to take their money, find others of like mind, and challenge the old league on the field, at the box office, and in the courts.

Prior to embarking on this venture, the two men had never met. Despite the commonality of oil money, they were physical and emotional opposites. Hunt, a 1956 graduate of Southern Methodist University, was a bespectacled, unassuming, slightly built six-footer who looked like the average office boy.

Despite his unimposing presence, Hunt came from one of the wealthiest families in the world. He was the youngest son of Haroldson Lafayette (H.L.) Hunt, who was, in the 1920s, an unsuccessful cotton farmer and owner of a gambling hall in the Arkansas mining town of El Dorado. The senior Hunt was financially strapped, supporting two wives and two families simultaneously. He saw opportunity in the petroleum business and, in 1930, acquired the rights to some leases from "Pop" Joiner, the legendary wildcatter who had made the first great oil strike in East Texas. The wells drilled on the leased land produced fabulously, and Hunt became one of the richest men in the world, supposedly earning $200,000 a day by 1960. Son Lamar was reported to have $50 million in his own name.

The senior Hunt was eccentric and a political arch-conservative (the last successful administration, he declared in the mid-1960s, was that of Coolidge) who was consumed by dual passions: making money and fighting the perceived onslaught of communism and socialism. "Everything I do," he once said, "I do for a profit." Hunt earned much and spent little. He lived in a house purchased for $60,000 in 1937, occupied a spartan office, and brought his lunch to work each day in a brown paper bag. Having made about as much money as a man could make, Hunt later in life turned his efforts to defending the world against communists and socialists, who he referred to as "The Mistaken." He funded a number of conservative causes and wrote a book, *Alpaca*, which described a utopian society in which the wealthy had greater voting power, as did those who eschewed government benefits. Hunt saw "The Mistaken" everywhere, threatening to corrupt capitalists in a myriad of ways, from cradle to grave, "placing nurses with babies who will inherit wealth, governesses, tutors. It can be through Mistaken playmates, classmates, or teachers skillfully working at the job. It can be through conspiracy planned marriages, and, for those not available for marriage, lovers. The Mistaken will not overlook the proper approach to woo the senile."

H.L. Hunt's only connection to football was a passion for gambling on college games. According to one of Harry Wismer's numerous acquaintances, Hunt wagered a million dollars each week. It was well known by Hunt's staff that any call from his bookie was to be put through immediately, no matter what Hunt might be doing.

Young Lamar Hunt appeared to possess none of his father's eccentricities, but Bud Adams, on the other hand, was exactly what one would expect of a rich Texan. The owner of Ada Oil Company and son of "Boots" Adams, chairman of the board of Phillips Petroleum, Bud was a stocky, flamboyant man born in 1923, 10 years before Hunt. Adams maintained an enormous office at Ada that featured a barbecue pit and a lily pond.

In addition to being wealthy oilmen, the young Texans had two other things in common. Both played college football without notable success, possessing a love of the game that encouraged them to persevere despite a pronounced lack of athletic ability. Hunt's principal claim to fame had been backing up Hall of Famer Raymond Berry at SMU. The second common experience of Hunt and Adams was unsuccessful attempts to purchase the Chicago Cardinals of the NFL.

George Halas, owner and coach of the Chicago Bears, was one of the founders of the NFL and perhaps its most dominant personality. A.E. Staley, owner of the Staley Starch Works in Decatur, Illinois, hired Halas in 1920 to coach his company's football team. The Staleys became a charter member of the American Professional Football Association, which became the National Football League two years later. In 1921, Staley gave the team to Halas, who moved it to Chicago and, in 1922, changed its name to the Bears. The success of the Bears left little room for the rival Cardinals, owned throughout the 1950s by Walter and Violet Wolfner. Mrs. Wolfner inherited the club upon the death of her first husband, Charles Bidwill Sr., in 1947, and married Wolfner in 1949. By the late 1950s, the Wolfners, experiencing financial difficulties, went in search of a partner with deep pockets. Adams, whose pockets were as deep as any, approached Wolfner, but, when the Cardinals' owner offered only a 49 percent interest, Adams terminated the negotiations. He wanted to be the majority owner and move the franchise to Texas, which had been without professional football since the ill-fated Dallas Texans left for Baltimore after the 1952 season. Hunt likewise entered into discussions with Wolfner with the intention of relocating the Cardinals franchise. Like Adams, he was unsuccessful.

There was a third man, in addition to Adams and Hunt, who wanted the Cardinals out of Chicago. That man was George Halas. Through 1961, each NFL team had its own television contract, which allowed it to air its road games. In 1960, nine teams were with CBS, two with NBC, and two with independent stations. League rules prohibited a club from broadcasting into a market in which another NFL game was being played, even if the game was sold out. When the Bears were on the road, the Cardinals were generally home, and vice versa. Thus, neither Chicago franchise was able to televise in its local market, severely diminishing the value of their broadcast rights. Halas reportedly offered Wolfner half a million dollars to move out of town. Wolfner, feeling he was negotiating from a position of strength, played hardball with Adams, Hunt, and Halas, and failed to strike a deal with anyone.

Frustrated in their efforts to obtain an existing NFL franchise, Hunt and Adams set their sights on convincing the league to expand. This was unlikely, for unanimous approval of the owners was required to admit an expansion franchise. Again, broadcast revenue was a deciding factor. Washington owner George Preston Marshall was steadfastly against expansion, for he relied heavily upon television revenue from southern markets when his team played on the road. He was not interested in sharing his audience with a new club. The Wolfners also depended on the southern markets and were against having a franchise in Texas, unless it was their own.

During Hunt's final meeting with Wolfner, which took place in Miami, the Cardinals' owner tried to strengthen his negotiating position by dropping the names of several other bidders. On his flight back to Dallas, Hunt realized that if so many men of means wanted a professional football franchise, he might be able to gather enough of them to start his own league. Hunt flew to Houston in March 1959, and had lunch with Adams at the latter's Charcoal Inn restaurant. On the way to the airport, Hunt asked Adams if, provided Hunt could find investors for four additional teams, Adams would join him in a new league. Adams said he would.

The time was ripe for the expansion of professional sports. Major League Baseball had been static since 1901, despite its ever increasing popularity. There had been 16 teams in the first year of the century, and there were still 16 teams in 1959, despite the population of the United States having increased from 76 million to 181 million. New York, with a population of nearly eight million, had only the Yankees, as both the Dodgers and Giants had fled in search of greener pastures. There was tremendous pressure for expansion from cities that ached for major league sports. Yet, both the American League and National League resisted, testing the patience of Washington politicians, who kept threatening to review baseball's unique exemption from anti-trust laws if it did not add new franchises.

A further irritant to the baseball hierarchy was an organization called the Continental League, which intended to be a third major league, or, as subsequent events hinted, assumed that stance to pressure the established leagues into adding new teams. The president of the Continental League was 77-year-old Branch Rickey, the legendary baseball executive best known as the man who signed Jackie Robinson. Behind Rickey was

William Alfred Shea, a 52-year-old New York corporate attorney whose principal desire was to bring a major league club to his city. In 1958, Shea had been appointed by New York mayor Robert Wagner to a four-man committee dedicated to bringing a National League franchise to New York. Failing to convince the Philadelphia, Pittsburgh, or Cincinnati clubs to relocate, and equally unsuccessful in persuading the National League to expand, Shea announced in November 1958 that he was involved in the formation of a third league.

Shea had been only mildly interested in baseball as a youth, attending NYU and Georgetown on football and basketball scholarships. He had been an associate of Dodgers owner Walter O'Malley in the 1930s and briefly operated the Long Island Indians, a short-lived minor league football club. By 1959 he had become very interested in baseball, and he and Rickey positioned the Continental League to begin play in 1961.

With the Continental League applying relentless pressure for recognition, major league owners decided that expansion was inevitable. At a monumental summit meeting in Chicago in August 1960, the existing leagues agreed to expand immediately and include four of the Continental League cities. In return, Rickey and Shea would abandon their plans for a third league.

The expansion was announced that fall. The American League would allow the Washington Senators to move to Minneapolis and would add teams in Washington and Los Angeles. The National League would move into New York and Houston. When the locations of the new teams were announced, Shea and Rickey were livid. While the National League had honored its agreement, the American had not. By that time, however, the impetus of the Continental League was spent, and Rickey's threat to reactivate the league was hollow. Yet his efforts had added four teams to major league baseball, including one in New York.

Similarly, in 1960, the American Basketball League was formed as a competitor to the National Basketball Association, which had been holding steady at eight teams for several years. The new league signed some top college players and introduced the three-point basket. The Cleveland ABL franchise, owned by an excitable young shipbuilder named George Steinbrenner, pulled off the biggest coup by signing Ohio State All-America Jerry Lucas. Although the ABL was short-lived, its initial efforts put a scare into the formerly complacent NBA.

Why should football be different from other sports? The NFL had not added a franchise since the assimilation of three All-America Football Conference teams in 1950. There were only six professional games on Sunday afternoons, and in 1959, attendance averaged 43,617 per game, setting a record for the eighth consecutive season and representing a 72 percent increase from the 1950 average of 25,353 per game. The nationally televised, sudden-death overtime 1958 NFL Championship Game between the New York Giants and Baltimore Colts was a watershed event that awakened American sports fans to the drama and excitement of professional football. If ever there were a time for a new league, it was 1960. On August 1, 1959, NFL Commissioner Bert Bell announced that there were three groups attempting to organize leagues of their own. The Trans-American League, whose spokesman was former Giants quarterback Travis Tidwell, and the International League were given little chance of success. Hunt's new league was granted the best odds of cracking the NFL monopoly.

In the months following his meeting with Adams, Hunt had been a busy man, making phone calls, flying to meetings, lining up investors for the new league. Knowing he needed a franchise in New York, Hunt approached Shea. Shea was too involved with his baseball plans to join Hunt, but arranged to meet with Harry Wismer, a well-known sports announcer who owned 25 percent of the Washington Redskins. The two men met at the Sands Point Country Club on Long Island, where Shea told Wismer of Hunt's plans. He asked if he could have Hunt call Wismer directly. Wismer could scarcely contain himself. Of course Hunt could call him. As Wismer remembered the conversation, Shea said that if Wismer were unable to raise sufficient funds to operate the club, money could be obtained from other sources, sources Shea did not reveal. Nor did Shea say how much would be available.

Wismer had money of his own, but was a relative pauper in comparison to Hunt and Adams. He was born on June 13, 1913, in Port Huron, Michigan, and grew up in modest circumstances. His father was the manager of a clothing store, but the son dreamed of reaching greater heights, devouring the stories of Horatio Alger and Frank Merriwell. "I'd wipe the dishes for my mother," he recalled later, "and I'd say, 'Don't worry. Someday you won't have to worry about all those bills. I'll take care of everything.'" Wismer attended St. John's Military Academy in Delafield, Wisconsin, from 1929 through 1932, where he played quarterback on the football team, and also participated in baseball, basketball, and track. He spent a year at the University of Florida, where he endeared himself to head football coach Charley Bachman by organizing a petition drive to make Bachman coach of the College All-Stars in the annual game against the NFL champions. Wismer, using many names that were suspected to have been copied out of the phone book, brought Bachman home second, which turned out to be first when winning coach Frank Thomas of Alabama had to decline after an attack of the gout. (Several years later, in 1937, Wismer helped Gus Dorais obtain the All-Star coaching position by taking signed political petitions he found in the county building and substituting the name of Dorais for that of the political office seekers.) When Bachman became head coach at Michigan State, Wismer followed.

Like Hunt and Adams, Wismer was an enthusiastic but untalented player in college. He was the third-string quarterback for the Spartans when an injury sent him to the broadcast booth. He made his debut serving as spotter at a Michigan State–Carnegie Tech game for legendary announcers Bill Stern and Graham McNamee. Wismer was mesmerized by the drama the two veterans brought to a rather dull contest. "I couldn't believe," he later wrote, "I was watching the same game they were describing." After the game, Wismer told Bachman, "If those two guys can do it, this is the business for me." Broadcasting was indeed the business for Harry, and he soon became a sportscaster for WKAR, the campus station, and the regular announcer for the Spartans' games.

While organizing his petition drive for Bachman, Wismer had made the acquaintance of Detroit Lions owner George Richards, who also owned radio station WJR. After serving as sports director for the college station in 1934, he moved to WJR, where from 1935 to 1940 he broadcast Big Ten games on Saturday and Lions games on Sunday. Wismer later claimed he was earning $20,000 after one year and was grossing $100,000 by age 25.

In 1941 Wismer moved to NBC in New York and began broadcasting Notre Dame football. He relocated to Washington the following year and added the games of the Washington Redskins, who were led by star quarterback Sammy Baugh. In Washington, Wismer met many political figures and elbowed his way into the city's social set. He had a natural advantage; in 1941, he married Mary Elizabeth Bryant, niece of Henry Ford. In 1946, at the age of 33, Wismer was named one of the 10 outstanding young men of America. J. Edgar Hoover, another friend, had nominated him. One of the other recipients was a young Congressman from Massachusetts, John F. Kennedy.

Throughout the 1940s and 1950s, Wismer was a household name to sports fans; his enthusiastic voice could be heard all over the country describing college and pro football. He also served as sports director for the American Broadcasting Company, and got in on the early stages of the bowling boom, earning a considerable fortune by investing in the stock of Brunswick Corporation.

By 1950, Wismer had acquired an interest in two NFL clubs, an admirable and semi-legal feat. Richards of the Lions had become ill and had gone to California to recuperate. Wismer claimed that, in Richards' absence, he virtually ran the club until its sale to Fred Mandel. By 1947, Mandel was looking to unload the franchise. Wismer formed a group of seven investors who each contributed $20,000. They added a $25,000 loan to raise the total purchase price of $165,000. Although he had intended to be one of the seven owners, Wismer discovered that Richards was angry with him for attempting to acquire part of his old club. Wismer therefore used his father-in-law, Roy Bryant, as a straw man to hold his shares. In 1950, when George Preston Marshall needed working capital, Wismer purchased 25 percent of the Redskins for $44,000. Although it was against NFL regulations to own stock in more than one team, Bryant's nominal ownership of the Detroit shares enabled Wismer to skirt the restriction.

Not content with minority ownership, Wismer was eager to hear of Lamar Hunt's plans for a new league. In July 1959, he met with Hunt and former NFL quarterback Davey O'Brien at the Belmont Plaza Hotel in New York. This was the first time Wismer and Hunt had ever met, although Wismer numbered Hunt's father among his many acquaintances. Wismer recalled that during their conversation, Hunt expressed his admiration for Wismer's ability to "generate publicity and controversy." He also said that during the two-hour session Hunt did most of the talking, a difficult feat for anyone engaged in conversation with Wismer. By the end of the meeting, Wismer agreed to invest in the New York franchise. When he called Shea to tell him he was committing to Hunt, Wismer said Shea told him that construction of a new stadium in Flushing Meadows was now a certainty.

Hunt still needed three more franchises to fulfill his promise to Adams. Forty-one-year-old Ralph Wilson of Detroit had been a Lions fan since the 1930s. His family had been very successful in the trucking business, and Wilson himself was active in insurance, road building, and oil drilling. He had a small ownership interest in the Lions, and, like Hunt and Adams, had sought his own NFL franchise for several years. In July 1959, Wilson heard that Hunt was forming a new league and wrote the young Texan a letter. Hunt phoned and asked Wilson to come to Dallas for a meeting. Wilson flew to Texas and told Hunt he would like to start a team in Miami, where his family maintained a home. Wilson's reception in temperate Miami, however, was rather chilly. The city's AAFC Seahawks had gone broke, and local politicians were not confident that a new franchise would be able to compete successfully with the college game. Discouraged, Wilson called Hunt, who told him he had heard of interest in Cincinnati, Louisville, Kansas City, St Louis, and Buffalo, and suggested Wilson visit those cities.

On October 16, 1959, Wilson went to Buffalo to determine the level of interest in the city, which, unlike Miami, had strongly supported its AAFC club. Paul Neville, editor of *The Buffalo Evening News*, was a staunch advocate of a professional franchise in Buffalo and told Wilson he could gather the necessary local support. Although Wilson had not intended to make any decisions that day, he committed to place a team in Buffalo if a satisfactory stadium lease could be arranged.

Four more investors committed to join Hunt, including 32-year-old Barron Hilton, son of hotel magnate Conrad Hilton, who was approached by Hunt through a mutual friend, tennis pro Gene Mako. Hilton agreed to fund a franchise in Los Angeles. Bob Howsam, whose family owned the Denver Bears of baseball's American Association, agreed to head up a Denver team. Bill Sullivan was a long-time Bostonian, former public relations man for Notre Dame, and a friend of legendary Irish coach Frank Leahy. Now president of the Metropolitan Coal and Oil Company and head of a 10-man syndicate, Sullivan approached Wismer, who he knew from the days when Wismer broadcast Notre Dame football. At that time, the AFL's expansion committee consisted of Leahy, Wismer, and Hunt. The first two, who knew Sullivan well, easily convinced Hunt to grant Boston a franchise.

Max Winter, owner of the NBA's Minneapolis Lakers, led a group that intended to place a team in Minnesota, which would round out the league with an even eight clubs. Winter's partners included H.P. Skogland, an insurance magnate, and William Boyer, an automobile dealer and chairman of the Minneapolis Chamber of Commerce. Like Hunt and Adams, both Winter and Howsam had bid for the Chicago Cardinals. Each of the eight teams tendered a $25,000 check and posted a $100,000 bond, to be forfeited if the franchise defaulted. The owners privately labeled themselves "The Foolish Club" and prepared to go public. "They were a strange group," said a reporter who covered professional football at the time. "The AAFC was formed by football and baseball people. This new group just looked like a bunch of millionaires. They had the money to keep going forever."

On August 14, 1959, Hunt and the other owners met at the Chicago Hilton and officially announced the birth of the new league. Eight days later, they took the name American Football League, the fourth time an organization with that name had taken form. Charles C. "Cash and Carry" Pyle, best known as the agent for Red Grange, started the first AFL in 1926. Pyle, like Hunt and Adams, had been frustrated in his attempts to obtain an NFL franchise and formed his own nine-team circuit, featuring Grange and former Notre Dame stars Elmer Layden and Harry Stuhldreher, two of the legendary Four Horseman. The first AFL lasted only one season, but Pyle achieved his original goal, as the NFL absorbed his New York Yankees. Two other AFLs had brief lives, one from 1936–1937 and the other 1940–41. Neither was a serious threat to the NFL, despite the latter organization signing Michigan All-America Tom Harmon.

The NFL was determined that the fourth AFL would suffer the same fate as the first three. Expansion, which had long been prevented by the recalcitrance of George Marshall, now became a reality, spearheaded by George Halas. Marshall did not yield gracefully. "The only reason for expansion I've heard from other owners is that we could destroy the new league," he said. "If that's the only reason, then we are guilty of monopolistic practices. No one can give me an intelligent reason for adding a couple of more franchises." Marshall's statement was an NFL lawyer's worst nightmare, but the crotchety old Washington owner was a lone voice. Realizing that there would be teams in Texas whether they liked it or not, the owners of the old league's franchises decided that they should be theirs. Halas recommended that Houston and Dallas, strongholds of AFL founders Adams and Hunt, be granted NFL franchises that would begin play in 1961.

While Halas wanted to challenge the new league head on, NFL commissioner Bert Bell favored a conciliatory approach, having learned a valuable lesson from the earlier conflict with the All-America Football Conference. Several men who later became AAFC owners approached Bell's predecessor, Elmer Layden, regarding the possibility of obtaining NFL expansion franchises. "These men have asked me for permission to join our league," Layden said, "I told them to come back when they got themselves a football." The remark was highly publicized and helped touch off a war that not only destroyed the AAFC (the teams of which allegedly lost $11 million in aggregate) but also did great harm to the established league. In the AAFC's final season, it was reported that only two professional teams, the Bears and Redskins, made a profit, while the NFL clubs in aggregate lost $2.5 million. AAFC clubs lost $3.6 million. Bell was much more politic than Layden in his remarks about potential competitors. Testifying before the U.S. Senate committee investigating monopolies and possible antitrust violations on July 28, 1959, he said, "The more football there is and the more advertisement of pro football the better off we are. We are in favor of the new league."

Hunt wanted a pro franchise, not a debilitating war, and was eager to accept Bell's offer of amity. He asked a mutual friend, Davey O'Brien, to act as intermediary and arranged a meeting at Bell's Atlantic City farm in early August. He asked Bell to serve as commissioner of both leagues, an offer the latter declined. Bell did, however, leave Hunt with the distinct impression that he would not oppose his efforts to form a new league and indicated that there would be no NFL franchise in Texas for years to come. He also agreed that, while there would undoubtedly be heated competition for unsigned players, neither league would tamper with those under contract.

On October 11, Hunt's hope for peaceful co-existence received a crushing blow when Bell, attending a game between the Eagles and Steelers in Philadelphia, suffered a fatal heart attack during the final minutes. There were now no restraints on Halas and his allies. At Bell's funeral, Halas pitched his fellow owners on the idea of adding new teams. Adams said both he and Hunt were offered NFL franchises if they would abandon the AFL, while Hunt said Clint Murchison later offered him his proposed Dallas franchise with the same caveat. Both immediately declined the offers. Ed Pauley, one of the Rams' owners, reportedly offered Hilton an interest in his NFL franchise if he would desert the AFL.

With all of these temptations, AFL owners kept close tabs on each other. When Hunt told Wismer, in late October, that he had to leave a meeting unexpectedly to catch a flight to the West Coast, Wismer became suspicious. He called the airport and discovered that no flights were leaving for California until the following morning. Wismer therefore had a detective follow Hunt to Idlewild Airport, where he watched him board a flight to Chicago. There was only one reason Hunt could be going to Chicago, Wismer surmised, and that was to visit George Halas and make a deal to join the NFL. He therefore tipped off the wire services that Hunt was in Chicago, and received a bonus in the form of Bud Adams, who had rendezvoused with Hunt. If there was a meeting with Halas, however, nothing of import resulted from the session.

While the AFL was holding an owners' meeting in Minneapolis on November 22, a crack appeared in their solid front. Max Winter, who had learned of the NFL offer to Adams and urged him to stand by the AFL, had been simultaneously negotiating with both leagues for three months. On the 22nd, he hinted to Ralph Wilson that, if the NFL put a franchise in Minneapolis, as it had announced it might, the competition would make it impossible for him to field an AFL club. He made no mention that he would be the NFL franchisee.

That evening, the Minnesota group hosted a banquet for their fellow owners at the Cedric Adams Hotel. In addition to the AFL investors, approximately 200 members of a Minneapolis booster club were in attendance. Wismer, who arrived late after broadcasting a Notre Dame game, had a sense that something was amiss. He claimed that Frank Leahy, the new general manager of the Chargers, shared his suspicions. During dinner, Wismer was summoned from the room to take a call from Mims Thomason, a friend from UPI, who informed him that Minneapolis was definitely going to receive an NFL franchise.

Wismer returned to the gathering and walked up to the dais. "Boys, it looks like it's the Last Supper!" he shouted. Winter was Judas Iscariot, he declared, and anyone who knew Wismer, an incurable egomaniac, could guess the role in which he envisioned himself.

Wismer, Winter, and Hunt went outside, where Wismer grabbed Winter's lapels and demanded the truth. Hunt tried to calm Wismer, who told Hunt to shut up and continued shouting at Winter. According to Wismer, Winter admitted that he and his partners were about to join the NFL.

Wismer got in a car with Boyer and started for the site of the owners' meeting. As he had done with Winter, Wismer demanded to know whether the Minneapolis owners planned to desert the AFL. Boyer denied the allegation, said he wasn't feeling well, and asked to be dropped off at his home.

When the formal meeting got under way, Hunt began with several points of order. Already in a state of frenzy by this point, Wismer jumped up and shouted that this was no time for administrative trivia. He again demanded an answer of Winter, this time in front of the other owners. When Winter refused to confirm or deny, Harry told him and Skogland to get out. Later, someone brought in a copy of the *Minneapolis Tribune*, which confirmed Thomason's report and carried the story of the Minneapolis NFL franchise. After weeks of speculation, the AFL announced on January 3 that the Minneapolis group would be allowed to withdraw their application. The league was down to seven clubs.

Hunt realized that the battle was on and announced his determination to fight the NFL. He enlisted the help of attorney Edward Guinn to attempt to dissuade the NFL from expanding into Texas and began a search to find another investor to replace the defectors from Minnesota. The league also conducted a player draft on November 24, a draft with a most unusual format. None of the new clubs had a viable scouting system, so the league relied upon Leahy, Dallas general manager Don Rossi,

Denver general manager Dean Griffing, and Houston director of player personnel John Breen for talent evaluation. The four men selected the 24 best college players at each of the 11 positions, ranked in groups of eight, that is, 1–8, 9–16, and 17–24. Since college football was essentially a one-platoon game, there was no distinction between offensive and defensive players.

The draft started with territorial selections, in which each club obtained rights to a player whom it believed was of star quality and a potential drawing card. The Titans selected quarterback George Izo of Notre Dame.

The names of the top eight players at each position were placed in a box, and each club drew in turn. After 11 rounds, therefore, each team held the rights to a player at each position. After two more boxfuls of players, the 9–16 and 17–24 best at each position, all clubs held the rights to three complete teams. Two weeks later, the same process was repeated for an additional 20 rounds.

On November 30, Joe Foss, World War II flying ace, winner of the Congressional Medal of Honor, and former governor of South Dakota, was elected commissioner of the AFL. Foss was 45 years old, robust, and handsome, with a full head of dark curly hair. "He is a worn but still rugged piece of leather," wrote Wells Twombly. "His hair is curly and his face is handsome, only his features look like they were left out in the wind and snow all winter." Foss possessed a politician's charismatic manner coupled with a heroic virility. He was a powerful salesman, remarkably accomplished, and possessed of an iron discipline, following a steady regimen of exercise to maintain his weight at 180 pounds, exactly the same as when he entered the Marines 20 years earlier. Perhaps the greatest insight into Foss's masculine appeal can be gleaned from the following endorsement of his autobiography: "Any man who doesn't give this book to his son is derelict in his duty as a father."—G. Gordon Liddy.

Foss was Hunt's third choice, approached only after Fritz Crisler, athletic director at the University of Michigan, and Rip Miller, athletic director at the Naval Academy, turned the job down. According to Wismer, Crisler was prepared to accept, but at an annual salary of $100,000, plus a large insurance policy. Unlike the first two choices, Foss had no experience in football, other than as a guard at the University of South Dakota. He had seen just two pro football games in person and only about

30 on television, for reception in Pierre, South Dakota, was poor.

Foss, even more than Wismer, personified the fictional tales of Horatio Alger, as he overcame numerous obstacles in his path to success. His father died when Foss was 18, and the youngster ran the family farm for a time. His first son was stillborn, and a second died shortly after birth. Two of his surviving children, a son and a daughter, suffered from polio and cerebral palsy, respectively.

While his personal life was filled with sorrow, Foss's professional life was one of almost uninterrupted success. He worked his way through Augustana College and the University of South Dakota, then served in the Air Force during the Second World War, equaling Eddie Rickenbacker's World War I record by downing 26 Japanese planes. After the war, he began a career in politics, serving two terms in the South Dakota legislature, followed by two as governor, starting in 1954. A statutory, two-term limit prevented Foss from running again in 1958.

Ineligible for re-election, Foss received more than 30 job offers. He turned down Rickenbacker, who wanted him as a vice president of Eastern Airlines, and accepted a job as vice president of Raven Industries, a manufacturer of high-altitude research balloons based in Sioux Falls, South Dakota. The largest single investor in Raven was H.P. Skogland, president of North American Life and Casualty. When Foss had to go to Los Angeles on business, he hitched a ride with Skogland on the latter's private jet. Skogland, one of the owners of the AFL's Minneapolis franchise, was on his way to California for a league meeting, and invited Foss to cocktails and dinner with his fellow owners. At dinner, one of the owners mentioned to Foss that they were looking for a commissioner and asked if he was interested in the job. Foss agreed to an interview, which took place the following day.

The day after the interview, Barron Hilton leaked a story stating that Joe Foss would definitely not be the commissioner of the American Football League. When he read this, Foss announced that he had no interest in the job, and considered the matter closed. A few weeks later, Lamar Hunt called Foss and told him that if he were still a candidate, he should be available for a conference call the following day. During the call, in which Hunt, Adams, and Howsam participated, Foss was offered and accepted a three-year contract at $30,000 per year.

Meanwhile, following Bert Bell's death, the NFL sought its own commissioner. After 21 ballots on January 25, 1960, no candidate had the nine votes needed to produce a decision. Marshall Leahy, a San Francisco attorney, had seven staunch supporters, while Austin Gunsel, the interim commissioner, had four votes. George Halas, not wanting to offend anyone as he pushed his expansion plan, abstained. When it became apparent that neither side would yield, Paul Brown of Cleveland and Wellington Mara of the Giants suggested a compromise candidate, the relatively unknown, 33-year-old general manager of the Los Angeles Rams, Pete Rozelle. Eager to end the stalemate, the Leahy and Gunsel camps united behind Rozelle.

The new commissioner was cut from an entirely different cloth than Bell. Bell had been born to wealth, the son of a Pennsylvania attorney general and the grandson of a congressman, but his demeanor was anything but aristocratic. Bell was a football man, one who knew what it was like to play football and to operate a franchise on a shoestring. Rozelle, like Foss, was not a football man. He was a marketer, wise to the ways of Madison Avenue. One of his first acts as commissioner was to move the league office from Philadelphia, Bell's home base, to New York, in order to maintain better relationships with the league's advertising agencies.

Many thought that the youthful Rozelle would be a mere figurehead, while Halas and others wielded the power. Upon assuming office, he threw his full support behind the Bears' owner in his quest to destroy the AFL, discarding Bell's supportive position. The new commissioner had not been in office a full day when the league rule regarding expansion was amended to require only 10 votes, not all 12, to approve the addition of a new franchise. The next day, despite warnings from Foss and Hunt that a move into Dallas would mean war, the NFL owners voted to do just that. They awarded a Dallas franchise to Clint Murchison Jr. and Bedford Wynne for $50,000, plus $550,000 to pay for players chosen in the expansion draft.

True to their word, the AFL struck back. Foss sent a self-serving letter to Halas, leaked to the press, setting forth the NFL's historic refusal to expand and its current efforts to destroy the AFL. "The professional football war is on," wrote Howard Tuckner in *The New York Times*, "and Texas is the battlefield."

"This is an out-and-out attempt to wreck our league," said Foss. "By putting a team into Dallas they strike at the heart of our league. We're going to fight them down the line." What about New York and Los Angeles, NFL cities that had been invaded by the AFL? Foss cited the large populations of those two areas, compared to Dallas, which had a population of only about 750,000. He compared putting a second team in Dallas to placing a Christmas tree on a birthday cake. Ironically, two weeks earlier, the battling leagues had taken the opposite position regarding New York. In a letter regarding the case of Mississippi fullback Charlie Flowers, who had signed with the Giants and the Los Angeles Chargers, Wellington and John Mara stated, "It is our opinion that every city is a one-team city." This provoked a quick response from Wismer, who volunteered his opinion that New York had plenty of room for two teams. If a city the size of New York was a one-team city, Wismer now asked, why was the NFL planning to go to Dallas?

Foss and Hunt appealed to the U.S. government to intervene. Senator Estes Kefauver of Tennessee, head of the Senate Anti-Monopoly Subcommittee, said he would not interfere in the battle over Dallas, and that no club or league had an exclusive claim on any city. "It is a question of who has the better product in a city," he said. Paul Rand Dixon, counsel to the subcommittee, added, "They are businesses in commerce. Rather than restraint, there is supposed to be competition."

Apparently, while Kefauver felt no team had the right to a city, he was prepared to grant exclusive ownership of a day of the week. Three months earlier, when the AFL announced that it planned to play on Saturday afternoons, Kefauver said he would propose legislation banning professional telecasts by a station within 75 miles of any college game. Given the plethora of colleges throughout the United States, the ban would essentially cover the entire country. The AFL changed its plans, citing, through Wismer, a concern to avoid damaging the college game.

Having failed to persuade Kefauver to act, the league took its fight to the courts, filing a $10 million antitrust suit against the NFL in April 1960. Wismer claimed he was against the lawsuit from the beginning and had persuaded Washington insider Clark Clifford, in a conference call, to tell his fellow owners their case had no merit. The suit was unsuccessful, for, after two years, Judge Rossel C. Thomsen ruled in favor of the NFL. Thomsen found that the existing league had not gone beyond normal competitive business practices in its duel with the AFL. The fact that the new league had survived and was on the verge of making money was a powerful argument against its claim that the NFL had unfairly prevented it from competing. The only damage suffered by the established league was approximately $300,000 in legal fees expended to defend the suit. Each AFL club, on the losing end, was assessed roughly $50,000 for its share of the league's legal costs.

While the fight with the NFL over Dallas held center stage, the AFL addressed the need to replace Minneapolis as its eighth franchise. The two front-runners were groups from Atlanta and Oakland. At the eleventh hour, George McKeon, a construction executive, showed up at a league meeting in Dallas on January 29 and announced that he wanted to put a team in San Francisco. After a brief discussion of McKeon's proposal, it was rejected and the contest devolved to one between Oakland and Atlanta. Groups from both cities made presentations to the seven remaining owners. The AFL bylaws, like those of the NFL, required a unanimous vote to admit a new franchise. The first ballot produced four votes for Oakland and three for Atlanta. On the second ballot, New York and Denver switched to the Atlanta camp, giving the Georgia city a 5–2 advantage. At that point, a deadlock ensued, with Billy Sullivan of Boston and Barron Hilton of Los Angeles anchored solidly in the Oakland camp. The meeting adjourned and reconvened the following day.

At 9:15 on the morning of January 30, a new vote produced the same 5–2 margin. Foss left in the afternoon for a speaking engagement and told the owners they were going to stay there until a decision was reached. By evening, Sullivan was convinced to break with Hilton, and the hotelier stood alone.

The league's attorneys favored the Atlanta option. They planned to sue the NFL for antitrust violations, and placing a team across the bay from the San Francisco 49ers smacked of the same predatory spirit as the NFL's attempts to put teams in Dallas and Houston. The previous September, Hunt had indicated that the league wanted two teams in California, but now he was publicly silent on the issue, casting his vote in favor of Atlanta. However, the Georgia city posed a potential public relations problem, for, at least in 1960, an Atlanta franchise would be forced to play in segregated Grant Field.

Hilton desperately wanted a West Coast rival for his Chargers. He brought his attorney, Maury Rosenfeld, to the meeting and attempted to convince the other owners that the legal concerns were not compelling. At 12:30 a.m. on January 31, a voice, supposedly that of Hilton, could be heard bellowing, "I'd rather talk about economics and let them talk about the legal aspect. I'm a businessman, not a lawyer." By 2:15 a.m., Hilton either convinced or exhausted the opposition. The Oakland group of eight investors, headed by building contractor Chet Soda, Wayne Valley, and Robert Osborne, would be the AFL's final franchise. The Atlanta group received a consolation prize in the form of a promise that they, along with Chicago, would be given expansion franchises for the 1961 season. This pledge, of course, was never fulfilled.

One of the first tasks facing the Oakland club was the selection of a nickname, for which a contest was announced, with the person who submitted the winning entry to be awarded a trip to the Bahamas. One of Soda's long existing—and predictable—habits was saying "Hello, señor" in greeting when seeing an acquaintance or meeting someone new. Therefore, reporters cringed when Soda announced at a press conference that the new team would be known as the "Oakland Señors." Valley and Osborne were both embarrassed, and, after graciously sending the woman who had suggested the name Señors to the Bahamas, they decided upon "Raiders."

In addition to the nominal problem of selecting a nickname, the Oakland owners had a more substantive issue with which to deal. The Minnesota investors, knowing they were probably going to withdraw, made no effort to sign any of their draft choices. Oakland had a franchise, but no players. The league developed a plan under which each team could freeze 11 players. Oakland would then be allowed to select five of the unprotected players from each of the other seven clubs. The Raiders never recovered from their belated start, however, and brought up the rear of the Western Division standings until the arrival of a cocky young genuis named Al Davis in 1963.

CHAPTER 3

CONGRATULATIONS!

With a full complement of clubs, the league embarked upon its next important quest, finding a network to televise its games. Due to his former affiliations with ABC and NBC and his excellent connections within the broadcast industry, Wismer was named chairman of the television committee.

Professional football had a 20-year history with television, beginning on October 22, 1939, when station W2XBS, the predecessor of WCBS, broadcast a game between the Brooklyn Dodgers and Philadelphia Eagles. Despite the tremendous growth of the television industry, the NFL was slow to grasp the importance of the new medium. In 1947 Halas sold the television rights to Bears broadcasts for $900 per game. Paul Brown, one of the shrewdest coaches and executives in the league, could get only $5,000 for the rights to all Cleveland's games in 1950, the year the Browns entered the NFL following four consecutive AAFC championships. As late as 1956, the Packers received only $35,000 for their annual broadcast rights. Each franchise's ability to make its own deal was clearly to the advantage of the New York Giants and Los Angeles Rams, with their sizable local markets, and led to the type of problem experienced in Chicago. The situation was strikingly similar to that which exists in Major League Baseball today.

Wismer favored a proposal that was certainly not in his self-interest as the owner of the New York franchise, insisting from the beginning that the AFL should sell its television rights as a package, with all teams dividing the revenues equally. With typical egotism, he referred to it as "The Wismer Plan." The equal division of receipts was not a completely novel concept, for William Shea had envisioned just such an arrangement for the baseball clubs in his abortive Continental League. Wismer recognized that for the league to survive, all teams would need to prosper. There was little hope that clubs from smaller metropolitan areas, such as Buffalo and Denver, could procure a local television contract lucrative enough to ease the pain of the anemic attendance that all the owners knew was a distinct possibility in the early years.

With the concept agreed upon, Jay Michaels of Music Corporation of America (father of current ABC announcer Al Michaels) was sent off by league officials to find a network. At the same time, Foss went to Madison Avenue to convince potential advertisers that the AFL was viable. Wismer, of course, was deeply involved in the negotiations. The climactic meeting with the American Broadcasting Company took place in his apartment at the Park Lane Hotel. Wismer opened the discussion by asking for $2 million per year, which ABC's Tom Moore told him was ridiculous. This caused Wismer to jump from his chair with such force that he tipped it over. He stormed out through a door, but, unfortunately, had chosen the door to his closet rather than the one leading to the hallway. He remained closeted with himself for a full 10 minutes before re-entering the room and continuing the discussion.

In early June, ABC announced that it would pay $10.625 million over a five-year period, subject to annual renewal, to broadcast the games of the American Football League. Payments started at $1.785 million in 1960 and increased each year thereafter. According to Wismer, an ABC caveat was that the AFL be able to sell at least half of the available advertising time. With the help of the Young and Rubicam advertising agency, the league was able to meet its quota, and the contract was finalized.

Despite the role of Music Corporation of America, there is no doubt that Wismer was a key figure in the acquisition of the contract and in establishing the method for the distribution of the proceeds. Regardless of what happened during Wismer's stewardship of the Titans, everyone associated with professional football owes him a debt of gratitude, for without him, there might not have been an American Football League.

Unlike the old AAFC, which had to rely solely upon gate receipts, the new league had a guaranteed source of revenue even if not a single fan passed through the turnstiles.

Having their games on the air also exposed the AFL to millions of fans who would not initially venture out to see a game in person. "The smartest thing they did was put the games on at four o'clock," said Gino Cappelletti, former Patriots star and currently a color commentator on the club's radio broadcasts. "Here's the whole country, watching a single game at one o'clock, and they were hungry for more football. So now, at four o'clock, they could watch this other league—a rinky-dink, mickey-mouse league they used to call it. But they started watching, and we began to grab a fan base we could build on because the games were exciting, high-scoring affairs. They saw a lot of touchdowns being scored."

The equal distribution of revenue also helped prevent the imbalance that hastened the AAFC's demise. While Hunt, Adams, and Hilton could withstand large losses at the gate, Howsam and Sullivan could not. The more than $200,000 per team that came in during the first year of the ABC contract was crucial to the survival of the league, although in the end it was not enough to save the architect of the plan.

Perhaps the greatest compliment to the AFL's foresight came shortly afterward in the form of Pete Rozelle's announcement that he intended to pursue an identical contract for his own league. During the interval between the 1960 and 1961 seasons, Rozelle signed a $9.3 million, two-year contract with CBS. This represented a tremendous increase in revenue that, in 1959, under individual contracts, totaled $3.5 million.

In 1953 Judge Allan K. Grim of the United States District Court in Philadelphia had ruled that the NFL's blackout rule was not in violation of anti-trust laws. In July 1961, Grim decreed that the new NFL television package did violate anti-trust statutes and declared it void. The decision sent shockwaves throughout the sports industry, for not only did the AFL have a similar agreement, the NBA and college football also had all-inclusive contracts. Said Joe Donoghue, executive vice president of the Philadelphia Eagles, "Without packaged TV all sports as we know them will be out of business within two years." He conveniently forgot that his own club had been operating with an independent contract since the beginning of televised sports. Rozelle, with a similar lack of historical perspective, told Judge Grim during the NFL's appeal that half of the league's teams would be without a television contract if the decision were allowed to stand. Without broadcast revenue, Rozelle said, even the champion Colts would have lost money in 1959. The commissioner gratuitously pointed out that there were a number of other athletic associations that had contracts identical to that of the NFL. Grim asked Samuel Gordon, a government attorney, whether in Gordon's opinion, the contracts of other sports were legal. Gordon replied that he doubted they were.

Joe Foss quickly attempted to differentiate his league's arrangement by pointing out that the AFL televised one "Game of the Week" in the eastern part of the country and another in the west, whereas the NFL planned regional telecasts. The NCAA made the argument that anti-trust laws applied only to professional sports, not colleges.

The issue was resolved in September 1961, when President Kennedy signed a bill sponsored by Representative Emanuel Cellar of New York, which specifically exempted professional sports leagues from the anti-trust laws when negotiating television contracts. In January 1962, the NFL signed its first legal contract with CBS.

Wismer lost no time in taking credit for procuring the ABC contract, for the Titans' owner was the consummate egomaniac. He craved attention like cigarette smokers crave nicotine and went to extremes to make sure people noticed him. Wismer's entrances demonstrated his complete lack of subtlety. He would barge into a room and greet one person after the other with "Congratulations!" on the premise that they had probably done something they were proud of. "Congratulations can mean anything!" Wismer said. "It rings a note! It's wonderful! And it's a great opening line. 'Congratulations!' and they say, 'How do you know?' And I say, 'I keep pace.'"

Wismer also was known for starting false rumors. "So they shot Castro," he would say at a party. "It was his brother Raul. They weren't getting along." "You get a lot of emotional reaction from people," he observed. If anyone questioned Wismer's veracity, he would reply, "Well, that's what I heard."

Attracting attention was always paramount to Wismer. When the Titans deplaned at an airport, the public address system blared, "Now arriving at Gate 12, Harry Wismer and the New York Titans." On other occasions, he would have himself paged, then identify himself to everyone in shouting distance. "He'd say, 'That's me! That's me! I'm the owner of the Titans!'" remembered former player Dewey Bohling.

Wismer employed the Titans' first quarterback, Al Dorow, as a scout and public relations assistant during the offseason. Dorow gave speeches, often for free, and, along with tackle Sid Youngelman, sold tickets over the phone. Dorow was also a frequent companion of the owner. "We'd walk down Park Avenue, and he'd have these little firecrackers. You didn't have to light them, and if you threw them on the sidewalk real hard, there'd be an explosion. He'd throw one against the side of a building. Everyone would look up and say, 'Hey, there's Harry Wismer.'"

Wismer's daily routine was predictable. "He had a circuit he made every morning," said Dorow. "He'd walk to the New York Athletic Club from Park Avenue, a one-and-a-half mile walk. We'd stop at the Bull and Bear. John Roosevelt was there, and they'd have a drink, and then we'd hit another place, and Harry would have another drink. We'd always hit the Plaza, because it was right around the corner. In each one of these places, his buddies were there. We'd finally get to the Athletic Club and have a good workout and work our way back to the office. He'd be on the phone the rest of the day, and I'd line up my speaking engagements."

Needless to say, by the time Wismer reached the office, located in his apartment at 277 Park Avenue, he was often inebriated. His favorite eye-opener was a concoction called a bull shot, a mixture of vodka and beef broth. "By two in the afternoon," said Dorow, "he was rip-roaring. He had all those belts in him, and he could be like a rattlesnake." When intoxicated, Wismer's judgment frequently failed him, and the afternoon phone conversations were often injudicious. "Wismer was a very difficult man to deal with," said a reporter who covered the Titans. "I never saw him breathe a sober breath when I was dealing with him. He was bombastic and up to his eyeballs in BS and everybody knew it."

Wismer suddenly flew into rages or, alternatively, became manic. Dorow recalled a visit to the garment district, where Wismer was attempting to borrow enough money to carry him through the 1961 season. "They had quite a conversation," said Dorow of Wismer and the prospective lender. "Harry was yelling and screaming and the other guy was the same way. He gave us the money and we jumped into a limo and went to a haberdasher where Harry had his suits custom made. He ordered six or eight new suits. I saw a sports coat I liked for about seventy-five dollars. Harry said, 'You like that, you got it.' Then I found a pair of alligator shoes. I'd always wanted a pair of alligator shoes. They were a hundred and twenty-five dollars. He said, 'You want those, they're yours.'"

When Wismer was in one of his manic moods, there was no one more generous. Frank Tripucka, the Denver quarterback, was a New Jersey boy who had played in Canada for several years. When he led the Broncos into New York, many of his family and friends wanted to come to the Polo Grounds to watch him. Among them was Tripucka's high school coach, Bill Foley, who had suffered a stroke and was a semi-invalid. Tripucka called Wismer and asked if it would be possible to drive Foley onto the field in a car and park it against the stadium wall. Wismer readily agreed and, as Tripucka remembered, went out of his way to accommodate Foley.

That was the good Harry. There was no one more belligerent or offensive than the bad Harry. Murray Goodman, one of several publicity men for the Titans, said, "I've never seen anybody like Wismer. He had a multiple personality, which could run its course in an hour's time. He could be a charmer, kind, vicious, or mean."

"One minute," said a former employee of the Titans, "you'd want to kiss him for his kindness and a few minutes later you'd want to hit him over the head with a chair."

Wismer's friends loved him for his effusive enthusiasm, tolerated his embarrassing attention-getting techniques, and tried to avoid him when he was in one of his dark moods. A friend was quoted in *Sports Illustrated* as saying, "If you knew Harry for a month or two, you'd hate him. After a year you'd begin to reverse yourself. If Harry would only let his accomplishments speak for themselves instead of letting himself speak of his accomplishments, he'd be much better off." Said another friend in the same article, "Harry's the greatest contact man in the United States. He's always maneuvering. If he had someone to curb him, he'd be a very great man."

In Wismer's mind, he *was* the Titans. Ask the club for some autographed pictures, and you would receive photographs not of the players, but of the owner. Dainard Paulson, a New York defensive back, remembered being taken to the team's offices with his fellow rookies and departing with a cocktail glass bearing a picture of Wismer and an autographed photo. The owner's picture dominated the team's ticket advertising. "It is my pleasure to bring more major league sports to New York fans," read the quote over a photo of, as Bill Wallace wrote, "Harry looking like Bing Crosby, circa 1936."

When asked to compare Wismer with George Steinbrenner, current owner of the Yankees, an associate of Wismer's said the two men were "very similar. Of course," he added, "Steinbrenner has much more money." The money enabled Steinbrenner to survive mistakes of the kind that buried the financially strapped Wismer, and that often led Wismer to do things that did not endear him to his players or fellow owners. "I don't know what his relationships were with the other owners," said the same associate, "I think they liked him, but I'm not sure he was true to his word under pressure."

Like Steinbrenner and Dallas Cowboys owner Jerry Jones, Wismer wanted to be actively involved with game strategy. For a time, he had a direct line from his box to the sideline, and sent down play-calling and substitution suggestions. "I think Sammy Baugh finally tore that out," said Dorow. "Once in a while I'd call a play and Harry'd say, 'Wasn't that one of those plays I gave you?' I'd say, 'Yeah, that was one of them.'" Occasionally, Wismer ventured into the locker room to deliver a pep talk. Before a game with San Diego, he exhorted the troops with, "Guys, if you can't beat a team this close to the Mexican border, you can't beat anybody."

Wismer loved the limelight and his associations with famous people. "An immortal name dropper," wrote one columnist, "Wismer is likely to interrupt a league meeting with, 'As I told Jack Kennedy when he called me this morning, I don't think the Pope is going to go for that...and believe me I know what the Holy Father is thinking.'" Harry collected inscribed photographs of well-known personalities and stocked his office with them, visible signs of his success. Eisenhower, Nixon, Truman, Omar Bradley, and many others stared down from the walls of Wismer's office. "Some people work for dollars," said a friend. "Harry works for pictures."

A live celebrity was even better, and Wismer collected a number of them. Florida Senator George Smathers, a fraternity brother at the University of Florida, was a director of the Titans. John Roosevelt, Franklin's son and a partner at Bache and Company, was a vice president. From his Washington days, Wismer knew Clark Clifford, who he engaged to negotiate the Shea Stadium lease, and whom he approached for favors from time to time.

When he was announcing sporting events, one of Wismer's favorite techniques was to spot celebrities in the crowd, even when they were not there. "I do that a lot," he said. "I play my friends. I say, 'Dean Acheson is here. President Eisenhower just walked in. There goes Dick Nixon.'"

"Wismer was known as the name-dropper of football broadcasts," wrote Arthur Seigel in *The Boston Globe*. "His rapid-fire description of a contest was colorful, but often confusing, because it was hard to tell whether Bing Crosby and Bob Hope had just come into the booth or had completed a pass."

"If occasionally I happen to mention someone who doesn't happen to be there," Wismer wrote in his autobiography, "no one is hurt and that person still enjoys the play."

Wismer expected other announcers to return the favor. Titans fullback Joe Pagliei remembered being with Wismer on a night that Les Carter was broadcasting a big fight from Madison Square Garden. Wismer phoned Carter before he went on the air and asked him to tell his listeners that he was at ringside. "But you're not here," Carter protested. Tell them anyway, Wismer responded.

While most of the players did not care for Wismer, particularly when paychecks began bouncing, his ultimate fate evoked their sympathy. "Very few players liked him," said one member of the Titans' staff, "but many felt sorry for him the last year."

"No matter what people say about the man," said Art Powell in the dark days of November 1962, "I hate to see him lose that much."

"He was arguably the most eccentric owner in pro football history," said quarterback Lee Grosscup. "He was a very strange man." Tight end Karl Kaimer joined the club as a rookie in 1962 and, for reasons totally unknown to him, became a favorite of the owner. "Where do you find guys like Harry Wismer?" he asked recently. "He was a Runyonesque character. He always had a half a dozen gofers. He'd come into the locker room and pull out a cigarette, and five guys would flip their lighters. He'd hold the cigarette in his mouth, look around, honor somebody, and light up."

Linebacker Bob Marques said, "I only met him once. That was the night I got hurt and was in the trainers' room. He came in and said, 'Who the hell are you?' and turned around and walked out. I almost hit him over the head."

Professional football was the ideal place for Wismer. He had visibility, he was in New York, and he had influence in the new league. There was one thing, however, that Harry Wismer did not have. That was money. He, the Titans, and the entire league would learn the importance of this shortcoming during the next three years.

CHAPTER 4

SLINGIN' SAMMY

During the final month of 1959, the Titans began to build an organization. On December 7, Wismer announced the appointment of Steve Sebo, his former teammate at Michigan State, as general manager. Sebo, 45, was a respected veteran of the college coaching ranks who had served as athletic director at tiny Alma College, assistant coach at Harvard, and head coach at the University of Pennsylvania. He had become available due to a somewhat unusual sequence of events.

In 1954 Sebo took on a formidable task, the head coaching job at Penn, which had little talent and a punishing schedule, including national powers Notre Dame and California. As Arthur Daley wrote in *The New York Times*, "the team was de-emphasized, but the schedule was not." In Sebo's first two years, his team did not win a single game, losing 19 consecutive times in all. During the succeeding three seasons, he gradually built a competitive club, while simultaneously acquiring a schedule more compatible with an Ivy League school. After five years, Sebo's overall record was 11–34. Since the losing streak, it had been 11–15.

Sebo's progress was too slow to suit the Penn alumni, and he was told prior to the 1959 season that his contract, which expired at the end of the year, would not be renewed. As a lame duck, he led the Quakers to the Ivy League championship with a 7–1–1 mark, Penn's best record in 12 years. The team's excellent performance did nothing, however, to change the decision of the school's administration. They proceeded with their plan to fire the coach and replaced him with John Steigman, the incumbent at Rutgers. Within a week of losing his job at Penn, Sebo agreed to accept a three-year contract as general manager of the Titans. His announced salary was $25,000, a substantial increase from his coaching income.

Sebo's first task was to select a coach, a mission he hoped to accomplish by the end of the year. In fact, it happened much sooner and, as with most decisions related to the Titans, it was Harry Wismer, not Sebo, who made it. On December 17, 1959, the Titans announced that at one o'clock the following afternoon they would hold a press conference at which "one of the biggest names in the history of football will be announced as the head coach of the Titans."

The biggest name in the history of football had not been Wismer's first choice. In early November, Heartley "Hunk" Anderson, a former Notre Dame player and coach and a line coach under George Halas in Chicago, said that Wismer had offered him the head job. Anderson was an odd choice, for he was in the steel business and had been out of football for 14 years. It was probably for the best that he and Wismer never came to terms.

The Titans' owner, with his Michigan State background, openly coveted Spartans head coach Duffy Daugherty, but New York's negotiations succeeded only in getting Daugherty a better contract in East Lansing. Wismer was also reported to be interested in former Santa Clara coach Dick Gallagher, who, as chief talent scout, had helped build the Cleveland Browns into a powerhouse. Gallagher, however, accepted the position of general manager of the Buffalo Bills. Otto Graham, the former quarterback of the Browns, and former Illinois coach Ray Elliot were also rumored to be in contention for the job, but neither appeared to have much interest.

With his top candidates out of reach, Wismer was at the Deepdale Golf Club watching a telecast of the Giants–Redskins game on November 29 and happened to see Sammy Baugh, the former Redskins star who was the head coach at Hardin-Simmons University, interviewed at halftime. A light bulb went on. Baugh was a big name that might put some people in the seats. He knew the game and had been a decent coach at Hardin-Simmons. Wismer reached Baugh in the press box and arranged a meeting for the next day. Baugh had a connecting flight through New

York and arranged to meet Wismer at Idlewild Airport. The process moved along quickly, and on December 18, Wismer introduced Samuel Adrian Baugh as the first coach of the New York Titans.

Baugh was born on March 17, 1914, in a farmhouse near Temple, Texas. As a youngster, he excelled at baseball, playing third base well enough at Sweetwater High School to attract attention from professional scouts. Later, after graduating from college, Baugh was signed by St. Louis Cardinals great Rogers Hornsby, and played shortstop in the Cardinals' farm system, splitting the 1938 season between Columbus and Rochester. There were two obstacles, however, between Baugh and the major leagues. The first was rangy, 20-year-old shortstop Marty Marion, who would join the parent club two years later and become an anchor of the great Cardinals teams of the 1940s. The second was Baugh's batting. He hit just .220 in 16 games at Columbus and .183 in 37 games at Rochester. "I could hit everything but the curveball, the fastball, and the changeup," he said 20 years later. When the Cards balked at allowing him to leave in August for football training camp, Baugh decided to give up baseball.

Baugh also played football in high school, but it was his ability as a baseball player that caused Dutch Meyer, the coach at Texas Christian, to recruit him. Baugh was inclined to go to the University of Texas, but the Longhorns' coaches told him that he could play only baseball, and would not be allowed to play football. Baugh therefore opted for TCU, where he was a three-sport performer, twice earning All-America honors at tailback and leading the Frogs football team to a 29–7–2 record. Meyer became the head football coach during Baugh's sophomore season and introduced a ball-control passing game more sophisticated than that used by many pro teams. The next year (1935) was a spectacular one for the Frogs. TCU and rival SMU each won their first 10 games, setting up a historic encounter in Fort Worth on November 30. SMU won 20–14, but then lost to Stanford 7–0 in the Rose Bowl. On New Year's Day, TCU played LSU in the Sugar Bowl in a torrential downpour. It had rained in New Orleans virtually the entire week, and the field was an absolute quagmire. The referee had to hold the ball between plays; otherwise, it would float away. Baugh's passing ability was of little use in such elements, as the game was one of limited offense and continual maneuvering for field position. However, his 14 punts kept LSU in its own territory for most of the afternoon, and TCU was able to eke out a 3–2 victory. The Williamson Rating Service ranked the Frogs No. 1 in its final poll, giving Baugh an unusual distinction. He, Joe Namath, and Joe Montana are the only three quarterbacks to lead their teams to championships at both the college and professional level.

The 1936 season, Baugh's last at TCU, brought no repeat of the national championship, but he had an excellent year, leading his club to victory over Marquette 16–6 in the inaugural Cotton Bowl game on New Year's Day, 1937. Following his graduation, the Washington Redskins selected Baugh in the first round of the NFL draft. Pro football was still well behind the college game in terms of popularity, and Baugh had heard of neither the draft nor the Redskins. He thought of becoming a high school coach, but decided to ask Redskins owner George Preston Marshall for the outrageous salary of $8,000. If Marshall agreed, he would play pro football. The odds were against him, for Marshall was notoriously penurious, and would pay Cliff Battles, the league's leading rusher, only $2,700. Yet, Marshall was a born promoter and recognized a potential marquee star. He agreed to Baugh's demand, starting him on a Washington career that lasted for 16 years. Beginning as a single-wing tailback, he became a quarterback when the Redskins adopted the T-formation in 1944. By the time he retired, Baugh held virtually every NFL passing record. When Baugh entered the league, professional football was a leather-helmet, bone-jarring game played by the likes of Bronko Nagurski and Johnny Blood (McNally). The skinny Texan seemed as though he would be raw meat for such bruisers. "If you sign him," legendary sportswriter Grantland Rice warned Marshall, "insure his arm for one million dollars because these pros will tear it off." In those days, the "roughing the passer" rule had yet to be enacted, and defenders could chase the quarterback all over the field, even after he had released the ball. Rice's fears were unfounded, for it was not Baugh who was torn apart. It was the game of football that would never be the same. The rookie brought finesse to the playing field and established the pass as the most dangerous offensive weapon in the game.

Although the forward pass had been legalized in 1906, a number of rules discouraged its use until the 1930s. Any incomplete pass into the opponents' end zone was a touchback and loss of possession, and passes could only be thrown from five yards or more behind the line of scrimmage. An incomplete pass out of bounds or two incompletions during the same series also resulted in a loss of possession. The lack of passing, and the resultant ability of the defense to stack the line against the run produced a dearth of scoring. In 1932, the Bears opened their season with three 0–0 ties and a 2–0 loss. The Boston Braves managed only 55 points in 10 games, yet finished 4–4–2. Four of the eight NFL teams scored 77 points or less, about a touchdown a game. The Bears followed their four consecutive shutouts with a veritable offensive explosion, and wound up leading the league with an average of 11 points a game. Arnie Herber of the Packers paced the league's passers with 37 completions in 14 games.

Before the next season started, the NFL made several rule changes designed to liven up the games with more scoring. The goal posts were moved from the back of the end zone to the goal line to make field goals more achievable. Passing was allowed from anywhere behind the line of scrimmage and hash marks were established 10 yards from the sidelines so that any play following one that ended out of bounds would not have to begin from the sideline.

The amended rules set the stage for offensive heroics, but the star actor did not arrive for four years. In 1963 Arthur Daley wrote in *The New York Times*, "Baugh was the man who revolutionized football and altered all previous strategic concepts. Until the Slinger arrived on the scene, an unwritten pattern of play had been established. No team ever passed from within its 25-yard line. For the next 50 yards it was acceptable to pass on third down. Complete freedom was permissive only within the other team's 25-yard line."

Baugh threw the ball from anywhere on the field. In his first pro game, against the Giants, he completed 11 of 16 passes. For the year, he led the league with 171 attempts, 81 completions, and 1,127 passing yards. While these totals are minuscule by today's standards, they were enough to lead the Redskins to the championship game against the Chicago Bears. In a key December game at the Polo Grounds, Baugh went up against a Giants defense that was considered one of the best of all time. After losing to the Redskins 13–3 in the season opener, the Giants allowed a total of only 47 points in their next nine games. In the season finale, Baugh led Washington to a 49–14 win, racking up more points in a single game than the rest of the league had managed all season.

The championship game was played on an icy field with a temperature of 15 degrees, conditions hardly conducive to a passing attack. On Washington's first play from scrimmage, however, Baugh dropped back to pass out of his own end zone and threw a 43-yard completion to Battles. By the end of the day, he had thrown 33 times, completing 18 for 354 yards and three touchdowns, leading the Redskins to a 28–21 victory and their first NFL championship.

Between 1940 and 1945, Baugh led the Redskins to four title games. Although in some years he shared the passing chores with Frank Filchock, Baugh rolled up impressive statistics, leading the NFL in passing six times. In 1947 he set records with 354 attempts, 210 completions, and 2,938 yards, while passing for 25 touchdowns—six in a single game against the Cardinals. In 1945 he had a record completion percentage of 70.3 percent.

Baugh was not a one-dimensional player, however. He was an excellent safety, intercepting 28 passes during his career, including a league-leading 11 in 1943. Against Detroit in November of that year, he threw four touchdown passes and had four interceptions. Baugh was also perhaps the greatest punter of all time, leading the league four times. He averaged 51.4 yards per kick in 1940 and 45.1 for his career, both figures remaining the best in NFL history. In 1943 he led the league in passing, punting, and interceptions.

Baugh retired at the end of the 1952 season, and returned to Texas as an assistant at Hardin-Simmons, a small Baptist school in Abilene. In 1955 head coach Murray Evans resigned, and Baugh was asked to take his place. After much arm-twisting, he was finally convinced to accept.

Baugh brought a heretofore unseen, pro-type passing offense to the Border Conference. He scrapped the single wing and put in the pro T-formation. The Cowboys put men in motion and filled the air with footballs, routinely throwing more than 30 passes in a game. "We were the BYU of the '50s," said Dewey Bohling, who played for Baugh both in college and with the Titans. In 1957 quarterback Ken Ford—a sturdily built drop-back passer—led the nation in passing. After Ford graduated, Harold "Hayseed" Stephens—a 5'9" 170-pound scrambler—took over at quarterback. Baugh changed the offensive scheme to incorporate more running and rollout passes, and Stephens repeated Ford's feat.

Baugh had an uncanny ability to read defenses and quickly determine what would work against them. "Offensively," said long-time pro quarterback Cotton Davidson, "I don't know too many people who had a better mind than he had."

Fred Julian and Dick Jamieson, former Titans who became outstanding coaches, claim to have learned a tremendous amount by watching and listening to Baugh. They had to listen carefully, however. Tackle Buddy Cockrell, comparing Baugh to Paul Brown and Weeb Ewbank, said, "Sam knew more football than all of them. His problem was that he knew football so well, knew what every defensive man's reaction should be on every play, that he had a problem getting it across to players. He assumed everybody knew what he did." Communication was limited, meetings were rare, and most instructing was done right on the field.

There was little formal structure to Baugh's practices, with a heavy emphasis on improvisation. "Sammy could draw better plays in the dirt than most coaches could draw on the board," said Larry Grantham. Drawing plays in the dirt, however, was no way to run a football team. And while this was not always the case with Baugh, improvisation generally triumphed over preparation.

Baugh, Frank Filchock of the Broncos, and Buster Ramsey of the Bills were typical of the coaches in the early years of the AFL. They had been great players and understood strategy, but most of their knowledge was intuitive. "With a guy like Frank Filchock," said former Broncos quarterback Frank Tripucka, "there was no such thing as a playbook. I'd make things up almost like a guy playing a game of touch in the street. He hated practice, he hated looking at movies, and he hated playbooks."

Within three years, coaches who disdained playbooks and practices were rarely found in the AFL. The good old boys had been replaced with structured, businesslike coaches such as Jack Faulkner, Weeb Ewbank, and Al Davis. Players were no longer sent on the field to improvise. "Al Davis never put a person on the football field," said Cotton Davidson, "who wasn't ready to handle any situation that could possibly come up in that ballgame. He gave you the tools. In every training camp with Al Davis you started as if you knew nothing about football. He never took anything for granted."

Baugh was the antithesis of Davis, with his laid-back personality and a belief that players would take responsibility on their own shoulders. "I think you can get as much out of the players if you work them right and pay attention to them," he said recently. "I never liked to chew on anybody if they made a mistake. I've made too damn many myself. I was taught at TCU to never chew one of your players out if he misses a ball, misses a block, misses a tackle. As long as he's doing the best he can do, that's all you can ask. That's how I feel about it today."

On only one occasion does anyone recall Baugh sitting the team down and reading the riot act. After four consecutive losses in 1960, he got the Titans together in the locker room and told each player, one at a time, what he should be doing to improve his play. "He spent an hour," said Roger Ellis, "and went around the room and basically chewed our ass. He told the prima donnas who they were right in front of everybody. He ripped every one of the 35 guys, as only Sammy Baugh could do it. I don't know of any better expression than to say that he just tore ass. Not a single player complained, and, you know what, we played better football after that. But it's the one and only time he ever did it." For many coaches, such as Vince Lombardi, such an act was a daily event. For Baugh, it was a last resort, after self-discipline had failed. Would he have gotten better results if he did it more often? Perhaps, but that simply was not Sammy Baugh.

Everyone who played for Baugh agrees that he was a wonderful human being; indeed, according to many, the finest man they have ever met. "The chief reason for the Titans' high morale," wrote Howard Tuckner before the opening game of the Titans' first season, "appears to be their fondness for Baugh."

"Coach Baugh was probably one of the most honest people you'd ever meet," said Curley Johnson. "He's a fine, fine man."

"Most of us loved the guy," said Dick Jamieson, "He held the team together in spite of a lot of tough things that happened to us."

"Sammy Baugh is one of the finest people I ever met in my entire life," said Roger Ellis. "I'll bet of the 150 or so guys who didn't make it (in 1960 training camp) not one of them left with hard feelings toward Sammy Baugh. He was such a decent guy, so well-liked, that even though he brought you in, gave you one practice, then called you in and said, 'Hey, George, I just don't think you're going to make it here,' there were no hard feelings. He was just a wonderful human being."

Blanche Martin, a highly touted running back from Michigan State who was let go early in the 1960 season, confirmed Ellis's opinion. "I was upset because they gave up on me so quickly, but Sammy was kind of a neat guy."

"There'll never be another Sam Baugh," said fullback Pete Hart. "There's not a player who played for him who didn't like him. Sam always took up for his players and always gave them a fair shake. He was fighting a big battle with a small stick. He didn't have the players that LA, Houston and Dallas had."

Given the variety of personalities on the Titans, Baugh's universal popularity was remarkable, for nearly every coach has his supporters and detractors. And although some have commented on his lack of organizational skill, no one has had anything but the highest regard for his character.

"Sammy is one of the nicest gentlemen I have ever met in my life," said Thurlow Cooper. "That's why he didn't last. He was just too nice a guy to be a pro coach." Treating professional athletes as mature adults is a risky proposition, but doing the same with a group of college boys is even more likely to lead to disaster. According to those who played for Baugh both in college and the professional ranks, he acted exactly the same in both situations. When he coached at Hardin-Simmons, there was little emphasis on fundamentals. "Sam treated everybody like we were professional football players," Dewey Bohling said of his college days. "Most of our practices were like the pros."

Because of Baugh's reputation, Hardin-Simmons, which had a total enrollment of fewer than 1,500 students, played an incredibly challenging schedule. In 1958 they won the Border Conference and lost 14–6 to Wyoming in the Sun Bowl. In October of that year, they faced LSU in Baton Rouge. The Tigers, featuring eventual Heisman Trophy winner Billy Cannon at halfback, were on their way to the national championship. They were fired up for the Hardin-Simmons game, as the father of starting quarterback Warren Rabb had died just hours earlier. Before he passed away, Amos Rabb told his son he wanted him to play Saturday night even if he should die.

"We shouldn't have been in the same park with them," said Pete Hart. Baugh wanted to keep the ball away from Cannon and the volatile LSU offense, so he developed a game plan that emphasized ball control. Hardin-Simmons made 22 first downs and sustained a 22-play, 94-yard touchdown drive. Hart equalled Cannon with 83 yards rushing. With 1:30 left in the first half, Hardin-Simmons, trailing only 13–6, went into punt formation on fourth down. Backup center Cleatus Drinnon bounced the snap to punter Fletcher Fields, who was tackled on his own 11-yard line. LSU scored to take a 20–6 halftime lead. There was no scoring in the second half, although Baugh's club threatened repeatedly. They reached the LSU 1, 9, 44, and 38-yard lines without putting a point on the board. A potential touchdown pass was dropped in the end zone. Although they lost the game, the small school from Abilene scored a tremendous moral victory. That same season, Baugh's club played Auburn (ranked fourth), Mississippi (eleventh), Arkansas, Baylor, and Tulsa, all recognized national powers. Amazingly, Hardin-Simmons finished 6–4.

Hardin-Simmons' ability to play with the best teams in the nation was not entirely due to Baugh's ability as a strategist. He also used his country charm to recruit some talented players. Hayseed Stephens had quarterbacked Abilene High School to three state championships and was planning to attend the University of Oklahoma, then a perennial powerhouse under legendary coach Bud Wilkinson. Hayseed, as one might suspect, was a farm boy. One day, as he was working in the fields on his tractor, he saw Baugh walking toward him. Baugh asked Stephens if he would be interested in attending Hardin-Simmons. No, he said, he was going to Oklahoma. That was good, said Baugh, for the Sooners had a great program, a great coach, and terrific players, really good players. But Stephens was also a good player, Baugh said, and probably by his senior year he would be a starter. Of course, at Hardin-Simmons, quarterback Ken Ford had just completed his junior year and if Stephens were to stay home in Abilene, he would be a starter for three years. "Son," Baugh asked, "are you a benchwarmer or are you a player?" For a star high school athlete, there was only one answer. Stephens went to Hardin-Simmons.

Baugh also pirated Dewey Bohling from the University of Denver at the eleventh hour. He coached Bohling in a high school all-star game in Memphis and suggested that, even though the youngster had committed to coach John Ralston at Denver, he stop in Abilene on his way home to Albuquerque, New Mexico. "Of all the coaches I talked to," said Bohling, "he was the one I liked and really trusted." When things started to go sour with Denver, Bohling took Baugh up on his invitation. He was toured all around Abilene, everywhere, Bohling remembered, except the campus. "I didn't even know it was a Baptist school," he said later. In the end, the charm of Baugh won out and Bohling enrolled at Hardin-Simmons.

Coaching at Hardin-Simmons was the ideal situation for Baugh. Abilene was only 75 miles from his ranch, and his duties essentially ended when the playing season came to a close. He was a hero in Abilene and probably could have stayed at the school until he chose to retire.

Yet, when Harry Wismer asked Baugh to come to New York and coach his newborn Titans, he accepted, for reasons that were never completely clear. Reportedly, he had rejected offers to coach the Oilers and Texans, much closer to his home. Yet he said yes to the Titans. Why? Baugh had been acquainted with Wismer when the latter announced the Redskins' games, but the two could never have been considered close friends. Wismer's considerable persuasive talents were undoubtedly a factor. The money was certainly attractive, a three-year contract at $20,000 a year, more than Baugh had ever earned as a player.

For whatever reason, Baugh was on his way to New York for the December 18 press conference. Nearly 40 years after the fact, he still could not explain what had made him take the job. "I didn't want to go to New York," he said. "I'd been to New York all I wanted to. I don't know how I let him talk me into going up there. It was the biggest mistake I ever made. I should have stayed at Hardin-Simmons."

As assistants, Baugh selected three of his old teammates, Hugh "Bones" Taylor, Dick Todd, and John Steber. Taylor, one of Baugh's favorite receivers in Washington, coached the ends and helped with the offense. Like Baugh, he was a players' coach. "He'd go out and have a beer with you and kick around," said one former Titans player. Like Baugh, Taylor did not believe in playbooks. Coincidentally, he had been the leading receiver for the Redskins in 1954, the year Al Dorow, who led the Titans in 1960 and 1961, did most of the quarterbacking for the Washington club.

Todd, an All-America at Texas A&M, Baugh's Washington roommate, and briefly head coach of the Redskins, worked with the backs, and Steber, a Redskins guard for five years, tutored the linemen. "I just liked them real well, and they knew football," Baugh said of his selections. As his final aide and defensive coach, Baugh chose John Dell Isola, the former Giants lineman. Baugh had attempted to lure Giants star Andy Robustelli as a player-coach, but Robustelli declined. So Baugh tabbed Dell Isola, who played with the Giants from 1934 through 1940, was an All-Pro in 1939, and coached the Giants' linemen from 1957 through 1959.

Dell Isola was 48 years old in 1960, but looked much older than Baugh, two years his junior. The old Giants lineman had grown heavy, and his hair was steel-gray. Perhaps his biggest contributions to the Titans were the players he acquired through his Giants connection: Bob Mischak, John McMullan, Thurlow Cooper, and Roger Ellis—nearly an entire offensive line—plus flanker Don Maynard.

It is easy to see why Baugh was so fond of his assistants, for they were by all accounts fine men. Their skill as players was undeniable. All four had been named All-America in college, and all but Steber had been All-Pro. However, few players can remember receiving much useful advice from any of the New York staff. Their input was mainly limited to evaluating talent and exhorting their charges to greater effort. Few pro assistants had any training in instructional techniques, and their knowledge came principally from their experience as players. Guard Bob Mischak, for example, could articulate the nuances of offensive line play far better than Steber. Ted Daffer, who played for the Bears in the 1950s, said, "In the pros, they didn't have time to talk to you about individual responsibilities. They just put you out there and said, 'You're an end' and by god you'd better do it right in a hurry." Most coaching staffs were assembled from the friends and former teammates of the head coach, and part of their duties was to provide companionship for the top man.

Baugh and Wismer were the oddest of couples. To the same degree that Wismer was pretentious and needed the constant adulation of the public, Baugh was unpretentious and completely comfortable with his own personality. A constant bone of contention between the owner and the coach was Baugh's steadfast refusal to lend his presence to Wismer's shameless attempts to generate publicity. Captain Mischak often attended the Titans' weekly press luncheons rather than the coach. "Wismer was a man who liked to draw attention to himself," Baugh said recently in a substantial understatement. "At lunch he'd yell at people across the room. It was embarrassing as hell for me."

The day after each season ended, Baugh was on a plane back to Rotan. The next time he appeared on behalf of the Titans was the first day of training camp the next summer. Unlike modern coaches, who spend 16 hours a day in the offseason studying films, Baugh spent the late winter and spring months working on his ranch and playing golf. "I didn't stay one day longer than I had to," he said. "What [Wismer] needed was a coach who was going to be there all the time. He understood that when I took the job. That's the only way I'd take it. I didn't like New York. I don't like any big city."

Baugh spoke with a deep Texas drawl, and used profanity prolificly, rarely uttering a sentence without a "damn" or a "hell" in it. The cuss words were not obscenities, however, merely adjectives or punctuation, such as: "Hell, if you can't get the damn ball to the damn receiver, what the hell good is it?"

There was generally no anger in Baugh's use of language, for he was remarkably even-tempered. On one occasion, the Titans' bus was weaving through a rough neighborhood near the Polo Grounds, when a piece of fruit sailed through an open window and hit Baugh squarely on the chest. While the players waited apprehensively for the coach's reaction, he got up, used a newspaper to wipe off his shirt, shrugged, and said, "Well, it could have been worse. It could have been a sack of shit."

Wherever he went, Baugh carried two things with him, a chaw of tobacco and a large wad of currency. Even when delivering a speech, he carried a Coke bottle with him and paused to spit every few sentences. George Blanda, who played for Baugh at Houston, and didn't think much of his coaching ability, said, "Sammy's real ability as a coach was his skill at hitting a bucket ten feet away with a chaw of tobacco." The Titans players always tried to avoid the seat directly behind the coach on the team bus, for if both windows were open, Baugh would let fly and anyone behind him was likely to get a face full of tobacco juice.

The wad of currency was of much greater benefit to the players than the wad of tobacco. When Wismer's financial difficulties began to cause problems for the Titans, the coach often acted as unofficial banker. Cur-ley Johnson recalled the time he had just bought a new house in Dallas. He got a call one day from his wife saying that his paycheck had bounced and she had no money to make the mortgage payment. Johnson went to Baugh and told him of his dilemma, hoping that the coach might inter-cede with Wismer to make the check good. Instead, Baugh asked the full-back how much his mortgage payment was. "I don't want you to lose your goddamn house," he said, and peeled off $250 as a loan.

When Johnson's check finally came through, he went to Baugh to repay the advance. "What's that for?" Baugh asked. When reminded about the loan, Baugh said, "Goddamn, I forgot all about it." This was not atyp-ical, for other players spoke of similar experiences, including the same lack of concern about repayment. Jack Klotz said, "We had a linebacker, Hubert Bobo, who'd been to Hollywood and made some movies. But he couldn't handle all that and had personal problems. He went in and wanted to borrow $100 from Sam. I think Sam gave him $500 and blew him away. He said, 'If you can pay me back, fine. If you can't, that's fine, too.'"

Punter Joe Pagliei joined the Titans at the end of September 1960. An inveterate card player and bettor on horses, Pagliei was a free spirit who gave himself the nickname, "The Big Dog." One December night in Denver, a number of Titans players were walking through a snowstorm in search of a late-night snack. Pagliei stopped in the middle of the street, reached into his pocket and pulled out a handful of change. He threw it into the snowy street, then turned to his companions and noted solemnly, "The Big Dog carries nothing but the folded stuff."

When the club was in Houston that season, the Big Dog ran out of the "folded stuff." When he found that his paycheck was no good, Pagliei called Baugh and said he was going home. "I can't play for nothing," he told the coach. Baugh assured him that eventually things would get straightened out and that both the AFL and the Titans would prosper. He pulled out his wallet and peeled off, as Pagliei remembered, about eight one-hundred-dollar bills.

Four or five weeks went by before Baugh mentioned casually, "Son, do you owe me any money?" Pagliei, a hustler from Philadelphia, replied with a straight face, "Hell, no. You never loaned me any money." "Shit," said Baugh, " I thought I loaned you five or six hundred dollars." When

Pagliei continued to profess ignorance, the coach decided he must have been mistaken. "Of course," Pagliei said, "about an hour later, I went over and gave him his money."

It is almost certain Baugh came out a loser on some transactions, and that some players never repaid him. It's also almost certain that he never lost any sleep over it, for he didn't keep track of his loans, believing that a man's word was his bond.

Even after his relationship with Wismer began to deteriorate during the 1961 season, Baugh handled it in a way that Wismer could not: with honor, dignity, and humor. While the owner abused him in the press, and tried to force his resignation and avoid paying him by humiliating him, Baugh refused to be bitter. "I felt sorry for Mr. Wismer," he said recently, "because if he could have held on until he got into that new stadium, he would have made a go of it." Jack Klotz recalled Baugh, at the height of the feud, calling the team together. "He said, 'Boys, there isn't anyone in this room, including me, or Bones, or John Steber, or Johnny Dell, who's bigger than the game. The game is the thing, not me, not Mr. Wismer.' He gave a great talk on what a tremendous game it was, the respect he had for it and all the years he had put into it."

In 1964, when Baugh was head coach of the Houston Oilers, he took his club to New York for a game with the Jets at Shea Stadium. At the Oilers' hotel, he received a call from Wismer, who said he had not been to a game since giving up ownership of the Titans, and asked if he could ride to the stadium on the Oilers' bus. Most people would have told Wismer to go to hell. Baugh agreed to take him to the game and allowed him to stand on the Houston sideline. Klotz, then playing for the Oilers, remembered the scene well. "I felt very sorry for Harry Wismer," he said. "I remember him standing on the field—he was inebriated—looking up at the fans, kind of with tears in his eyes, thinking, 'this could have been mine.'"

Baugh recalled that during halftime, Wismer went up to the press box to visit with some writers and encountered trouble on the journey. "Someone punched the living hell out of him," said Baugh. "When he came back down for the second half, he had blood all over his shirt and it looked like his nose had been hit. His eye was swelling up. Someone had punched him good. I felt sorry for him."

At the press conference on December 18, 1959, neither Baugh nor Wismer envisioned that their relationship would end that way. Before he would enter the room in which the reporters were gathered, however, Baugh wanted his entire salary, in cash. Fortunately, Joe Arcuni, Wismer's minority partner, routinely carried large amounts of currency. He peeled off $20,000 and handed it to Baugh, who put it in his pocket. Only then did he agree to talk to the press. The writers asked about the style of offense the new coach planned to employ with the Titans, and Wismer stood by beaming, his dream of a successful football team one step closer to reality.

CHAPTER 5

THEY'LL NEVER FIND ENOUGH GOOD PLAYERS

Before the AFL's first season, a writer asked Buddy Parker, coach of the Pittsburgh Steelers, what he thought of the new league's chances of survival. Parker, a veteran who had guided the Detroit Lions to NFL championships in 1952 and 1953, was a man who knew football. He quickly dismissed the chances of the new league. It was hard enough for the existing teams to find 33 players, he said, and the AFL would not survive because they would not be able to find enough quality ballplayers.

However, such players were around in abundance. Indeed, sportswriter Leonard Schecter commented in 1961, "The theory that there are just so many good players and no more is disputable. That's always an argument against having more teams—expansion—and it never works out as an important problem in the long run."

In 1959 professional football in the United States consisted of just 12 teams in the National Football League. Each club was allowed a 33-man roster, providing a total of 396 jobs for all those who desired to make their living on the gridiron. Yet, college teams were graduating roughly 5,000 seniors per year. Said Al Dorow, "There were enough players for five leagues." Even Bert Bell agreed. "There are plenty of players," he said in September 1959. "There are 250 kids graduating from college every year with pro football ability. We keep about five per team, a total of 60. That leaves 190 unemployed in football." The NFL draft consisted of 30 rounds, or 360 players in total, of which only a small fraction would ever play pro football.

As soon as the Titans opened their doors, they were inundated with letters from those who wanted to take a shot at the pro game. A typical communication read: "Dear Sammy: This letter is to inform you that I am ready to take over your offensive left end position. I am 6 feet 4 inches tall and 235 pounds of solid rock. I run the 100-yard dash in 10 seconds. I am 25 years old, a veteran of 10 years outstanding experience in football. I can only say that Ray Berry of the Balto. Colts is all-pro. But I consider myself just a little bit better. If I were to go back to college, I would be a sure-fire All-America, costing you more money. Please contact me as soon as possible, as I am giving you first crack at my services."

While some erstwhile Titans may have exaggerated somewhat, talented, unemployed football players were everywhere. Gino Cappelletti, who became one of the AFL's finest receivers, was tending bar at his brother's Minnesota restaurant after having been cut by the Detroit Lions. "The NFL was such a tightly wound cocoon," he said. "The veteran players never wanted any rookies coming in and taking a job from one of their buddies that they'd been playing with for years."

There were rookies, like Bill Mathis, a halfback from Clemson, for whom competition for an NFL job would be at very long odds. Drafted by the San Francisco 49ers in December 1959, Mathis perused the 49ers' roster, spotted the names of future Hall of Famers Joe Perry and Hugh McElhenney among the running backs and decided his opportunities might be more promising with the Denver Broncos of the new AFL.

The 1959 NFL champion Baltimore Colts drafted Larry Grantham, an end from Mississippi, who was told by coach Weeb Ewbank that the Colts were looking to add one rookie to the roster from among the 20 draftees. The previous season only two of 30 had made the squad. Grantham also opted for the new league and signed with the Titans.

Jack Kemp was a collegiate star at Occidental, a small school just outside of Los Angeles. On the banquet circuit, Kemp recounts how his college coach pulled him aside during his freshman year and told him that he was the only player on the squad with pro potential. He asked him not to tell the other players of the conversation, and promised that, if Kemp were willing to give his all, the coach would work with him and see that he developed his potential. Kemp kept his side of the bargain for four years, pouring his heart and soul into his play. He found out later that the coach held the same conversation with each player on the team.

In Kemp's case, however, the coach was correct, and when the quarterback graduated in 1957, the Detroit Lions drafted him in the 17th round. The Lions were deep at quarterback, with Hall of Famer Bobby Layne and solid veteran Tobin Rote, and Kemp was released. He signed with the Steelers as a backup to Earl Morrall, and played in four games in 1957. The following year, the Steelers acquired Layne and released Kemp.

Kemp spent 1958 on the taxi squad of the New York Giants, but ran into a roster problem the following year. The Giants already had Charley Conerly, along with veteran backups Don Heinrich and George Shaw. In 1959, they drafted Lee Grosscup, an All-American from Utah, in the first round, and gave him a no-cut contract. They even tried all-pro halfback Frank Gifford at quarterback. There was no room for Kemp, and he found himself on the move once again, this time to Canada.

At Calgary, he again found himself the victim of a no-cut contract, this one held by Joe Kapp, a highly touted rookie from California who later led the Minnesota Vikings to Super Bowl IV. The Stampeders were not about to waste one of the few spots allocated to Americans on a backup. Kemp returned to the United States and joined the taxi squad of the 49ers. Early in the 1959 season, Y.A. Tittle, the 49ers' starter, was injured and the club tried to activate Kemp. Commissioner Bell ruled the youngster ineligible for the NFL, since he had played two games in Canada early in the season.

When the AFL was formed, Kemp got in touch with Chargers coach Sid Gillman, who quickly became a fan of the young quarterback. Kemp had a very strong arm, a great attitude, physical toughness, and intelligence. The latter quality was important, for, after a few years of bouncing around, Kemp was making contingency plans. He decided that if he was not successful in pro football by the age of 26, he was going to quit and enter another profession. Kemp was studying for a Master's degree in political science during the offseason and, as Bill Wallace of the *New York Herald Tribune* pointed out, "he is no dope."

In 1960, Kemp was 25, with one season left to prove his worth. Had there been no AFL, he might have started his political career much sooner. Without the notoriety provided by his outstanding years in professional football, however, it might have taken place in obscurity. Given a fresh chance with a new league, Kemp went on to lead the Chargers to two Western Division titles and the Buffalo Bills to two AFL championships.

Many future stars suffered the same tribulations as Kemp. Lineman LaVerne Torczon from Nebraska was chosen by the Cleveland Browns in the 18th round of the 1957 draft. Upon reporting to camp, he learned from coach Paul Brown that Cleveland would keep five defensive linemen. The four starters were set, and Torczon would battle another rookie, Henry Jordan, for the lone backup position. The Browns elected to keep Jordan, who eventually became a perennial all-pro with Green Bay.

Torczon was left without a spot on the roster, despite the fact that he possessed enough ability to make All-AFL teams in 1960 and 1961. "I was good on kickoffs," said Torczon of his performance in training camp. "In today's age, they would have kept me because I was good on special teams. But in those days, if you didn't start, your chances of surviving were limited." Two future all-stars fighting for a single backup position was not an unusual occurrence in the NFL of the late 1950s. It was a situation that delighted the owners, and eventually helped the teams in the American Football League.

With the limited playing opportunities in the NFL, there were many athletes who were at least as skilled as the last three or four men on NFL rosters, but remained on the fringe, eager and able to contribute to Lamar Hunt's new league. Most AFL teams began their search for talent with late cuts from 1959 NFL camps. Many of those players were north of the border, in the Canadian Football League, where teams were permitted to keep up to eight Americans on their rosters.

The Cleveland Browns drafted Thurlow Cooper, a tight end from the University of Maine, in the 16th round in 1956, following his junior year. Cooper was one of the finest all-around athletes in Maine history, earning letters in football, basketball, and track, and All-Yankee Conference honors on the gridiron. At 6'4", he was tall enough to be a basketball center, and limber enough to set the state AAU record in the high jump. The Maine football team employed a conservative offense, and Cooper caught very few passes. He was known mostly for his ability on defense, and had no thoughts of playing professionally. He intended to go into high school coaching, and was shocked to hear that the Browns had drafted him.

Cooper performed well in training camp as a rookie and, in addition to playing tight end, was given an opportunity to perform the kick-off chores because of a leg injury to the legendary Lou "the Toe" Groza. He was hopeful of winning a spot on the Browns' roster until he saw Groza in action for the first time. "He came back," Cooper recalled, "put the ball down, took three steps and kicked it out of the end zone. I said 'I guess they don't need me.'" Head coach Paul Brown concurred and Cooper was dropped from the squad on the final cut.

Upon receiving the news of his release, Cooper drove straight home to Maine, where his parents told him he had received a phone call from a Canadian Football League club that was interested in his services. The next day he was on a plane to join the British Columbia Lions. At his third practice, however, he suffered a severe ankle injury and was subsequently released. In the middle of the 1958 season, Cooper surfaced in Montreal, replacing injured Alouette receiving star Harold Patterson. After seven solid games, he was cut again. Patterson had healed and Cooper was looking for work again.

The following year, he went to training camp with the New York Giants, and played in every exhibition game in place of injured starter Bob Schnelker. He knew full well, however, that when the season began, the starting ends would be perennial all-pro Kyle Rote and the reliable Schnelker. No matter how well Cooper played, he had no chance of breaking into the lineup. Once again, he found himself on the waiver wire at the end of the pre-season schedule.

Americans who played in the CFL considered themselves quite lucky, for the life of an American in Canada was a good one. The imports were much better compensated than the native Canadians. Cooper was paid at the rate of $11,000 per year for his time in Montreal, while his Canadian teammates earned less than half that amount.

The compensation was so attractive that there were some Americans who were in Canada by choice, not because they were cut from an NFL roster. In 1953 the CFL had increased the quota of Americans from three to eight per team and began actively poaching NFL players, attracting a number of good ones with salaries well in excess of what was being paid in the States. "They could afford to do it," said Frank Tripucka, who played seven seasons in Canada, "because there were only eight Americans getting paid any kind of money." Don Allard, a quarterback from Boston College, was chosen in the first round by the Washington Redskins in 1959 (the fourth selection overall), and offered a salary of $7,000 by Redskins owner George Marshall. Marshall, like his counterpart in Washington, Senators owner Calvin Griffith, was notoriously thrifty; even though his quarterback, Eddie LeBaron, was completing law school and contemplating retirement, Marshall was unwilling to spend more than $7,000 on an unproven rookie. The Saskatchewan Roughriders of the Canadian League offered Allard $13,500, plus an opportunity to start immediately, rather than sit on the Washington bench or fill in at defensive back. At that time, the Canadian dollar was worth slightly more than an American dollar, and Allard barely hesitated before signing with the Roughriders.

Most Canadians had to hold a second job in addition to football in order to make ends meet. They worked all day and practiced in the evenings. The Americans enjoyed themselves during the day and explored the beautiful Canadian cities. "I had a great, great time in Montreal," remembered Cooper, who was a carefree bachelor at the time, and quite disappointed to leave the CFL behind. Although the Americans were much better compensated, they were generally well received by their Canadian teammates. There were some who resented the Americans, said Allard, but most felt that without the marquee players from the United States, there might not be a Canadian Football League. "They knew that the Americans were the ones drawing the crowds," said Tripucka.

The Canadian game required some adjustment for those who played college ball in the US. The field is 10 yards longer and 35 feet wider than the American gridiron and the end zone is 25 yards deep. The offense has only three downs, rather than four, to make a first down, leading to a much more wide-open game and more passing. Canadian teams typically employed more zone defenses than were found in the NFL. Twelve men to a side, as many as four men in motion, and the prohibition on downfield blocking further complicate the strategy. "I went up in the middle of the week and played both ways two days later," said Cooper, who was totally unfamiliar with the Canadian rules. "On defense, the first play, everybody was coming at me. Everybody was running and the ball hadn't even been snapped." Cooper didn't try to grasp all the intricacies of the new game, but simply played aggressively, the way he had played at Maine.

"I was penalized severely," he remembered. He adapted quickly to the new rules, however, as did virtually all of the American players. "It's the same game," said linebacker Jerry Fields, who played two years in Canada after being released by the Jets in 1963. "It's hitting and execution and tackling."

For many, the CFL game was much more suited to their skills than that played in the NFL. Players tended to be smaller, and linemen who were quick but not quite heavy enough for the American game could find a home in Canada. The three-down, wide-open nature of the offense suited others. Doug Flutie, the former Boston College star, is a prime modern example. Initially a journeyman in the NFL, he became a star in the CFL. Thirty years earlier, a Michigan State product named Al Dorow, another scrambler, had a similar experience. "I really liked it up there," he said. "It was a wide-open game, a quarterbacks' game, with an extra receiver, a longer field."

Despite the monetary and aesthetic benefits, many Americans passed up the Canadian League because it had been their lifelong dream to play professionally in the States. Larry Grantham, an undersized college end who would have been well suited for the CFL, had an opportunity to go to Canada following his junior year at Mississippi, but elected to stay for his senior season and the chance of being drafted by the NFL. Defensive lineman Bob Reifsnyder, who graduated from the Naval Academy in 1959, said, "I wanted to play in the NFL. Canada was the place that guys who couldn't play in the NFL went." Limited offseason employment opportunities in Canada, so important to a player making $10,000 or so per year, presented another reason to try for a career in the United States.

One American playing north of the border in 1959 was a skinny speed burner and former track star from Texas Western University (now the University of Texas at El Paso) named Don Maynard. Maynard had NFL experience, having spent the entire 1958 season with the Giants, playing in the overtime championship game against the Colts. He was utilized primarily as a punt returner and played a bit at halfback and defensive back. Maynard really wanted to be a pass receiver, however, and all season he watched Rote and Frank Gifford and studied their moves.

Despite having lasted a full year in the NFL, Maynard's position in New York was tenuous. In addition to the Herculean task of supplanting

Rote, he faced another obstacle in his quest to stay with the Giants. Maynard was a non-conformist at a time and in a place where conformity was a highly valued commodity. Most aspirants for positions in the NFL sported crew cuts and wore conservative jackets and ties on the road. Maynard, on the other hand, wore sideburns, cowboy boots, and a tall cowboy hat, and marched to the beat of his own drummer.

During the offseason, Allie Sherman had taken over as offensive coach of the Giants, replacing Vince Lombardi, who assumed the head job in Green Bay. Maynard's strange habits did not sit well with Sherman, a man who did not cotton to anyone who was "different." He was itching for an opportunity to rid himself of Maynard, and let it be known that he doubted Maynard had the intellectual capacity to play pro football.

Sherman found his chance during the 1959 exhibition season. During a key 1958 game against Cleveland, Maynard had dropped a punt, an incident that unfairly branded him with a reputation as a fumbler. The following summer, the Giants played the Packers at Bangor, Maine, in a stadium that was far below NFL standards. The lights were suspended so low that nearly every punt soared above them and out of sight. Maynard fumbled again and Sherman cut him the next day.

The young speedster went to Canada and joined the Hamilton Tiger Cats. Shortly thereafter, Lombardi acquired his rights and asked him to come to Green Bay. "It took them about a week to find me," Maynard recalled, "and by that time I had played a couple of games." "Do I have to come?" he asked Lombardi. When the coach said no, he elected to finish the season in Hamilton. Upon hearing of the formation of the AFL, he contacted Baugh and asked for a chance to make the New York team. "I knew he was going to throw the ball a lot," said Maynard. Baugh remembered Maynard from his college days, when he had coached him in the Blue–Gray Game and against him during the regular season. "We played against him for three years and we couldn't cover him," Baugh said. "So I figured they couldn't cover him up here either." John Dell Isola also remembered Maynard from his tenure with the Giants and encouraged Baugh, who sent assistant coach John Steber to sign Maynard.

Linebacker Bob Marques was unimpressed with his first glimpse of the new Titans receiver. "I can still picture him getting off the bus," said Marques. "A cowboy hat, dungarees, cowboy boots, and one of those big belt buckles. I thought, 'Who the hell is this guy?' He was so skinny, I thought somebody was going to break him in half ... that shows you how much I know."

Another person with misgivings about Maynard's ability was Roger Ellis, who had been in the Giants' camp with Maynard in 1959 and had also signed with the Titans. "He'll never make the team," Ellis confided to Dell Isola. Of course, Ellis had never seen Maynard at flanker.

When he lined up wide in training camp, the 24-year-old from El Paso showed Ellis, Marques, and the rest of the Titans the skills that had eluded Allie Sherman. The most impressive facet of Maynard's game was his blinding speed. "Maynard could run as fast as he wanted to," remembered Thurlow Cooper. "I never, ever saw him get caught from behind." Maynard seemed to have an overdrive gear, and occasionally one would see a defender gaining on him, only to have Don accelerate and pull away. Quarterback Hayseed Stephens said, "He'd be going as fast as he could, but if he had to pick up a step or two to catch up to the ball, he could do it." Despite his slight frame, he was also fearless when it came to running crossing patterns over the middle. In Baugh's passing offense, Maynard would learn to use his speed to develop into one of the finest receivers in football.

While Sherman and the Giants had been drastically mistaken regarding Maynard's ability as a football player, they were right on target regarding his eccentricity. "I love him to death," said Bill Mathis, a good friend from their days in New York, "but you have never, ever met anyone like him. He was unique."

Maynard was perhaps most legendary for his frugality. Nearly every one of the old Titans has at least one story concerning Maynard's appreciation of a dollar, and sometimes much less than a dollar. On one occasion, after taking a cab from the airport, he gave the driver a five-cent tip. The cabbie looked disdainfully at the nickel, and threw it back out onto the street, saying, "If you need the money that bad, keep it." As the cab screeched away, Maynard bent down, picked up the coin and put it in his pocket, saying, "Well, I sure do need it."

One teammate recalled how, before making a long-distance call, Maynard would decide in advance how long he was going to talk. He held a stopwatch and, after reaching the predetermined time, hung up regardless of what stage the conversation had reached.

Some of Maynard's schemes were ingenious. He discovered that a

Mexican penny was the same size as a U.S. quarter, and would stand by a jukebox with a supply of the former. When someone wanted to put in a quarter, Maynard would give him one of his pennies in exchange for the quarter. The penny activated the machine and Maynard pocketed the quarter.

Mathis recalled the period when Maynard stayed with him for the last two weeks of the season after the latter's family had returned to Texas, driven south by the cold New York weather. Mathis put him up, fed him, and drove him to practice every day, footing all of the bills. Finally, one night he suggested that Maynard pick up something for dinner. Maynard ventured out to the neighborhood grocery store and returned with, as Mathis remembered, "two little bitty cans of beanee weinees." That was dinner, Maynard-style.

When the Titans went on road trips, Maynard carried two suitcases, one with his clothes and the second empty. When the club returned to New York, the second suitcase was filled with toilet paper, towels, and other assorted items bearing the names of the western hotels the Titans had stayed in.

Given Maynard's attention to financial detail, it was suggested to Larry Grantham that perhaps the Titans would have had a better chance of survival if Maynard had been the owner and Wismer played flanker. "Hell no," Grantham replied, "we would have all had to quit and go home in mid-season. Maynard never would have paid us a living wage."

There are endless stories regarding Maynard's attention to finances, one in particular which shows the planning that went into his efforts. During his early years with the Titans, Maynard, who was a car buff and self-proclaimed "drug store mechanic," discovered that he could power his Ford with propane fuel, which could be purchased at a fraction of the cost of conventional gasoline. "Using propane cuts fuel costs by 20 to 30 percent," he said recently, "and the engine lasts two to three times longer." The only problem was that propane was much more difficult to find than gasoline. To overcome that obstacle, Maynard had a switch that allowed him to run the engine on either propane or gasoline and installed an enormous fuel tank, which Mathis estimated at 300 gallons, in the trunk of his car, enabling him to get all the way from El Paso to New York. "If people realized the danger of gasoline," Maynard said, "they'd all use propane.

If you dropped a tank of propane from the top of the Empire State Building, the only thing that would happen is that the tank would get dented. The gas has to leak out for several hours before a match would set off an explosion. You can't start a fire inside a propane tank."

Maynard's actions while with the Titans might have been born of necessity, as money was always scarce under Harry Wismer, but he continued to keep close watch on the purse strings even after Sonny Werblin and Leon Hess brought the franchise stability and economic security. On one of the Jets' late-season trips to Oakland in 1966, Maynard, Mathis, and backup quarterback Mike Taliaferro were sitting by the hotel pool, wearing their kelly green Jets traveling blazers. It was a chilly day, and the pool was deserted. Mathis and Taliaferro dared Maynard to dive off the high board into the freezing water fully dressed. Maynard thought it over for a few seconds, calculating his price. He decided that he would do it for a hundred dollars if they would allow him to take off his watch and boots. Mathis and Taliaferro scampered off to take up a collection from their teammates and were quickly successful in subscribing the entire amount. Maynard, true to his word, removed his watch and boots, dove neatly into the icy water and pocketed his earnings. He put the green blazer into a small hotel dryer, so he could put it back on before coach Weeb Ewbank found out what he had been up to. Unfortunately, Maynard had not tested the shrink resistance of the garment, and when he put it back on, found that the sleeves ended in the vicinity of his elbows.

The pool incident was one of the few times off the playing field that Maynard ever removed his boots. He wore them everywhere. Years after they retired, Thurlow Cooper convinced Maynard to play in a charity golf tournament at the University of Maine. Cooper picked Maynard up at the airport and drove him to the club, where they agreed that it was too hot to play in long pants, and they would change into shorts. Emerging from the clubhouse, Cooper was astounded to find his old teammate attired in shorts, a cowboy hat, and a pair of white cowboy boots. "Don," he said, "they won't let you play in those!" Maynard grinned and lifted up one foot to show Cooper the golf spikes in the bottom of his boots. "People still tease me about them," Maynard admitted. "They say 'Here comes the majorette. Where's your pom-poms?'"

While there were many American players in Canada, others unable to crack the NFL remained in the States. Some had gone into coaching. Tommy O'Connell, who quarterbacked the Cleveland Browns to the 1957 Eastern Division championship, left the coaching ranks to join the Buffalo Bills. Sammy Baugh convinced his old neighbor and Hardin-Simmons fullback, Pete Hart, to abandon his post at Port Neches High School to take a shot at pro ball. With a family to support, Hart hesitated, but consented when Baugh assured him he was almost certain to make the squad. Jim Swink, a TCU All-America who had initially spurned professional football for medical school, signed with the Texans.

The Titans discovered other players in the employment of Uncle Sam. The quality of football on the service teams of the 1950s was astoundingly good. Between the military draft and college ROTC programs, most young men of that generation, including football stars, wound up putting in time in the service. "Football was practically a branch of the armed services in the early fifties," wrote Mark Ribowsky, the biographer of Al Davis, who obtained his first head coaching job at Fort Belvoir in 1953. "No gunnery skill or officer training could turn a base commander's head as fast as a GI, tar, flyboy, or marine who could effectually throw or carry a pigskin. Pros, All-Americans, and lettermen became instant VIPs, granted immunity from the rigors of military subsistence and assigned to bases for 'special services'—which might entail little other than arising at the crack of noon and playing ball against a schedule of service and small-college teams."

"When I joined the Bolling Air Force team," said Dick Felt, who later became a defensive back for the Titans, "every starter had at least one year in the NFL or Canada." One of Felt's teammates at Bolling was Bob Skoronski, who later became the offensive captain of the great Green Bay Packer clubs of the 1960s. Joe Ryan played at Fort Dix with three players who had, the previous year (1956), taken part in the NFL Championship Game.

Between stints at Yale and Rutgers, Alex Kroll, who would later play for the Titans, served two years in the Army. When Kroll was stationed at Fort Campbell, Kentucky, camp commander General William Westmoreland, who later became commander of U.S. forces in Vietnam, decided that Fort Campbell was going to field the best football team in the service. In order to find the toughest 11 players, Westmoreland ordered full scrimmages in the grueling heat of July. It was a battle of attrition, a prelude to the general's strategy in Southeast Asia. Westmoreland also used his extensive network to comb the Army for former college players who might help his team. "About every two days," said Kroll, "a helicopter would land on the north side of the field and out would come a kid who'd played quarterback at Oregon State and had just been drafted. If he could throw better than Bobby Stone, our regular quarterback, he had a place. If not, two days later, the helicopter was on its way up. It was a presage of the Titans' experience."

Westmoreland's efforts bore fruit. "It was positively the best football team I ever played on," said Kroll. With such an abundance of talent, the Fort Campbell team had a perfect record until losing to a club from Fort Carson. The commander did not take the defeat lightly. "We heard that the general was very upset," Kroll recalled. "We had disgraced the division and the post. He was going to make sure we kept playing football until we had a record Fort Campbell could be proud of." The team kept playing, week after week, until the rematch with Fort Carson. They won and faced another big game against Fort Bragg, which could make or break the season. "We figured if we lost that game we'd have to play until Easter," said Kroll. With the United States at peace, this was the direst threat Westmoreland could muster. During the Korean conflict, Al Davis's Fort Belvoir team was told that, if they didn't play well before a visiting general, all 21 officers on the squad would be immediately dispatched to the front.

Westmoreland's milder threat was enough to motivate the Fort Campbell squad. "We were grim," Kroll recalled. "There was never a group of mercenaries quite like the Fort Campbell team that played and routed the team from Fort Bragg." Following the impressive victory, Westmoreland declared the season ended.

Dick Felt played at Bolling Air Force Base, where he set a rushing record with 809 yards, and was named the Air Force MVP in 1959. Felt was a 27-year-old from Brigham Young who graduated late after spending two years on a mission for the Mormon Church. He had been a great offensive player at BYU, once scoring four touchdowns in a single quarter against San Jose State. Felt wanted to take a shot at pro football, but there was one hitch. He had joined the Air Force in 1958 with a three-year commitment, and still had one year to go. His coach was a civilian named George Makris, who previously worked at Michigan State under Biggie Munn and Duffy Daugherty. Harry Wismer, who attended MSU, was always partial to anyone with a Michigan State connection. When Makris told the Titans about Felt, Wismer listened. Despite competition from newly hired Charger assistant Chuck Noll, the Titans got Felt on their negotiating list and offered him a contract. Although he had 14 months remaining in the Air Force, Felt "had some people at the Pentagon with some juice," who got him released early.

Other Titans came from the semi-pro leagues. Unlike baseball, with its hierarchical farm systems through which players made a steady climb to the major leagues, football's minors were loosely-knit organizations which operated on a precarious basis. Teams and entire leagues failed regularly. Some semi-pro clubs were known as "town teams" and played independently rather than as part of an organized league. "These were mostly guys," said Roger Ellis, "who'd played in high school, were working in construction, and had big beer bellies." The town teams had very few paid players, often only the quarterback, and sometimes played teams that were members of a league. Many players were not paid at all, and others recalled being paid in change, as owners took collections from the gate and concession stands and parceled it out right at the stadium. Practices were held infrequently, most teams played in high school stadiums, and the 'program' was often a mimeographed sheet with one roster on each side. The first step down from the NFL was a giant one.

In the anonymity of the minors, some players were able to perform for more than one club at a time, which might require the use of an alias. Ellis played for Brockton under an assumed name, while using his real identity to compete for another team. He figured he was safe, since he didn't know anyone in Brockton except the proprietor of the specialty shoe store where he bought his 15AAA brogans. One night the shoestore owner came up to him on the sidelines and addressed him by his alias, adding a sly wink.

Minor league players competed not for the money, but for the love of the game, or with the chimeric hope of landing a spot in the NFL. Some had legitimate talent, but had not been able to survive academically in college. Since players could not be drafted until their class graduated, they bided their time with minor league clubs. The inspiration for all of the semi-pros was Johnny Unitas, who at one stage played for the Bloomfield Rams for six dollars a game. The minors were teeming with players for whom the prospect of eight new teams was like a dream come true.

While there was an occasional future NFL or AFL player in the mix, most of the minor league rosters consisted of former high school or college players who simply could not give up their connection with the game. Paul Zimmerman, a guard for the 1961 Mt Vernon, New York, Eagles, explained the lure of the semi-pro game. "There's a certain pride you have. You just don't like to play for nothing. The money isn't much, but it helps and it means something. I play, though, because I enjoy it."

Zimmerman's teammate, Leo Dragami, was 32 years old and had been playing football since he was a 14-year-old freshman in high school. "I got $25 for the opening game with this team last season," he said. "That's more money than I made during the other 16 years of football combined. Until last year I never made a penny. I got that $25 for three games and then the money ran out so we played the rest of the games for fun."

There were more celebrities in management than on the field. Johnny Most, legendary radio voice of the Boston Celtics, was general manager of the Boston Sweepers. In 1966 Jackie Robinson was the general manager of a Continental Football League club called the Brooklyn Dodgers.

As professional football expanded, so did the semi-professional brand. In 1962 the Atlantic Coast Football League came into existence with six teams and became the pre-eminent minor league. By 1964, the ACFL had expanded to 14 teams, consisting of the Atlanta Spartans and 13 clubs from the northeast. That same year, the Jets established a relationship with the ACFL's Jersey Giants, under which the Giants would have the first opportunity to sign any player cut by the Jets, while the latter had first choice of any player on the Jersey roster. By the mid-1960s, many ACFL teams had established similar affiliations with AFL and NFL clubs. The Montreal Alouettes of the CFL used the Sea Dogs of Portland, Maine, as their farm club. The parent clubs sent taxi squadders and late cuts to their affiliates in order to give them game experience. If injuries depleted the major league club's roster, they looked first to the ACFL club for reinforcements.

The Midwest featured the United Football League and other smaller circuits. As in the early Atlantic Coast League, there were no affiliations, although both major leagues looked to the UFL for replacements for injured or waived players.

Roger Ellis, a teammate of Thurlow Cooper's at Maine, was typical of the top minor leaguers of 1959. He lacked superstar ability but was a dedicated worker determined to have a career in pro football. After three weeks of training camp in 1960, Baugh said, "There isn't anybody in camp who hustles more than he does. He's really here to play." The role of underdog was a familiar one for Ellis, who was not recruited heavily out of high school and had to ask for a tryout at Maine. He quickly became a starter and, in his senior season (1958), was selected the team's most valuable player. In 1959 Ellis found himself in the New York Giants' training camp, a 15th-round draft choice. A natural center, he had to compete with perennial all-pro Ray Wietecha, who was an iron man, hardly ever missing as much as a single play. There were five rookie linemen in the Giants' camp that summer and only one would make the team as a backup. With a 33-man roster, most clubs carried only two spare linemen.

Ellis pulled out all the stops to garner that one precious opening. In drills he went up against massive, 300-pound Rosey Grier, where the 240-pound Ellis's only hope was to attempt to cut Grier's legs out from under him. Roger had the foresight to plant a friend of his in the stands to watch practice. Each time Ellis was successful in upending Grier, his friend would shout loudly, "Way to go, Ellis!" in order to make sure that head coach Jim Lee Howell had noticed.

In the end, however, all the careful planning went for naught, and Ellis was cut after the fifth exhibition game, which was played in Bangor, Maine. As a local hero, Ellis was cheered mightily, but Howell was not swayed. For a young man who desperately wanted a career in pro football, the release was a devastating episode. "I don't think I came out of the house for two weeks," he said. "I was so depressed. I was so embarrassed. I didn't want to see anybody." For the remainder of the 1959 season, he played for the North Attleboro Jewelers for $25 a game. The quarterback and coach of the Jewelers was Ed "Butch" Songin, a 35-year-old Boston College graduate and a veteran of the Canadian League. Songin was the highest-paid Jeweler at $250 per game. He and Ellis became close friends. When John Dell Isola became an assistant coach for the Titans, he remembered Ellis and recommended that the new club sign him. Songin signed with the Patriots.

The player who took perhaps the most unusual route to the Titans was defensive back Fred Julian. Julian was a versatile two-way performer at the University of Michigan who led the Wolverines in rushing in 1959, his senior year, although he netted only 289 yards, the lowest total ever to lead Michigan in rushing.

When he graduated in June 1960, Julian told his parents that the only present he wanted was $100 to buy a plane ticket to New York. He got his wish, and convinced his college coach, Bump Elliot, to arrange a tryout with the Titans. Julian landed at La Guardia, took a cab to a Bronx hotel, and, the following morning, July 7, walked across the bridge to the Polo Grounds, where he found a group of about 100 players who would shortly try to impress Baugh and his assistants.

Baugh liked Julian's ability at one-on-one coverage and invited him, along with five others, to training camp in Durham, New Hampshire. He told the youngster to meet him at his suite in the Manhattan Hotel the next day. Scared stiff, Julian knocked on the door of Baugh's suite and was admitted, where inside he found the coaching staff lounging about in their skivvies. Baugh took out his wallet, peeled off five or six twenty-dollar bills and handed them to the youngster, telling him that he was responsible for getting himself and the other five signees to Durham. With the money, Julian bought train tickets and meals for the would-be players, and brought his charges in safely, alighting from the train at the University of New Hampshire, where he joined Maynard, Cooper, Felt, Ellis, and many others who were prepared to compete for a job in pro football.

CHAPTER 6
THE GAMES THEY PLAYED

Roster size, which ranged from 33 to 36, largely defined the professional game of the late 1950s and early 1960s. With the coaches allowed to keep only a limited number of athletes, they had to make certain to choose those who could do a number of things reasonably well, rather than those who could perform one specialty exceptionally well. An intelligent athlete who could learn a variety of assignments quickly was a valued commodity.

Specialists were a luxury few teams could afford. "When you carry only 33 men," said Baugh in 1960, "a kicking specialist must be really good if that's all he can do." Gino Cappelletti, a college quarterback who knew he didn't have a major league arm, asked Patriots coach Lou Saban for a tryout as a kicker. Saban told him he would have to earn a spot as a defensive back first. A kicker would be chosen from among the players who had already made the team at other positions.

Some veteran players performed principally as kickers, but virtually all had been regulars in their younger days, and remained backups in their original positions. This meant that practice time for kicking was limited, for kickers and punters had to stay after the regular drills to work on their specialties. In addition to a lack of practice time, regulars who kicked or punted had a distinct disadvantage compared with today's specialists, who stay on the sideline between kicks, stretching and kicking into a net. Cotton Davidson was a starting quarterback who also punted and did some field goal kicking. "Imagine a guy," he said, "who's played three quarters of football, his leg is tired, and he has to kick a fifty-yard field goal! As a punter, I'd play the whole ballgame at quarterback and then have to punt in the latter part of a game. That old leg just doesn't have the snap that it did in the first quarter."

These factors particularly impacted field goal accuracy, as did natural turf and hash marks that were five yards closer to the sidelines than under present-day rules. In 1959, NFL players attempted 248 field goals and were successful on only 116 occasions (46.8 percent). The great Lou Groza of the Cleveland Browns made only five of 16 attempts, and Paul Hornung of the Green Bay Packers just seven of 17.

While accuracy was well below the standards of the 1990s, when a misfire from less than 40 yards might land a kicker on the waiver list, the range of kickers in 1959 was not drastically less than that of their modern counterparts. A 50-yard field goal was an admirable feat, but not unheard of. Bert Rechichar of the Baltimore Colts kicked a 56-yarder in 1953, a mark that was not broken until Tom Dempsey launched his remarkable 63-yard rocket for the New Orleans Saints in 1970. In a 1960 scrimmage, Bill Shockley of the Titans connected from 54 yards and hit the crossbar from 59.

One of the reasons for the lack of accuracy was that all kickers used a straight-on approach, rather than the soccer style that became prevalent by the 1970s. The first soccer-style kicker was Pete Gogolak of Cornell, who joined the Buffalo Bills in 1964. Jack Klotz remembered that when they first saw Gogolak line up to kick off from an angle, he and his teammates started screaming to beware of the onside kick. They had never seen anyone approach the ball that way.

In his rookie year, Gogolak connected on 19 of 29 field goals, helping the Bills to the AFL title and starting a trend that eventually made the straight-on kicker obsolete. In 1996 NFL kickers made 732 of 915 field goal attempts (80 percent). In 1998 Gary Anderson of the Vikings made all 35 of his field goal attempts.

Another factor that inhibited the development of kickers was the substitution rule in the college game. Once a player left a game, he could not re-enter in the same quarter. If a kicking specialist was inserted for a field goal attempt, the player he replaced could not come back in until the next period. Thus, the place-kicker was almost always one of the starters. A player such as Gogolak, who could only kick, had no place in the collegiate game of the 1950s, except perhaps for desperate last-minute attempts. The result was that not many talented kickers emerged from the college ranks. In 1959 George Grant of Colorado State set a single-season NCAA record with seven successful field goals. Jim Turner, who later became one of the NFL's greatest field goal specialists with the Jets and Broncos, had a grand total of three during his senior season at Utah State.

On the other hand, punters, at least in terms of distance, have shown little improvement during the past 40 years, despite the advent of artificial turf. The records of Baugh and Detroit's Yale Lary have not been excelled with the finality of those of their placekicking counterparts. Averages in the mid-40s generally led the league, as they do today.

While the physical nature of the game has changed, so has the mental phase, particularly for the quarterback. In 1960 the signal-caller was also the play-caller, not only barking the snap count, but determining what play would work in a certain situation against a particular defense. Paul Brown of Cleveland, who used alternating guards as messengers, was the only coach who called all the plays. Frank Tripucka, Denver's quarterback from 1960 through 1962, said: "I played fifteen years of pro football and four years of college football and never had a coach call a play for me." Some coaches occasionally sent in plays, but for the most part, the quarterbacks were in charge, and took their leadership role seriously. When Sid Gillman of the Rams started calling plays for Norm Van Brocklin, the Dutchman quit rather than take orders from the sideline.

Although calling plays and having to think ahead added an extra burden to the position, not one of the quarterbacks who played for the Titans believed that it made his job more difficult. "I felt I was down there in the middle of the field, where the action was," said Al Dorow. "I had a better feel than anybody in the press box or on the sidelines could ever have. You're thinking of the yardage, the distance, the time of the game, and the plays that are working for you. You've got to bank all that stuff. It's part of being a quarterback." Although Baugh had been one of the best quarterbacks in history, he was in total agreement and let Dorow call nearly all the plays.

Hayseed Stephens echoed Dorow's sentiments. "In the huddle, I could look into a running back's eyes and see when he really wanted the ball." He could also tell when the back was out of gas and needed to rest for a play.

Lee Grosscup added a further dimension. "It was really the leadership aspect," he said. "The name for the quarterback was 'field general' or 'coach on the field.' Now the quarterback is more like a robot. He just responds to signals. In our day, there was always a lot of communication in the huddle, especially with the Giants. Charlie Conerly would ask Ray Wietecha, the center, what looked good with the running game and ask Kyle Rote what looked good with the passing. They would always talk in the huddle and on the sideline." Although Conerly was the leader of the Giants, Don Heinrich often started at quarterback in order to let Conerly watch the opposing defense from the sideline and develop his strategy.

Dorow relished the challenge of trying to outsmart the defensive signal caller, generally the middle linebacker. "That's why I play," he said in 1960. "There is much more satisfaction to me in making a good call on a third-down, two-to-go situation and fooling some linebacker than throwing a sixty-yard touchdown pass. This is a brain game." Archie Matsos, a fellow Michigan State graduate, played in the middle for the Buffalo Bills. "I used to run a lot of quarterback draws," said Dorow recently. "I'd go up under center, look him right in the eye and say, 'Archie, I'm going to run the quarterback draw.' He'd start yelling and screaming and adjusting his guys. He wouldn't believe me. He'd run out of there to cover the tight end and I'd run the quarterback draw. The next time I'd do it again and he'd say, 'I don't believe you.'"

In a 1961 game against Dallas, Dorow called five straight running plays up the middle. With the defense bunched toward the center of the line, he called a bootleg and carried the ball for 40 yards. This was the type of cerebral jousting he loved.

While all preferred calling their own plays, there was disagreement among the old quarterbacks over whether it would be possible with today's sophisticated offensive and defensive schemes. "I think it would be difficult, but it could be done," said Grosscup. "I believe that some of the reluctance is that a lot of people would be out of work if quarterbacks went back to calling their own plays. I really think it's taken something away from the game."

Dick Jamieson, a quarterback for the Titans and recently the offensive coordinator for the Arizona Cardinals, disagreed. "The preparation is such that players would have to do a lot more work in the offseason and put in a lot more time on Monday and Tuesday than they're really able to. I've been around some guys who were very sharp. Ty Detmer was sharp. Rodney Peete was very sharp. But the guys I've been around are very comfortable in being given the latitude to change plays, but not having to go through the rigor of calling them."

Cotton Davidson, another quarterback who spent more than 20 years in coaching, disagreed with Jamieson. "I think if I call a play that I like," he said, "and I know will work, I think I'll come a lot closer to making it work than a play that's sent in that I don't have confidence in. I think, as a coach, that if I spend a couple of hours each day with the quarterback, when a certain situation comes up, we'd call the same play." He did not believe the complexity of modern offenses should take responsibility out of the quarterback's hands. "In most cases," he said, "teams could take half their offenses out and they'd be a better football team. Players make mistakes because they're running plays they haven't practiced that much. Why did the Green Bay sweep work for Green Bay? Because they ran it about fifty times a day in practice."

Frank Tripucka agreed that a coach and quarterback became of like mind if they frequently discussed strategy. "It's amazing," he said, "how many times I came out of a game and the coach said, 'That's exactly what I would have called.'"

The defenses that the quarterbacks of 1960 faced were much simpler than those of the present day. The 4-3-4 was the standard formation, with no nickel backs or situational substitution. Defenders became fatigued, and the smart quarterback was able to sense weaknesses in the secondary and take advantage of them. The basic pass defense was man-to-man, enhanced by simple zones. The bump-and-run did not make its appearance until the mid-1960s. In 1955, the Los Angeles Rams drafted K.C. Jones, the basketball star from the University of San Francisco, in the 30th and final round. During training camp, Jones played defensive back in a way no one had before. He defended the same way he did on the basketball court, maintaining contact with the receiver and hand-checking constantly. Although Jones never played for the Rams, defensive backfield coach Jack Faulkner remembered his technique. When Faulkner became head coach of the Denver Broncos in 1962, he taught the style to cornerback Willie Brown. When Brown went to Oakland in 1967, he passed it on to Raiders defender Kent McCloughan. Titans defensive back Dainard Paulson explained the effectiveness of the bump-and-run by comparing pass defense to dancing. "When you hold your partner close," Paulson said, "she can follow your moves and move with you. But when you're far away, she really can't follow you unless you telegraph your moves."

If dancing were the standard, most AFL defensive backs did the minuet, keeping a respectful distance from their partners, rather than a cheek-to-cheek tango. "Defensive backs are hard to come by," said former Patriots coach Mike Holovak. "It's a tough job. You've got to be able to run, backpedal instead of going forward, go sideways and every which way. Every time the receiver goes deep, you've got to be able to run with him and go for the ball. And everybody knows it if you get beat."

Tom Rychlec, Buffalo's leading receiver in 1960, played tight end for the Detroit Lions in 1958 and 1959. "The biggest difference in the two leagues," he said, "was that in the NFL, the linebacker would hit you at the line and try to check you. You had to use all your moves and finesse to get into the pattern. In the AFL, nobody touched you. You could get right into the secondary, and even then they gave you a lot of room, because they didn't want to get beat deep."

In 1962 Tripucka said, "The biggest difference in the three leagues? (NFL, AFL and CFL) I'd have to say it's the linebackers. They let you complete passes. They don't move fast enough."

The lack of quality pass defense was not entirely an accident. If the AFL could not achieve immediate parity with the NFL in terms of talent, it was determined to surpass them in terms of excitement. As its official ball, the AFL adopted the Spalding JV-5, which was 1/4 inch longer and 1/4 inch thinner than the NFL Wilson model, and therefore slightly easier to throw. As Leonard Schecter wrote, the AFL was "a league which hasn't learned enough about the game to make it dull." Owners expended the majority of their efforts in signing skilled offensive performers, and relied to a large extent on undrafted rookie free agents to man the defense. The two major court battles between the rival leagues involved running backs Billy Cannon and Charlie Flowers. Lamar Hunt made it clear that his new league could not survive by trying to develop diamonds in the rough. It needed recognizable names that would draw spectators, and most familiar names lined up on the offensive side of the ball.

The Titans signed veteran quarterback Dorow, Maynard, and 49ers draftee Bill Mathis for the offensive platoon, and later added former Eagles end Art Powell. Their four starting defensive backs, on the other hand, were all rookie free agents. Dick Felt, a Titans rookie in 1960, said: "You think you've learned a lot about playing defense in college and service ball. But when you get into the pros, it's like moving into a new world." For the most part, college football was still a "three yards and a cloud of dust" game, and professional rookies had had very little experience defending against the pass. In 1960 the *New York Post* described a "sparkling aerial show" by Richie Mayo of the Air Force Academy, one of the leading passers in the nation. Mayo had completed eight of 19 attempts for 147 yards.

With their stable of seasoned quarterbacks and a dearth of quality defenders, AFL teams took to the airways with enthusiasm. In 1959 NFL teams averaged about 26 passes per game. The following year, AFL clubs threw more than 33 times per contest. Tripucka and Kemp each passed for more than 3,000 yards, a feat never before accomplished in pro football. In a 1962 Denver–Houston contest, the Broncos threw 53 passes and the Oilers 44. Like most AFL encounters, the game was not an artistic success, as the Oilers had eight interceptions and the Broncos five. The same year, against Buffalo, Tripucka had 56 attempts. In 1960 George Blanda threw 55 passes and Jack Kemp 37 in a Houston–Los Angeles game. "Today they talk about the West Coast offense," said Tripucka. "Hell, we had the West Coast offense going in 1960. My theory was, if I can throw a quick little hitch pass and pick up five yards, what's the difference between that and running an off-tackle play to pick up five yards."

"We were having a ball," said Dorow. "We had mostly experienced people on offense, because the owners wanted to throw the ball, while the defense was mostly rookies. The secondaries were so vulnerable and inexperienced that anything you called to Maynard or Powell, they were going to be open." Receivers did not have the benefit of the tacky gloves they wear today, but the pass catchers of 1960 created their own advantages. "We used a lot of resin," said star Oilers end Charley Hennigan, "and if it got wet we would use flesh-colored band aids, clip off thumbtacks, and put them on the tips of our fingers." That was illegal, of course, but it made the inexperienced defenders' lives even more trying.

The new league was a quarterback's dream. "I still have a lot of warm feelings about the old AFL," said Grosscup. "I thought it was a lot more fun. Later on, the AFL started to look more like the NFL. There are a lot of people who wish the merger had never happened."

Pass defense in the early AFL was so difficult that, in 1962, a Boston Patriots fan decided to help his team's undermanned secondary. In a late-season night game, the Dallas Texans drove inside the Boston 10, where quarterback Len Dawson spotted tight end Fred Arbanas open in the end zone. As he pumped his arm to throw, however, someone darted between Dawson and his receiver, causing him to draw the ball back. Game films showed that the shadowy figure in the corner of the end zone was one of 12 men on the defensive side of the ball. As Alex Kroll wrote, "The one wearing a long black overcoat was not on the roster."

Not only were the defenders inexperienced, they received limited help from the pass rush. "We used to blitz a lot," said Holovak. "I guess deep down we were hiding our pass coverage. We were trying to help them by not giving the other team as much time to throw the ball."

Blitzing helped, but there were few defensive linemen who could strike terror into a quarterback's heart. For the most part, the front four were big, slow men geared to stop the running game that was prevalent in the NFL. It was not until the mid-1960s, in response to increased passing, that quick linemen like Deacon Jones, Merlin Olsen, and Alan Page became dominant figures. "The punishment that quarterbacks take now is incredible," said Jamieson. "We got beat around a little bit, but nothing like what they get today. The defenses are so much bigger and faster and geared to getting to the quarterback. I would not want to be standing back there taking the shots these guys take."

Virtually all of the old Titans admit that today's players are stronger and faster. "Speed is the biggest difference in today's game," said Julian, now an outstanding junior college coach.

Today's players are undeniably bigger. "The biggest change in the game," said Holovak, whose football career spanned nearly 60 years, "is weightlifting. Everybody's lifting weights. Players are stronger today and they're faster. Today, if you've got a guy who weighs 250 pounds, you make a linebacker out of him because he's too small for the line." The average weight of the Titans' starting offensive line in 1960 was listed at 247 pounds. Even that figure is questionable. Buddy Cockrell, who was listed at 250, said he actually weighed only 230–235. If the other linemen exaggerated similarly, the Titan line was much lighter than 247.

The defensive front four averaged 254 pounds and the linebackers 210. A 300-pounder was a rarity at that time, and the Titans had none. As late as 1986, there were only eight 300-pounders in the NFL. Only four years later, the Dallas Cowboys' offensive line averaged 296 pounds, and by 1998 there were 250 NFL players who topped the 300-pound mark, led by Minnesota's Korey Stringer at 359. The Raiders boasted 13 such heavyweights, and the Giants and Packers each had 12 men above 300 pounds.

In 1960 none of the teams had weight rooms, and most players did not work out from the day the season ended until the first day of training camp the following summer. Buddy Cockrell prepared for camp by punching a heavy bag and doing some running on his ranch. A handful of conscientious athletes began getting in shape a few weeks prior to the start of camp, but most showed up and sweated off excess poundage under the eyes of the coaches.

One reason players did not train during the offseason was that they had to hold down jobs to supplement their football income and prepare for life after their playing career was over. The unofficial pay ceiling for professional athletes was $100,000, and only a rare superstar earned anywhere near that amount. In 1962 Willie Mays was the highest-paid baseball player at $90,000. Mickey Mantle earned $85,000 and Roger Maris, in 1961, the year he hit 61 home runs, pulled down only $32,000, despite an MVP season in 1960. Salaries in football and basketball were much lower. In 1959 the NFL minimum salary was $6,500 per year and the league average was $9,000. Jimmy Brown, perhaps the best player in the league, was reported to draw a $32,000 salary as late as 1961. Al Dorow, the Titans' highest-salaried player in 1960, said he now earns more from his NFL pension that he made in his peak years as a player.

Although the advent of the AFL increased salaries somewhat, compensation was still not at a level to provide lifetime financial security. In 1963, when the Titans filed for bankruptcy, the salaries of the 1962 club were made public in the court records. Grosscup was the highest paid, earning $17,000. Maynard, with three outstanding seasons under his belt, was next in line at $15,000. Surprisingly, Wayne Fontes was third at $14,500, ahead of all-stars Mathis, Grantham, and Mischak. Most of the linemen received less than $10,000, with Nick Mumley, a three-year starter, earning only $8,500. Bobby Fowler, a running back signed late in the year, brought up the rear, earning only $8,000 per year.

Compared to today's multi-million-dollar incomes, the 1962 salaries appear almost ludicrous. "My kids found my contract a few years ago and laughed themselves silly," said Karl Kaimer, who earned $9,500. "They asked me if I cashed my check at a toll booth on the way home."

Jack Klotz was an assistant coach at the Pennsylvania high school where Joe Klecko, a star defensive lineman for the Jets in the 1980s, played. He remained friendly with Klecko and later found himself discussing salaries. Klotz told the younger man how he had skillfully negotiated his way into a $5,500 contract with the Rams for his rookie year. Klecko heard only "55" and assumed Klotz must have meant $55,000. "Fifty-five thousand wasn't bad back then," Klecko replied. When he heard the true number he thought Klotz was kidding.

The relatively low salaries did not stop people from describing professional athletes as overpaid and pampered. In early 1964, when Houston's Bud Adams signed Scott Appleton, the Outland Trophy winner from the University of Texas, Arthur Daley wrote in the *Times,* "his salary and fringe benefits could bring him $40,000 per annum, for four years, an utterly ridiculous sum to pay for an untried lineman. It would also be a ridiculous sum to pay to anyone less than a Jimmy Brown, a Paul Hornung, a Y.A. Tittle, or a Johnny Unitas." (Indignation over salaries paid to professional athletes can be found as early as the 1870s, when legendary sportswriter Henry Chadwick complained about the "preposterous salaries" earned by baseball players. "Just imagine a ballplayer receiving twenty five hundred dollars for eight months' service," he wrote in 1871.)

The players had little leverage in those days, for there was no union, and no agents. "One year," said Art Powell, "I scored fourteen touchdowns

and got a contract the next winter offering me a cut in salary. Those were
the games they played in those days because we didn't have anybody to
represent us."

The Los Angeles Rams drafted All-America center Alex Kroll of Rutgers. Having played at Yale and Rutgers, Kroll had become rooted in
the New York area and had no desire to move to California. When the
Rams came to New York to play the Giants, he arranged a meeting with
Los Angeles general manager Elroy "Crazylegs" Hirsch and asked if he
could be traded to the Giants. Later in life, Kroll, as CEO of Young and
Rubicam, an international advertising agency, spent a great deal
of time opening new markets in Communist bloc countries. He compared
the look he received from Hirsch to that which he got in Eastern Europe
when he asked a question that was politically or culturally inappropriate.
"It wasn't that they weren't able to process an answer," Kroll said. "They
couldn't process the question. The question, 'How about trading me to
the Giants?' didn't exist in Crazylegs' world at that time. The notion that
one of the indentured servants would request to be traded to another
plantation was so implausible that it wasn't that he wasn't going to answer.
He wasn't going to accept the question."

If a player didn't like his contract offer he could send it back unsigned
and wait for a better one. Since free agency was not an option, the player
could negotiate with only one team. If agreement could not be reached,
the only alternative was to hold out. The club could then negotiate
through the press, hinting that the player's demands were unreasonable,
and they were hurting the team with their selfishness. Powell viewed the
negotiating process as a one-way street. "Management would say that we
had to spread the ball around and get other people involved in the offense.
Then you'd come in for negotiations and they'd say, 'You didn't catch as
many balls as you did last year.' You never won the negotiating game. You
tried to get as much as you could and then saddled up and went out and
played."

In 1961 Powell held out and didn't sign until the day training camp
started. The following year, he took the most drastic action a player of that
era could take. He refused to sign a contract with the Titans and played out
his option. Playing one's option year without a contract called for an automatic 10 percent reduction in salary, but gave the player the freedom to

negotiate with any team for the following season. The danger was that free agency would be only a euphemism for unemployment, for several players had been unofficially blackballed from pro football for daring to buck the system. Powell himself had already experienced that type of treatment in the NFL. In the case of marginal players, the owners generally made their point by relegating troublemakers to Canada or the semi-pros. "The NFL had a monopoly on pro football," said Proverb Jacobs. "If you did anything wrong, they'd say, 'We'll see that you don't play football in the U.S. anymore.' With only twelve teams, they could dictate that." For a player of Powell's tremendous ability, however, there was work available. Al Davis, newly installed as coach of the Oakland Raiders in 1963, made Powell the first of his renegade signees, a move that proved greatly beneficial for both club and player.

While salaries were low by today's standards, they were still much more than a college graduate could expect to make in nearly any other professional endeavor, and most players considered themselves fairly compensated. "I got eight thousand dollars my first year," said quarterback Bob Scrabis. "People laugh, but you've got to remember that with a BS in accounting, people were getting four hundred twenty-five dollars a month. With a Master's you could get six hundred and fifty dollars a month. My salary was for four and a half months."

"I was an engineering major at Maine," said Roger Ellis, "and went for some interviews my senior year. I would have had to work for no more than five thousand dollars a year. With the Titans I was making nine thousand for six months. In 1960, after the season was over, I took my last check and bought a brand new Impala Super Sport for three thousand dollars."

"When I got that five-hundred-dollar bonus my senior year," said Dewey Bohling, "I was the richest man in the world. I didn't even bother to go to my second semester classes."

It was not just the money that made players feel privileged. Whether they earn millions or just a few thousand, professional athletes have always received plenty of media attention, become heroes to youngsters, and live a somewhat glamorous lifestyle if they so choose. Many considered themselves special and had an identity that relied heavily upon their football career. When Joe Pagliei first came to New York to sign with the Titans, he spotted his favorite actress, Lauren Bacall, in a bar near Penn Station. He approached her and said, "I'm not an ordinary person. I'm a pro football player and would really like to say hello. Can I buy you a drink?"

Making a modest salary playing professional football was infinitely better than earning the same amount of money in a more pedestrian occupation. When the Detroit Lions released Tom Rychlec in 1959, he returned to his hometown and just hung around. "I really wasn't interested in a job," he said. "You feel you're superior to everybody. You're in the limelight." Rychlec was thrilled to receive an offer the following year to play for the Buffalo Bills for $11,000. "I just wanted to keep playing," said Joe Ryan of signing with the Titans. "That way I didn't have to get a job."

Off-the-field opportunities for additional income were limited, with endorsements available only to recognizable superstars. Bohling recalled a number of speaking engagements during his days with the Titans. "We'd get ten to fifteen dollars," he said. "We'd get invited by the Elks or some other club and they'd give us lunch. I made about five appearances and never got more than twenty dollars."

Retirement benefits were non-existent prior to 1959, when the NFL pension plan was established. When the AFL was formed, it had no retirement plan. In 1961 Wismer announced his intention to set aside 25 percent of his profits for the players, but 25 percent of zero is zero. A league-wide plan was finally instituted in 1964, and was retroactive to include players who started their AFL careers in 1960.

The low salaries sometimes discouraged marginal players, particularly those with family responsibilities, from taking a shot at the pros. Thurlow Cooper and Roger Ellis, who stuck with football until they finally made the grade, were both single. They were in the minority, as a high percentage of college players married young. From the late 1940s through the mid-1950s, many college players were war veterans, first from World War II and then from Korea. They were often in their mid-twenties, matured from their battlefield experiences and able to handle the responsibilities of classroom, football, and family. When the vets graduated, however, the marriage rate among players continued at the same high levels. Sixteen of the 22 Arkansas starters on the 1960 Gator Bowl team were married, which coach Frank Broyles saw as an advantage. "We think marriage helps a boy in his studies," Broyles said. "The wives make 'em bear down." Not everyone shared Broyles' beliefs, and several schools instituted rules against marriage. This was somewhat tricky, since neither a coach nor a university could legally prevent two consenting adults from joining in holy matrimony. What they could do was revoke the player's scholarship. This was the policy at Auburn.

Dewey Bohling of the Titans was married at 16 (with Baugh as his best man) and, by the time he arrived in New York at the age of 22, he had a three-and-a-half-year-old son and a one-and-a-half-year-old daughter. His fellow rookie Blanche Martin likewise had two children. Jim Moran, a 22-year-old rookie with the Giants in 1964, was the father of five. These men, with their family responsibilities, could not afford to spend years pursuing a dream.

Limited earning power also meant that the athletes of 1960 could not achieve lifetime financial security through sports. They needed to prepare for life after football. Commissioner Bert Bell visited the players from each NFL team annually and always urged them to pursue meaningful offseason employment. Just prior to the 1960 draft, the league produced a marketing brochure aimed at graduating seniors. One section read, "Football should not be your life's work, merely a stepping stone...so we want to tell you about this dynamic city [Pittsburgh] and how it will fit into your future."

Salary levels also had an impact at the end of a player's career. In today's game, most players do whatever they can to squeeze out an extra year of active play. One season of professional sports will earn them many times what they could hope to realize in their post-football career. In the era of the Titans, many players had to make the difficult decision to end their playing career at a time when their physical ability would have allowed them to continue on. A trade that would take them away from their offseason business was often the reason for a premature retirement.

Dick Guesman summed up the players' dilemma. "During the winter of 1964, I had to make a decision. I was not getting a good job in the offseason. Corporations didn't want to hire you unless you made a commitment to come with them full-time or you were a superstar, which I was not. I was twenty-seven, had recently gotten married and decided to embark upon a career. I went to work for the Shell Oil Company in New York."

Others saw football as a means to an end. "I was using football as a stepping stone," said defensive lineman George Strugar. "I wanted to play long enough to get enough money to get into business. When the business could afford to pay me more than football, that was it."

Although virtually none of the old Titans resent modern players for their astronomical salaries, many old veterans are disgusted by the deportment of today's players. When Dennis Rodman appeared on the cover of *Sports Illustrated*, longtime reader Larry Grantham wrote a letter of protest and canceled his subscription. "When a guy won't go into a playoff game! That's not what sports is all about," he said.

"One of the things that's changed in football is the specialists," said Joe Ryan. "With guys only being in the game for three or four plays, that's why we've got these dandies running around in the end zone doing their dances and shaking their behinds. In the old days you played all offense or all defense. If you ever did anything like that to show up the other team, somebody would come and level you. But now, they're only out there for a few plays, so you don't really get a shot at them."

Playing both ways also necessitated conserving one's energy, rather than expending it by dancing. Maynard, who played both offense and defense in college, said: "When you held somebody on the one-yard line, you didn't whoop and holler. You just got up and said, 'Well, we've got ninety-nine yards to go.'"

Hank Soar, a former Giant from the 1930s and 1940s, has a similar disdain for the end zone dandies. "They're getting paid to tackle players and score touchdowns," he said. "I remember one time we had a game in Brooklyn, and the fans were giving it to us good. I ran about twenty yards for a touchdown, and when I got to the end zone, I bowed. When I came off the field, Steve Owen [the Giants' coach] chewed me out like you wouldn't believe. He said, 'You're not on the stage'. It drives me up a wall when they spike the ball. Steve Owen must be turning over in his grave."

No one can deny that the game and the players have changed. The players of 1960 were slower, smaller, and poorer, and they played a game that was much less sophisticated than today's computerized version. It was a very different game, but it was every bit as competitive, and competition is the essence of sports. Titans captain Bob Mischak commented, "Every time I competed it was a private game against the guy on the other side of the line. It was a personal battle between me and my opponent." That was what drove the players to excellence, not the promise of a big paycheck. The concept of competition is timeless and the game of 1960 was every bit as fierce as that of 1990, or 1920. It was professional football.

CHAPTER 7

THE FIRST TRAINING CAMP

On the morning of July 9, Baugh met 26 members of his new football team in front of the Manhattan Hotel. The players represented a curious mixture as they stood on the sidewalk, trying to appear nonchalant and unconcerned. Some were veterans looking for a final chance; others were pursuing a quixotic dream, while a handful were NFL regulars who had every expectation of making the team. Among the latter group was Bob Mischak, a guard who had been drafted by the Cleveland Browns upon his graduation from West Point in 1954. After serving three years in the Army, Mischak went to the Browns' camp in 1957, but left prior to the start of the season. He incurred some nagging injuries, his wife was pregnant, and he decided to go home. The next year, Mischak joined the New York Giants and was the starting guard in the overtime loss to the Colts in the title game. The following spring, he had his appendix removed, was forced to sit out the entire season, and took a position as supervisor of the repair department of New Jersey Bell Telephone Company. Only 26 years old at the time, Mischak, who had been ambivalent about pursuing a pro career due to its lack of security, discovered that he was not ready to give up athletics for life behind a desk. During his year in the business world, he found that he really missed football. John Dell Isola, who had coached Mischak with the Giants, signed him on behalf of the Titans.

Mischak was an outstanding athlete. "He was quick, fast, had good hands, good strength, good coordination," said Roger Ellis. "He just did everything right." During the Titans' first training camp, Steve Sebo said, "He is a great player; he has everything needed to be a greater player—brainpower, poise, leadership, speed." A fullback in high school, Mischak switched to tight end at Army. When he reached New York, he found that the Giants were set at tight end, but needed an interior lineman. He had never played guard before, but was tutored by New York assistant coach Vince Lombardi, who knew Mischak from the days when Lombardi was an assistant under Earl Blaik at Army. He learned so well that he became a starter in his first season.

In addition to his athletic ability, Mischak brought maturity to the young Titans team. The players respected him as much or more than they did the coaching staff. He was well spoken, had the bearing of the military officer he had been, and, while most players headed off to the bar every day after practice, limited himself to an occasional beer. According to lineman Joe Ryan, "Other guys would be going out to have a beer after a practice or game, while Bob would go to a coffee shop and have coffee." The hobbies of most players tended toward hunting and fishing, but the Titan program listed Mischak's principal outside interest as "studying corporation financing and proxy fights."

"Bob was a very special person as far as I was concerned," said Cotton Davidson, who later played with him at Oakland. "He was a great football player, but he was also a unique individual, so serious about everything. I have a ranch in Texas, and Bob wanted to know everything about cows and horses and tractors. Every subject that was brought up, he would want to know all the details about it."

Years later, the members of the Titans still speak of Mischak as if he were a level above the rest. He combined the ability that would make him an AFL All-Star with the character of a classic All-American sports hero. Larry McHugh, a rookie guard in the 1962 training camp at Stroudsburg, remembered how, while most veterans were doing whatever they could to protect their jobs, Mischak went out of his way to help young McHugh with his technique, even though they were competing for the same position.

"If I like people," said Mischak, "I'm willing to give whatever information I have. I never felt threatened." It was that confidence, which never showed itself as cockiness or arrogance, that gained him the respect

of his teammates, coaches, and opponents. Departing for his first training camp with the Titans, Mischak said, "Money's a little better here, and
the conditions are, too." If asked the same question three years later, when
the Titans were history, Mischak might well have wanted to amend his
answer.

Sid Youngelman, the other NFL veteran standing in front of the Manhattan Hotel, was almost the opposite of Mischak. As much as Mischak
was polished and professional, Youngelman, a Brooklyn native, was bois-
terous, brash, and earthy. "Everybody liked Sid Youngelman," said Bill
Wallace, who covered the Titans for the *New York Herald Tribune*. "Sid realized that this wasn't going to last very long, but let's have a good ride while
it's going." Wallace found much of Youngelman's loud, brash persona to
be a front, and learned that he was in fact quite an intelligent man.

Youngelman, a 28-year-old defensive tackle, had ballooned to a rather
paunchy 265 pounds. "He had started to pouch a little," recalled an old
teammate. "Sid was not much on conditioning," said another. Youngelman was also missing three teeth as a result of being kicked in a pileup in
college. He had played at Alabama, participating in two bowl games, and
for five years performed in the NFL with the 49ers, Eagles, and Browns.
He was a regular for the Browns in 1959, but was released following a lingering dispute with an assistant coach. He also had worked the pro
wrestling circuit, earning $300 a week in Buffalo and Cleveland as an
"honest" wrestler.

Despite his increasing girth and missing teeth, Youngelman could
be charming; he always had a great deal of success with women. The other
Titans envied him his stable of attractive escorts, and often marveled at
how he managed to attract them. "He wasn't the best-looking guy in the
world," said one, "but he always had a way with women. He'd take them
to dinner and feed them nice drinks. He'd get the limos and everything."

In the locker room, Youngelman was loud, humorous, and sometimes
just odd. "He had an unusual way of protruding his chin and upper lip and
looking down at his thumbs," said Jack Klotz. "Sid would always check
his thumbs. He would hold them about a foot and a half in front of his
nose, right together, look at his thumbs, put them away, put them up,
check them again."

Youngelman could also be downright crude. Thurlow Cooper once invited his cousin, a doctor from Bar Harbor, Maine, to a game. The doctor was a rabid Titans fan, so dedicated that he drove his car to the top of Cadillac Mountain and plugged a portable television into the cigarette lighter in order to watch his cousin in action. When Cooper invited him to watch a game, visit the locker room, and mingle with the players, the doctor was ecstatic. He drove to New York, saw the game, and then went to a post-game party at Cooper's apartment. Youngelman was talking to the doctor when he suddenly dropped his pants, turned around, bent over, and said, "I've had piles, doc. How do they look?"

On another occasion, Youngelman had been hit so hard in the stomach during a game that, while giving a post-game interview in front of his locker, he lost control of his bowels. He continued talking, without missing a beat while, as a teammate said, the flies began to gather. "Sid was very cool. It didn't bother him at all. He delivered."

On the field, the veteran tackle was known for vicious play that often went beyond the boundaries of the rules. He went to Alabama on a basketball scholarship, but was banished from the team early in his freshman year. One day, he was repeatedly run into a pick, and berated by the coach for his inability to stay with his man. Finally, Youngelman blasted through the screening player. "I guess I hit him in the teeth with my elbow," he said later, "and knocked him half across the floor. Then the coach hit the ceiling, and he threw me out of the gym and told me not to come back." Fortunately, the Crimson Tide football coach was in the gym and recruited Youngelman for his team, where such tactics were more appropriate. "I learned to clothesline and all sorts of other things," he said.

"Sid couldn't differentiate," remembered Karl Kaimer. "He'd bite and kick his own guys." On several occasions during his two seasons with the Titans, he was ejected from a game for fighting. On the Friday before a key 1960 game with the Oilers, a game that would decide first place in the Eastern Division, Youngelman gave a lengthy interview to the *New York Herald Tribune*. Among other things, he said, "There's no excuse for mental mistakes." Two days later, he was thrown out of the most important game of the year for fighting.

Youngelman's style was exemplified in one exhibition game. The day was brutally hot, and all the players were complaining, particularly those linemen carrying a few extra pounds. Rather than merely complain, Sid told everyone he intended to do something about it. Early in the game, he ran over to a pileup and began kicking everyone in sight. He was immediately ejected, which carried with it an automatic $50 fine, equal to the pay for each exhibition. Youngelman departed happily, however, boasting after the game that it had been well worth $50 to avoid playing a meaningless exhibition in the punishing heat.

In addition to veterans such as Mischak and Youngelman, there were some setting out in pursuit of a nearly impossible dream. Bill Wohrman was a 27-year-old halfback with a wife and young child; he had had a brief tryout with the Cleveland Browns in 1955. He had since played two years in the Navy and in a semi-pro league in Bloomingdale, New Jersey. Wohrman quit a coaching job at Dickinson High School in New Jersey for one last shot. "I could never have lived with myself if I hadn't tried once more to play pro football," he said. "I know it's about time I settled down, but this game gets in your blood. I have to find out definitely if I have it. I think I do." Wohrman, like most others who passed through the Titans' camp that summer, learned that he did not have it. Hampered by two huge blisters on his feet, he was cut before the exhibition season began.

After a seven-and-a-half-hour drive, the Titans' bus arrived in Durham, New Hampshire, a small town located 12 miles from the Atlantic coast. Durham is best known as the home of the University of New Hampshire, a state school with a current enrollment of approximately 16,000. In 1960 the entire town of Durham had a population of 4,800 and the University was even smaller, with an enrollment of only 4,000.

Dick Young of the *Daily News* described the town for his New York readers. "It is a typical New England campus: red brick colonial buildings covered with spreading ivy; narrow sidewalks lined by breeze rustled trees. Across the street, side-by-each, is the malt shoppe on the corner...the haberdashery, the sundries store and the glass-enclosed public phone booth. Around the corner is the movie house, open on Tuesday and Thursday evenings only. This is the business district of Durham, New Hampshire, a town that pills could take to fall asleep." Worst of all for the writers, "Not only is Durham small and quiet, it is dry. In this town, when you buy a teammate a refreshing drink after a workout, it's a milk shake—and you had better drink all of them you can before 6:30, because the malt shop is closing. The midnight curfew set by general manager Steve Sebo is superfluous. Nobody stays out; there is simply no place to stay out in." The Titans were housed in Fairchild Hall, which was without air conditioning and in which smoking was prohibited.

It was in Durham that Baugh faced the task of finding 35 football players from a squad that numbered anywhere from 100 to 110, depending on the source. He did not have much time to judge the many prospects, for in just three weeks, the roster had to be reduced to 45. By July 16 it was down to 73, and a week later it was 63. Two days after that it was 50, and by the time the club left Durham at the end of the month, it was down to the maximum of 45. However, due to the substantial number of players coming and going, the exact size of the roster at various points in time was difficult to pin down with any degree of exactitude. *The Daily News* reported that there were only 58 players left after just 10 days in camp.

Paring the roster was not a job that Baugh relished. "Some of these boys will be eating dirt from the first day," he said before the bus left New York, "but they won't quit. Then you have to tell them, and some go away and cry." When the team arrived in Durham, he observed, "This is like waking up on Christmas morning and looking at the pretties. I reckon it's time to find out which toys will hold out." Releasing players was a part of pro coaching that Baugh could never accept. "Some boys wanted to play so bad," he said nearly 40 years later, "they hung around for a week after we let them go. You feel a little bad about cutting anybody. They think they're good enough to play. I never have liked that part of it. I don't think you get used to it either."

Throughout the summer, Baugh and Sebo would be forced to tell many a hopeful player that their dream had ended and they would not be on the final roster. The coach was correct in his assessment that players almost always thought they were good enough to make the squad. Self-confidence is a necessary ingredient for any successful athlete, and even those cut in the first days of camp had succeeded at some level of competition. Most had been cut before, and it was the conviction that they had been misjudged that brought them to Durham. When speaking decades after their careers ended, many made the sincere claim that they had more potential than the coaches and front office allowed them to

realize. Backups felt they should have been starting, and many cut early
on believed they were the best at their position and were the victims of
favoritism or inadequate opportunities. Few realized they were overmatched and left camp of their own volition.

The players who assembled on the first day of practice were just the
initial wave. As NFL and other AFL clubs cut their rosters, the Titans
brought the released players in for tryouts. "A bus would pull up and
unload ten or twenty and pick up ten or twenty," said Roger Ellis. As one
of the poorer AFL clubs, New York had often been last in line when signing players in the offseason. Now they had a second chance at some they
had failed to get the first time around. The AFL clubs divided up the NFL
teams and determined which had first choice of released players. The
Titans, for example, had the first shot at anyone let go by the Baltimore
Colts. Only if they decided not to sign a Baltimore cut could the other
teams approach that player. Every day, the league sent telegrams to each
club listing all players that had been placed on waivers. Every evening,
Sebo went over the list with his coaches to see if there were any familiar
names who might be of assistance.

New Hampshire Route 4, which runs west from the coast into
Durham, was heavily traveled by football players arriving and departing
from the Titans' base. An article published in *Sport Magazine* in 1971 stated
that 234 players went through the camp. In September 1960, Sebo put
the total at 238. Many who were there thought the number was much
higher. "I imagine we ran 400 ballplayers through there," said Baugh.
"It was an absolute circus," Dewey Bohling recalled. "Everybody who had
ever thought about being a professional football player was there." They
came in all shapes and sizes, as hundreds of Walter Mittys trudged to
Durham, Colorado College of Mines, Chapman College, the University
of Massachusetts, and the other AFL training sites. In the early summer,
the Chargers held an open tryout that attracted 300 hopefuls. "We got
just about every truck driver and bartender," recalled Chargers coach Sid
Gillman. "We had several hundred guys who thought they might be football players." Only one, defensive back Bob Garner, made the team.

It was estimated that the Patriots ran 280 players through their camp
at Amherst, including three named Bob Lee, Bob Fee, and Bob Dee. Mike
Holovak, who eventually became Boston's head coach, was initially signed

as director of player personnel. "Billy Sullivan handed me an airline ticket and a credit card," he recalled, "and said, 'Get some players.'"

"It was a madhouse," Gino Cappelletti said about the first Patriots camp. "There was an exodus of vans and trucks driving from Amherst to Logan Airport bringing guys to fly back home and picking up guys who were flying in. After every practice, after the evening meal, you'd go back to the dormitory, where they'd post a list of players who were to see the coach. Boy, you just sweated it out and hoped your name wasn't on that list."

The Bills tried out 215, including future major league umpire and author Ron Luciano. The Broncos, in Golden, Colorado, had a similar experience. "We had people coming in and out of camp like crazy," said Frank Tripucka. "I said that unless they're here two weeks, I'm not going to bother to learn their name."

The camps were not, for the most part, in luxurious settings. The Dallas Texans trained in Roswell, New Mexico, under the baking, blistering desert sun. "We stayed out there forever," recalled Cotton Davidson. "It seemed like we practiced for three months. We went to Oakland for an exhibition game and it was such a relief to get on a plane and get out of that place."

Of the many players passing through the Titans' camp, some stayed only briefly. One player drove all night from New York City for his tryout, and was a bit late getting out to the practice field. An assistant coach saw him running out to join the group and asked who he was. When told that it was the player from New York who had just been signed, the coach snapped, "He can't run. Cut him." The young man, who had quit his job to pursue an opportunity with the Titans, returned to the locker room without having broken a sweat, disbelieving and unemployed.

"With the league just starting," said Holovak, "everybody was anxious to make a good showing right from the start. Every owner wanted it. Every coach had the pressure of trying to do it. If someone didn't catch your eye the first day, you just passed them by and looked at somebody else."

"Every time there was a cut," said safety Roger Donahoo, who made the Titans' starting lineup as a rookie, "you'd see guys coming into camp with a pair of shoes slung over their shoulder, either high cuts or low cuts."

When he saw the high cut shoes, Donahoo would relax, for he knew that it was either a lineman or Johnny Unitas, and there was little chance of the latter appearing in the Titans' camp. If the newcomer had a pair of low-cut spikes, Donahoo knew that he might represent competition for one of the precious roster spots and took the necessary measures. "We'd say, 'Art Powell, he's slow on the inside, he can't beat you deep.'" Then he'd watch as Powell beat the rookie deep and drove another nail into his coffin. "It was dog-eat-dog," said Donahoo. "There were fights. There was kicking. There was punching."

"You were there to win a job," said Bob Marques. "You weren't there to make friends. I learned that the first or second day. I asked Sid Youngelman for some advice and he just snorted at me. I took care of myself from then on."

Unlike today's game, where players come to the professional ranks as specialists, virtually all college players of the 1950s had played on both offense and defense. When they arrived in camp, they were tried on both platoons until it was determined where they were most effective. New arrivals were immediately thrown into scrimmages, to see whether they had any promise. If they failed to make an immediate impression, they were on the bus out of town the next morning. The early practices were hectic, for the Titans had equipment for only about half the players in camp, necessitating two sessions in the morning and two in the afternoon.

With so many players passing through, and with multiple practice sessions, it would seem imperative that the operation be fine-tuned and smoothly organized. Organization and detail, however, were not Baugh's long suits. Practice was an informal event, which proved greatly disconcerting to some players who came from highly structured college programs like Penn State, Michigan State, and Notre Dame. A number had been in the Cleveland Browns' camp, which was operated with military precision by Paul Brown. Brown administered IQ tests to the players and held endless strategy sessions. Every minute of practice was scheduled in advance and each player's activity was accounted for. With the Titans, many players had the impression that the coaching staff showed up at practice each day and then decided what to do on a catch-as-catch-can basis. "You didn't know from one day to the next what the hell you were going to do in practice," said one. Dick Felt thought he had made progress after several days when Baugh asked him his name.

Baugh was only 46, in excellent condition, and if the plays were not being run the way he wanted, he would jump in under center, a big chaw of tobacco in his cheek, and show his young Titans how it should be done. "He could still throw the ball," said tight end Thurlow Cooper. "He threw the softest pass. You didn't have to catch it. It just landed in your hands."

In passing technique, Baugh had little use for style and a textbook spiral. The most beautiful pass in the world, he always preached, was the one that was complete. It could be a wounded duck, or thrown end over end, but if it got to the receiver, Baugh was happy. He was not called "Slingin' Sammy" for nothing, as he delivered the ball sidearm, off-balance or from odd angles, rarely planting his back foot before unloading. "It was shuffle, shuffle, shuffle, throw," remembered Al Dorow. Hank Soar, the longtime baseball umpire and former professional football player, recalled playing against Baugh one day at the Polo Grounds. "He was near the sideline," said Soar, "and he was going to pass. Our guys rushed in on Sammy, with their hands up in the air to stop the pass. He threw the ball underhand from one side of the field to the other. The ball never got more than three feet off the ground, and Wayne Millner caught it. As he got up, he said to me, 'Did you ever see anything like that?'"

Bob Scrabis recalled, "He told me, 'Scrabis, you've got to learn how to move. Anybody can stand in the pocket and throw the ball. You've got to learn to move to your left and throw it this way, move to your right and throw it over your shoulder, throw the ball off balance.'" At Penn State, Scrabis had been taught to pivot and sprint back as quickly as possible, then turn and plant. Baugh had him backpedal so that he never lost sight of his receivers and could watch the patterns develop.

Baugh was perhaps most effective in working with the punters. He taught the Titans' punters how to drop the ball properly and how to hold it to get both distance and direction. He had the remarkable ability to kick the ball to a spot on the field, or drop it out of bounds near the opponents' goal line. Baugh was a directional kicker before the term was invented. He would play catch with Bones Taylor in a game where Taylor would throw the ball to Baugh, who would kick it back to Taylor. Rarely did Taylor have to move more than a couple of steps to catch the ball.

Jack Gregory, coach at East Stroudsburg State at the time the Titans trained there, recalled Baugh sending a player downfield, as if he were running a pass pattern, then punting the ball and trying to hit his receiver in stride. "He could punt the ball to wherever the guy was going to run," said Gregory. "He was exceptional." Baugh would have contests with the Titans' punters, Joe Pagliei or Curley Johnson, placing practice vests at certain spots on the sideline and attempting to place kicks out of bounds between the vests. Rarely did he lose. "He'd beat my butt every night," remembered Pagliei. Unlike today's punters, who prefer high spirals that drop dead near the goal line, Baugh kicked line drives that sailed out of bounds wherever he wanted.

One of the problems facing Baugh during his first week in Durham was that he had neither a punter nor a skilled quarterback to coach. After the club's first intrasquad game, Dick Young wrote in his "Quick Kicks" section, "Game pointed up Titans' crying need for a punter. Kremblas is best, but one of his boots netted only 12 yards."

The lack of a quarterback was a more serious issue. Other AFL teams loaded up on offense, signing experienced quarterbacks such as George Blanda, Frank Tripucka, and Babe Parilli. The Titans, on the other hand, did not have a single quarterback with professional experience on the day they opened camp. George Izo of Notre Dame, the Titans' No. 1 draft pick, signed with the Cardinals. Ken Ford, Baugh's old Hardin-Simmons quarterback, who the Giants cut in 1959, and Bob Colbrunn, a Little All-American from Miami of Ohio, were the two most prominent quarterbacks in camp. There were also a number of other candidates, including Scrabis, Frank Kremblas, James Reese, Larry Bielat, Neal Buckman, Billy Joe Caldwell, Terry O'Brien, and Tom Dimitroff, none of who appeared to have the experience or ability to lead a pro team.

On July 23, the Titans traded linebacker Jim Baldwin to the Dallas Texans for Dick Jamieson, the only Texan quarterback of any repute who did not have a guaranteed contract. Jamieson played football, baseball, and basketball at Bradley University for two years before leaving school to sign a contract with the Pittsburgh Pirates. He played in the Pirates' farm system for two years as a catcher, but when his class graduated, signed with the Philadelphia Eagles, who selected him in the 1959 draft. Jamieson went to training camp, where he found Norm Van Brocklin entrenched at quarterback. Released by Philadelphia, Jamieson was signed by the Colts and placed on their taxi squad. For the entire 1959 season, he backed up Johnny Unitas, ran the scout team in practice, and then changed into civvies for the games. Baltimore carried only one quarterback on the active roster and, in the event Unitas was injured, defensive back Ray Brown was the emergency replacement.

When the AFL began organizing, the Patriots and Texans contacted Jamieson, who opted to sign with the latter franchise for $12,000, twice the value of his first contract with the Eagles. After two weeks in the Dallas camp, he realized he had no shot at a regular job, and asked to be traded. The Titans, without a viable starting candidate in camp, were eager to give up Baldwin, a marginal player who did not make the Dallas roster.

Jamieson's days in the sun were limited, for, in late July, Wismer signed Al Dorow, a 29-year-old veteran who played in the NFL for four seasons with Washington and Philadelphia. In 1956 he played well enough to be selected to the Pro Bowl. In 1958 and 1959, Dorow had been in Canada, playing for the Toronto Argonauts in the latter season. Any Michigan State alumnus drew Wismer's attention, and the Titans' owner had pursued Dorow (MSU class of '52) since the previous December. Wismer had first-hand knowledge of Dorow's ability, for he had been a broadcaster for Notre Dame in the early 1950s when Michigan State, with Dorow at quarterback, was one of their most dangerous opponents. The Spartans lost only one game during Dorow's junior and senior seasons, and started a 28-game winning streak that continued well after his graduation. Wismer also broadcast the Redskins' games in the mid-1950s when Dorow was the Washington quarterback. Living in Altadena, California, Dorow hoped to hold out and provoke a trade to the Chargers. By late July, with the teams already in training camp, he gave up and agreed to report to the Titans.

Although only 29 (28 according to Dorow), the new quarterback was a Y.A. Tittle look alike, almost completely bald, with only a fringe of blond hair around the edges. Dick Young wrote in the *Daily News*, "Dorow's hairline starts like himself, about a quarterback." At one time, Dorow possessed an extremely strong arm, but after several years of pro ball, it was a little the worse for wear. A scrambler, he loved to roll out and run with the ball, a penchant that caused him to have his nose broken four times. "That's nothing," Dorow said. "You don't miss a game for that." He was tough and aggressive, possessing all the leadership qualities one expected of a field general, both on and off the field. "Al knew where all the parties were," said one teammate. Tom Rychlec, who played with Dorow for the Buffalo Bills in 1962, said, "Al was a party guy, the center of attention, a comedian. He always had a joke."

Finally, Baugh had a quality, experienced quarterback with whom to work. "Dorow wasn't what I'd call a great quarterback," Baugh said recently, "but he was a damn good quarterback. We were fortunate to get him." That was not what Baugh said when Dorow first reported to Durham. "Dorow is going to have to win [the job] for himself," the coach said. "After all, he hasn't exactly set the world on fire the other places he's been." The new quarterback blended in quickly, for Baugh's offense was essentially the same system Dorow had run with the Redskins. Although Ken Ford had gotten most of the work in camp, and many reporters made him the choice to be the starter, there was no way he would beat out an experienced NFL veteran. After the first exhibition game, Baugh conceded what virtually everyone knew from the day Dorow reported: "There is just no question that he has to be the starter."

After 27 days in Durham, the coaching staff and the 45 survivors took off from Logan Airport in Boston on a journey that would cover 8,200 miles, last for more than five weeks, and encompass a like number of exhibition games at locations spanning the continent. The first stop was Los Angeles, then a 10-hour journey by air. Many of the players on the plane were those who expected to make the team, such as Mischak, Maynard, and Youngelman. Also on the plane, in the 45th and last seat, as his teammates told him, was Fred Julian. Julian, one of the two surviving signees from the tryout camp (tackle Joe Katchik was the other), injured his ankle in his first practice in Durham, and appeared on the field thereafter only on crutches as a spectator. Expecting to be cut any time, he waited out the days without hearing a word from the coaching staff or front office about his fate. When the list of those flying to Los Angeles appeared, however, his name was on it, and when the starting lineup was posted, he found his name on that as well, for reasons he did not understand.

The 46th spot belonged to quarterback Terry O'Brien, the last player cut in Durham. O'Brien had to fly with the team to Chicago, where the other 45 players caught a flight to Los Angeles and he boarded one to his Abilene home. "I hate to think I'm through at 22," he said. He was. (Despite having been cut, O'Brien was listed on the program for the Dallas exhibition at Abilene. This is most likely because the promoters thought the promise of seeing a local boy might boost attendance, and placed his name on the roster.)

On August 6, 1960, the Titans took the field in massive Los Angeles Coliseum to play the first game in their history. They wore blue jerseys with gold lettering, gold pants with dark blue stripes, gold helmets, and blue stockings with gold stripes. The blue and gold colors were those of Wismer's favorite college team, Notre Dame. The Titans' opponents, the Los Angeles Chargers, clad in blue and white with the trademark lightning bolts on their helmets, were expected to win. They had more money than the Titans, more experienced players, higher expectations, and better coaching. While Baugh had hired his old Redskins cronies, Chargers coach Sid Gillman brought in talented young assistants Chuck Noll, Al Davis, and Jack Faulkner, who all would eventually become successful head coaches. Don Klosterman, who would carve out a long career as an NFL executive, was the Chargers' scouting director. "They all had fine football minds," Gillman said recently. "Noll played with the Browns for several years, and we knew he had to come away from Paul Brown with some knowledge. Jack Faulkner had been with me for several years, and I also knew Al Davis." Davis, who had already been involved in recruiting scandals at The Citadel and USC, found the more liberal world of professional football much to his liking. He was a master at persuading players to sign with the new league, and became the chief recruiter for the Chargers.

Head coach Gillman, 49, was an NFL veteran, former coach of the Rams, and a strategic genius. He developed the long passing game that Davis later took to Oakland and called his own. Gillman also utilized men in motion, two tight ends, and two wide receivers to one side of the field. Although aggressive, Gillman's system was anything but freewheeling. It was as complex and structured as Baugh's was loose and spontaneous.

Attendance for the Titans–Chargers game was 27,778. Scattered throughout the 100,000 seats, the crowd looked even smaller, and was a severe disappointment to owner Barron Hilton. A high school all-star game in the same stadium had attracted 46,000 the previous evening. Yet, this would be the largest crowd that would watch the Chargers at home all season.

Los Angeles won the toss and elected to receive. Bill Shockley of the Titans teed the ball up, referee John McDonough blew his whistle, and Shockley drove the ball five yards deep into the end zone. Waiting for the kick to come down was Paul Lowe, a 23-year-old graduate of Oregon State, who was married with four children and had failed in a previous trial with San Francisco. When the AFL was formed, Lowe was working in the mailroom of Carte Blanche, a credit card operation owned by the Hilton family. After a brief negotiation, he signed with the Chargers for an $800 bonus. "Of course, I would have signed for nothing," Lowe said later. "I had a big family to support and I thought I could make some money in football."

When the exhibition season started, the unheralded Lowe was the fifth running back on a club that planned to keep only four. As he backpedaled under Shockley's kick, Lowe knew that he would not make the Chargers with touchbacks. He gathered the ball in and took off up the center of the field. At the 20, he broke for the sideline, got a key block, and cut back toward the middle. By the time he reached the Los Angeles 40, Lowe had cleared the defenders. He raced into the end zone to complete a 105-yard kickoff return against the Titans on the first play of their existence. A press box pundit indicated that it was a new league record.

"Everybody was standing on the sideline like I was, dumbfounded," said Bob Marques. "This guy caught the ball and went down the field about ninety-five miles an hour. We thought, 'What the hell did we get ourselves into?'" As Roger Ellis left the field, he said to the player beside him, "I guess it's going to be an awfully long season."

Bob Reifsnyder kicked the extra point and, less than 20 seconds into their first game, New York trailed 7–0. Upon receiving the ensuing kickoff, the Titans failed to move the ball and punted. The Chargers drove 79 yards for a second touchdown, Jack Kemp rolling out to his right and dashing 24 yards into the end zone. With just over five minutes elapsed, the score was 14–0.

The Titans' best opportunity of the first half came when Roger Donahoo intercepted Kemp on a crossing pattern over the middle and returned the ball to the Chargers' 9. After moving to the 1, however, fullback Pete Hart fumbled and Los Angeles' Jimmy Sears recovered. (Sears was a 29-year-old who had been an assistant coach at USC in 1959. When the head coaching position became vacant, Sears thought he would get it. Bypassed in favor of John McKay, he decided to come out of retirement and join the Chargers.)

Trailing 20–0 in the fourth period, New York finally scored with 2:38 left on a six-yard scramble by quarterback Dick Jamieson, who entered the game after Dorow and Ford had been unable to move the club. Los Angeles added a final touchdown for a 27–7 victory. The Chargers' offense dominated the New York defense, gaining 202 yards on the ground. "We aren't anywhere near ready yet," Baugh said. Sebo was more optimistic, praising Jamieson for the way he moved the offense and singling out Fred Julian as the best defensive back on the field.

The second stop on the Titans' tour was Sacramento, where they played the Raiders on August 13. Prior to the game, the club accepted an invitation to visit Aero-Jet General Corporation, manufacturer of the Titan missile, largest in the US arsenal. The complex, located just outside Sacramento, was a model for 1960 American industry, with a sprawling recreation area, including a swimming pool for the workers. The players arrived by bus, brought their bathing suits and swam in the pool, and afterwards signed autographs for the employees. Roger Ellis, who had been named captain for the Oakland game, stood at a podium and mumbled a few words of thanks.

The outing at the missile facility was the best reception the Titans received in Sacramento, as the Raiders rallied from a 17–7 deficit to inflict a 23–17 defeat upon the New York club. Despite the loss, an encouraging sign for the Titans was their ability to put together two long touchdown drives of 73 and 81 yards. Maynard turned in the best performance, catching 9 passes for 135 yards.

From Sacramento, the Titans flew to Abilene, Texas. The game, sponsored by the Shrine Club of Suez Temple, was the first professional contest ever played in Abilene. Wismer was hoping that Baugh's popularity would draw a good crowd to the city where he had coached college ball. It did not, as only 4,000 showed up at Abilene Public Schools Stadium, which had a capacity of roughly 15,000. The Old West atmosphere surprised a few of the more cosmopolitan Titans. They remembered, above all, the heat and the dust, and the fact that cattle were allowed to roam unmolested through the streets. The cattle had no impact upon the game, but the heat did, for it was 90 degrees at kickoff. The Titans lost to Lamar Hunt's Dallas Texans, 38–14, and were out-gained 478 yards to 164.

After more than two weeks on the road, the Titans had established a routine. On days when there was no game, they practiced from nine until eleven and again from three until five. Conditions were not always the best, and Baugh noticed that the players hungriest to make the team, the poor farm boys and those from small colleges, complained the least. The heat, the food, the travel, nothing seemed to bother them.

In the evenings, far from home, the players got to know each other. In Durham, they had come together from 100 different directions, has-beens, those who never were, and a few talented athletes who only needed a chance to play. Some knew each other from NFL camps, but most were strangers. "In Durham," said Jamieson, "you didn't get a chance to know anybody because they changed so quickly."

Now, for more than a month, the Titans practiced together, played together, traveled together, ate together, drank together, and formed a bond that was timeless. They played cards for the small stakes they could afford. Most of the players had little money, for they were not paid at all during camp and received only $50 for each exhibition game. Road trips meant an additional $9 a day for meal money. Those who had received a signing bonus were living on whatever was left, and the rest were subsisting on savings or checks from home. Since none of the players could afford expensive entertainment, they had only each other's company, over a few beers. If the recreational drugs that plague today's players had been prevalent in August 1960, they would have posed no temptation to the Titans, for no one could have afforded them.

"Nobody knew who we were," said Dewey Bohling. "You could go into town, have dinner and a few drinks—everybody did things together. Everywhere we went, there'd be ten, twelve, or fifteen people who were always together." After practice, groups of players headed for the bars, where they talked about football and women, played cards, and, in many cases, formed lasting friendships. "I think that's why we became such a close-knit group that first year," said Bohling. "We were on the road and we all had to live together for six weeks."

Dick Guesman, who recently attended a reunion of former Denver Broncos, reminisced about the closeness of the older players. "At the reunion, I was with about six guys at the Marriott Hotel and we were sitting in the lobby playing poker, just like we did thirty years ago. The only thing that changed was time. The friendship and relationships were still there. We had great camaraderie. When I meet guys like Ray Mansfield and Fuzzy Thurston, who I'd never met before, after an hour I feel like I've known them all my life. There was more team spirit then. Hell, we used to go out, have a few beers, and sit around and talk. Now I think they jump in their limousines and fancy cars and go their separate ways."

When the team returned to New York, economic necessity resulted in continued bonding. Thurlow Cooper, Roger Ellis, and Bob Marques shared an apartment that held three beds in the single bedroom. "The first year," recalled Nick Mumley, "Larry Grantham, Dick Jamieson, and I and our wives were apartment hunting in New Rochelle. The first day, only one apartment was available. Three guys who only knew each other from training camp and three wives who had never met—one from West Virginia, one from Mississippi, and one from Illinois—were together in one apartment for a few days. We had a hell of a good time. We all got to know each other and remained friends for all our years in New York."

Throughout the Titans' epic journey, the roster continued to evolve. At every stop, half a dozen players would show up looking for a tryout, and cuts were made every week. Joe Biggs, a lineman who had played for Baugh at Hardin-Simmons, was cut in Abilene, near his hometown. Linebacker Eddie Bell, a CFL cut, and Joe Ryan, a defensive lineman cut by the Eagles, joined the Titans in Texas. The quarterback situation became clearer. Frank Kremblas was cut in Sacramento. He had been expected to make the team as a punter, but his performance had been disappointing. When New York acquired Rick Sapienza from the Patriots prior to the game against the Chargers, Kremblas became expendable. That left Dorow, Jamieson, Scrabis, and Ford competing for the quarterback position. Scrabis, who was fighting for a backup spot, felt that the

Titans would keep Ford at least until after the Abilene game, as he, like Baugh, was a local hero. If Ford was going to be dropped, thought Scrabis, it would happen after that game. He was right. Despite the fact that Ford played reasonably well in the loss to the Texans, he was released.

From Abilene, the Titans took a train, an unusual mode of transportation even in those days, to Mobile, Alabama, for a game with the Oilers. In Mobile, the Titans lost again, 30–14, but made an acquisition that was to serve them in good stead for many years. The Denver Broncos had originally drafted Bill Mathis, a halfback out of Clemson. In his senior year in college, Mathis led the ACC in scoring, with 70 points, and played against Texas Christian in the Bluebonnet Bowl in Houston, where he met Oilers owner Bud Adams. Adams asked Mathis if he would be interested in playing for the Oilers if they could acquire his rights from Denver. Mathis said he would and, when training camp opened, was wearing a Houston uniform.

Mathis did not remain Oiler property for long. By signing with the AFL, he had avoided competing with Hugh McElhenney and Joe Perry of the 49ers, but now found himself playing the same position as the 1959 Heisman Trophy winner, Billy Cannon of LSU. The Oilers had staged a costly and highly publicized court battle to win Cannon's services from the Los Angeles Rams, and there was no doubt that he would be the starting halfback. Further, Mathis did not take well to the Marine-like camp conducted by Oilers coach Lou Rymkus. Baugh had coached Mathis in a postseason college all-star game, and arranged a trade to bring him and halfback Bob Crandall to the Titans as delayed payment for the Titans having assigned Houston the negotiating rights to a New York draftee who refused to play anywhere but Texas.

When he learned of the swap, Mathis had to go back to Houston, retrieve his car, fill it with his belongings, and make the long drive to Mobile to join his new team. Loaded down with suitcases, he appeared at the door of his hotel room to be greeted by his new roommate, Don Maynard. Maynard looked up in amazement at the number of suitcases under Mathis' arms. "You're planning on staying, aren't you?" he said. Mathis was, and he did, remaining with the franchise through the 1969 season.

CHAPTER 8

WE DON'T TOTE NO COLOREDS

Just before the final exhibition game in Buffalo, after four straight losses, the Titans were the recipients of an extremely fortunate stroke of luck. "The thing that made our season," Baugh said nearly 40 years later, "was when we got Art Powell."

Powell was an end who played college football at San Jose State under the tutelage of a man named Bob Bronzan. Two of his teammates were future coaches Claude Gilbert and Dick Vermeil, while a recent graduate named Bill Walsh was an assistant coach. It was a good place for anyone wanting to learn about modern football, for Bronzan, like Baugh at Hardin-Simmons, masterminded a sophisticated passing offense that was unusual in college football in the 1950s. The offense that gave Walsh his reputation as a genius, according to Powell, was that of Bob Bronzan.

Powell flourished in the wide-open system, and led the nation with 40 pass receptions as a sophomore in 1956. He left school early and played in the Canadian League, the only professional option for premature departees. By 1959 he found himself in the NFL with the Philadelphia Eagles. Although drafted as a receiver, Powell played almost exclusively as a defensive back and kick returner, for Philadelphia had Tommy McDonald, Pete Retzlaff, and Bobby Walston, three all-time greats, at the receiving positions. That year Powell returned a punt for a touchdown in the game during which commissioner Bert Bell died.

During the 1960 exhibition season, the Eagles were scheduled to play a game in Norfolk, Virginia. Just before the club was to depart, Powell learned that the black players would not be allowed to stay in the same hotel as the white players. "All your life," said Powell, "as an athlete, you're told that this is a team sport. You play together. Well, you can't just play together on the field and then send me off somewhere else to stay. The places they sent us to were places you wouldn't send your worst enemy. They were horrible." Powell refused to go; a decision he knew was likely to have serious consequences. "It wasn't something I set out to do," he said recently, "but it was right in front of me and I didn't think it was right. In life, sometimes when you make choices, even if you think your choices are correct, other people may differ, and they can be costly."

Although the other black players told Powell they too would boycott the game, they backed down under pressure from management, and Powell was left alone. This was not the first time he had run afoul of the Eagles' management, for during his rookie season Powell had had problems with defensive coach Jerry Williams. When Williams singled Powell out for poor play during a scrimmage and told him to run 10 laps, Powell refused and was fined $300. Shortly afterward, he was having a beer with a number of his teammates following an exhibition game in San Francisco, when Williams came by and threatened to fine him again. "Just me out of about forty players!" Powell complained later.

Following the incident in Norfolk, the Eagles decided that Powell was expendable, and that it was necessary to make an example of him. Trading him to another NFL team was out of the question, for, recognizing Powell's talent, the Eagles did not want him playing against them. Therefore, Philadelphia gave him his release.

At the time, none of the reasons underlying Powell's abrupt departure were made public. Bill Wallace wrote, "Just how or why this fellow, who ran a kickoff back 95 yards on the Giants last year, was waived out of the National League and no other club made a claim on his services is mysterious." Harold Rosenthal followed up six days later, "a lot of eyebrows went up when [Powell] was waived out of the National Football League two weeks ago."

"I don't care what they call it," said Powell after joining the Titans. "I was blackballed." In the short run, Powell's actions appeared to have cost him dearly, but in the long run they spared him another season of apprenticing with the Eagles and freed him to enter a situation where his skills would be used to their fullest.

Norfolk was not unique among southern cities in 1960. Virginia law decreed that segregated accommodations had to be maintained in places of public assembly and virtually the entire area south of the Mason-Dixon line was solid in its stance on segregation. While racism unquestionably existed in the north, it was practiced quietly, was not sanctioned by law and not defended in public. In the deep south, however, governors such as John Patterson and George Wallace of Alabama, Ross Barnett of Mississippi, and Orval Faubus of Arkansas presided over administrations that were openly committed to maintain a legalized separation of the races.

In November 1961, the State of Alabama announced that it had retained Dr. Wesley Critz George, a retired faculty member of the University of North Carolina School of Medicine, to conduct a study of race. Ralph Smith, a Montgomery lawyer who was coordinating the project, said, "Scientific data support the contention that the white race, intellectually is superior to the Negro, and that is the point we seek to make with this study. It was my feeling, shared by Governor Patterson, that we should explore every avenue in our efforts to preserve racial segregation." Roy Wilkins, executive director of the NAACP, responded, "Is Governor Patterson confessing, through the initiation of this study, that for all these decades the segregation policy of the State of Alabama has been based upon guesswork?"

While southern blacks had lived with segregation all their lives, those who were accustomed to the laws and ways of other regions, including Powell, who grew up in California, were appalled by the conditions they encountered when visiting the south. By 1960, Americans were more mobile due to the rapidly expanding interstate highway system. As more northerners were exposed to segregation, the closed society of the south came under intense pressure to change its ways.

The NFL, with no teams in the deep south prior to the expansion Cowboys, had been relatively free of any embarrassing episodes, other than during the exhibition season. Several blacks, most notably Fritz Pollard and Paul Robeson, played in the NFL during the 1920s, Pollard as a player-coach. After a 13-year period of segregation, the newly relocated Los Angeles Rams signed former UCLA halfback Kenny Washington and

Woody Strode in 1946, the same year Paul Brown brought Marion Motley and Bill Willis to the AAFC. None was heralded as a pioneer in the
manner of baseball's Jackie Robinson, even though they played a year
before Robinson joined the Dodgers. Despite the early integration, however, the number of minority players remained small throughout the 1950s.
"There were always an even number of blacks on a team," said Proverb
Jacobs, "because when you went to a hotel, you had to have a roommate. There was never an odd number, because when you went on the
road, somebody would have had to stay by himself."

The AFL was not lacking in black players but, with franchises in Dallas and Houston, had to deal more directly with the segregation issue. In
Jepperson Stadium, home field of the Oilers, black spectators were
restricted to designated sections of the stands. The NAACP picketed
Houston's 1961 opener, and asked five black players on the visiting Raiders
to boycott the game. They did not. In November, the NAACP asked the
nine black members of the San Diego Chargers to sit out the team's
December 3 game against the Oilers. Sid Gillman, coach and general manager of the Chargers, showed little sympathy and hinted that players might
be fined or suspended if they refused to play. In the event, all of the Chargers decided to play, but the team, perhaps distracted by the controversy,
suffered its first loss of the season after 11 straight victories, falling to
Houston by a score of 33–13. The largest crowd in the history of the AFL,
37,845 of both races, filled their designated sections.

The seating in most southern stadiums was similar. Blanche Martin,
one of the few black players on the Titans, remembers the 1960 exhibition
game the club played at Ladd Stadium in Mobile, Alabama. The end zones
were packed with black spectators and the rest of the stadium was virtually empty. Martin grew up in the north, and was often taken by surprise
by the unique customs of the south. During the train ride from Abilene to
Mobile, the entourage stopped for lunch at a station along the way. Martin walked up to the counter and sat down with a number of his teammates.
Although he wondered why none of the black players were at the counter,
he assumed they had just not arrived yet. When the waitress ignored him
and waited on patrons who had come in after him, he asked her why. Embarrassed, she told him that she didn't make the rules, but that if he wanted
to eat, he would have to sit over in the corner, where Martin now realized
his black teammates were gathered, laughing at his naiveté.

Powell, a proud, defiant man, often addressed such situations head-on, and frequently paid the price by being branded a rebel, a loner, or anti-social. Martin, on the other hand, preferred to use guile rather than confrontation. Following the 1960 AFL Championship Game, in which Martin played for the Chargers, he had to catch a plane back to Michigan to interview for graduate school. He had only about two hours to shower, say good-bye to his teammates, and get to the Houston airport. With little time to spare, Martin stood in front of the hotel as one empty cab after another passed him by.

Finally, a sympathetic white cab driver stopped and asked what his problem was. When Martin explained that he needed to get to the airport quickly, the driver said, "You don't understand, do you?" "Understand what?" Martin asked. "We don't tote no coloreds," the man replied. Martin told him it was worth a lot to him to catch that plane and offered $20, a significant sum of money at the time. The driver stared at the bill in Martin's hand and mentally weighed his role as a southern white man sworn to uphold segregation against the prospect of earning more than a day's pay for one run. He looked around to see if anyone was watching, and growled, "Get in and get down!"

Martin knew the cabbie wasn't asking him to dance. He jumped into the cab and laid on the floor for the entire ride to the airport. When he arrived back in Michigan in time for his interview, he swore he would never return to the south. "That was 1960, for crying out loud!" he said later.

Bill Shockley, another black member of the Titans, was a quiet, dignified man who, regardless of what he might have felt, said nothing about the disparate treatment he received in the south. The word most frequently used by his former teammates to describe Shockley was "gentleman."

Linebacker Eddie Bell was a veteran who had experienced segregation in college and the NFL, and accepted the situation as the status quo. He remembered traveling to Maryland with the University of Pennsylvania in the early 1950s. Like Martin, he went to a lunch counter with his teammates. Bell was refused service and left in the company of his white friends, all of whom walked out in protest.

Most of the white players, however, didn't give much thought to the disparate treatment. "Nobody thought a lot about it back then," said one.

"We, the white guys, didn't see it as the black guys being discriminated against. They were just being put up in another place. Until about ten years ago, when I realized it, I never thought of it as degrading. I just figured, this is the south. We stay in this hotel and the black guys go to another hotel. They're going to have their fun over there and chase their women and raise hell just like we were going to do in our hotel."

"There was no problem," said Cotton Davidson of an exhibition game in Arkansas when the Dallas Texans had to occupy separate accommodations based upon race. "They took it in stride. We didn't like it, because they were part of our team, but there wasn't anything we could do about it."

"One time," said Jack Klotz, "Proverb Jacobs came out of a game after making a heck of a play. I patted him on the head and said 'Great job.' Oh, man, did he get upset! He told me that was a racist thing, patting blacks on the head for good luck." Klotz is a deeply religious man, but even he was then oblivious to the impact of segregation. "I never realized it," he said. "The black ballplayers at that time were very sensitive about it and they had every right to be."

Management appreciated the cooperative behavior of Bell, Shockley, and Martin, since it enabled the Titans to book lucrative exhibitions in the south and compete in the regular season against Dallas and Houston, two of the stronger AFL teams. Powell, on the other hand, was branded as a troublemaker.

Baugh, although he hailed from rural Texas, was, by all accounts, color-blind. "All he was interested in was what you could do on the gridiron," said Martin. "If you could catch the ball, he didn't care if you were chartreuse." When Powell arrived in Buffalo to join the club, one of the Titans' assistants warned Baugh about the receiver's reputation and asked how the head coach intended to handle him. "If he can help this football team," Baugh was reported to have replied, "I don't care if he sleeps with my wife."

Indeed, Powell made a tremendous contribution to the struggling New York club. Although not as fast as Maynard, Powell was a rangy 6'3" and had tremendous moves, incredibly sure hands, and the ability, like Maynard, to shift gears almost in mid-stride. "Art had fingers that seemed about seventeen inches long," said Perry Richards, who played with Powell in 1962. "He had moves I'd never seen," said Baugh. "He had moves you wouldn't believe."

"The best moves I've ever seen," remembered Dorow. With his height and strength, Powell could also jump and outfight a defensive back for the ball, much like the Cowboys' Michael Irvin in more recent years. "It was a joy for me to throw to Arthur," said Grosscup.

During the first four exhibition games, Ken Campbell, a good blocker but mediocre receiver, had been starting at split end. Without a receiving threat opposite him, Maynard had been consistently double-teamed. When Powell arrived, defenders could no longer key on Maynard, and the Titans' passing game emerged as a genuine threat. "Until we got Art Powell," recalled Pete Hart, "things looked pretty bleak. Thank the Lord they got him. He showed up on Wednesday, and got there early for the afternoon practice. He went up to Dorow and said, 'Al, throw me a double out.'"

"What the hell is a double out?" wondered Dewey Bohling. Bohling watched as Powell sprinted downfield, broke to the outside, turned it up the field, and then broke to the outside again, changing speeds all the while. Another favorite maneuver was the "stumble and run," in which Powell feigned falling to lull the defensive back to sleep, then scrambled to his feet and looked for the open area.

Powell had his shortcomings. He did not like practice, and saved his best efforts for game day. "If he'd had Raymond Berry's temperament and work habits," said one former teammate, "there's no telling how great he would have been." Further, like so many outstanding athletes, Powell had tremendous confidence in his ability. He always wanted the ball, a preference he made known with such regularity that it became a sore point with Dorow. "He was very temperamental," said Dorow. "You'd call a pattern where the primary receiver was Maynard or somebody else, and he'd start cussing and kicking the dirt. Maybe two plays later, you'd call his pattern and he'd say, 'No, throw it to your buddy Maynard.'"

"No matter how many people were covering him," said Grosscup, "he always thought he was open. He wanted the ball on every play." With Powell's ability to catch the ball in traffic, Grosscup admitted, he almost always *was* open.

The benefits of Powell's acquisition were immediate. In the first quarter of the Buffalo exhibition, with the Titans holding a 3–0 lead, Powell caught a two-yard touchdown pass from Jamieson. In the second period, with New York leading 17–3, he hauled in a 28-yard scoring toss from Dorow. In the third period, he caught two more passes from Jamieson, of 35 and 42 yards, each for a touchdown. "I don't think there was a Buffalo defensive back within five yards of Powell that day," said Roger Ellis. His four touchdown receptions carried the Titans to a 52–31 victory, their first win ever.

CHAPTER 9

OPENING DAY

The Titans team that reached New York was very different from the group that assembled at Durham for the first workout in July. As other clubs made their cuts, Sebo skillfully picked up a player here and a player there to augment the New York roster. "We didn't have a good ball club in camp," said Baugh, "but we have one now." Neither of the two quarterbacks, Dorow and Jamieson, was at the first workout. Powell, who caught four touchdown passes in the final exhibition game, was a late pickup. On the defensive platoon, ends Nick Mumley (a Dallas Texan cut), Joe Ryan, and Bob Reifsnyder and linebacker Eddie Bell were added during camp. Early in the season, defensive linemen Dick Guesman and Ed Cooke, cut by the Baltimore Colts on the last day of training camp, joined the club. In all, 10 members of the opening-day roster had not set foot in Durham, and, including those signed during the first weeks of the regular season, 14 were added during a three-week period. Only three New York draftees (Grantham, Martin, and Dave Ross) made the team. (Although Ross had been drafted by the Titans, he went to camp with the Detroit Lions. Cut by the Lions, he joined New York early in the season.) By mid-October, only 16 members of the 35-man roster had been in the Titans' training camp.

In the scramble before the start of the regular season, the Titans had acquired a number of serviceable players, but no big name that could attract fans to the Polo Grounds. Wismer had been searching for a star from the day he acquired the franchise. One of the first players he signed, in late December 1959, was Martin, a 195-pound halfback from Michigan State, who had been clocked at 9.8 for 100 yards. The New York publicists gave Martin a big buildup, based upon his performance during his first two years at MSU. They glossed over the fact that he had missed the entire 1958 season after suffering a severe knee injury during the spring alumni game. Following major surgery, he returned in 1959, but was only a shadow of his former self.

After Martin graduated, Pete Rozelle, then general manager of the Rams, offered him a $12,000 salary and a $2,000 bonus. Sebo countered with $12,500 and $2,500, and Martin joined the Titans. Despite his preseason buildup and a four-touchdown performance in a late July scrimmage, he couldn't recapture the brilliance he had shown before his injury. "My knee was never the same again," he said later. Martin appeared to favor the knee in camp and re-injured it during the exhibition game in Abilene. When the regular season began, he was on the bench. He carried the ball only a dozen times before his release in mid-October.

A second big-name college halfback also failed to make the grade. On August 31, Wismer traded defensive back Marshall Harris and a seventh-round draft pick to the Patriots for Gerhard Schwedes, star of the 1959 Syracuse national championship team. The Orangemen fielded a dominant team that year, one that was undefeated while outscoring the opposition 390–59. Schwedes scored 100 points and led Syracuse to victory over Texas in the Cotton Bowl by throwing an 85-yard touchdown pass, the longest completion in Cotton Bowl history. He arrived in New York with injured ribs and a big question mark over his head. The ribs had been damaged on the final play of a Boston exhibition game. The question mark was due to the fact that the Patriots had given up so quickly on a player who had been such a big star in college. They virtually gave him away to the Titans and didn't even require Wismer to assume his sizable no-cut contract.

The Patriots were right. Schwedes was simply too slow to be a pro halfback. Former reporter Bill Wallace said later, "The innocence of the professional leagues' scouting at that time was no better demonstrated than in the case of Gerhard Schwedes. I think the assumption was, 'Here's a good guy. Syracuse is the national champion. He's got a great coach. Let's get this guy.'" In addition to his absence of speed, Schwedes also seemed to lack the consuming desire that fired so many of the free agents. "He appeared to be the kind of guy," said one of the Patriots, "who wasn't really sure he wanted to continue to play football. He was very well schooled and had a good academic record. The guys in the AFL in those early years were hungry to play. They wanted to express themselves as football players or they just didn't have a whole lot going for themselves in anything else at that point in their lives. Schwedes didn't seem to have that burning desire to go on and play."

Wismer's hope for a bankable star never materialized, and New York gave up on Schwedes as quickly as the Patriots. In mid-September, he was given medical clearance to begin practicing. Within two weeks, he was cut and, since Boston was still obligated under his contract, Schwedes was returned to the Patriots. Boston paid up, but rarely allowed Schwedes to get into a game. He played a total of 10 games for Boston in 1960 and 1961, and then retired.

Both Titans starting running backs, Dewey Bohling and Pete Hart, were virtual unknowns who had been in camp since day one and, for three years previously, had played for Baugh at Hardin-Simmons. Bohling was released by the Steelers in training camp in 1959 and spent a year selling sporting goods at Montgomery Ward in his hometown of Albuquerque, New Mexico. He was a steady runner and good blocker but lacked breakaway speed. He was also an excellent receiver who would be the Titans' third-leading pass-catcher behind Maynard and Powell. His receiving skills had come a long way since his first meeting with Baugh, as a member of a high school all-star team. Bohling experienced flight delays and ran onto the field just as the first practice was starting. He had been a single-wing tailback in high school and had run and passed, but not caught. Baugh was playing quarterback in a drill and told Bohling to run to a certain spot and then turn. Bohling did as he was told, turned, and Baugh's pass hit him right in the nose. "The next time you turn, son," Baugh drawled, "look for the ball." Bohling learned to look for the ball, and catch it as well. When the regular season began, he alternated with Ted Wegert, a Long Island high school star and former service player who had not attended college. Wegert was a two-year veteran of the Eagles.

Hart, at 5'9" and 190 pounds, was a fireplug, a ferocious blocker, a poor receiver, but a hard runner from fullback. "I wasn't real fast," he said recently. "I wasn't real anything. I just ran hard and low." In another offense, he might have had difficulty surviving, but Baugh's formations spread out the defense and opened holes for the compact Hart to get through. He ran well enough to keep Mathis on the bench.

When the season started, the lineup for the Titans was as follows:

OFFENSE		DEFENSE	
FL	Don Maynard	E	Nick Mumley
TE	Thurlow Cooper	T	Tom Saidock
T	Joe Katchik	T	Sid Youngelman
G	John McMullan	E	Bob Reifsnyder
C	Mike Hudock	LB	Eddie Bell
G	Bob Mischak	LB	Bob Marques
T	Buddy Cockrell	LB	Larry Grantham
SE	Art Powell	CB	Fred Julian
QB	Dick Jamieson	CB	Dick Felt
HB	Dewey Bohling	FS	Corky Tharp
FB	Pete Hart	SS	Roger Donahoo

Cockrell and Saidock were the offensive and defensive captains, respectively. Cockrell was part of an offensive line that was one of the club's greatest strengths. Mischak was all-star material, and center Mike Hudock was a steady performer who lasted eight seasons in the AFL. Jack Klotz, who soon replaced Katchik at tackle, was a strong pass blocker, while McMullan was better with the running game. Upon turning pro, most college linemen had to learn how to pass block, since nearly all of them came from teams that were run-oriented. In the AFL, with its greater emphasis on the passing game, the change was more drastic than in the NFL. "You had to learn how to use your hands to keep the defense away from you," said Hudock. "On a run block, you try to get into a person to control him and turn him the way you want him to go. In pass blocking, you try to stay away from them and not let them get their hands on you and pull you. You have to learn how to knock their hands off."

The Titans' linemen faced a unique challenge protecting the scrambling Dorow, who received the majority of playing time at quarterback. Hudock liked the fact that the quarterback had great maneuverability and could dodge anyone who got through the forward wall. Klotz, who later in life wound up acting as a bodyguard for Robert Kennedy and Mother Theresa, found Dorow more difficult to protect than either of them. Dorow was likely to be anywhere, which Klotz found frustrating. He might drive his man exactly where he wanted, only to find that that was where Dorow had ended up.

McMullan, a Notre Dame grad, was strong, but heavy-legged and without Mischak's quickness. He was emotional and high-strung, to the point that he vomited before almost every game. McMullan spent two years in the Army, earning all-service honors in 1956 and 1957, and then went to training camp with the Giants, where his Irish temper resulted in a rapid departure. "He was hot headed," recalled Cockrell, "a talker, an agitator."

"John was hyper-emotional," said Mischak. "Most players accepted the coach as a dominant figure. John would up to a point. Then he would get anxious about what was happening and might bark at the coach." That was not a good idea when the coach was Giants assistant Vince Lombardi. McMullan was having a bad day in camp, and Lombardi was riding him hard, calling him a big Mick, or something to that effect. McMullan shot back a few epithets concerning Lombardi's Italian heritage, and that was the end of his career with the Giants.

Cockrell, another Hardin-Simmons product, had chronic knee problems. After his first operation, which took place while he was still in high school, Cockrell went to the University of Oklahoma. As a sophomore, he played on the Sooners' national championship team, but, following the season, had a falling out with coach Bud Wilkinson over his rodeo activities. Wilkinson, a stickler for following the rules, was concerned that Cockrell's professionalism on the rodeo circuit, where he earned approximately $3,000 per year, might affect his amateur status on the gridiron. Rather than give up bulldogging and calf roping, Cockrell quit school. Despite the disagreement, however, he maintained the highest regard for Wilkinson. "He's one of the finest men I ever knew in my life," Cockrell said, "just a peach of a gentleman. What impressed me about Bud Wilkinson was that any boy could walk into his office, and there might be three millionaires waiting to see him, but the boy always got in first. He had a Master's degree in English, and the biggest thing he stressed was education. Every time you cut a class, you had to run the stadium steps twenty-five times under clock. If you didn't run them fast enough, you started again the next morning. I never cut a class."

Cockrell went back to Texas and resumed farming and cattle trading, which he had been doing since his high school days. He had no intention of playing football again until Baugh, a longtime acquaintance, called and asked if he was interested in playing for Hardin-Simmons. "What about the rodeo?" Cockrell asked. "You know what I think about that," replied Baugh, who was quite a calf roper himself. Said Cockrell, "The dumbest thing I ever did was quit OU and the smartest thing I ever did was go back to school."

He played at Hardin-Simmons for two years, enduring another knee operation, and was drafted by the Browns. Cockrell injured a knee once more and was cut, ending up in Canada with the Saskatchewan Roughriders. When Baugh was named head coach of the Titans, he called Cockrell and offered him a job. "I guess it's like being a habitual drinker," Cockrell said of his return to football. "You just can't stay away from it."

As might be expected of a rodeo bulldogger, Cockrell was a rugged individual who prided himself on his ability to play with pain. In 1961 he broke three ribs, but put a pad over them and played the next week. Cockrell was not afraid to mix it up on the field when necessary. "I never picked a fight in my life," he said later. "I'm a real easy going guy." If that is the case, it is remarkable how many people picked fights with him.

Larry Grantham, starting at the weak side linebacker position, had been a pleasant surprise in training camp. Despite having been voted most valuable lineman in the Hula Bowl, Grantham was largely unheralded, principally because of his size. He played end at Mississippi, and Baugh, remembering him from the Ole Miss–Hardin-Simmons game, was glad to see the Titans had been able to sign him.

Grantham came to the New York camp expecting to play offense. "Then I looked at Maynard, who was fast, and the tight ends, who were big, and I thought I was going home," he said. Johnny Dell Isola suggested he try linebacker, even though Grantham weighed only 195 pounds. "They said I was too small to play football," he said. "I've been hearing that all my life." For the next 14 years, Grantham proved that size was not the only determinant of a man's ability to play football.

"Larry had a knack for tackling that you can't teach," said Dewey Bohling. "I don't know how he did it, but he was always there."

"I didn't try to kill people like they do today," Grantham said. "I felt that my job was to tackle them, get them on the ground, then get up and make the next play." Grantham also realized that a small linebacker had to be smart, and spent hour after hour watching films, studying opposing offenses and other linebackers.

The opening game of the Titans' first season pitted them against the Buffalo Bills at the Polo Grounds in New York. When the visiting Bills entered the old stadium, Buffalo tight end Tom Rychlec took a moment to pause and gaze toward the upper deck. He recalled a Sunday a number of years earlier, when he was still in grammar school, and his father had taken him from their home in Meriden, Connecticut, to the Polo Grounds to watch the Giants play the Redskins and their star quarterback, Sammy Baugh. He wandered away from his father and found a good vantage point at the railing of the upper deck, from where he looked down at the players and dreamed that someday he might wear the uniform of a professional football player and perform upon that field. Now, in his white Buffalo uniform trimmed in blue and red, he looked up to where the young boy had stood and realized that the boy's dream had come true.

While Rychlec was looking up, however, most of his teammates were staring down, amazed at the horrible condition of the old playing field, which had a long and storied history. The site on which the stadium was built was part of a farm granted to John Lion Gardner by the King of England in the seventeenth century. The first field to carry the name Polo Grounds was opened for baseball in September 1880. Located at Sixth Avenue and West 112th Street, it was a two-diamond complex that was utilized by both the Giants of the National League and the Metropolitans of the American Association, which at that time was considered a major league. The field was the site of the first World Series, contested in 1884 between the Metropolitans and the Providence Grays, champions of the National League.

A second field known as the Polo Grounds, at 155th Street and Eighth Avenue, opened in July 1889, and was occupied by the Giants. When major league players revolted against the owners and formed their own league for the 1890 season, the New York entry played its games in a third stadium, located just north of the second incarnation of the Polo Grounds. Bounded by 157th and 159th Streets to the north and south, respectively, and by the Harlem River and a 115-foot rise known as Coogan's Bluff on the east and west, the park became known as the New Polo Grounds. When the Players League folded after one unsuccessful season, the National League Giants began occupancy in 1891.

On April 14, 1911, a fire engulfed the wooden park and destroyed everything but the outfield bleachers. By the end of June, the facility had been almost completely rebuilt. While the wooden bleachers remained in the outfield, the seats around home plate and outside the base lines were anchored in concrete, the first use of that material in a sports arena. This reconstructed facility was the park in which the Titans would play.

Known in the early 20th century as Brush Stadium after Giants owner John Brush, the field was used by both the Giants and the New York Yankees from 1913 until the opening of Yankee Stadium in 1923. From then on, the Giants had been the sole summer occupants. During the next 35 years, some remarkable moments transpired in the shadow of Coogan's Bluff. Carl Hubbell struck out five Hall of Famers in succession in the 1934 All-Star Game. Jack Dempsey fought Luis Firpo, and Joe Louis rallied to beat Billy Conn. Many of the Titans players were sports fans and appreciated the history of the grounds they played upon. "Growing up playing baseball," said Hayseed Stephens, "I knew all about the Polo Grounds and the great plays that had been made there. To be out there playing football on that great field was pretty awesome and overwhelming."

"My favorite part of the Ken Burns baseball special," said Roger Ellis, "was watching Willie Mays make that catch." As Ellis watched Mays race back to catch Vic Wertz's drive in the first game of the 1954 World Series, he saw the steps to the old clubhouse, the last major league clubhouse located beyond center field, the steps Ellis had climbed many times as a Titans player.

The first Polo Grounds football game took place on December 4, 1920, when the Buffalo All-Americans defeated the Canton Bulldogs, featuring Jim Thorpe, 7–3. When Tim Mara brought an NFL franchise to New York in 1925, his Giants played all of their home games in the Polo

Grounds. They were in residence there through the 1955 season, moving across the Harlem River to Yankee Stadium in 1956.

By 1958 the football Giants were playing in Yankee Stadium, the baseball Giants were performing in Seals Stadium in San Francisco, and the storied Polo Grounds was without professional sports for the first time since the 1880s. The neighborhood surrounding the old ballpark had deteriorated through the years, and parking facilities were limited. The baseball Giants had seen their attendance drop from a high of 1,600,793 in 1947 to 629,179 in 1956. When they departed for the West Coast, the old park sat empty. A sign hung on the 8th Avenue gate of the stadium read, "If no answer, see parking lot attendant one block south." On April 27, 1958, the American Committee for Israel rented the facility for a celebration of the 10th anniversary of Israel's creation. Later in the year, the Jehovah's Witnesses held a weeklong convention at the park. The only ongoing activity was midget auto racing, which took place on an asphalt track constructed around the perimeter of the field.

When the formation of the Titans was announced in mid-August 1959, they had yet to find a home field. Speculation centered around the Polo Grounds and Ebbets Field, which had been unoccupied since the Dodgers moved to Los Angeles in 1958 and had previously housed a number of NFL and AAFC clubs. On September 12, Wismer announced that he had signed a two-year lease for the use of the Polo Grounds. The Titans would pay rent equal to 13 percent of their gross revenue, with a minimum of $7,500 per game. They would receive no income from parking or concessions.

The lease was a complex document, for the Coogan family owned the land upon which the Polo Grounds rested. The National Exhibition Company, the corporate name of the New York Giants baseball team, owned the stadium itself. The National Exhibition Company leased the land from the Coogans under an agreement that was due to expire in April 1962. Despite moving to California, the Giants had continued to pay rent, and thus had the right of occupancy. Under the terms of the lease, they also had the right to sublet. The document Wismer signed was an agreement to sublease the stadium from the Giants.

When the Titans arrived at their new home prior to the opening game, the players were shocked at the condition of the field. There were several inherent problems with the facility, the most prominent being drainage. Old city maps, one from as early as 1609, showed the Polo Grounds parcel under the Harlem River. By the early 1960s, the water table was only two to six feet below the surface, rendering the turf extremely soggy after a heavy rain. Water also drained down from Coogan's Bluff toward the stadium, compounding the problem. In 1949 the Giants spent nearly $130,000 to raise the playing field four and a half feet, improve the drainage, and resod the field. Unfortunately for the Titans, their opening game was played in a steady rain, the residue of Hurricane Diana, and the turf was muddy and treacherous. Harold Rosenthal wrote, "The Polo Grounds playing surface, which would have been deplorable even in bright sunshine, was unspeakable."

Increased usage and lack of maintenance were a dangerous combination. The stadium had been relatively dormant in 1958 and 1959, but activity picked up in 1960. In June, Floyd Patterson defeated Ingemar Johansson there for the heavyweight championship. Every Sunday throughout the summer, the Polo Grounds hosted games of the International Soccer League. The increased wear and tear took its toll on the playing surface, and the Giants, who were generating more expenses than revenue from their lease, did little in the way of maintenance. "It was like going out and playing in a vacant lot," said Maynard. In some places the grass was at mid-calf level, while in others, the ground was barren. "The field was overgrown," remembered Rick Sapienza. "They had cut it, but it looked as though they'd cut it with a mower that wasn't sharp enough. It was very clumpy, a slow field."

There were holes and divots, and a ravine between the 40-yard lines that Maynard referred to as "Wismer's Gully." "I never did like to play at the Polo Grounds," said Baugh. "It had that damn hump and dip in it." Maynard recalled a Denver player intercepting a pass and having an open path to the goal line in front of him. While ascending the far side of Wismer's Gully, which Maynard likened to climbing a flight of stairs, the Bronco went sprawling. The 12th Titans defender had prevented a touchdown.

Wismer fired off a blast at the National Exhibition Company, and sent them a bill for repairs done to prepare the field for the opener. "The place need[ed] a lot of work," he said in an uncharacteristic understatement. "There were holes and ruts all over the place, and some of the drainage covers were bare. I had a twenty-five-man crew working all day Friday and Saturday putting down new turf and topsoil...If anybody breaks a leg Sunday, I'll sue. The situation is disgraceful. Horace Stoneham has no interest in New York fans and the poor conditions prove he hopes the Titans fail." Wismer complained that the stands and seats were encrusted with grime, and many seats were broken.

"It was the dirtiest damn place you ever stepped in," said Baugh. Reporters entered the press box for the opener and encountered three years' worth of pigeon droppings. Some of the players recalled coming into the locker room to find that rats had gnawed away the edges of their shoulder pads.

The field conditions and sloppy weather mattered little to the 35 Titans and their counterparts from Buffalo who stood on the sidelines waiting for the game to begin. These athletes, from the collegiate ranks, the Canadian Football League, the military, the semi-pro leagues, and the ranks of the retired, had made the roster of a major league football team. A poor field and a little rain and wind were mere inconveniences.

At 2:08 p.m. on Sunday, September 11, 1960, the first regular-season game in the history of the New York Titans began when the Bills' Darrell Harper kicked off toward the open end of the field, in the direction of the clubhouse. Powell caught Harper's kick at the 6 and made a fine runback to the 45. Jamieson trotted onto the field as the starting quarterback, based upon his five-touchdown performance in the final exhibition game. Dorow watched from the sidelines as the two offenses moved sluggishly in the rain. During their first two years in the league, Buffalo had a feeble and rather unimaginative attack. The team went through a succession of quarterbacks—Richie Lucas, Tommy O'Connell, Bob Brodhead, Johnny Green, M.C. Reynolds, and Warren Rabb. No Buffalo quarterback was able to move the ball consistently until the team acquired Jack Kemp midway through the 1962 season.

The weak offense was perhaps a reflection of the Buffalo coaching staff. Head coach Garrard "Buster" Ramsey had been a lineman with the Chicago Cardinals, a defensive coach for the championship Detroit clubs of the 1950s, and knew little about the offensive intricacies of the game. He chose his assistants as Baugh had, taking old cronies from his playing days. His clubs therefore possessed strong defenses, but an unimpressive offense. In 1960 the Bills allowed the fewest first downs of any team in the league and also led with 33 interceptions. On offense, however, the club ranked seventh among the eight AFL teams in points scored. Only Boston, with 286 points, was below Buffalo's 296. In the muddy turf of the Polo Grounds, the Bills' offense didn't have a chance.

With eight minutes to go in the first period, Harper kicked a 35-yard field goal that gave the Bills an early lead. On the Titans' first possession of the second quarter, Jamieson hit Maynard with a 56-yard completion to the Buffalo 11, which set up a 16-yard field goal by Bill Shockley. Following Shockley's kickoff, the Titans' defense smothered Buffalo deep in its own territory, leaving them in a fourth-and-18 situation on their own 12-yard line. Billy Atkins barely got a punt away from his own goal line, and it rolled to a stop in the mud on the Buffalo 45. At this point, Dorow entered the game. On third and three, he hit Maynard for 20 yards and a first down on the 18. Two plays later, he scrambled 14 yards to the 4. Two running plays and an incomplete pass brought the Titans to a fourth-and-goal situation at the 2. Dorow waved toward the sideline, indicating that the field goal unit would not be needed. He called his own number, faked a hand-off into the line, put the ball on his hip and took off around the left end. Behind a rare block from Maynard (a "tree-felling" block according to Howard Tuckner of *The New York Times*) Dorow reached the 1-yard line, where he was hit hard by safety Atkins. He fell forward into the end zone with the first touchdown in Titans history.

On the first play following the ensuing kickoff, defensive end Nick Mumley recovered Wray Carlton's fumble on the Buffalo 45. Dorow completed three straight passes that brought the ball to the 15. He dropped back to pass once more but, unable to find an open receiver, took off for the right corner of the end zone. Dorow had a nerve-wracking habit of carrying the ball out in front of him, in one hand. Wrote Leonard Schecter: "He handles a football at arm's length, as if it were loaded with explosives and a short fuse." Waving the ball in front of him, Dorow dove just inside the flag for a 17–3 Titans lead. "If there was a crowd," Dick Young wrote, "it would have roared." Since entering the game, Dorow had carried five times for 31 yards and two touchdowns. Under Buster Ramsey, the Bills stacked their defense to the inside and forced teams to beat them to the outside. Dorow, with his inside fakes and bootlegs, was doing just that.

The second half was uneventful, but more comfortable, as the rain let up. The final score of 27–3 reflected a solid effort by the Titans and a miserable offensive performance by the Bills. Buffalo gained only 113 yards of total offense and managed just nine first downs. Quarterbacks O'Connell, Lucas, and Brodhead completed only five passes between them against a New York secondary that would prove quite porous against the league's top passers. Both O'Connell and Lucas left with injuries, leaving Brodhead to finish up.

The Titans were undefeated. Wismer picked up the tab for a big party at Mama Leone's and basked in the glory of his new team. The modest attendance, announced at 9,607 in total and 5,727 paid, failed to dampen his spirits, even though the Giants drew 50,000 to an exhibition game at the Yale Bowl the same weekend. Although Wismer had predicted a crowd of 30,000, he was sanguine. "The fans liked what they saw," he said. "All we lost was a little money." The Titans' next victim would be the Boston Patriots, who were coming to the Polo Grounds the following Saturday.

CHAPTER 10
THE PUNTS

Prior to the start of the season, *Sports Illustrated* ranked the Chargers, Oilers, and Patriots as the three best teams in the AFL, based upon their performances during the exhibition season. The Titans and Broncos were judged the weakest. The Broncos not only played poorly, they looked bad, wearing uniforms that Denver general manager Dean Griffing bought second-hand from a high school all-star game. The costume featured hideous socks with broad brown and yellow vertical stripes. Joe Pagliei, a fullback who wound up with the Titans, found the stockings so unattractive that he refused to negotiate with Denver after he saw their uniforms. "I didn't like the way Denver's socks looked," he said. "They looked like hell. I said, 'I've got big legs, they won't look good on me.'"

The socks may not have been pretty, but Denver owner Bob Howsam, operating without the financial resources of Lamar Hunt and Bud Adams, went head over heels over the price. In Dean Griffing, who came from the CFL, Howsam had selected the ideal man to run a shoestring operation. "If you want to run a club at the lowest possible cost," said Frank Tripucka, "you hire Dean Griffing. The first time we ever kicked an extra point in the Denver stadium, all of a sudden there's a big tussle behind the goal posts. Who the hell is it but Dean Griffing wrestling the ball away from one of the fans."

Denver lost all of its exhibition games, one to the Patriots by a 43–6 margin, and was outscored 200–53 overall. Boston was therefore established as a 16-point favorite in the new league's first game on September 9. The underdog Broncos surprised everyone by taking the lead on a 76-yard punt return by Gene Mingo and a 59-yard screen pass and run from Tripucka to Al Carmichael. The Broncos' defense thwarted a late Patriots rally, and Denver held on for a 13–10 upset win.

In the season's second week, the Patriots bused down to the Polo Grounds to meet the club judged the other weak link in the AFL. The game was initially scheduled for Friday night, but was moved to Saturday to avoid a conflict with the Yankees, in the midst of a pennant race and playing a key game against the Baltimore Orioles on Friday. This caused problems with the telecast, and ABC requested a delay in the start time until nine o'clock. The change in date also cost Wismer some fans. A bus filled with Patriots rooters had been scheduled to motor to the Polo Grounds, but when the date was changed, the trip was canceled. Many who had signed up also planned to go to the Boston College–Navy game on Saturday afternoon, and chose college football over the Patriots and Titans.

The first professional night game played in New York in 15 years, the Titans–Patriots clash exposed another deficiency of the Polo Grounds. When the lights were tested earlier in the week, it was discovered that the baseball Giants had removed about 300 bulbs and sent them to their Phoenix training site. Other bulbs had simply burned out, necessitating a number of replacements prior to game time.

By halftime, the Patriots perhaps wished that the game was being played in semi-darkness, for, with the Titans holding a 17–7 lead, the Boston club was in danger of suffering a second straight loss to the two teams rated the worst in the league. New York added a touchdown in the third period and held a 24–7 advantage entering the final quarter. Titans middle linebacker Bob Marques was enjoying himself tremendously at this point. A graduate of Boston University, Marques was well-acquainted with Patriots assistant Mike Holovak, who was a former Boston College star and coach, and Alan Miller, the Boston fullback who had also played at BC. Marques shouted a number of uncharitable remarks across the field to Holovak as the Titans built their sizable lead and was quite vocal about the poor performance of the Patriots. During one Boston drive, on fourth down and one, Marques blitzed and tackled Miller in the backfield. He lay on top of him after the whistle, holding Miller down and forcing the fullback to wrestle himself free.

In the fourth quarter, the Patriots came storming back, closing the gap to 24–21 on a fourth-down pass from Butch Songin to Jimmy Colclough with 1:50 left. When the ensuing on-side kick was recovered by the Titans' Thurlow Cooper on his own 46, however, it appeared as though the game was safely in the Titans' win column. On the first play from scrimmage, the overeager Patriots jumped offside, giving New York a first down on the Boston 49, leaving them only five yards to gain on three plays to get another first down and run out the clock. Pete Hart ran to the left and was dropped for a four-yard loss. Approaching the sideline and knowing he had to stay in bounds to keep the clock running, Hart dropped to the ground, and then was rolled across the white boundary line. Despite the protests of Baugh, the officials stopped the clock. Two more runs by Ted Wegert failed to move the ball past the Patriots' 48, and the officials stopped the clock when the Patriots were slow to get up from a pileup, again over Baugh's objections. This brought up fourth down and four with 30 seconds left in the game. The Patriots were out of time-outs and the clock continued to tick. Rather than attempting to run out the clock with another play from scrimmage, Baugh sent Rick Sapienza in to punt.

Sapienza had played halfback and flanker at Villanova and was signed by the Eagles following his graduation in 1958. He was cut during the exhibition season and played for the semi-pro North Attleboro Jewelers in 1959. A Boston native, Sapienza was signed by the Patriots when the new league was formed, but was released early in camp. This greatly disappointed Sapienza, since he had dreamed of playing with the local club and felt he was performing better than many of the running backs in camp. Reportedly, the Patriots had 20 players with no-cut contracts, many of whom were running backs. Sapienza was then picked up by the Titans, who were in desperate need of a punter, prior to the first exhibition game. Now, playing against the Patriots, by whom he still felt he had been treated unfairly, he had a chance for revenge.

Sapienza moved slowly onto the field and into the huddle. On the sideline, Bob Marques was unwrapping the tape from his hands, still yelling at the Patriots' side of the field. "At that point," Holovak said

recently, "you hope something happens, but mostly it's just wishful thinking. That day, something *did* happen."

The Titans broke the huddle and deployed into punt formation.
Sapienza looked up at the clock. When he opened his hands, giving the
signal to center Mike Hudock to snap the ball, there were seven seconds remaining. Hudock delivered the snap knee high. Watching the film
later that week, the Titans saw that, just as the ball was approaching
Sapienza's hands, he lifted his head and looked up to check the heavy rush,
taking his eyes off the ball for a precious second. The snap hit Sapienza
right in the hands, and he dropped it. He reached down to try to pick it
up. "You know how when you bend down to pick something up, your foot
gets in the way and you accidentally kick it away from yourself?" Sapienza
asked. "People have done that a lot of times, but not during a football
game."

The Patriots poured in on Sapienza. One of the rushers knocked him
away from the ball and fell on top of him, removing any chance of the
punter recovering his own fumble. There was a mad scramble in the backfield, with six or seven players touching the ball and losing it. Boston middle linebacker Tony Sardisco kicked at the ball with his left foot, squirting
it free and sending it toward the Titans' goal line. As Sardisco attempted
to fall on the ball, New York's Bill Mathis hit him, and the elusive pigskin
was free once more. Chuck Shonta, a Boston defensive back, chased the
ball, picked it up at about the New York 25, and, with a half dozen teammates as a trailing escort, carried it across the goal line as the final gun
sounded. While the players stood around looking at each other in confusion, the officials signaled a touchdown that gave the Patriots a 28–24
victory.

Marques, greatly embarrassed, sprinted to the clubhouse before
Holovak and the rest of the Patriots could find him. Sapienza sat dis-
consolately in the dressing room, suffering through the lowest moment
of his young life. Baugh came over, told him not to worry, and recounted
the story of the 1945 NFL Championship Game, which his Redskins
lost to the Cleveland Rams 15–14. Early in the game, Baugh attempted
a pass from punt formation in his own end zone. The ball hit the goal
post, which according to 1945 rules resulted in a safety and the deciding points of the game. Sharing the story was a noble gesture on Baugh's

part, but it did little to console Sapienza.

By the time the reporters entered the locker room looking for him, Sapienza had exited through a back door. Numbly, he walked to the subway station to catch the train back to his hotel. "I looked down at the tracks and I wanted to jump in front of the train," he recalled. "I was twenty-three years old and I was crushed. It was the most devastating thing that had ever happened to me."

Upon returning to the hotel, he took a call from his father and assured him, with false courage, that he was fine. A reporter from *The Inquirer* in Philadelphia, who knew Sapienza from his days at Villanova and with the Eagles, appeared and asked for an interview. "Rick," he said, "let me tell you something. You become famous two ways, when you do something real good or when you do something real bad." After a pause, he added, "Tonight, I think you did something real bad."

There was no practice scheduled for Sunday. On Monday, it rained and practice was canceled. For those two days, Sapienza secluded himself in his hotel room, seeing no one and replaying those fatal seven seconds over and over in his mind.

Meanwhile, Wismer sprang into action. After the game, he had called Baugh's decision to punt "stupid football." "They didn't build guided missiles with that type of thinking," he said in the locker room.

"I don't give a God damn what Mr. Wismer thinks or says," Baugh responded. He told reporters that, in the same situation, he'd do the same thing again, with one exception. He'd tell his punter not to fumble. The next day, Wismer filed a protest with the league office, claiming that the Patriots' touchdown should be voided, since their players had kicked the ball before picking it up. Paradoxically, in this game called football, any kicking of the ball in such a situation, intentional or not, was illegal. Bob Austin, a 15-year veteran NFL official who was the AFL supervisor of officials, reviewed the game film and found a double foul. "The Titans have a legitimate beef," he said. Sardisco had indeed kicked the ball, as had the Patriots' Gino Cappelletti, but so had Sapienza, although a bit later and for a much shorter distance than he had intended. The double infraction should have resulted in a replay of the down, and another punt by the Titans. Austin said he would inform Commissioner Foss of his findings. He did so and Foss, while essentially admitting that the Titans' claim was valid, disallowed the protest. "There has never been a result changed in the history of pro football," Foss said. "If I should rule in the case it would make history. The game films showed there was an error in judgment by the officials on the game's final play, but our games will always be decided on the field and not by viewing movies after the contest."

On Tuesday, Sapienza appeared at practice and, due to an injury to Art Powell, worked with the first team at flanker. He expected to start against Denver. On Wednesday, however, Baugh called the young man in and told him he was being released. It was Wismer's directive, the coach told him. Sebo insisted that Sapienza was dropped because of his poor punting, not because of his fumble. In two games, he had averaged only 32.4 yards on eight kicks.

Sapienza approached Denver coach Frank Filchock, in town for that week's game, and asked for a tryout. Filchock, who had been involved in a gambling scandal before the 1946 NFL Championship Game, told Sapienza that Denver couldn't sign him because there had been rumors that he had thrown the game against the Patriots, a ridiculous assertion, but another blow to the poor man's ego. Returning home, Sapienza signed with North Attleboro once again. He played semi-pro ball until he was 36 years old, while pursuing a full-time career as a physical education teacher and coach. Yet, the specter of the Saturday night game with Boston, his last major league football game, remained with him. "There hasn't been a single month that I haven't thought about that game," he said 36 years after the event. "I hear people talk about it and I say to myself, 'I wonder if I was ever there? Maybe it was just a dream.' It was the most traumatic experience."

It was not a dream. The Patriots had gained the first win in their history and the Titans had suffered their first loss. New York's next game, against Denver, featured, by an incredible coincidence, an exact reversal of the ending of the prior week's contest. The Broncos, after their miserable showing during the exhibitions, had won their first two regular-season games, and were a team to be taken seriously. Like the Titans, they had picked up a number of key players as other teams made their cuts, and now boasted a potent offense. Frank Tripucka, who began his professional career in 1949, had gone to the Broncos' training camp to assist Frank Filchock and Dean Griffing, both of whom he had known in

Canada. He had no intention of playing. After about three weeks in camp, the Broncos played an intrasquad game. The first half was miserable. "I don't think they completed a pass," recalled Tripucka. "No touchdowns. Nothing. Filchock said, 'Gee, the people paid five dollars a head to see the first pro football game in Colorado and the guys aren't doing anything. How about getting dressed and going in for the second half and giving them their money's worth?'" Tripucka dressed, played the second half, and wound up starting the season at quarterback. In addition to Tripucka, the Broncos had versatile Gene Mingo, a rookie with tremendous physical talent who had never attended college, honing his football skills in the Navy. Mingo ran from scrimmage, caught passes, returned kicks, could throw the option pass, and was one of the league's top kickers. Al Carmichael, his running mate at halfback, spent six years in the NFL, and held the record for the longest kickoff return (106 yards).

Denver led the Titans 10–7 at halftime. Late in the third quarter, the Broncos widened the lead on a four-yard touchdown run by Bob McNamara. Following the score, Leon Burton, the Titans' speedy, 5'9" running back, dropped back to receive Denver's kickoff. Burton, as a halfback at Arizona State, led the nation in scoring and rushing as a junior in 1957, gaining 1,126 yards and averaging a phenomenal 9.6 yards per carry. During his college career, he averaged 8.5 yards per carry. He had supposedly been clocked at 9.6 for 100 yards, but, ignored by the NFL, played briefly in Canada and had been working in a department store for $75 a week before signing with the Titans. In warmups prior to the Denver game, Burton collided with Roger Ellis. Ellis was knocked silly and Burton limped off the field with a leg injury. He was well enough to play, however, and took the Broncos' kickoff straight up the middle, stumbled toward the sideline, regained his balance, and covered 88 yards to once again bring his club within a field goal at 17–14.

Midway through the final period, Dorow (who averaged 44 yards a punt in Sapienza's absence) led the Titans on an 11-play, 68-yard drive culminating in a 10-yard scoring pass to Thurlow Cooper, putting New York in front 21–17. With just under three minutes remaining, Denver had the ball on the Titans' 32-yard line. Lionel Taylor, a former Chicago Bears reserve, had joined the Broncos the previous day and was playing split end. He told Tripucka in the huddle, "I think I can beat this guy on a short post." Tripucka looked at Taylor. Not only had he just arrived, he had been a defensive back, not a receiver, with the Bears. Frank remembered, however, watching Taylor make acrobatic, one-handed catches in his first practice. "We'll try it," Tripucka answered. True to his word, Taylor broke free, and Tripucka hit him for a touchdown that gave the Broncos a 24–21 advantage.

Dorow had one more chance to win the game, and passed his club to the Denver 42. With 1:15 to go, however, he was intercepted, seemingly snuffing out the Titans' last hope. The New York defense held and, by calling all their timeouts, forced the Broncos into a punting situation at their own 26. Only 16 seconds remained.

The Titans knew their only chance of winning the game was to block the kick. They put on a ferocious rush, and Nick Mumley and Roger Donahoo pulled a stunt, Mumley going inside and Donahoo to the outside. Mumley, 6'6" and a former all-state basketball player in West Virginia, found a clear path to rookie punter George Herring. He leaped high and smothered the ball on the 10-yard line. "The halfback who was supposed to take me just ran by," he said. "He missed the block and the ball just hit me on the chest." It bounded off to the side, where Herring, like Sapienza, tried to pick the ball up. At that moment he was blocked aside, and Donahoo grabbed the ball. He looked up, saw no one between him and the goal line, and sprinted in with the winning touchdown. For the second week in a row, a botched punt on the final play decided the game. "This time," wrote Al Buck in the *New York Post*, "the Titans got the girl."

"When I plan a game," Baugh said in the locker room, "I plan it right."

The fourth week of the season found the New York club in Dallas to face the formidable Texans, meticulously assembled with Lamar Hunt's sizable bankroll. "They've had a strong bunch since the beginning," Baugh said. "They haven't had to pick up players cut by the other league like most of us have had to do." Dallas won all six of its exhibition games, including the one-sided 38–14 victory over New York, and was favored by 13 points over the Titans.

The Texans' offensive backfield was loaded with talent, including three rookie running backs: Abner Haynes of North Texas State, Jack Spikes of TCU, and Johnny Robinson, Billy Cannon's backfield mate at LSU. Haynes was the backbone of the Texans' attack. A speedy, shifty breakaway threat, he could run, return kicks, and catch passes with equal skill. "Abner was a great ballplayer," said Cotton Davidson. "He was probably the most complete player we had. Abner was a great pass receiver and a great runner and he was also a very good blocker. You couldn't find a lot of flaws with Abner."

Elusiveness was Haynes' great talent. "He left me tackling the air a couple of times," remembered the Titans' Paul Hynes. Haynes was such an integral part of the Texans' offense that at the end of one game at the Cotton Bowl, the public address announcer cautioned the departing fans, "Drive carefully on the way home. The life you save may be Abner Haynes'."

For the trip to Dallas, the Titans added a permanent replacement for Sapienza—Joe Pagliei, who had spurned Denver because of their striped socks. Pagliei was a fullback who played in Canada and for one season in the NFL with the Eagles. During his college career at Clemson, he twice led the ACC in punting. The Titans' stockings passed Pagliei's inspection but their helmets did not. Wismer had purchased Wilson helmets, which rested flat on a player's head. Many Titans preferred the newer style Riddell suspended helmet. The Riddell helmet looked better and, many thought, provided greater protection. Pagliei bought his own helmet and spray painted it in his hotel room, rendering a good portion of the drapes Titans blue and gold in the process.

"The boys want this one awful bad," said Baugh the week before the game. "I think we'll play a real good game." It was not only the boys who wanted to win. *The New York Times* reported that during practice that week, Baugh "frequently gave his commands with a bark. Everything the coach said seemed to have more bite than was his custom." Baugh was returning to his native Texas, and he wanted to make up for his team's poor showing in the Abilene exhibition game.

Sunday, October 2, was a beautiful day in Dallas, with bright sunshine and temperatures reaching 85 degrees. The crowd was estimated at 37,500, twice what the NFL Cowboys had drawn two days earlier. The attendance figure deserves an asterisk, however, as many had been admitted for free. It was Barber's Day, and all barbers were let in without charge, as were several thousand students who presented their ticket stubs from Friday night high school games, and several thousand more children wearing complimentary Texan T-shirts. Still, a crowd of 37,500 was nothing to sneeze at. By mid-October, Lamar Hunt's team would be leading the AFL in attendance, belying his claim that Dallas was a one-team town.

The Titans' offense was as hot as the weather, taking less than two minutes following the opening kickoff to reach the end zone. Following two penalties against the Texans, Dorow hit Powell, who was several strides behind Dave Webster, for a 36-yard touchdown. Dallas, however, countered with seven points of its own less than two minutes later. The key play was a 72-yard pass from Davidson that bounced off the hands of New York's Chuck Dupre and into the arms of Dallas's Johnny Robinson. The Titans regained the lead when Maynard leaped high in the end zone and wrestled the ball away from Dallas's Don Flynn for a 26-yard touchdown. The defenses finally rallied and there was no further scoring until midway through the second quarter.

Powell again got behind the Dallas secondary and hauled in a 49-yard pass from Dorow, setting up a five-yard touchdown toss to halfback Bill Shockley. Dallas countered with a quick touchdown, but Leon Burton ran the ensuing kickoff back 50 yards to set up a 37-yard scoring pass to tight end Dave Ross, which made the score 27-14 Titans at halftime.

In the second half, the Titans had to fend off Haynes. He ran from scrimmage, caught passes, returned kicks, and almost single-handedly brought his team back. For the game, he carried the ball five times for 46 yards; caught six passes, some on spectacular grabs, for 80 yards; returned two kickoffs for 58 yards; and returned three punts for 74. With about a minute to play in the first half, he took a punt from Pagliei on his 13-yard line. He started to run with the ball, then lateraled to Johnny Robinson. Robinson danced around, then tossed it back to Haynes, who was finally tackled on the 35. On New York's first possession of the third quarter, Shockley attempted a 53-yard field goal. The kick was short, and Haynes fielded the ball on the 7-yard line. He ran straight up the middle, burst out of a pile of players and went 93 yards. Fortunately for the Titans, one of the Texans was detected clipping and the play was called back.

In spite of the penalty, Davidson led his club to a score, but New York came right back on the running of Shockley, who gained 45 yards on a drive that put the Titans ahead 34–21. New York's offense in the second half consisted principally of a ground attack, as Dorow, who had completed 16 passes in the first half, connected only once more.

Despite a 36-yard kickoff return by Haynes, the Titans held on Dallas's next possession. Early in the fourth quarter, however, Haynes scored on a five-yard run to bring the Texans within six points. The next time New York had the ball, Shockley kicked a 32-yard field goal that turned out to be the margin of victory. Dallas countered with a touchdown, and the Titans got the ball on their 20 with 2:25 left, needing to run out the clock to preserve a two-point victory. On third down, Dewey Bohling picked up a first down on a pitch to the right side. Two plays later, with 15 seconds left, Bohling carried again and was hit hard by defensive end Mel Branch. The ball came loose and began rolling toward the Titans' goal line as a mad scramble ensued, and the prospect of a third consecutive bizarre ending flashed in front of Baugh's eyes. On the 6-yard line, Branch tried to pick the ball up and run with it. He dropped it, and finally, on the 8-yard line, as time ran out, New York guard John McMullan outwrestled a Texan for the ball.

New York fans watching the game on television were spared the nerve-wracking ending, as the local affiliate, WABC, cut off the telecast at precisely 6:30 PM, with the Titans leading 37–35. A Walt Disney special featuring Davy Crockett and his sidekick, Mike Fink, was scheduled, and ABC executives wanted to be certain the audience would not miss a single moment of their quest to "make the Ohio River safe for honest boats."

ABC quickly discovered that a number of viewers preferred Harry and Sammy to Davy and Mike. "The [switch]board lit up like a Christmas tree seconds after the game went off," said a network executive. It was a presage of the "Heidi game" of 1968, when NBC cut away from the dramatic Jets–Raiders game to begin showing the classic movie. Unlike the "Heidi Game," there was no further scoring in the New York–Dallas match, and the Titans, at 3–1, were in first place in the Eastern Division. Rather than return to New York, the team stayed in Texas, where they were scheduled to meet the Houston Oilers the following week.

CHAPTER 11

TRAGEDY IN HOUSTON

The Houston Oilers had perhaps the most talent of any team in the AFL. They had an adequate defense—in a league where defense was not a long suit—and a formidable array of offensive talent at what are now referred to as the "skill" positions: quarterback, running back, and receiver. At quarterback was 32-year-old George Blanda, a player made to order for the wide-open AFL, an experienced veteran with a right arm that still had several years of life in it. Blanda started his professional career with the Chicago Bears in 1949 and was a mediocre player in the NFL. He clashed repeatedly with Bears coach George Halas, didn't see regular duty after 1954, and spent 1959 out of football. Halas approached Blanda before the 1959 season started, told him he would not be on the active roster, and offered to pay him $6,000 to stay in shape in case the Bears needed him. After Blanda accepted, he realized he had been taken. Halas had not released him, so Blanda was not free to join another team. When the Colts expressed interest, Halas wouldn't let him go. Blanda attempted to report for duty with the Bears, but Halas wouldn't take him. In desperation, Blanda threatened to sue the NFL. On October 8, Bert Bell announced that he would examine the case, but, three days later, Bell died. Rather than continue to fight the establishment, Blanda decided to seek opportunity in the AFL, where all eight clubs were looking for a passer with his qualifications. John Breen, the Oilers' director of player personnel, said, "My first thought was if you're going to play in a new league, go and get the best-throwing quarterback you can find and have him put the football in the air, because it will be a year or two before anyone can get the kind of defensive backs that will be able to stop him." He convinced Blanda to sign with the Oilers. Halas, so intent on driving the new league into the ground, delivered one last dig at his old antagonist. "The American Football League can't be anything but a Mickey Mouse league," he said. "How can it be anything else? Isn't George Blanda a first-string quarterback over there?"

The experienced Blanda was like a coach on the field for the Oilers. The son of a Pennsylvania coal miner, he was a rugged 215-pounder who had played linebacker for the Bears in 1950. He was an emotional, hardnosed player who could dish out verbal and physical punishment to opponents and teammates alike. Once, when Broncos linebacker Jerry Hopkins sacked Blanda and then laughed at him, Blanda got up, ran over, and kicked Hopkins in the backside.

His attacks upon those wearing his own colors were limited to the verbal variety. "We were playing an exhibition game in 1960," said star receiver Charley Hennigan, then a struggling rookie. "George called a pattern, but the coverage was shifting toward the way the pass was going, so I broke off the route. The next thing I saw was George coming after me. He said, 'You SOB, you can do what you want on your own time, but if you want to play with me, you go where I tell you to go.'"

Jacky Lee, Blanda's young backup, could have started for most AFL clubs. In November 1960, in his second professional game, Lee's first three completions were touchdown passes of 73, 78, and 92 yards. The following year, he set a single-game passing record with 457 yards.

At halfback was Billy Cannon, the 1959 Heisman Trophy winner from LSU. After winning the Heisman by the biggest margin in history, Cannon was selected as the territorial choice by Houston and also by the Los Angeles Rams, who held the first pick in the NFL draft. Both clubs made generous contract offers.

Money was very important to Cannon. He married during his freshman year at LSU and, by December 1959, had three daughters ranging in age from two years to two and a half months. Immediately after his selection by the Rams, he announced his intention to play in the NFL and sign with Los Angeles immediately after the Sugar Bowl. He did, in fact, sign with Los Angeles, but much sooner than his stated timeframe. The Rams' contract was dated November 30, more than a month prior to the end of Cannon's collegiate eligibility. It called for a salary of $10,000 for the 1960 season and $15,000 for 1961 and 1962. He received a $10,000 signing bonus and $500 for expenses.

By late December, Cannon was wavering. He said he was leaning toward signing with the Oilers "because the money was too great to resist," reportedly a $100,000 offer for three years. The proposed agreement was a personal services contract with Houston owner Bud Adams, assuring Cannon that he would be paid whether the league succeeded or not. It was rumored that Adams planned to open a chain of Billy Cannon Health Centers, or that Cannon would receive lucrative contracts to operate service stations for Adams. (This was not the only example of Adams being an innovator in the area of compensation. Willard Dewveall, full-time split end and part-time insurance agent, sold a $1 million life insurance policy to Mrs. Adams. The sizable commission was a nice complement to his Oilers salary. In 1964 Houston signed tackle Scott Appleton from the University of Texas, the country's best collegiate lineman, to a package that included a filling station, cattle for Appleton's father's ranch, and a franchise for a company that had developed a new chemical fodder process.)

The contract Adams offered was sufficient to pry the Heisman winner loose from the Rams. On December 30, Cannon sent a letter to the Los Angeles club, along with uncashed checks totaling $10,500, representing his bonus and expense money. The letter, undoubtedly drafted with some assistance from the Oilers' attorneys, stated that, since Cannon had been ineligible to sign until after his final college game, the document executed in November was only a proposal to sign a contract in January. After the Sugar Bowl, which LSU lost 21–0 to Mississippi, Cannon stood beneath the goal posts and signed a personal services contract with Bud Adams.

In the early months of 1960, Foss and Rozelle, the commissioners of the two leagues, re-affirmed the earlier agreement of Bert Bell and Lamar Hunt that there would be no tampering with any player under contract to the other league. By July, Rozelle claimed that the AFL had violated the pledge by signing Cannon and Charley Flowers of Mississippi. The issue was whether the players were under valid contracts when the AFL signed them. While Rozelle obviously thought they were, Foss just as strongly believed they were not.

On January 11, 1960, the Rams filed a lawsuit in federal court to enforce their contract. Cannon's answer to the suit claimed that Rozelle, when he had been general manager of the Rams, had told him the contract would not take effect until after the Sugar Bowl, and by rescinding prior to that date, he had rendered the agreement void. Rozelle was in a difficult position. In order to prove the November 30 document binding, he would have to admit signing a collegian whose eligibility had not yet expired. Now that he was commissioner, Rozelle's position was even more treacherous.

The trial commenced in mid-June. On June 20, Judge William J. Lindberg ruled the Rams' contract invalid and cleared the way for Cannon to join the Oilers. Lindberg stated in his opinion that Cannon was a naive country boy who had been misled by the sophisticated Rozelle regarding the character of the document he signed. The 22-year-old halfback was now, by 1960 standards, a very rich naive country boy.

Cannon was a rare talent, a muscular 6'1" 210-pounder who was exceptionally fast, having once been clocked at 9.4 in the 100-yard dash. The combination of power and speed was extremely rare at the time, for most speedsters were little, jitterbugging backs incapable of breaking tackles. The big backs were plowhorses who ran over people but could not run around them. In the open field, Cannon was as hard to bring down as a charging fullback. Pete Hart recalled playing defense against the Heisman winner when Hart was at Hardin-Simmons. He was at cornerback when Cannon rounded the end at full speed on a sweep. "I came up and hit him so hard I thought I broke his leg," said Hart. He went back to the huddle, where one of his teammates told him to take a look at what Cannon's leg had done to his helmet. "He just mashed that Riddell helmet. There was a big old hole in it. It was crushed. It looked like you'd taken a sledgehammer and smashed it."

Cannon and Blanda were only two of a number of Houston offensive threats. Fullback Dave Smith led the league in rushing for a good portion of the season, and wound up with 645 yards. Bill Groman and Charley Hennigan, the two ends, were talented pass catchers who in 1960 combined for 116 receptions and 18 touchdowns. Groman, from little Heidelberg College, led the league in yards per catch in both 1960 and 1961. "Bill had the most beautiful pair of hands you've ever seen," said Hennigan. "He had real good speed and great body control. He was loose. He was one of those guys who'd go out there and dance and everything would move."

Hennigan set a professional record with 1,748 receiving yards in 1961, and in 1964 caught 101 passes for 1,546 yards. Dick Felt of the Titans thought he was the toughest receiver he ever defended. "Hennigan ran like he was going to fall apart," said Felt. "He could be at full speed in a couple of steps, make his move, and I swear he wouldn't lose any speed at all in the break."

Hennigan played at Northwest Louisiana State, then briefly with the Edmonton Eskimos of the CFL. "In Canada," said Hennigan, who has a doctorate in education, "they told me I was too dumb to learn the plays and I couldn't block. One of those is true." He was back home in Robiline, Louisiana, teaching high school biology, when he learned that a new league was being formed. Hennigan called the sports editor of a Shreveport paper and was told that the nearest franchise was in Houston. A call to Oilers coach Lou Rymkus produced an invitation to training camp, so Hennigan recruited his Northwest Louisiana teammate, Charley Tolar, hopped into a borrowed station wagon, and made the drive to Texas.

Since being cut by Edmonton, Hennigan had lifted weights and bulked up from 170 to 188. He had improved his technique by working with former Cleveland Brown receivers Dub Jones and Mac Speedie. When he went to the Oilers' camp, however, he was so nervous he couldn't catch the ball. At the end of the exhibition season, Speedie, an assistant coach, approached Hennigan, who thought he was going to be released. Speedie said, "Rymkus wanted to cut you, all the assistant coaches said to cut you, and Adams said we couldn't keep you. I told him I'm putting my job on the line for you. So you'd better catch that ball or we're both gone." Hennigan more than repaid Speedie's confidence, setting several professional receiving records before retiring in 1967.

While Blanda, Cannon, and Hennigan grabbed most of the headlines, many of the Titans felt Charley Tolar, a 5'6" fireplug and a reject from the Pittsburgh Steelers, was the most punishing offensive player on the Oilers' club. He blocked for Cannon from the fullback position, and ran low and hard. "Charley was so low to the ground and so powerful," said Hennigan, "he had just destroyed people in college. Every little man remembers Charley Tolar." The Steelers cut Tolar after a defensive end hurdled him during an exhibition game and tackled quarterback Bobby Layne. He tried the CFL, then went to graduate school and coached for a year. Tolar was too short for the NFL, but AFL clubs were prepared to take a chance on a player with less than classic proportions. A number of New York defenders stated emphatically that they would rather go up against Cannon than Tolar. "He was so hard to tackle," said Bob Marques. "There was nothing to hit. It was all knees and shoulders. There was no middle of him. He was like a little bowling ball going down the field."

"Tolar was murder," said defensive end Joe Ryan. "It was tough getting your arms around him. He was an impossible person to tackle. He wasn't tall and when he bent down all you saw was elbows and knees. He had big legs and was a tough guy to wrap around."

In addition to their explosive offense, the Oilers, unlike most AFL teams, could play defense. "Most teams could score, but didn't have real good defenses," Baugh said. "Most teams were about like us, except Houston. When we hit a team with a good defense, we couldn't move the ball."

With such a formidable club, many expected the Oilers to dominate the AFL East. Yet, when the two teams met in Houston, the Titans, with a 3–1 record, held a half-game lead over the 2–1 Oilers. Cannon, slowed by a knee injury and a tendency to fumble, had been unimpressive.

Both offenses started slowly in the October 9 matchup. The only scoring in the first quarter was two field goals by Blanda, from 22 and 36 yards, giving Houston a 6–0 margin. Dorow, overcome by the intense 91-degree heat, departed after failing to complete any of his eight passing attempts. The heat was so brutal on the field that Houston linebacker Mike Dukes, who had received a pain-killing injection for his injured ankle, began shaking violently and had to be taken to the hospital and packed in ice to lower his body temperature.

In the second period, Jamieson hit Powell with two scoring passes to give New York a 14–13 halftime lead. The turning point of the game came midway through the third period, when Houston blocked a field-goal attempt by Shockley and recovered on the Titans' 38. Shortly thereafter,

Cannon scored his first professional touchdown on a run from the 1-yard line. Another New York turnover—this time a fumble recovered on the Titans' 49—resulted in a 40-yard touchdown run by Tolar, which sealed Houston's 27–21 win and catapulted them into first place in the Eastern Division.

The loss was insignificant, however, compared to what happened to the Titans' Howard Glenn after the game. Glenn was a reserve offensive lineman from Linfield College in Oregon; he had been cut by the Giants and played in 1959 with Maynard on the Hamilton Tiger Cats. He returned to the Giants in 1960, was cut in mid-September, and signed with the Titans before the game against the Patriots. In the pre-weightlifting era, Glenn was an anomaly. He was a 240-pounder with a thin waist and a powerful upper body. Married and the father of one, he was a bright, likable fellow who, although reserved and quiet, had quickly become popular with his teammates. A talented artist, he drew caricatures, including some excellent ones of Maynard with his cowboy hat and boots.

During the game against Dallas, Glenn suffered what appeared to be a minor injury, yet it had taken some time to revive him. Throughout the next week, although not normally a complainer, he was quiet and moody and spoke of frequent headaches. In Houston, he was inserted at left guard in place of Mischak, who was injured early in the game. Shortly before the end of the first half, the Titans ran a trap play up the middle, and Glenn was caught between two stunting defenders. He lay on the ground after the play was over and had to be helped to the sideline. When he reached the Titans' bench, he said he felt tired and leaned on Fred Julian for support. Julian, thinking Glenn was merely fatigued from the heat, got him seated and went back in the game.

As the Titans did not have a doctor with them, Glenn sat unattended on the bench. "He was a very quiet guy," said Joe Ryan. "After he got hit, he walked around for a while and he was even more quiet, more sullen. He just withdrew. Guys were coming and going and everyone was watching out for themselves. I don't think too many people realized how hurt he was."

When the game was over, Glenn went to the locker room, showered, took some salt pills, had a soft drink, and then began acting strangely. He became belligerent and started looking for a fight. The players attempted to calm him and sat him down in a metal folding chair in the middle of the locker room. Suddenly, Glenn started shaking violently and slid off the chair onto the floor. His eyes rolled back in his head.

The other players looked on in shock. Maynard had hunted small game all his life, and when he saw Glenn quivering on the floor, realized in horror that that was exactly how rabbits looked just before they died. John McMullan screamed, "For God's sake, get a doctor!" The Titans had no doctor, and it was quite some time before Houston's team physician, James Whitehurst, came in and administered an injection to Glenn. He was rushed to Hermann Hospital, and the players were told he would stay overnight rather than accompany them back to New York.

Glenn never emerged from Hermann Hospital alive. After he was taken out of the locker room, his badly shaken teammates dressed and proceeded to the airport. While they sat aboard the aircraft, Sebo and the coaching staff remained outside, long after the equipment had been loaded and the plane was ready to go. Finally, they came on board. "All you boys," said Baugh, "pay attention." He told the players that Glenn had died. Taken from the locker room at 5:30, he was pronounced dead at 6:10. The cause of death was officially listed as a broken neck. The county medical examiner, Dr. Joseph A. Jachimczyk, said the symptoms were not instantaneous because the fracture had to cut through the spinal column before death occurred.

"You thought, how could a man like that—he was built like a god—how could a thing like that happen?" said Marques. Pagliei recalled that television reports had indicated only that one of the Titans had died following the game in Houston. The victim had not been identified. While the team was in the air, none of the families knew whether their loved one had perished. As soon as the plane landed, Pagliei ran to a phone and called his wife to let her know he was all right.

"I never saw a bunch of men so down in my life," said Baugh that week. "Howard was a fine boy, and his loss is a great shock." In the wake of Glenn's death, the Titans took some tangible measures to see that the tragedy would not be repeated. First, they engaged Dr. James Nicholas as the team physician. Nicholas was Wismer's personal doctor, having treated the owner for gout for the previous three or four years. He also ministered to a number of the rich and famous, having assisted at one of the spinal surgeries on President John F. Kennedy. Among his other celebrity patients were Greta Garbo, Claudette Colbert, Angela Lansbury, and Peter Lawford. As team doctor of the Titans, Nicholas went to all home games and occasionally made road trips.

The club also took greater precautions with injured players. For the first time, they ordered x-rays. "Guys found out they had broken legs at one time and didn't know it," said Pete Hart. Hart had been injured in the Houston game, but was not believed to be seriously hurt. He had been hit with an elbow between his shoulder blades, but continued playing despite the pain. X-rays showed that Hart had a fractured cervical process. "If Glenn hadn't died," said Hart, "I probably would have kept playing." Shaken by the guard's death, the 27-year-old Hart decided to retire rather than risk permanent injury.

Marques had been injured during the Dallas game and, for a frightening moment, lay immobile on the ground. "That was probably the most scared I was at any time in my life," he said. "I was lying on the field and I couldn't move. I didn't think I was ever going to move again." During the next week, Marques could not get out of a chair without assistance from his roommates. After the tragedy in Houston, he insisted on having x-rays, which showed two fractured transverse processes. Marques did not play again that season and, although he tried to come back in training camp the next summer, his professional career was over. "I was lacking something," he said of his attempted comeback. "Maybe it was fear of injury. That's something I never figured out." Perhaps it was the specter of Howard Glenn that hovered over Marques.

There was one further ramification. Some of Glenn's teammates believed that he might have taken Benzedrine, or "bennies" in an effort to enhance his performance. Bennies were freely distributed in pro football locker rooms. The concept of recreational drugs was not a national issue at that time, and many players took the drug quite innocently known as a "pep pill." Recently one former player related proudly, "I can tell you one thing. I never knew a ballplayer, the whole time I was playing, who took any kind of drugs, none whatsoever, other than a bennie on game day."

Blanche Martin remembered being offered something to pick him up a little before a game. He said sure and was given a bennie. "I'd never had anything like that before," he said. "I felt like I was running on air. It looked as though nobody could catch me. I said, doggone, I should have had some of this a long time ago." Said another player who took bennies occasionally, "I used to play a whole game, get on the airplane, and I couldn't close my eyes."

"I remember that first time vividly," said Lee Grosscup of his initial experience with the drug. "It was before an exhibition game and I was throwing the ball eighty yards in warm-ups. The only trouble was, my receivers were only out about forty yards. I didn't care. I just felt so happy. The pills made me reckless, too. I was never known for my running, but in that game I just felt I could run right over tacklers."

Glenn's death put an abrupt halt to the use of bennies by several Titans players. Although no one knew for certain whether he had taken one the day he died, the mere thought that he had was enough to put a severe scare into the other players. They relied upon natural adrenaline and prepared to go on with the season.

CHAPTER 12

OUT OF QUARTERBACKS

The first game following Glenn's tragic death was against the Bills in Buffalo. Some of the players were still shaken, and it showed in the quality of play, which was ragged on the part of both teams. Al Dorow was a one-man show, running or passing on 56 of New York's 79 offensive plays. He threw 35 passes and ran 21 times, gaining 158 yards in the air and 72 on the ground.

Dorow's most critical dashes came in the fourth quarter, after the Bills took a 13–10 lead. Following a Buffalo punt, the Titans took over at the 50 with five-and-a-half minutes left. On the first play, Dorow completed a seven-yard pass to tight end Dave Ross. Joe Pagliei ran for six yards and a first down at the Bill 37. Two plays gained nothing, and, on third and 10, Dorow was unable to find a receiver. He scrambled for 21 yards to the 16.

Two plays later, he took off again, getting almost to the goal line before he collided with Buffalo safety Billy Atkins. In the opener at the Polo Grounds, Dorow had been hit by Atkins and fallen forward across the goal line. This time he bounced at the one-foot line. On the next play, Dorow leaped over right guard for the touchdown that gave the Titans a 17–13 win.

The victory set up a key game on October 23, when the Titans, 4–2, met the Oilers, who led the Eastern Division with a 4–1 record. In addition to the chance to gain sole possession of first place, the game also represented financial opportunity for Wismer; the Giants had the day off and Wismer had the city to himself. From day one, the Titans' owner had set his sights on the Giants. He supposedly chose the name Titans because in Greek mythology titans were larger than giants. The choice of names was also very efficient. When the new club took down the Giants' sign from the Polo Grounds and replaced it with one reading 'Titans', they needed only to substitute a "T" for a "G" and rearrange the remaining letters.

Wismer built a team with an exciting offense, which he hoped would produce a style of play more appealing to the fans than that of the defense-oriented Giants. He also took every opportunity to taunt the NFL club. In an ABC interview with Jack Buck during halftime of the Titans–Chargers game in December, Wismer challenged the Giants to a charity game. He said the Titans could beat at least five NFL teams and that Al Dorow was as good as any quarterback in the other league, including Johnny Unitas. Giants president John Mara responded icily to Wismer's challenge. "We just don't want to dignify it with an answer," he said. "This is a desperate attempt to get some sorely needed publicity for the AFL and we want no part of it." Don Smith, the Giants' publicity man, added, "That's like a Class B minor league club asking the Yankees for a post-season game."

Wismer always insisted his club could beat the Giants. When Pagliei joined the Titans, Wismer told him, "We could take on the Giants right now and we'd knock the pants off them." John Roosevelt, sitting next to Wismer, laughed.

Such remarks did not amuse Baugh, who knew it would be the Titans standing in their undershorts if the two teams ever met. "He made the statement that we could beat the Giants by three touch-downs," Baugh said. "That turned my stomach. The Giants would run us right off the field."

In his autobiography, even Wismer admitted that his statements were pure bravado. "I know that if the NFL had picked up these challenges, we probably would have been handed our heads," he wrote. "It was all a publicity gimmick."

Taking on the Giants, either on the field or at the box office, was a formidable task, for they were a championship club that had been in

New York since 1925. From 1956 through 1960, they averaged 56,000 fans at each home game. In October 1960, Mayor Wagner held a ceremony at City Hall and presented John Mara with the City's Medallion. The mayor then read from a proclamation, which read in part, "whereas the Giants are New York's major league football team..." As *The New York Times* noted, "Apparently, the city's proclamation writers have taken little notice of the new American Football League or the New York Titans of that league."

Wismer had a paranoid suspicion that the NFL intentionally strengthened the Giants in order to run his club out of New York, assuming that without a viable franchise in America's largest city, the fledgling AFL could not survive. "If they can knock off the Titans," said Wismer, "they knock off the league." In 1961 the Giants obtained Y.A. Tittle and Del Shofner in what turned out to be very favorable transactions, which Wismer insisted were part of the NFL plot to destroy him. He even accused Wellington Mara of hiring kids to let the air out of the tires of cars in the Polo Grounds parking lot. On another occasion, Wismer said that a New York columnist was anti-Titans because his son was the Giants mascot. The writer provided the ultimate rebuttal with the fact that he had no children.

After a 1962 home game with the Chargers, Gordon White of *The New York Times* approached Wismer at the foot of the clubhouse stairs, looking for a quote. There were 30 or 40 fans milling around, and Wismer was preparing to climb the steps to the Titans' locker room. "Harry, have you got a minute?" White asked. Wismer spun around, saw White, grabbed him forcefully by the collar, and started to shake him. "Harry! Harry!" White shouted, "You'd better let go or we're both going to be in trouble. You're going to have a lawsuit you can't afford, and I might do something I don't want to do."

"Harry finally dropped his grip on me," White recalled, "and then said, 'Gordon White, you and your boss, Jim Roach, have each taken ten thousand dollars from the New York Giants to write bad things about us.' Then he went upstairs to the locker room and made the same statement loud and clear in front of everyone."

As Wismer ascended the steps, White stood at their base in shock. Not only was the thought of accepting money from the Giants preposterous, he had not even written anything negative about Wismer's team.

Other papers were far more critical than the *Times*, known for its straight-forward reporting of facts. White's story on the day he was accosted by Wismer was an innocuous piece previewing New York's game against San Diego.

Suddenly, the reason for Wismer's outburst dawned upon White. The *Times* had recently begun strict enforcement of a policy that forbade staffers from accepting gifts. It had been common practice for professional teams to send liquor or candy to sportswriters at holidays, and just as common for the writers to accept. Wismer had just sent cases of whiskey to White and Roach as Thanksgiving gifts. Both men, in light of the newspaper's new policy, had returned them unopened. To the paranoid Wismer, that could mean only one thing. They were in the pay of the Giants.

Everybody was out to get Wismer: the NFL, the city, the Giants, the *Times*, and even the Yankees. With the Giants out of action and out of the headlines, the Yankees chose the week before the game against the Oilers to announce the dismissal of manager Casey Stengel, usurping the front pages of the sports section and burying any news of the Titans' upcoming game.

While Wismer took aim at the Giants' owners, the players on the two teams got along much better. Many lived at Concourse Plaza, an old hotel near Yankee Stadium, and often socialized together at P.J. Clarke's, a popular Manhattan watering hole for athletes. Pagliei, Klotz, and Eddie Bell of the Titans commuted from Philadelphia on the train with Jim Katcavage and Tom Scott of the Giants. New York guard Darrell Dess attended North Carolina State with Dick Christy, who played with the Titans in 1961 and 1962, and was a link between the players on the two teams.

The Titans and Giants often met at banquets, and rival quarterbacks Al Dorow and Charley Conerly became good friends. Said Dorow, "My line was that within five years there would be one league and a big championship game. Some NFL players never believed for a minute that the AFL would last more than two or three years. Sam Huff was adamant about that. He'd say, 'I hope that when I get as old as Al Dorow I'll have a league I can play in.' He was the only one who was bitter. Conerly and Gifford and the other guys from the Giants were all for the league."

In 1960 Wismer carefully scheduled around Giants home games so that the two teams never went head to head. In order to get the jump on his rivals, he arranged for the Titans to play three times in the Polo Grounds before the Giants' first home game. Even the Titans' road games were scheduled so that they would not be on the air when the Giants were playing live at Yankee Stadium. Despite repeated boasts that his team could beat the Giants on the playing field, Wismer did not dare challenge them in separate venues. This strategy, however, often forced Wismer to schedule games on Friday and Saturday nights, not prime viewing times for pro football, especially when the weather got colder. Television audiences were equally sparse for, as Howard Tuckner observed in the *Times*, "New York fans prefer Rawhide to pigskin on Friday nights."

To play at home when the Giants were on the road was perhaps a less desirable alternative than going head to head in New York. While Yankee Stadium could hold only 65,000, millions could watch road games telecast back to New York. Home games were blacked out, accessible on Hartford's Channel 3 only to those New Yorkers with a strong antenna or the willingness to spend Sunday afternoon in a Connecticut motel room. When the Titans played at home and competed against the black-and-white, two-dimensional images of Conerly, Gifford, and the others, weather conditions became a key factor. Bad weather caused people to stay home and watch the Giants from the warmth of their living rooms rather than venture out to see an AFL game. Pete Rozelle was well aware of this and made sure that, whenever the Titans were home, local fans had a televised alternative. Even though the Giants were idle on October 23, the NFL piped two games into the New York market. Still, the Houston game was probably the best chance the Titans had to win a New York following. There were no Giants, either live or on television, and Wismer's crew played an exciting game against a quality opponent.

With climate such a key to Wismer's hopes, it was particularly unfortunate that the Titans were cursed with horrible weather in 1960. Their opener caught the tail end of a hurricane, and almost every home game was plagued with rain, cold, and wind. A brilliant fall day in New York was referred to as "Mara weather," for it seemed the Giants had magnificent luck with the elements. Wismer had none. Perhaps the heavens were also conspiring with the NFL to drive him out of business, although it was probably unnecessary. Dick Young wrote in 1962, "Harry Wismer got some Mara weather but drew a Wismer crowd."

For the game against the Oilers, however, the Titans got Wismer weather as well, which kept many fans at home. The day was rainy and gloomy, a presentiment the New Yorkers should have heeded, for it was indeed to be a dark day for the Titans. The game started well, as Dorow hit Powell with an eight-yard pass to give the Titans a 7–0 lead. From that point on, however, things began to go downhill very quickly. Following the touchdown, Shockley boomed his kickoff four yards deep into the end zone. Speedster Ken Hall gathered it in and ran right through the Titans' coverage for 104 yards and the tying touchdown. The New York offense stalled, and Oilers quarterback George Blanda took charge, throwing three touchdowns to Bill Groman, who, according to Young, "was faking Fred Julian into the Harlem River." Blanda also scored on a quarterback sneak to put Houston in a commanding 35–14 lead.

Dorow suffered a rib injury after being hit with a knee following a 12-yard scramble late in the first quarter. He was replaced by Jamieson, who brought the Titans back by throwing touchdown passes of 55 yards to Maynard, 49 yards to Dewey Bohling, and 44 yards to Art Powell. It was his finest regular-season performance as a pro passer. With about five minutes left in the third quarter, however, Jamieson called a screen pass. The intended receiver was covered, and Jamieson broke out of the pocket and started to run. He was brought down hard and landed on his right shoulder. He got up and returned to the huddle, but when Jamieson got under center to take the next snap, he found he couldn't put his hands together. Baugh told Dorow to take the ice pack off his sore ribs and go back in the game.

With the Titans trailing only 35–28, the New York defense stiffened, containing Blanda, Cannon, and Tolar. Julian, who had pulled down two interceptions against Buffalo the previous week, picked off two more. Cannon had one of the worst games of his career. He gained only nine yards rushing and was benched in the second half. Despite being urged on with chants of "Go! Go! Go!" from the small crowd, the New York offense was unable to score, thwarted by two interceptions. With five minutes left in the game, Dorow was blindsided while attempting to pass, and hit hard in the back of his right knee. He was carried off the field on a stretcher and, with Jamieson already down, the Titans found themselves with a dilemma.

Baugh asked if anyone had ever played quarterback. Julian, who had played the position in high school, volunteered. Baugh told him to warm up in a hurry. Julian tossed a few passes on the sideline; he later said that, full of adrenaline, he was not the least bit nervous about the prospect of entering the game. He now admits he should have been. "I probably would have run for my life," he said.

Finally, Baugh decided upon Bohling, who had done some passing from the single wing in high school. "I could throw the ball fairly decent," Bohling said. "There's a big difference, though, between throwing the ball in practice and throwing it in a game situation."

Since Bohling had never taken a snap from the T-formation, Baugh went to the shotgun and sent in the plays himself. The scene was somewhat chaotic. Powell, of course, wanted the ball, as did Maynard. Both were certain they could get free in the Oilers' secondary. Bohling was less certain he could get the ball to them. He remembered the nervousness in the huddle, trying to get the play called, and both wide receivers yelling at him to throw the ball to them.

Bohling threw four passes, without a completion. "That's what made me aggravated," he said. "I just felt bad I didn't complete any passes. It happened so blurry and so quick I really didn't have time to savor it. I guess that's one of the highlights for the Titans...or maybe the lowlight." The Oilers tacked on a final touchdown on a pass from Blanda to Charley Hennigan and widened their division lead with a 42–28 win.

During training camp, the *New York Herald Tribune* ran a story headlined "Titans Chief Headache: 6 Passers, 6 Problems—Too Many Quarterbacks." By late October, that problem had been neatly solved, for now the Titans had no quarterbacks. During the next week, Baugh and Sebo concentrated on finding someone who could start the Friday night game against the Oakland Raiders. Stan Isaacs of *Newsday* suggested that Baugh activate himself, a bit of advice the coach dismissed immediately. The scheduling, done with the intention of avoiding a conflict with the Giants, now conspired against the new club, as Dorow would have only five days, rather than seven, to pull his battered body together.

Jamieson was definitely out with his shoulder injury. He had been examined on the field, and told he had a separated shoulder, which was taped tightly together. Standing on the sideline during the fourth quarter, Jamieson was in excruciating pain. After the game, Larry Grantham drove him to the hospital, seemingly hitting every red light en route. "I was almost delirious by the time I got there," said Jamieson, who was still wearing his uniform. When the doctor cut the tape from his arm, the shoulder hung loose, with a gap at the shoulder blade. The joint was dislocated, not separated. After waiting for muscle spasms to subside, the doctor popped the shoulder back into place.

Jamieson was admitted to the hospital and placed in the same four-bed room as Dorow. It was there that he discovered the strength of the Michigan State connection. On the table next to Dorow's bed was a flower arrangement from Wismer. Jamieson's table was barren. "I knew right then," he said, "that I was a second-class citizen as far as Harry was concerned."

Jamieson's roommate, Dorow, was questionable with his assorted ailments. X-rays revealed no rib fracture, but his right knee was still painful the day after the game. He attempted to check himself out of the hospital, but was sent back. With Dorow's status uncertain, the club activated Bob Scrabis from the taxi squad and prepared to start the game against the Raiders with him at quarterback.

Scrabis was a strapping 6'3", 225-pounder who played at Penn State as the backup to future Browns and Lions starter Milt Plum and then to All-American Richie Lucas. Lucas was a versatile athlete who was most dangerous as a runner, while Scrabis was a classic dropback passer with perhaps the best arm of any Titans signal caller. "He fires it good," said Baugh. "He's got the strongest arm we got, and maybe the most accurate." Scrabis had little opportunity to use his powerful arm in college, for the Nittany Lions had a very conservative, run-oriented offense under veteran head coach Rip Engle and his enthusiastic young assistant, Joe Paterno. "Passing was one of the things Joe was not very fond of," Scrabis said.

Paterno was then a bachelor and, according to Scrabis, obsessed with football. The quarterback remembered how many of the players earned spending money ushering at other sporting events. Paterno was often in attendance, and the players always dreaded seeing him approach, for they knew he wanted to talk football, the last thing they wanted to discuss in their free time. Paterno even jokingly suggested at meals that the players arrange their mashed potatoes in the form of a football, in order to keep their minds on the game. "It was always, business, business, business," Scrabis recalled, "but he was a hell of a nice guy. You couldn't really tell then that he was going to be the coach that he is now, but he was special. He always had the interest of the kids at heart and he was genuine."

When Scrabis graduated in 1958, Baltimore expressed some interest, but the Colts had Johnny Unitas, then in his prime at age 27, entrenched at quarterback, so Scrabis returned to Penn State to pursue a master's degree in business administration. He was the backfield coach for the Nittany Lions' freshman team, and continued to work out. When the Titans emerged a year later, Scrabis decided to take a shot at pro football. Penn State agreed to hold his graduate assistantship open in case he didn't make the team.

When he reported to Durham, Scrabis weighed 240 pounds, well over his playing weight. He gradually reduced to 225 and had the honor of taking the first snap in the first Titans practice. He survived most of training camp, but was told just before the final exhibition game that he was going to be released. Scrabis was offered a place on the taxi squad, a group of inactive players so named because former Cleveland Browns owner Arthur "Mickey" McBride had at one time given these athletes jobs driving his company's cabs while they practiced with the team and waited for an opportunity. By 1960 taxi squadders were paid at the rate of about $200 per week.

Scrabis decided against joining the taxi squad, electing instead to return to Pennsylvania to continue his studies. He arrived home on Friday and planned to start classes on Monday. Encouraged by his father, however, Scrabis changed his mind and went back to New York. He was single, with no responsibilities, and might as well give football another shot. He could always start a career in accounting, Scrabis reasoned, but a chance to play pro football would not come again. Apparently, he had made the right decision; for now, a month later, it appeared as though he would be the Titans' starting quarterback.

In the week preceding the game against the Raiders, Scrabis was the center of attention, taking nearly every snap in practice and coming under close observation from the reporters who followed the club. He was a smart player who picked up the system quickly. "I really didn't pay much attention to the newspapers," he said. "I had confidence I could get the job done. There was no pressure. I was just anxious to play."

Meanwhile, the status of Dorow was the subject of constant speculation. On Monday, after being released from the hospital, he declared confidently, "I am going to play Friday." Although it had at first been feared that he would be hospitalized for an extended period and probably miss the rest of the season, Dorow claimed he would sleep all day Monday and appear at practice on Tuesday. "The ankle will come around," he said. "The knee is a little sore, but it will come around too. The neck and the jaw don't matter. The ribs may be sore, but I'll just tape them up."

While Scrabis practiced diligently with the first unit, Baugh remained hopeful that Dorow, rather than the untested rookie, would be able to line up under center on Friday night. Not only was Scrabis without professional experience, he had played very little in college. "I'm not gonna put Al in and get him killed," Baugh said, "but if he's ready to go, I'm gonna go with him." On Wednesday, Dorow appeared at the Polo Grounds, but spent the afternoon in the whirlpool. "I'll play," he said, "but I don't know how much." On Thursday, he practiced for the first time and was encouraged. On Friday, true to his prediction, Dorow, sore ribs, knee, neck, ankle, jaw, and all, took the field with the Titans' starting offense when they trotted out to do battle with the Raiders.

It would have been a great story if Dorow could have risen from his sickbed and led the Titans to victory. The scene was perfect for drama, a raw, windy, and rainy night, classic Wismer weather, with only about 10,000 hardy souls scattered throughout the Polo Grounds. On the Titans' first possession, Dorow led a 76-yard touchdown drive, capped by a 47-yard scoring pass to Maynard. After Oakland tied the score with about six minutes left in the first quarter, the Raiders' Larry Barnes sailed his kickoff into the end zone. As Bill Shockley waited to catch the ball, Leon Burton ran over and collided with him. The ball hit Shockley and bounced out to the 1-yard line, a live ball. Burton picked it up, headed for the right sideline and streaked 99 yards down the field for the go-ahead touchdown, his second scoring kick return of the season. "I had to run,"

Burton said after the game. "It was Shockley's ball and I knew he was going to give me hell about it."

The two teams traded long touchdowns, Raiders quarterback Tom Flores hitting Al Hoisington with a 61-yard bomb, and Dorow finding Powell with a 76-yarder, giving the Titans a 21–14 lead at the half. Dorow, despite the plastic padding he was wearing to protect his ribs, had completed 10 of 16 attempts for 165 yards and two touchdowns. Powell had caught five of Dorow's passes for 108 yards.

The only scoring in the third quarter was an 18-yard field goal by Shockley. Early in the fourth period, the Raiders closed to 24–21, with a drive during which they seemingly ran at will against the Titans' defense. The two teams then traded interceptions, Larry Grantham returning a pickoff of Babe Parilli, who had replaced Flores at quarterback, to the Oakland 37. On third and 10 from the 26, Dorow dropped back to pass. Unable to find an open receiver, he forgot about his injuries and scrambled for 11 yards and a first down. Four plays later, Shockley kicked a 24-yard field goal for a 27–21 lead with 6:13 left in the game.

During Oakland's next drive, the Titans' defense appeared helpless against the running of J.D. "Jetstream" Smith and Tony Teresa. Coach Eddie Erdelatz told Parilli to keep running the ball until the Titans showed they could stop it. The Titans couldn't stop it. Nine plays and less than three minutes later, Smith scored his second touchdown of the game, this time from nine yards out. The extra point gave Oakland a 28–27 lead. The Titans had two more possessions, but could muster only five incomplete passes and a fumble on six plays. On the final snap Dorow was flattened by Oakland's Charley Powell (Art's older brother) and Ray Armstrong. As he picked himself up off the turf, he could look back on a courageous effort, having played every offensive down. In the second half, however, he had worn down, completing only five of 17 passes for 36 yards.

In the locker room, Dorow blasted his own defense. "Boy, some defensive team," Dorow told reporters. "We have to score eighty points to win. You score twenty-seven points; you figure you're going to win. But not this team." Making remarks like that in public was not likely to win friends on the defensive unit. Defensive captain Tom Saidock responded, "You don't blame one guy when the team is going badly. We lost that game as a team." Saidock then took a direct shot at Dorow. "No one guy is that important," he said. "I mean, say Dorow is out. We have enough confidence in Scrabis to win it."

At 4–4, the Titans were just a game and a half behind the 5–2 Oilers, but had lost three of their last four. During the next two weeks, the team proceeded to all but eliminate itself from contention by losing at home to the Chargers and to the Patriots at Boston University.

The Chargers put tremendous pressure on Dorow, hitting him often and causing his passing to be erratic and ineffective. The Titans had only three first downs in the first half, and Dorow lost the ball twice on a fumble and an interception. For Los Angeles, Paul Lowe had a brilliant 62-yard touchdown run. The final score was 21–7, the last Chargers score coming after the recovery of a Dorow fumble deep in New York territory. The Titans' defense, inspired after the criticisms of the previous week, played well. It was Dorow and the offense that let the club down, a point that was not lost on the defensive unit. "We got the ball enough, didn't we?" said Sid Youngelman in a veiled comment about the lack of offensive production.

The offense played better against the Patriots, but the defense completely fell apart. Before the game, Baugh said he intended to use Powell both on defense and on kick returns. He never followed through, but perhaps he should have. The Patriots ran up 20 first downs and 377 yards, while punting only once during the entire game. Jim Colclough, the Patriots' star end, beat Dick Felt badly, catching six passes, two for touchdowns.

The final score could have been much worse than 38–21, for two more Boston touchdowns, including a 76-run by Dick Christy, were nullified by penalties. The two most potent Patriots on offense, Christy and quarterback Ed "Butch" Songin, would both later join the Titans, but on this day they were busy shredding the New York defense. Christy rushed for 105 yards on 11 carries, and also caught four passes. Songin, who had only a mediocre season against the rest of the AFL, completed 19 of 34 passes for 234 yards and three touchdowns. After throwing an interception late in the game, Dorow became involved in an altercation with Patriots tackle Art Hauser and was ejected.

Now 4–6 and in third place in the Eastern Division, behind Houston and Boston, New York faced a Thanksgiving morning game at the Polo Grounds against the Texans, who were 5–5, only a game behind the Chargers in the Western Division. The Titans were bolstered by the return of tight end Thurlow Cooper and safety Corky Tharp, two starters who had been abruptly released a week earlier for reasons that were not completely clear. Since the cuts reduced the New York roster to 31, four players below the limit, it was suspected that the whole affair was a Wismer economy move. "Sam thought those fellows weren't helping us," said publicity director Art Susskind, a statement the coach immediately branded as untrue. Sebo said the move was intended to ensure that the Titans ran a "tight, efficient operation." He also indicated that the threat of being cut might act as an incentive to the remaining players, and rumors spread that the squad would be cut to 28.

This unleashed a tempest. Lineman Dick Guesman approached a reporter and told him, "If I'm cut, I'll give you a story that will curl your hair." The quote was printed in the *New York Post*, but Guesman's identity was not revealed. When Wismer saw the anonymous remarks, he was livid. A few days later, he dispatched Sebo to the locker room to distribute a questionnaire to each player. There was only one question. It asked whether, after the Boston game, the player had said, "If I'm cut, I'll give you a story that will curl your hair." There were two boxes, labeled yes and no, and each player was asked to check the appropriate box.

When the players read the question, they started to laugh. Sebo "turned red as a beet," according to one player, and Baugh grabbed all of the papers and threw them on the floor, putting an abrupt end to Wismer's investigation. There were no further roster reductions, and Cooper and Tharp returned a week later.

Cooper felt Wismer had wanted him gone from the start, since he was little known, from a small college, and unlikely to put many people in the stands. Neither was Sebo a big supporter. Baugh, on the other hand, liked Cooper's blocking ability (the "tight tackle" they called him) and his reliability as a receiver, and was as determined to keep Cooper as Wismer and Sebo were to cut him loose. The tight end remembered walking off the practice field on the last day of training camp and hearing Baugh say, "I don't care what you hear today. You're not cut." Although the comment somewhat unnerved him, Cooper stayed around and started every week until the Boston game.

Cooper had decent speed, good hands, and was a smart, dependable receiver. Yet, he rarely figured in the Titans' offense, catching only 36 passes in three years as a starter. "When you've got guys like Maynard and Powell," Dorow said, "you don't throw to your tight end a lot." In the early 1960s, the tight end was just beginning to emerge as an offensive weapon, with John Mackey, Mike Ditka, and Ron Kramer—dangerous receivers as well as punishing blockers—entering the league. "The tight ends back then weren't very important," Cooper said. "I'd get in the middle and if the quarterback was running around, I'd try to get open so he could throw it to me. But they were looking to go deep most of the time. By the time they were looking for me, they were usually on their back."

When Baugh informed Cooper of his release, he told him he'd be gone for 10 days and then would be brought back. He didn't tell him why the whole process was taking place. "He said, 'Stay in shape and don't do anything stupid,'" Cooper recalled. He never learned what had prompted the move or why he was brought back.

The person happiest to see Cooper return was Maynard. Maynard had a number of superstitions regarding his equipment. He insisted on wearing number 13, a habit he adopted while playing six-man football in high school. After a boy named Charlie Smith, who wore that number, broke his leg on the opening kickoff of the season, no other player would touch the uniform. No one, that is, except Maynard, who took it and refused to wear any other number thereafter. Wearing 13 was but one of Maynard's lucky habits. He never wore a chinstrap. "If they want the helmet," he often said, "they can have it. But my head's not going to be in it." Maynard also wore a specially constructed pair of lightweight shoulder pads, which gave him increased flexibility. The only person allowed to pull Maynard's jersey down over those shoulder pads before a game was Cooper. "He would not let anyone touch that number 13 jersey except me," said Cooper. "A couple of times I sent Roger [Ellis] over and Maynard went berserk." The fact that Maynard caught five passes for 100 yards against the Patriots without Cooper's help did nothing to lessen his belief in the sacred ritual. A superstition was a superstition, and Maynard probably felt he had only dodged a bullet in Boston.

The Thanksgiving Day game, the first in New York in 24 years, was intended to be an annual tradition, a decision perhaps influenced by the time Wismer spent in Detroit, where the Lions' Turkey Day contest had been a fixture since 1934. The New York affair was christened the Mayor's Trophy Game. On Wednesday, November 23, Wismer attended a ceremony at City Hall during which he presented Mayor Robert Wagner with a football autographed by all members of the Titans (not, remarkably, an autographed picture of Wismer) and invited him to attend the game and present the winning team with a 30-inch antique English silver cup.

The New York Transit Authority ran two non-stop "Football Special" subway trains to the station at 155th Street and 8th Avenue, right outside the gate to the Polo Grounds. A 50¢ subway ticket, when presented at the Titan ticket office, gave the holder the right to purchase a $4 seat for only $1.25. In addition, any adult purchasing a $4 ticket could buy an adjoining seat for a child at the children's price. With these promotions, the lure of the Mayor's Trophy and the formidable Dallas club as competition, the Transit Authority announced that it was prepared to add more trains if necessary.

It did not prove necessary, for the official attendance was announced at only 14,000. Foss, who was there, claimed the actual count was no more than a thousand. Those who stayed home missed an exciting game, an offensive thriller that remained in doubt until the final minute. "The thing I remember about the Titans," said Texans quarterback Cotton Davidson later, "was that you had to score a lot of points to beat them. Every time you saw them, they were putting thirty or forty points on the scoreboard." On Thanksgiving Day, the Titans struck early and often. The first time New York had the ball, Baugh gambled on fourth and one from the Titan 35. Dorow got the first down on a quarterback sneak. Four plays later, from the Dallas 45, Dorow hit Maynard on the 32. The speedy flanker, bearing the luck Cooper brought him, eluded Duane Wood and Jimmy Harris and carried the ball into the end zone.

Dallas took the kickoff and drove down the field, but the Titans held on a fourth-and-one situation at the 6. They were forced to punt, but on the Texans' first play from scrimmage, Roger Donahoo picked a Johnny Robinson fumble out of the air and returned it 57 yards for a 14–0 lead.

Dallas broke through in the second quarter on a 14-yard field goal by Jack Spikes, followed by a dazzling 67-yard touchdown run by Abner

Haynes, during which he twice reversed his field. The Titans came right back on their next possession, with Dorow passing to Powell and Maynard for a total of 64 yards and carrying twice for 14 more, including the last three for the touchdown. Moments later, Dorow again teamed with Maynard and Powell, this time for four completions, the last to Powell for one yard and a 28–10 halftime lead. Dorow had thrown for 176 yards, all but three to Maynard and Powell. On the Dallas side of the ledger, Haynes had accounted for 129 yards on the ground.

Early in the fourth quarter, following a circus catch by Maynard for a 45-yard gain, Bill Mathis dove over right guard from one yard out and made the score 34–13. For most teams, this would have ended the suspense, but not for the Titans. In 1960 they were outscored 150–77 in the fourth quarter. Dorow was quoted as saying he never felt safe unless he had a 50-point lead with two minutes remaining. "In college," Dorow said. "Biggie Munn would never call the first team off until he had a twenty-eight-point lead. In this case, I felt it was almost double that. Points could be scored so fast. You never had a feeling on the sidelines that our defense was going to stop anybody."

Maynard and Baugh had the same doubts. "When the other team had third and eighteen," said Maynard, "it seemed like they'd always make it." Baugh said simply, "We couldn't stop anybody."

Sure enough, Dallas came back with two quick touchdowns and a two-point conversion to narrow the gap to 34–28. Aided by a 38-yard penalty for pass interference, the Titans increased their lead to 41–28, but Dallas responded instantly. On their first play from scrimmage following the Titans' touchdown, Chris Burford beat Fred Julian for a 50-yard gain. On the next play, Davidson hit Max Boydston, who had broken away from Roger Donahoo, for a touchdown that closed the gap to 41–35 with 2:15 left.

By this point, the Titans were like a bloodied fighter trying to hang on through the 15th round. With Julian and Donahoo having monumental difficulty staying with the Dallas receivers, Dorow didn't dare put the game in the hands of the New York defense. On second down from his own 38, he launched a bomb to Powell, who hauled it in for a 38-yard gain. One more first down, on a sneak by Dorow, sealed a harrowing win that lifted the Titans to 5–6. Dorow had thrown for 301 yards, Maynard catching 10 for 179 and Powell eight for 110. *The New York Times* reported that Baugh, afraid to look at the scoreboard, had asked a fellow subway rider what the final score had been.

The win over Dallas ended the Titans' home season, and sent them west for the final three games. The journey was a battle for survival. Wismer received only the minimum $20,000 guaranty in each city and claimed he lost $150,000 on the trip. With the Titans out of contention for the division title, and Wismer walking a fine line of financial solvency, the owner did not add to the roster to replace injured players. With only a 35-man squad to begin with, the Titans found themselves in California with only 27 or 28 healthy bodies. Baugh was forced to improvise to field a team, and depth was almost non-existent. Maynard filled in at defensive back. Although he handled the position reasonably well, the double duty took its toll on him, and he caught only five passes in the final three games.

Due to the simpler strategies employed in that era, it was easier for players to learn new positions. Hayseed Stephens, a quarterback on the 1962 club, recalled switching to defense when the New York secondary was decimated by injuries. "They said, 'There's your man. He's number twenty-four. Guard him.'" That was it. Receivers, linebackers, and quarterbacks would all fill in at defensive back for the Titans, and none suffered any major catastrophes. It was not easy, however. Stephens was assigned the task of guarding Houston's Hennigan, one of the AFL's leading receivers. "Charley was begging Blanda to throw him the ball," Stephens recalled. Jerry Fields, a linebacker, was moved to cornerback and put on Lance Alworth, San Diego's Hall of Fame flankerback. "When Alworth went across the middle," Fields said, "I'd just yell for help. That's all you could do."

The wide-receiver corps was also thin, and at one point center and linebacker Roger Ellis was the No. 1 backup. Ellis, a self-admitted lead-foot of legendary proportions, was selected because he had the best hands of any interior lineman and liked to run pass patterns after practice. Substituting Ellis for, say, Art Powell, would have resulted in a severe drop-off of talent.

In order to make the road trip interesting, Wismer promised to pay a $500 bonus to each player if the Titans won all three games. Such bonuses were frequently offered by the New York owner and were, under the rules of professional football, illegal. That never stopped Wismer from offering incentives for wins, touchdowns, sacks, or interceptions. He claimed that, prior to the season, he promised a bonus of $2,500 per man if the Titans won the division title and $5,000 each if they became AFL champions. One of the Titans' defenders remembered a game during which he was baffled by the fact that Larry Grantham, who gave the defensive signals, called his own blitz on nearly every play in the first quarter. Then it dawned on him that Wismer had offered $50 for every sack and Grantham, operating on a piecework basis, was trying to earn a little extra compensation.

Wismer usually frustrated such ambitions by failing to honor his promises. On many occasions, the Titans left the field thinking they had enriched themselves, only to wait for a payoff that never came. This was 1960, however, and the promise of a bonus still generated interest. "We didn't believe he'd pay us," said Dick Jamieson, who had returned to the active roster, "but we wanted to see what he'd do."

The trip started out well, with a 30–27 win over the Broncos in Denver, before only 5,861 spectators, many undoubtedly being discouraged by a morning snowstorm that rendered the field muddy and sloppy. Dorow threw for three touchdowns, all to Powell, and defensive end Nick Mumley, who had beaten the Broncos in New York by blocking a punt in the final seconds, intercepted a Frank Tripucka pass and ran it back 26 yards for a score. Once again, the Titans' defense made things exciting, allowing a 30–14 fourth-quarter lead to dwindle to the final three-point margin. The Broncos closed to 30–27 with five minutes remaining and it appeared as though the combination of Denver's proclivity for comebacks coupled with the Titans' inability to sustain a lead would result in a Broncos victory. Dorow, however, was able to direct a clock-consuming drive that finally sputtered out on the Denver 6 with 44 seconds left. Tripucka was out of miracles and the score held. Since Houston lost, the Titans still had a mathematical chance for the division title.

The following week, New York won another close one, 31–28 over the Raiders, as Dorow again threw for three scores and ran for a fourth, earning player of the week honors for the third time. He hit Powell with a 73-yard scoring pass on the second play of the game and Dewey Bohling with the 20-yard game-winner that erased a 28–24 Raiders lead. The crowd at Candlestick Park was disappointing, as only 9,037 turned out. (The Raiders drew only 69,000 for the entire season.) The Titans dominated the game to a much greater extent than the score indicated, running up 471 yards of total offense to Oakland's 275. Tom Flores, how-ever, kept the Raiders in contention until the final minutes with three touchdown passes. Dorow passed for 375 yards and ran for 43, account-ing for 418 of New York's 471 total yards.

An Oilers victory eliminated New York from the Eastern Division race, but the two victories put the Titans in position to earn Wismer's bonus when they faced the Chargers at the Los Angeles Coliseum on December 18. The Chargers had already clinched the Western Division title and were tuning up to face the Oilers in the first AFL Championship Game. The Titans, at 7–6, were trying to register a winning season.

Paul Lowe, the preseason long-shot who wound up gaining 855 rush-ing yards (missing the AFL lead by only 20 yards) and averaging more than six yards per carry, again tormented the Titans, starting with an adven-turesome 25-yard run midway through the first quarter. Lowe tried to sweep right end, was bottled up, reversed his field, went wide to the left and dashed into the end zone for the game's first touchdown. This set the tone for the game, which was an offensive masterpiece, each team matching the other point for point. "We had a hell of a game," said Baugh. "They'd score, we'd score, they'd score, we'd score. I think it's because our boys wanted to worry the hell out of Mr. Wismer. They played their hearts out. He was so worried on the sidelines, walking from one end to the other."

Clearly outmanned, the Titans matched the Chargers blow for blow, literally. Frequent fighting interrupted the contest and Howie Ferguson, the Chargers' fullback, was ejected for slugging in the second quarter. With nothing to lose and $500 a man to gain, the Titans gambled. On their first offensive series, they elected not to punt on fourth and one from their own 34. Dorow snuck for the first down. Pagliei ran for 25 yards and a first down on a fake punt. At the half, New York led 21–16. Dorow had thrown for 128 yards and two touchdowns.

After the Chargers took the lead in the third quarter, New York came back to score on a quarterback sneak by Dorow with 3:13 left. Shockley lined up to kick the extra point, but Jamieson, the holder, rose up and fired a pass to Cooper for two points and a 29–26 margin.

In the final three minutes of the quarter, each team scored on a quick drive, which left the score 36–33 in favor of the Titans. On the first series of the fourth period, Dick Felt intercepted a pass by Kemp and returned it to the Los Angeles 20. Two plays later, Leon Burton, seeing his first extensive action of the season, took a pitchout from Dorow and turned left end for 11 yards and a 43–33 lead.

Unfortunately, the Titans' defense again proved unequal to the task of holding a lead. A 10-point margin and 13 minutes were well short of Dorow's 50-point, two-minute standard. Blanche Martin, who had been such a disappointment with the Titans, narrowed the gap by scoring his only professional touchdown on a pass from Kemp. With 5:06 left, Kemp, who had left a sickbed to play and returned to bed after the game, scored on a five-yard run to give the Chargers a 47–43 lead, the fourth time in the game they had come from behind. Forty-one-year-old Ben Agajanian added a field goal to increase the margin to 50–43. The Titans had one last shot, but Dorow's desperation pass to Maynard was intercepted by Charley McNeil on the Los Angeles 17, McNeil's third interception of the game.

The Titans had unnerved Wismer, and put forth quite an effort, at least on offense. Dorow had his fourth consecutive outstanding performance, while Burton rushed for 90 yards, the best showing of the season by a Titans running back. Despite the heroics, however, the Titans had come up short, and finished the year at 7–7, which was good for second place in the Eastern Division, three games behind Houston. The season had been an uneven one, with a 4–2 start followed by four consecutive losses, three victories, and a narrow defeat in the finale.

Individually, Dorow had an excellent year, completing 201 of 396 passes for 2,748 yards and a league-leading 28 touchdowns. He also led the league's quarterbacks with 453 rushing yards. Maynard caught 72 passes for 1,265 yards, including a league record 11 for 174 yards at Houston. Powell had 69 receptions for 1,167 yards and 14 touchdowns. The Associated Press All-Star team included Powell, Grantham, and Mischak. UPI selected both Mischak and Youngelman. The Titans' running game was disappointing, as Dorow was the club's leading rusher. Bohling paced the running backs with only 431 yards. The most telling statistics, however, were the scoring totals. The Titans scored 382 points, the most in the league and more than any NFL club. The defense, however, yielded 399, also a league high.

On the day after the game against the Chargers, Baugh headed for Rotan, a relieved Wismer went back to New York, and the players headed for their homes. Dorow assumed his scouting duties and looked for defensive players who might give his offense a fighting chance.

CHAPTER 13

MY KINGDOM FOR A NEW STADIUM

On the first day of January 1961, George Blanda threw three touchdown passes and kicked a field goal to lead the Oilers to a 24–16 victory over San Diego and the first AFL championship. The game was played in Houston before 32,183 fans, the largest paying crowd in the league's short history. In the NFL title match, held on December 26, 1960, the Eagles had beaten the Packers 17–13.

If AFL Commissioner Joe Foss had his way, 1960 would be the last season in which the AFL and NFL champs went home after earning their respective titles. Shortly after being named commissioner in 1959, he mentioned the possibility of a playoff game with the NFL champions. On January 14, 1961, Foss announced that he had sent a telegram to Pete Rozelle proposing a championship game between the best teams of each league. "We . . . consider such a playoff game is necessary to the continued progress of professional football," Foss said, and asked for a response by April.

Harry Wismer, meanwhile, was trying to promote an AFL–NFL All-Star Game, which would take the place of the College All-Star Game, held annually each summer. "It's doomed," Wismer said of the college game. "The pros are too good. They used to pick the best college coaches, now they pick Otto Graham, who never coached anyone." (Ironically, when Jets owner Sonny Werblin threatened to keep prize rookie quarterback John Huarte out of the 1965 College All-Star Game,

Wismer leapt to the defense of the contest. "The College All-Star Game has been a great curtain-raiser for the football season," he wrote.)

While Wismer and Foss claimed that the caliber of play in the AFL was good enough to challenge the NFL, the financial results of the first season were well below those of the older league. Although attendance showed gradual improvement throughout the season, it was estimated that the eight AFL clubs lost a total of $3.5 million in their inaugural campaign. AFL visiting teams were paid 40% of the gate receipts, with a guaranteed minimum of $20,000. Wismer claimed that of the 56 games played in 1960, on only four occasions (two in Boston and two in Buffalo) did the payout exceed the minimum.

Houston, the league champion, dropped $710,000. Of that amount, $420,000 was an operating loss, while an additional $220,000 was spent on renovations to Jepperson Stadium and another $70,000 was expended on the court case involving the contract of Billy Cannon.

The Western Division champion Los Angeles Chargers, whose expenses exceeded their revenues by an estimated $900,000, suffered the largest loss. Attendance at the Coliseum had been poor, as an average of only 15,768 turned out for the seven home games. The Rams, playing in the same stadium, averaged 61,000. Only 9,928 appeared on December 11 to watch the Chargers clinch the Western Division title. In light of the lack of support, Barron Hilton petitioned the league to allow him to move his franchise to San Diego. Wismer leaked the news in December. "Barron Hilton will get mad when he hears this," Wismer said, "but don't let him deny it." The latter city agreed to expand Balboa Stadium to accommodate 33,000 spectators, more than sufficient to handle the crowds that had gone to the games in Los Angeles.

The losses of the other clubs were reported as follows:

New York	$450,000
Dallas	$400,000
Boston	$300,000
Oakland	$270,000
Denver	$270,000
Buffalo	$175,000

These figures were estimates set forth in *The New York Times* on

January 14, 1961. Different figures were reported in other sources. In his autobiography, Wismer said he lost $1.2 million. The Oakland loss was reported at $325,000 in a *Daily News* article of November 2, 1961, and the Boston loss at $566,233 in *The Boston Globe* of September 3, 1961. Approximately $250,000 of the Patriots' loss was attributed to stadium renovations at Boston University, which would mean that the figure set forth in the *Times* represented an operating loss.

In mid-January, the AFL owners predicted that the league, as a whole, would break even in 1961. All of the startup expenses of 1960 were behind them; the equipment had been bought, stadiums renovated, and other financial challenges met. Wismer forecast that average attendance would increase from 19,000 per game to 27,000, a 42 percent improvement. He promised to televise all seven of his own home games if at least 25,000 tickets were sold. A financial ray of hope was the fact that the contract with ABC was renewed. Under its terms, the amount each club would receive increased from $200,000 to $220,000.

An oft-repeated and probably apocryphal story had someone exclaiming to H.L. Hunt before the season started, "Your boy will lose a million dollars on his football team this year!"

"Well," the senior Hunt drawled, "I reckon at that rate he'll be broke in another hundred and fifty years."

While Hunt did not lose a million, he did drop nearly half that amount. Foss and Hunt had fought the NFL over Texas, but perhaps both leagues should have worried more about college football, which easily outdrew the Oilers, Texans, and Cowboys. In early November, the Cowboys and Rams drew 16,000 at the Cotton Bowl, where the previous day SMU and Texas A&M had attracted 35,000. On October 8, the Cotton Bowl hosted the traditional Texas–Oklahoma game, played before more than 75,000. The following day, the Texans and Raiders drew a crowd generously announced at 21,000.

Oakland, although it did not post the largest loss, was perhaps in the deepest difficulty. The team played in San Francisco, both in Candlestick Park and Kezar Stadium, rather than Oakland, and averaged less than 10,000 per game. They also did poorly on the field, finishing the season 6–8. Prospects appeared no better for 1961, for during the offseason, the owners were busy fighting amongst each other and failed to sign a single draft choice.

In January, 1961, Foss went to Oakland to attempt to resolve the ownership dispute. The stockholders had split into two camps—Bob Osborne, Ed McGah, and Wayne Valley in one, and Chet Soda, Don Blessing, Wally Marsh, Roger Lapham, and Charles Harney in the other. At the meeting with Foss, the discussion became so animated that Harney took a swing at Valley with his cane, barely missing Valley's head. Foss reached the conclusion that achieving harmony would be impossible and declared that one faction would have to buy out the other. A price was agreed upon and the two sides flipped a coin to determine which would remain. Harney called tails and lost, leaving Valley, McGah and Osborne in charge. Soda and his group departed. Adios, señor.

The partnership strife had been eliminated, but the Raiders still lacked quality players and a suitable place to play. Valley insisted that the franchise could never achieve financial success until it had a stadium in Oakland, rather than being forced to play across the bay in San Francisco. "You couldn't give sex away in San Francisco," wrote one columnist, "if the word Oakland was somehow associated with it." Valley's wish finally came true in 1962, when the club moved to Frank Youell Field, named after a local undertaker.

Wismer's Titans had lost nearly half a million dollars, much more than the Raiders. In late October, Wismer had predicted, "I won't lose more than $100,000 this season, and I've got news for you. I can afford to lose twice that for ten years." By those calculations, the actual results reduced the projected life span to five years. Wismer was temporarily bailed out by an inflow of cash at the end of the season. In November, he was ordered by Rozelle to sell his stock in the Redskins due to the conflict of interest arising from his ownership of a franchise in a rival league. Foss had made a similar demand earlier, but Wismer had been dilatory in complying. Finally, Rozelle grew tired of seeing one of his own team's stockholders lambasting the NFL in the media almost daily and forced the issue, threatening to seize the stock if Wismer did not sell it. In early December, Wismer sold his 25 percent stake to Bill McDonald, a Florida trailer manufacturer, racetrack owner, and investor in minor league baseball franchises, for $350,000. Assuming the stock had not been pledged as collateral for a loan, the sale provided Wismer with cash flow equal to a large portion of the Titan loss.

New York's official attendance was announced as 114,628, but that number was a figment of Wismer's imagination. The actual count of paying customers was probably not more than half that. During one game, Robert Fulton Kelly, one of many in Wismer's parade of publicity men, received a call from the owner. Wismer told Kelly to announce the attendance as 21,000. Kelly replied that he couldn't possibly make such a statement; anyone could see that there weren't more than a few thousand in the stands. "Announce it!" Wismer ordered. Kelly took the microphone and broadcast the following message to the press-box occupants: "I am told to tell you that there are twenty-one thousand people here. Do with it what you want." He repeated the message to make certain no one missed it.

Newspaper accounts contained sarcastic references to the fabricated figures, such as: "The announced attendance of 20,000 refers to arms and legs, or else 15,000 of the 20,000 people came disguised as empty seats."

"We never had to worry about hostile fans," Baugh later told a biographer, "because we always had 'em outnumbered." At least the low attendance proved a boon for memorabilia collectors. Because of the small crowds, only a limited number of game programs were printed. This made them more valuable as collectibles, a fact Roger Ellis discovered after he discarded his duplicates.

"As a business operation," wrote the *New York Herald Tribune*, "the Titans were a colossal bust. As predicted in some quarters, club president Harry Wismer succeeded in antagonizing a number of people who could have otherwise helped the team, and Harry also succeeded in spawning one of the most gosh-awful ticket operations the entertainment industry has ever experienced."

"Harry's office was in the hotel room where he stayed," recalled Gordon White of *The New York Times*. "You'd go in there and all the tickets were spread out on a double bed. What a way to operate! Things weren't as modern as they are now, and a lot of people did things differently, but you didn't operate with tickets on your bed."

"The New York Titans are dying from malnutrition of the turnstiles," wrote Arthur Daley. Joe Foss claimed that on Thanksgiving Day, 1960, he had been present at the Polo Grounds and shaken the hand of every one of the less than 1,000 in attendance. Even for a veteran politician, shaking the hand of every fan at a professional football game was a remarkable feat.

Dick Young blamed the attendance problems on the Titans' antiquated ballpark. After a 1961 game with the Patriots, he wrote, "It was a gorgeous day. It is an exciting team to watch. Still, the fans don't come out. There can be just one explanation: the Polo Grounds. The old joint has had it. The Yankees, with M & M [Maris and Mantle], couldn't draw there." Two weeks later, Young added, "The day was brisk and bright, fine football weather, but the Polo Grounds is still the Polo Grounds, and even a super attraction like the Chargers won't get the public to knock down the shabby old walls."

Wismer pinned his hopes for survival on the construction of a new stadium in Flushing Meadows. As Maury Allen wrote in the *New York Post*, "In his sleep at night, [Wismer] sees the beautiful dining club in the park. He rides up and down a modern escalator. He issues commands from the slick new office. He is burdened by endless lines of ticket buyers forcing their way up to the gates to see his team." Despite Wismer's nocturnal longings, however, it seemed as though the new stadium would never be finished. "Rome wasn't built in a day," wrote Young, "but it must have been started a lot quicker than the Mets' ballpark at Flushing Meadows."

In April 1957, legendary New York City Parks Commissioner Robert Moses first broached the idea of a new park in Flushing. Moses proposed the construction of a 50,000-seat domed stadium for the Brooklyn Dodgers. If the Dodgers were to remain in the New York area, however, Dodger owner Walter O'Malley wanted to stay in Brooklyn. He was not interested in moving his club to Queens.

Two months later, George V. McLaughlin, who had been involved with the financial management of the Dodgers in the 1930s, announced that he planned to acquire a major league club and place it in Moses' proposed Flushing stadium. His principal target was Horace Stoneham's New York Giants. Stoneham refused to negotiate with McLaughlin, and the National League informed him that there was no immediate prospect of expansion. Exit McLaughlin.

The concept of a new stadium was revived when Bill Shea arose as the principal of a New York franchise in baseball's abortive Continental League. To house the new team, Shea proposed, in 1959, a 55,000-seat facility with a retractable dome. Funding of the project would come from a self-liquidating city bond issue to be retired from stadium revenues. As 1960 began, engineers were busy preparing drawings for submission to the city, minus the dome, which had been eliminated from the plan. In April, Mayor Wagner displayed a $14,000 model of the new park and stated there was "no turning back now." Although the principal use of the stadium was to be baseball, a portion of the stands would be electronically movable on railroad tracks to reconfigure the seating for football.

A year later, with a $16,226,000 bond issue approved, the city solicited bids for construction of the new facility, which was to be called Municipal Stadium. Unfortunately, the sum of the lowest bids totaled $17,800,000, well above the authorized bond limit. Newbold Morris (Moses' successor as City Parks Commissioner) recommended that the city proceed with construction and sell general obligation bonds to make up the difference. "It isn't the cost of one snowstorm," he said. By this time, the identity of the principal tenant had changed. The Continental League was dead, but New York had been granted a National League expansion franchise scheduled to begin play in 1962. The extension of the franchise was contingent upon the construction of a new stadium.

In July 1960, the Titans announced their plans to play in the new stadium, commencing with the 1961 season. By December 1960, with construction bids not even submitted, that was clearly impossible. At a press conference, it was announced that occupancy was delayed until 1962, when "the stadium will certainly be completed, especially by October." Yet, as 1961 progressed, the prospect of a 1962 inaugural faded. Groundbreaking, which had been scheduled for April 1, was postponed until June 15, then July 1. Each date passed and, in mid-July, the ground at Flushing Meadows remained untouched. The Mets and the City of New York haggled endlessly, it seemed, over the terms of a proposed 30-year lease. The final issues, according to George Weiss, general manager of the Mets, involved insurance and liability concerns.

As negotiations dragged on, it looked as though neither the Mets nor

Titans would occupy the new stadium for the 1962 season. It also appeared as though both might have to vacate the Polo Grounds, due to difficulties in negotiations with the Coogan family, which held the soon-to-expire ground lease. The city attempted to remedy the situation by having the City Housing Authority condemn the Polo Grounds for low-income housing. Once the city had taken title to the property, it would delay the start of construction until both occupants had moved to their new home. Jay Coogan prepared to fight the city, and the future of both stadiums remained in limbo.

Dick Young fumed over the endless delays. "The lease hasn't been signed because both sides are debating interminably over such trivia as whether there should be five or six hot-dog stands in Section 10, and, if so, who is to supply the mustard pots. The lease, at last count, was well over 100 typewritten pages, the long, legal type. If the masterpiece is ever finished, it quite possibly could surpass *Gone With the Wind* in size. The United States of America became a nation via a document written on one sheet of paper, but lawyers have become much smarter in the last 180 years."

Finally, on October 28, 1961, with the Mets having signed a 30-year lease and the Titans a memorandum of agreement covering 15 years, ground was officially broken. Wagner, Weiss, and Wismer all turned ceremonial shovelfuls of Flushing dirt, and the festivities featured opera star Elaine Malbin and Guy Lombardo's Royal Canadians. Don Maynard, out of action with a shoulder injury, was also in attendance. Newbold Morris waved a Titans pennant and spoke enthusiastically of the club playing at Municipal Stadium.

The Mets' lease called for annual rents starting at $450,000 and gradually declining to $300,000. The Titans would pay the greater of either $5,000 per game or 10 percent of actual receipts. (In November 1962, the Parks Department declared that the Titans still had not signed a lease, although Wismer claimed he had.) Dr. James Nicholas, who was familiar with the negotiations, said, "The terms of the lease were very onerous. The Titans couldn't play if the Mets had a game. They couldn't practice at the stadium. I don't imagine they got any of the parking revenue or anything. Donald Grant (of the Mets) made Wismer sign the lease. He had to do it to save the team. That lease that Harry signed cost the team quite a bit. It led to Leon Hess going to the Meadowlands."

The fact that construction had finally gotten under way did not assure that the stadium would be completed according to the revised schedule. As with any undertaking of such magnitude, difficulties arose. The site had formerly been utilized as a landfill, and the pilings, which had to be dropped 125 feet below the surface, did not sit properly on the compacted garbage. Additional soil had to be added to level the pilings. In July 1962, while the Mets were suffering through their first season in the Polo Grounds, Ed Lustbader, president of P.J. Carlin Construction Company, the general contractor, announced that his firm was on schedule to meet the targeted opening of April 1, 1963. A total of 350 workers toiled on two shifts, six days a week. By starting at home plate and building simultaneously in two directions, Carlin was able to double up on resources and speed the work along. "If we have anything like the winter we had last year," Lustbader said, "we're a cinch. If we get as much [snow] as we had two winters ago… "

Unfortunately, the winter of 1962–63 resembled that of two years before, and, as the snow fell on Flushing, it became evident that the Mets would hold their home opener in the Polo Grounds. The new park, now called Shea Stadium after its principal advocate, was facetiously referred to as St. Bill the Undone's. In addition to the harsh winter, there were numerous other reasons for the continuing delay and increasing cost. The railing subcontractor filed for bankruptcy, there was a default by the subcontractor who was to precast the concrete tier units, and other subcontractors suffered from a series of union-instigated work stoppages.

The Mets planned to move in during July, then postponed it until August. In early July, the amended opening date of August 6 was formally abandoned and the Mets, like the Dodgers before them, adopted the slogan "Wait 'til Next Year." The city announced that the stadium would open in April 1964, and that the final cost would exceed $20 million.

The Mets had obtained a guarantee that the Polo Grounds would be available to them in 1963 in case the new stadium was not. They printed two sets of tickets, one for the Polo Grounds and one for Shea. The next year the Mets printed tickets for Shea alone. They had burned their boats. If the new stadium suffered another delay, there were no contingency plans. The press was given a tour of the new facility on March 1, and reporters noted that there was no turf and that the outfield fences had yet to be erected. Four days before the opening game in April, there was one last snafu. Local 3 of the International Brotherhood of Electrical Workers was proceeding smoothly with the installation of the telephone system until William Lyons, president of Local 1106 of the Communication Workers of America, allegedly saw a non-union worker on the site. The IBEW was pulled off the job and replaced by employees of Local 1106. Work was halted completely when the displaced electricians shut off power to the stadium.

The park opened without public telephones and telegraph wires, but, with the finishing touches virtually being put in place as the first customers passed through the turnstiles, the Mets christened the new stadium with a game against the Pittsburgh Pirates on April 16, 1964. The first AFL game was played that fall, but it was too late for Wismer, who had been stripped of his franchise.

As the 1961 season dawned, however, Wismer maintained the hope that the new stadium would be his salvation. In the interim, to increase attendance at the Polo Grounds, he hired Bill Tackmann, former director of sports promotion for the New York City Department of Commerce and Public Events. As business manager of the Titans, Tackmann assumed some of the duties of Sebo. His success in bringing top football games to New York gave promise that he would be able to effectively promote the Titans, and increase the dismal attendance figures of 1960. Tackmann spoke of plans to boost ticket sales and strengthen the club's ties to the community. As a further step to add to the professionalism of the franchise, Wismer announced his intention to move the club's offices from his Park Avenue apartment to legitimate office space. By early 1962, the offices were located in the Chatham Hotel, 33 East 48th Street.

Sebo, now concentrating his efforts on player acquisition, sought to place a better product on the field, in particular to upgrade the defense. The Titans received little help in the draft, as Wismer and Sebo were unable to sign most of their choices. Tom Brown, a guard from Minnesota who was the Outland Trophy winner and AP Lineman of the Year, was the No. 1 selection. He not only failed to sign with the Titans, but never played professionally. Two other players chosen in the early rounds, Herb Adderley of Michigan State and Tom Matte of Ohio State, became outstanding professionals, but not with the Titans. New York ended up signing only three of their selections: Bob Brooks, a fullback from Ohio University; Wayne Fontes of Michigan State, who joined the club in 1962; and Moses Gray, a tackle from Indiana. None made a significant contribution. In addition to Adderley and Matte, a number of Titans draftees went on to excellent careers in the NFL, including Mike Pyle, a center with the Chicago Bears; Bernie Casey, a wide receiver with the Rams and 49ers; Bill Brown, a Pro Bowl fullback with the Vikings; and Irv Cross, a defensive back with the Eagles and Rams.

Although the Titans fared worse than most, other AFL clubs were less successful than in the prior year's draft. In 1960 the new league had taken the NFL by surprise, signing six of the 12 NFL first-round draft choices. The following year, there would be no surprise, for the old league was fully prepared. They claimed that, of the players drafted for the 1961 season, the NFL signed 78 percent of those who wanted to play in the US. Rozelle stated that the schedule would expand to 14 games in 1961, in order to generate additional revenue with which to pay salaries commensurate with those offered by the AFL, which already played 14 games. Rozelle was confident that his league would prevail in the 1961 signing war; so confident that, as evidence that the NFL was taking the high road, he delayed the draft until December 27, 1960, more than three weeks after the AFL made its selections. The commissioner advised all graduating seniors to wait to sign until the NFL draft took place, and suggested that rookies might have a better chance of making an NFL roster because of expansion. The league also mailed 200 copies of a glossy marketing piece titled "The NFL and You" to graduating seniors. The brochure emphasized the business opportunities open to NFL players, and contained stories of ex-players who had succeeded in business or other professions following their retirement from the NFL. The virtues of each of the league cities were highlighted. As a further precaution, on draft day, NFL teams called prospective draftees to make certain they had not signed with the AFL.

The Titans, virtually shut out in the draft, were forced to search for diamonds in the rough among undrafted free agents. Al Dorow, scouting on the West Coast, uncovered the best rookie find of 1961. With today's sophisticated systems, not even a second-string offensive tackle from East Yahoo State Teachers' College can escape the scrutiny of professional scouts. In 1960, however, methods were much more primitive. Word of mouth, newspapers and magazines, a few game films, and a lot of networking were the most prevalent techniques. The Dallas Texans had perhaps the most unique set of scouts. Lamar Hunt sometimes took a couple of "lease hounds," the men responsible for acquiring land on which to drill, from his oil business and had them use their persuasive talents to sign college football players.

Sometimes, the news that another team was interested in acquiring a player was enough to recommend him. Prior to training camp in 1960, Sebo heard that the Bills were interested in signing a former Morgan State halfback named Jerry McArthur. Sebo had never heard of McArthur, but learned that he had been in camp with the Lions when Buffalo coach Buster Ramsey was a Detroit assistant. The fact that Ramsey was interested was enough of a recommendation for Sebo, who signed McArthur to a contract. The move almost paid off, for the young halfback was a star in the early days of camp. Once the exhibition schedule started, however, McArthur faded quickly. While he could run like the wind, he couldn't catch the ball, and was released.

Dorow had his own unique scouting methods. He usually worked out with a prospect, and then ran sprints with him. "I'm not the fastest man in the world or the slowest," he said. "If he can't beat me by five yards in fifty I figure he isn't fast enough for our team." Since the new player would also be a teammate, Dorow was careful to see that his personality blended well with the rest of the club.

Dorow had a friend at Oregon State who told him about a recently graduated tailback named Dainard Paulson. After two years at El Camino Junior College, Paulson became OSU's rookie of the year in 1958 and its most valuable player in 1959. He had not been drafted, but was interested in playing pro ball. Paulson was a fair offensive player, and a pretty good punter, but what really made him stand out was his aggressive play on defense. Dorow's friend told him that Paulson was the "hardest-hitting kid you'd ever want to see" and a solid citizen, a religious young man who would never cause any trouble. Dorow looked at some movies and agreed with his friend's assessment of Paulson's ability.

Paulson prided himself on his ability to deliver a blow. "I would hit anything that wiggled," he said later. Perry Richards, who played with him in 1962, said, "Dainard Paulson was the hardest-hitting guy. They worried about him. He came up and he'd pound and he'd pound and he'd pound. It got to the point where you'd say, 'Dainard, you've got to back off.' He'd put his head down and hit anything. The guys used to say he was going to start getting punchy. He was weird that way, nothing dirty, but he'd go head on. If there was anyone standing, he wouldn't be standing for long."

Unfortunately, Paulson, like Sid Youngelman, did not always distinguish between friend and foe. In his first training camp, eager to make an impression on Baugh, Paulson leveled Maynard, who was coming across the middle during a non-contact passing drill. As Maynard, who was not wearing pads, rose slowly to his feet, Baugh raced onto the field to deliver a profanity-laced tongue-lashing to the rookie. He had brought Paulson in to strengthen the defense, not cripple the Titans' most dangerous offensive weapon. Maynard survived, and the acquisition of Paulson went a long way toward beefing up the secondary, which had been New York's weakest link in 1960. With Paulson and Dick Felt, the Titans had two all-star-caliber defenders.

The addition of Paulson was part of a general overhaul of the Titans' defense. By the opening game of the 1961 season, three of the starting defensive backs from the initial campaign were no longer on the roster. During a training camp scrimmage, Roger Donahoo fractured his shoulder and sternum attempting to tackle 240-pound fullback Jim Joyce. "I thought I broke my neck," said Donahoo. "It scared me to death." The Howard Glenn incident was less than a year removed and still on everyone's mind. Donahoo never fully recovered from his injury and was released. He played one game with the minor league Toledo Blades and then retired.

Fred Julian, who had intercepted six passes in 1960, ran into difficulties of a different kind. He learned just before training camp that he was likely to be drafted into military service. Julian tried unsuccessfully to join the National Guard in both New York and Michigan, and reported to Bear Mountain with a Selective Service sword of Damocles above his head. He started every exhibition game, but was told at the end of camp that he was being released because of his imminent induction into the service. Julian called the Patriots, to see if they might be interested in picking him up, but they declined to sign him for the same reason. Ironically, Julian never did get drafted, but went back to Michigan, got a teaching job and became a player-coach for the semi-pro Grand Rapids team. It was the start of a long, distinguished coaching career.

On July 29, 1961, Corky Tharp, a third starter, was released. New defensive backs, in addition to Paulson, were Junior Wren, a five-year veteran of the Browns and Steelers; player-coach Bert Rechichar, another NFL veteran; and rookie Dave Ames from the University of Richmond. Felt was the lone returning starter.

Another key performer joining the defensive unit was Hubert Bobo, a rugged middle linebacker with a checkered past. Bobo had been tossed out of Ohio State after the 1954 season, for reasons that were the subject of great speculation. He told Dick Felt that, after failing English, and faced with academic ineligibility, he went back and threatened the professor with a beating if he didn't change the grade. The professor had been so frightened that he dropped dead of a heart attack on the spot. Bobo told Alex Kroll that he was expelled because, after the Rose Bowl, he went straight to Las Vegas, became the consort of a famous actress and did not reappear on campus until Easter.

Years later, when Felt related his story to a BYU professor who had attended Ohio State, the professor laughed and said that Bobo's expulsion was the result of a much more mundane transgression, such as failing grades or breaking team rules. In any event, Bobo left OSU, played in Canada, and then joined the Los Angeles Chargers in 1960.

Felt was apprehensive when he heard that Bobo would be joining the Titans, for he had heard about the linebacker's reputation. "Bobo said," Felt related, "'I've been in a fight in every bar in Columbus and slept with every gal in Columbus.' I believe it was true. You'd hear stories from guys that this was the dirtiest, meanest, wildest guy on two legs. The next thing we know, he's traded to the Titans. I thought, 'Holy smoke, do we want this guy around?' I was scared to death before he even got here. Then he got up here and was the greatest guy I've ever been around—the funniest guy. We became the greatest friends."

Many of the Titans believed that Bobo was involved in the movie industry, or had appeared in a film or two, but none could verify the fact. He was, in fact, movie-star handsome, with a muscular body and carefully coifed blond hair. "He reminded me somewhat of an oversized Albert Finney," said Lee Grosscup.

"I saw him later," said Felt, "when I was playing with the Patriots, and he was hanging around with some guys from Hollywood, mooching off them. He could take advantage of people, use them, and make them feel as happy as could be. He was fun. The wives of the coaches just loved him. You probably wouldn't turn your back on him, but he was more fun than you can imagine. Years later, maybe ten or fifteen years ago, I heard he'd almost gotten killed in a bar fight in Columbus, in a biker bar. They worked him over with chains. They said that for the first time ever, he probably wasn't at fault in starting the fight. He had gone to the defense of someone."

Bobo had great potential as a middle linebacker, but by the time he got to New York, his knees were shot. "He had a terrible limp," said Mike Hudock, who was known to his teammates as "Zipper Legs" and knew a thing or two about bad knees. "His knees were torn up bad. He was tough, but he couldn't keep up with anybody out of the backfield. He had the heart, but his body just didn't want to co-operate."

Dr. Nicholas remembered, "Hubert Bobo had two of the worst knees I'd ever seen. He had cruciate ligaments torn in both knees when we got him. His knees would pop out on almost every play. He'd go back in because there was no one to back him up."

"When he came out of a game," said Bob Scrabis, "he looked like he was used hard and put away dirty. He really went in banging and played a lot of times when he shouldn't have. A real tough, tough guy."

"He would have been one of the top middle linebackers of all time," said Ed Sprinkle, an assistant coach in 1962, "but he had a bad knee. He shouldn't even have been out on the field. He was out there on one leg. He couldn't cover anybody because he couldn't run."

Bobo had an unconventional, tortuous pregame ritual. He would stand on a table and have the trainer tape his knees locked in that position.

"Tighter! Tighter!" he'd scream as Buddy Leininger wound rolls of tape around his legs. By the time Leininger was finished, Bobo could barely hobble around. When the team went on the field, he would go down to the corner of the stadium and try to jog and break the tape. "It was a bizarre thing to watch," said Alex Kroll. "This man was running around in the corner of the stadium, screaming at the top of his lungs, hobbling at first. He had horrible knees, but he loved football and was going to keep playing as long as possible."

Bobo was typical of many early AFL players, in that he had ability but one major flaw, in this case, great promise unfulfilled because of injury. Teams in the new league were willing to take a chance on such players, hoping they could regain their form, or at least fill a hole until the league's talent improved. Another player in the same category was defensive end Bob Reifsnyder, winner of the Maxwell Trophy as college football's outstanding player in 1957, the year in which he led his Navy team to victory over Ole Miss in the Cotton Bowl. Prior to his senior season at the Academy, Reifsnyder was mentioned prominently as a contender for the Heisman Trophy. In pre-season practice, two weeks before the first game, Reifsnyder's world turned upside down. Running down on punt coverage, he felt a sudden pain shooting through his ankle, as if he had been shot. Although he had not even been hit, Reifsnyder suffered a ruptured Achilles tendon, which put him on the shelf for virtually his entire senior season (he played only in the Army game). Despite missing his final year, he had shown such ability in his first two seasons that he was drafted in the fourth round by the Rams. While playing in the College All-Star Game, Reifsnyder re-injured his ankle and wound up being traded to the Giants, where he spent the entire 1959 season on the taxi squad trying to strengthen his leg.

Treatment for the injury was primitive by today's standards. "They made this homemade device for me, connected by rubber bands," Reifsnyder said. "It was like a pedal with rubber bands on the front and back. I was supposed to manipulate it." Needless to say, the injury never healed completely. "I could never run the way I used to," he said. "One of my attributes as a college player was that I was very fast. I lost that step and a half or two steps which I guess spells the difference."

Reifsnyder decided that attempting to crack the Giants' starting defensive line of Jim Katcavage, Rosey Grier, Andy Robustelli, and Dick Modzelewski would be futile on one leg. Chargers coach Sid Gillman, who had coached him briefly with the Rams, signed him in 1960. At the end of the exhibition season, Reifsnyder, who had starred at Long Island's Baldwin High, was traded to the Titans, at his own request. He wanted to be closer to his pregnant wife in Long Island and tried to press the issue by walking out on the Chargers. Kicker Ben Agajanian, a 41-year-old resident of Los Angeles, was on the Titans' negotiating list, but wanted to play in California. A trade enabled each to realize his goal.

Reifsnyder performed creditably for the Titans in 1960 and was on the roster when the 1961 campaign began. After suffering a broken hand during the exhibition season, he was released in September, never having realized the potential he had shown prior to his injury. "Pro football's kind of a negative experience for me," he said recently, "because I'd always been on top of the pile. I was never the player I was in college. It's always been one of those things in the back of my mind. I've learned to put it to rest, but I always wonder how good I could have been if I was on two wheels."

A valuable addition to the defensive line for the 1961 season was Proverb Jacobs, another player for whom, like Maynard, the Titans could give thanks to Allie Sherman. Along with Moses Gray, Jacobs formed what sportswriters referred to as the "biblical tackles." He played at the University of California, and joined the Eagles as a rookie offensive tackle in 1958. His brashness drew the attention of Philadelphia coach Buck Shaw, who told Jacobs he was putting him in the starting lineup to see if he could back up his talk. On the first offensive play of his first game, Len Ford of the Packers ran right over Jacobs and sacked Eagles quarterback Norm Van Brocklin. Van Brocklin, an intense, hot-headed player who later became an intense, hot-headed coach with the Vikings and Falcons, jumped up and yelled over to Shaw, "Get this SOB out of here before he gets me killed!" Jacobs picked himself up, pulled himself together, and played well enough to be the starter for the rest of the year.

During the 1959 exhibition season, Jacobs was cut and returned to Berkeley to attend school. Early in 1960 he received a call from Giants owner Wellington Mara asking if he wanted to sign with New York.

Thinking it was a friend playing a joke on him, Jacobs asked for a phone number and called back. Realizing that it actually was Mara, he agreed to join the Giants and looked forward to another chance in the NFL.

"Then I ran into Allie Sherman," he said. Like Maynard, Jacobs was not Sherman's type. "He had trouble with guys who didn't fit his mold," Jacobs said. Many of the marginal Giant players who later ended up with the Titans shared the same opinion. They felt Sherman supported star players, while treating the reserves like dirt. "Frank Gifford walked all over Sherman," said one, "and Sherman worshipped him."

Switching back and forth between offense and defense, Jacobs was not able to attend all meetings of both groups and sometimes missed assignments, sending Sherman into a rage. "I thought, 'I graduated from one of the best schools in the country, and this jerk from some Brooklyn college is telling me how stupid I am. I've got a Ph.D. from Berkeley, and this jerk's calling me stupid.'" Jacobs played the 1960 season with the Giants, but when Sherman became the head coach in 1961, he was cut. On the recommendation of Art Powell, who had played with Jacobs in Philadelphia, the Titans signed him and stuck him into the starting defensive line.

The offense, which had performed so well in 1960, returned almost intact. The only significant addition was halfback Dick Christy, obtained in a trade from the Oakland Raiders for tight end Dave Ross and lineman Fran Morelli. Christy played for the Patriots in 1960 and went to Oakland in the trade that sent quarterback Babe Parilli to Boston. He was 25 years old, a chunky 5'10", 195-pounder, and a shifty, elusive runner. Christy was a versatile performer, a good runner, a fine receiver out of the backfield, and an outstanding punt and kickoff-returner. He still holds the Titans/Jets career record of 16.2 yards per punt return.

By the time Christy reached New York, he had a reputation as a slightly shopworn piece of merchandise; he had moved around quite a bit and never lived up to his potential. He was a gifted athlete, excelling not only at football, but also at track and gymnastics. "At a track meet," recalled Jack Klotz, "he'd win the hundred, the two-twenty, the discus, the pole vault...he'd see somebody else win an event and say, 'I can do that.' And he could."

At North Carolina State, Christy was a first team All-American, broke the school's scoring records and capped off his career by scoring all of his team's points in a 29–26 win over South Carolina in his final game. The last three points were a game winning 45-yard field goal at the final gun. Drafted by the Packers, Dick lost out to Jim Taylor for the final running back position. He moved on to the Steelers and played the 1958 season in Pittsburgh. In the late 1950s, the Steelers were a hard-drinking team, as quarterback Bobby Layne led the charge to the bar and many followed. Christy acquired a reputation as a drinker. When he arrived in New York, Baugh sat his new player down and told him what was expected of him, emphasizing the fact that he needed to settle down a bit. Baugh's exhortations had limited impact, for, although he played well on the field, Christy continued to have an active nightlife. One teammate recalled sitting in a bar at the Stardust Hotel in San Diego, where one could look through a glass wall into the hotel swimming pool. He watched as a golf cart, driven by Christy, who had consumed a few beers during the course of 18 holes, plunged into the pool and floated past.

On the field, Christy had an uncanny ability to avoid tacklers, looking like he was moving in slow motion, and then suddenly breaking into the clear for a long return. "He had a quick change of pace," said Mike Holovak, who coached Christy in Boston. "He wasn't a speed burner, but he ran hard. You couldn't bring him down with an arm tackle. He ran right through arm tackles."

While Christy was the only player added to the offense, New York had the equivalent of a new fullback, for Bill Mathis came to camp with a new body. The previous year, Mathis had reported late to the Titans, having been in the Denver and Houston camps. He lacked confidence in his ability and was awed by New York. The first professional game he played in was the first one he had ever seen.

Throughout that season, Mathis played on special teams and was used sparingly at halfback, gaining only 307 yards rushing the entire year. Following the 1960 campaign, Mathis returned to Clemson to complete his degree requirements. He worked out religiously, and increased his weight from 208 to 224, while actually improving his speed and quickness. "I began to eat like a fullback," he said. The seldom-used halfback was ready to become the starting fullback in 1961.

CHAPTER 14

A WAR AT WAR MEMORIAL

The chaos of the Titans' first training camp was missing in 1961, and, although there was a spirited competition for jobs, the club did not process a massive number of prospects as in 1960. The initial roster numbered only 65, a figure that would need to be reduced to 33 by the start of the regular season. AFL roster limits had been lowered from 35 on the assumption that clubs would be more settled in their second season. For the Titans, this was certainly the case. "They look like a football team this time, don't they?" asked Sebo. Baugh added, "It sure feels a lot better getting ready for this season than it did when we were just starting out a year ago."

The veterans found Bear Mountain, New York, much to their liking, as there was an abundance of nightlife. "It was the best training camp I've ever been in," said Dick Jamieson. "We had a nice practice field, nice rooms, and a bar [Hernando's Hideaway] we could go to." Proximity to New York City also brought out the fans. "We had more people watching practices at Bear Mountain than came to the Polo Grounds," said Grantham.

The most noteworthy aspect of camp was the intense heat, which affected a number of players. Tackle Dick Ledbetter, who had previously suffered a head injury, passed out and had to be revived with oxygen. There were a number of new prospects at Bear Mountain, including Mike Hagler, a scatback from Canada and a good kick returner, who nearly made the team after some bright moments during the exhibition season. Hagler was another Dorow discovery, an opponent from his days in Canada.

Dorow also brought in receiver Bob Jewett, a fellow Michigan State alumnus. Jewett had an excellent rookie year with the Bears in 1959, but lost two fingers on his right hand (between the first and second joints) in an industrial accident during the offseason. In training camp with the Bears the next summer, he couldn't catch the ball, was cut, and went to Canada.

Dorow worked Jewett out during the early summer of 1961, and found that his stumps had toughened to the point where he could catch the ball, Dorow believed, as well as he could before the injury. "After throwing twenty or thirty passes to Jewett," Dorow said, "I could see that he could catch them as well as ever...maybe better, because he was more careful to get hold of them." Jewett lasted through training camp and the entire exhibition schedule, but was cut the week before the regular-season opener.

Throughout the summer, Baugh concentrated on improving the running game and the defense. Linebacker was a particular soft spot, and Sebo invited seven new linebackers, along with 10 new defensive backs, to camp. Eddie Bell had retired due to the worsening condition of his knee, and Bob Marques had not recovered from his severe back injury. Larry Grantham remained as the only returning starter. Baugh moved defensive end Ed Cooke to linebacker and Sebo signed five-year Canadian veteran Jim Furey.

As it had been in Durham, punting was a weakness. Joe Pagliei, who kicked well on occasion in 1960, had gotten married and gained weight during the offseason; he was released before the exhibition schedule began. On August 19, the Titans signed 40-year-old Horace Gillom, a World War II veteran who spent 10 years with the Cleveland Browns and twice led the NFL in punting. Gillom retired after the 1956 season and had not played since. There was hope, however. The day after Gillom signed with the Titans, 55-year-old (by his calculation) Satchel Paige pitched three shutout innings in a Negro League All-Star Game at Yankee Stadium. Gillom was no Paige, however, and was released three days later. Two of the new defensive backs, Dainard Paulson and Junior Wren, tried their hand at kicking. The Titans' punting problems were finally solved just before the season started when they acquired Curley Johnson, who had been released by the Dallas Texans.

The 1961 exhibition season started as disappointingly as that of the previous year. The Titans lost their first game to Dallas, 39–28, in 93-degree heat, the New York high points being three touchdowns and 402 passing yards by Dorow and Jamieson and some good running by Mathis. Much of the aerial yardage, however, including two long bombs, came late in the game against the second-string Dallas secondary. The final touchdown came with one second left on a 71-yard pass from Jamieson to Leon Burton, who had performed so well in the 1960 finale and was bidding for a regular spot at halfback.

On August 10, the Titans lost again, this time to the Patriots and their new quarterback, Babe Parilli, in 90-degree heat in Boston. The Titans were held to only 46 yards rushing, and, for the first time in their history, failed to score a touchdown. Dorow, suffering from tendinitis in his right arm, could not throw long, and was unproductive.

A mere nine days later, the two teams met for the second game in a row, this time in Philadelphia. An immense crowd of 73,916, more than the actual total who had watched the Titans in their entire 1960 home season, was in attendance, but there was an explanation. The game was facetiously billed as the Grocery Bowl (or the "Ham and Egg Bowl" as Dick Young coined it), for anyone purchasing more than $10 worth of groceries at any of Philadelphia's Acme Markets was given a free ticket. Both clubs received financial guarantees from promoters Bud Dudley and George Kerrigan.

The Titans were inspired by the large crowd ("presumably well-fed" as Howard Tuckner of *The New York Times* described them) and gained their first victory by a 17–7 score. The game itself was not inspiring, as both teams mustered limited offenses. The Titans picked off five Boston passes—four in the second half—and allowed only seven completions for 65 yards in the game. "Plays were run chiefly between the 30-yard stripes as each eleven tried hard to get out of the other's way," Tuckner wrote. "At one point, the band played 'I'll Never Smile Again.' The song may have been dedicated to Joe Foss, the league's commissioner, who watched intently from the press box."

In the third quarter, Dorow, whose arm was feeling better, threw a 74-yard scoring pass to Maynard, enlarging a 10–7 lead to 17–7. There was no further scoring and the game ended when the fans tore down the goal posts with 15 seconds remaining. After the experience of 1960, Baugh was exhilarated by the fact that the Titans managed to maintain a 10-point lead for the last 25 minutes. Tuckner wrote, "The fans left buzzing about Dorow [who passed for 225 yards] and wondering if they should have Wheaties or Farina or Wheatina for breakfast."

At Greenville, South Carolina, in their final exhibition, the Titans lost to the Oilers 30–20. Powell accompanied the team but, in protest of the segregated conditions, did not play.

The opening game of the regular season pitted the Titans and Patriots, meeting for the third time in a month, on Saturday night, September 9, at Boston University Field. Although there were many new faces on the New York squad, 22 holdovers from 1960 made the final cut. The Patriots had measurably improved their roster from the team that finished last in the Eastern Division in 1960—only 10 players from the squad that faced Denver in the 1960 inaugural suited up to face the Titans.

The Patriots were favored by two touchdowns, but the campaign started auspiciously for the Titans. Rookie Ray Ratkowski of Boston fumbled the opening kickoff, and linebacker Pat Lamberti of New York recovered on the Patriots' 19. Seven plays later, from the Boston 1, Dorow bobbled the snap from center. It bounced off one arm, and then the other before Dorow got control. He looked for a hole and slithered through, scoring the Titans' first touchdown of the season, just as he had a year earlier against Buffalo. This was to be Dorow's day, as he accounted for all three New York scores, adding two touchdown passes to his one-yard run. The final touchdown came at the beginning of the fourth quarter, when, one play after a penalty nullified Boston's recovery of Dorow's fumble, he hit Maynard with a 43-yard pass for a 21–17 lead. On Boston's next possession, the New York defense forced a punt, which was fumbled by Dick Christy, playing his first game with the Titans, on the New York 23. The Patriots recovered the fumble, Christy's second of the game. The first had also been recovered by Boston and led to a Patriots touchdown. With eight minutes left in the game, Boston's Gino Cappelletti kicked a 32-yard field goal that brought the Patriots to within a single point. With four minutes left, Dainard Paulson, also in his first regular-season game with the Titans, was called for pass interference against Cappelletti on the New York 38. When the drive stalled, Cappelletti had another opportunity from the same spot as his previous field goal. This time, the kick sailed just wide to the right, giving New York a victory in its opening game for the second year in a row.

The next week, the Titans traveled to Buffalo for a nationally televised game with the Bills at old War Memorial Stadium. New York had defeated Buffalo twice during the 1960 regular season and once during exhibition play. Bills coach Buster Ramsey did not take defeat well. Ramsey was an unpredictable, volatile man given to violence at the slightest provocation. The former lineman had not curbed the physically aggressive nature that served him well as a player, but was not as appropriate for the coaching profession. Ramsey also liked his liquor, and Bills players learned to lie low on team flights when word spread that he had been drinking. One of the Bills recalled him getting into a fight with the groundskeeper and punching him in the mouth. Following the Titans' win during the 1960 exhibition season, Ramsey threw a violent tantrum and threatened to release the entire team. "Ramsey went nuts in the locker room," said one Bills player. "He started throwing chairs and said that everybody was cut. He had a temper like you wouldn't believe." Before the 1961 game with the Titans, Buster's team had lost seven straight, including exhibitions, and there were rumors that a loss to the Titans would cost him his job.

The game at War Memorial was a classic AFL offensive showpiece. The Titans jumped to a 17–7 lead on two touchdown passes from Dorow to Maynard. The Bills came storming back to take a 38–24 lead by the middle of the third quarter. One of the Buffalo touchdowns came on a 72-yard run on a double reverse by speedy flanker Elbert "Golden Wheels" Dubenion, who also scored on a 33-yard pass from quarterback Richie Lucas, making his first professional start. This was a rare bright moment for Lucas, the Bills' territorial draft choice from Penn State in 1960, a second team All-American who was runner-up to Billy Cannon in the 1959 Heisman balloting. Before his rookie season, Lucas was heralded as a potential star, but thus far his performance as a professional had been a huge disappointment. He was a fine all-round athlete, a running quarterback suited to the college game, but not really ideal for any position in pro football. Bob Scrabis, who played behind Lucas in college, said, "If I were a defensive coordinator, I would have made him throw the ball. He was much more dangerous when he pulled the ball down and ran." That worked well in college, but no professional quarterback could be successful without enough passing ability to keep the defense honest.

A free spirit, Lucas also lacked the leadership qualities necessary to quarterback a pro team. Today, he might have had a career as a valuable specialist, but the 33-man teams of the early 1960s had no room for a $50,000 specialist (that was the amount Lucas received under a three-year contract). Lucas played quarterback, halfback, and defensive back with only modest success before being released in 1962.

While Lucas was leading the Buffalo offense into the end zone, the Bills' defense was putting intense pressure on Dorow. They knocked him down repeatedly in the first half, often roughing him up after the whistle and accumulating 70 yards in penalties. After one particularly vicious hit, Buffalo defensive back Richie McCabe hit the prone Dorow with his fist and elbow. Although the New York quarterback jumped up and protested vehemently, the officials had seen nothing and did not call a penalty.

In the second half, following the touchdown pass by Lucas, Dorow rolled out on a play-action fake. The backs went left, Dorow went right, kept the ball, and went out of bounds near midfield in front of the Bills' bench. After he was clearly across the sideline, McCabe blasted him from behind. Dorow scrambled to his feet, saw McCabe lying in front of him, and fired the ball into his chest. Buster Ramsey, who was standing about 10 yards away from Dorow, came charging toward him and took a wild swing, hitting the Titans' quarterback on the shoulder pad. In a second, the Bills players followed and converged on Dorow, burying him under a pile of about 20 bodies.

Halfback Dewey Bohling had run a pass pattern on the left side of the field, well away from the action. Just as the play was ending on the opposite sideline, one of the Buffalo linebackers stepped in and belted Bohling near the eye with his elbow, opening a gash that would require eight stitches. Enraged, Bohling raced over to assist the embattled Dorow on the Buffalo sideline. Although he wanted to help his quarterback, Bohling's main goal was to get revenge for his bloody face.

Roger Ellis came charging over from his center position, as he put it, "like I was coming down on a kickoff busting the wedge." He soon found himself at the bottom of the pile, being kicked in a very sensitive place. "I remember running over full speed, hitting the pile, falling to the bottom, trying to cover myself and realizing I'd made a big mistake. My first thought was, 'My god, I'll never do this again.'"

Meanwhile, one of the officials ran to the pile, grabbed Dorow by the legs and pulled him from the melee. Bohling, Ellis, a few of their teammates, and most of the Bills continued to go at it, while Dorow, who had started the whole thing, watched from the periphery.

Maynard, Mathis, Felt, and Grantham, perhaps the four most talented Titans, proved among the four smartest as well. Grantham raced onto the field with the intention of coming to Dorow's aid, but when he reached midfield, realized he had forgotten his helmet. By the time he returned to the Titans' bench and strapped it on, the fracas was over. Mathis, Felt, and Maynard never left the sideline, although Maynard and Felt did stand up on the bench to get a better view.

Offsetting penalties were called on Dorow and McCabe, but neither was ejected. Shortly afterward, Dorow may have wished he had been thrown out, for on the next play, he was hit from the blind side while unloading a pass that was intercepted by Buffalo's Vern Valdez. Although he finished the game, the Titans' quarterback suffered a severe lumbar sacral strain in his back. He went to the sideline for medical treatment and a lecture from Baugh about the wisdom of starting a fight in front of the other team's bench.

Early in the fourth quarter, Dorow hit Powell with a 12-yard scoring pass. The Titans were unable to close the gap, however, despite having several opportunities at the end. Dorow was sacked twice deep in Buffalo territory and New York wound up on the short end of a 41–31 score.

Following the game, Wismer demanded that Foss bar Ramsey for life for his attack on Dorow. ABC, unlike CBS and NBC, had a policy of showing fights on the field. Thus, the entire incident was seen by a national audience and preserved on film. Ramsey swore he never hit Dorow, insisting he was a peacemaker who was merely trying to pull him off McCabe. Wismer accused the Bills of doctoring the films to eliminate any footage of Ramsey's actions. Foss, who was at the game, said afterward, "It did seem like a lot of people had their hands where they didn't belong." He stated that under league rules, any disciplinary action would be kept confidential. Said Dorow grimly after the game, "I hope [Ramsey] is still coaching them by then," referring to the Bills' upcoming visit to New York on Thanksgiving Day. Sources indicated afterward that Ramsey was fined a nominal amount, but he was not suspended.

Wismer spirited Dorow to a hospital on Long Island and kept him in seclusion, painting a dire picture of his physical condition. He hinted that Ramsey and the Bills had injured Dorow so severely that he would be unable to play in the next game against Denver. Dorow, who had only a minor back injury, did not know what hospital he was in and why he wasn't being allowed to go home. Back at the Polo Grounds, Baugh knew Dorow was not critically injured and was getting aggravated when by mid-week he had no quarterback with whom to prepare for the Broncos.

Jamieson, the Titans' other quarterback, had been suffering from an injured disc in his back since training camp. He returned to workouts the week before the Bills game and seemed to be improving, although he still had limited feeling in his leg. After the Buffalo game, with Dorow in the hospital, Jamieson was the only signal caller at practice, and worked hard with the first team. By the end of the week, he knew something was seriously wrong with his back. Wismer, with an eye toward economy, told trainer Jackie Copeland to take Jamieson to a chiropractor. Copeland took the quarterback to Dr. Nicholas instead. "I went in there thinking I had something wrong with my back and they were going to be able to treat it," Jamieson said recently. "The doctor came out of his office and said, 'You're done, your career's over. You can't play anymore.'"

"He couldn't pull his toes off the ground," recalled Nicholas. "He was trying to play with a drop foot, where the foot drops down and dangles." Jamieson had a congenital disc problem that required fusion, and, other than a brief comeback in 1965, his career was indeed over.

Jamieson's injury created another episode in the ongoing dispute between Wismer and Baugh. At his weekly press luncheon, undoubtedly fueled by a few bull shots, Wismer claimed that Dorow was a better quarterback than Baugh had ever been, and complained that Baugh and his staff did not remain in New York during the offseason. "Steve [Sebo] and

I had to do all the work alone," he said. Felt, who was at the luncheon, defended Baugh, and the coach later criticized Wismer for his unwillingness to spend enough money to acquire top-notch talent. Wismer, who had no money to spend, in turn carped at Baugh for not knowing the seriousness of Jamieson's injury and for not communicating that fact to the owner. The coach had thought it was only a minor muscular ailment.

Wismer also blamed Baugh for cutting backup quarterback Bob Scrabis at the end of training camp. Scrabis had been picked up by the Chargers and was now on their taxi squad. Unlike 1960, when Dorow and Jamieson were injured, Scrabis could not be activated with the stroke of a pen.

For the September 24 game against Denver, the battered Dorow was the only available quarterback. He appeared at practice on Thursday, still with a sore back. Bob Renn, the Titans' utility man who had played some quarterback in college, was given half a dozen plays and told to be ready in case Dorow went down. For the perennially short-handed Titans, Renn was a godsend. A Canadian veteran, he could play running back, flanker, defensive back, and could also punt. If Dorow had to leave the action, Baugh would find out whether he could play quarterback as well.

That was certainly a possibility, for Denver had a strong defensive line, anchored by 280-pound All-AFL defensive tackle Bud McFadin. McFadin was a 33-year-old product of the University of Texas who had played five seasons with the Los Angeles Rams. Between the 1956 and 1957 seasons, a friend of McFadin's was showing him his pistol when it accidentally discharged, nearly killing McFadin and leaving the bullet as a permanent memento in his stomach. When the 1957 season started, McFadin was in no condition to play and elected to retire. By 1960, although he still carried the bullet inside him, his health had improved considerably. Prior to a Denver exhibition game in Houston, near McFadin's hometown, a Broncos assistant coach and former Rams teammate asked McFadin if he would like to work out with the team the night before the game. McFadin agreed. Would he like to suit up and participate in pre-game drills? He would. Finally, during the fourth quarter, coach Filchock asked if McFadin would like to get into the game. It was the start of a second career that would see the big tackle earn All-AFL honors during the league's first three seasons.

As if the presence of McFadin weren't enough, New York was short-handed on the offensive line, as starting center Mike Hudock had broken his jaw in the game against the Patriots. "Heaven help the Titans if Al Dorow goes down," Bill Wallace had written in his pre-season preview in the *New York Herald Tribune*. Now, without Jamieson, the consequences were even greater. If Denver could take Dorow out of the game, Renn would be forced to reprise the Dewey Bohling role from the previous season. "I know they'll be after me," Dorow said before the game. "If I were a coach and I knew that the other team had only one quarterback—and a bruised one at that—I'd sure as hell tell them to pour in and get him."

As Dorow expected, Denver came at him full blast. Howard Tuckner wrote, "Every black helmet and padded white shoulder at the Polo Grounds was aimed at Dorow's Adam's apple." Despite being knocked down repeatedly, and in spite of the 90-degree heat, the Titans' quarterback persevered. In the meantime, Dick Christy showed why six professional teams had been willing to take a chance on him. With the score 0–0 and nine and a half minutes left in the first quarter, Christy took George Herring's punt on his own 31-yard line. He started down the sideline, weaving his way and using his blockers. "He had a knack for picking a hole and following his blockers," Bohling said. "It didn't even look as though he was moving, and all of a sudden he was crossing the goal line. It seemed like it took him half an hour to get down the field." Grantham wiped out Herring with a punishing block, and Christy registered the first six points of the game.

After a touchdown pass from Dorow to Maynard, Christy took another punt, this time on his own 36, and dodged four oncoming Broncos. Harold Rosenthal wrote, "Christy moved up the middle, using his teammates as posts to pivot around rather than as blockers." He made for the sideline and outran the last two defenders for a 64-yard return and a 21–7 lead. Two more scoring passes, to Maynard and Powell, gave New York a 35–7 lead early in the third quarter.

The rest of the game was a reprise of 1960. Denver kept scoring, and the Titans' defense struggled desperately to hang on. In the second half alone, Denver quarterbacks Frank Tripucka and George Herring threw 32 passes. Split end Lionel Taylor was the principal target, hauling in 11 for 126 yards. The 11 receptions tied the AFL record he already shared with Maynard.

In the end, however, the Titans withstood the Denver aerial onslaught and hung on for a 35–28 win. "When Dorow left the field," wrote Tuckner, "limping slightly, he did so with the proud expression of a man who had been a human target and had won."

With a 2–1 record and tied for first place with the Patriots, the Titans turned to the business of finding a backup quarterback. Wismer attended a press luncheon at the Roosevelt Hotel during which he first vowed to have a new quarterback by Sunday's game, then charged that Redskins owner George Preston Marshall had orchestrated his feud with Baugh.

This was not the first time Wismer and Marshall had locked horns. Marshall, like Wismer, was a promoter who brought life to the somewhat dull world of pro football when he purchased the Boston Braves in 1932. He formed a marching band, hired cheerleaders, and produced extravagant halftime shows. Marshall's wife, silent movie star Corrine Griffith (the "Orchid Lady"), and orchestra leader Barnee Breeskin took the melody from an old religious revival song called "Yes, Jesus Loves Me" and created a new hymn, "Hail to the Redskins." Like Wismer, Marshall liked to have input into game strategy and, early in his ownership tenure, would charge out of the stands to the sidelines and begin issuing orders.

It was inevitable that two men with the egos of Marshall and Wismer would clash. In Wismer's autobiography, he described Marshall with phrases that were often used to characterize Wismer. "He is a most complex person," Wismer wrote, "and anyone who thinks he knows the real George, finds himself facing a new George the next time they meet." He also said that when he was broadcasting the inaugural Pro Bowl game, Marshall, unmindful of the time difference, called from Washington at 4 a.m. and told him to mention at least five times during the broadcast that the game was Marshall's brainchild.

When Wismer was a minority owner of the Redskins, he had numerous disagreements with Marshall. In 1956, Redskins halfback Vic Janowicz, the former Heisman Trophy winner from Ohio State, was seriously injured in an automobile accident. When Janowicz was unable to play, Marshall cut off his salary, claiming that since Janowicz's injury was not football-related, the Redskins were not obligated to pay him. The Washington players took up a collection to pay Janowicz's salary, and Wismer criticized Marshall's actions on the air. According to Wismer, this precipitated the final break between the two men.

Wismer then sued Marshall for $500,000. He asserted that Marshall was padding expenses to avoid paying dividends on the Redskins' stock. When the relationship between Wismer and Marshall ended, Wismer claimed Marshall told him, "We'll get you! We'll break you!" Shortly afterward, Wismer's broadcasting assignments began to diminish, a circumstance he attributed to the fact that NBC sports director Tom Gallery was a good friend of Marshall's.

The feud with Marshall had not abated, for, as recently as November 1960, Wismer accused Marshall of thwarting his efforts to dispose of his interest in the Redskins. Now, Wismer said, Marshall was attempting to get Baugh to break his New York contract and coach the Redskins in 1962. He further accused Marshall of sabotaging the Titans' attempt to sign a quarterback. Wismer said he had been about to sign veteran signal caller Ralph Guglielmi, who Washington planned to release. When Marshall learned of his intentions, said Wismer, he changed his plans and traded Guglielmi to the Eagles, preventing him from becoming a free agent. Similar methods had been used, Wismer claimed, to prevent the Titans from signing Eagle Day, another quarterback.

Despite Marshall's alleged skullduggery, the Titans were successful in acquiring a quarterback, one already familiar with the New York offense. Bob Scrabis was not happy in San Diego. He missed the night life of New York, didn't like the California lifestyle, and found Sid Gillman's offensive system much more complex than New York's and difficult to assimilate.

In New York, Scrabis, a 25-year-old bachelor, had loved the Peppermint Lounge and the life it represented. In San Diego, he lived in a motel and practiced with the Chargers at the Marine Corps Recruiting Depot. "I used to sit there, when the airplanes went over," he recalled, " and say 'Why couldn't I be on one going back to New York?'" When Scrabis heard the Titans were looking for a backup, he convinced the Chargers to let him go.

Later in the season, the Titans added a third quarterback, Don Allard, who came to New York by a circuitous route. Allard had been drafted in the first round by the Washington Redskins, but elected to play in Canada for a higher salary and more playing time. In 1961 he was convinced by Boston coach Lou Saban to play out his option and join the Patriots. Although he was happy in Canada, Allard had been born and raised in the Boston area and dreamed of playing in his hometown. He went to the

Patriots' camp in Concord, Massachusetts, only to find after the first day that he had been claimed on waivers by Montreal, and was contractually obligated to report to the Alouettes. He played five games with Montreal, was released, and joined Saban and the Patriots in October. His first day in Boston, he dressed and went out to the field, only to find that practice was canceled. Saban, the man who had convinced Allard to leave Canada, had been fired and replaced by Mike Holovak. Holovak summoned Allard to his office and told him that, for the rest of the season, he planned to alternate incumbent quarterbacks Babe Parilli and Butch Songin. There was no room for a third quarterback.

Shortly after his departure from Boston, Allard received a call from Wismer, who wanted him to go to New York. Knowing of the feud between the coach and owner, as did anyone who could read a newspaper, Allard asked for a no-cut contract for the remainder of the season. Wismer readily agreed. When Allard got to New York, however, and read the contract, he saw that it did not contain the no-cut provision. Not wanting to repeat his experience in Boston, he packed up and headed for the airport. Wismer summoned him back and changed the contract to Allard's specifications.

Apparently Baugh had not been consulted about the signing, for when Allard reported for practice, he was greeted with, "Who the hell are you?" Allard introduced himself, and Baugh laughed. "I know who you are, Don," he said, "but I need another quarterback like I need a hole in the head." He told Allard about his troubles with Wismer and asked about the details of his contract. Baugh told his new player that he would be put on the roster for the Houston game, then placed on the inactive list the following Monday.

Allard had a difficult first day with the Titans. Not only did he find the head coach less than enthusiastic to see him, he left the Polo Grounds locker room to find that his car had been broken into. All of his personal possessions had been stolen. Finally, at the end of a long day, Allard made his way to Dorow's apartment, where he was spending a few days in order to get a crash course in the New York offense. He needn't have bothered. In Houston, Allard's only activity was on the opening kickoff, when he ran down in coverage. After the game, he went on the inactive list for the rest of the season.

With Scrabis signed, the Titans and Patriots met for the fourth time in seven weeks, this time in New York on October 1, with the winner to take sole possession of first place. The early part of the contest proved a complete reversal of the normal New York pattern, as the defense kept the club in the game despite the best efforts of the offensive platoon to hand it to the Patriots. On the Titans' first four plays from scrimmage, they fumbled three times, losing all three. On their fourth possession, they managed to hold onto the ball long enough to get to fourth down and a punting situation. Ellis, still subbing for Hudock at center, bounced the ball back to Curley Johnson, and Boston recovered for the fourth time.

The defense put up a valiant effort, and, despite four possessions deep in New York territory, all Boston could show was three successful field goals in four attempts. What could easily have been an insurmountable 28–0 lead was only 9–0, a margin quite capable of being erased by Dorow and his explosive receiving corps. That was exactly what happened, as the Titans took a 20–9 lead by halftime. It was fortunate that the Titans had Scrabis. Dorow was sacked hard by Harry Jacobs and Rommie Loudd just before the end of the half, suffered a strained neck muscle and had to leave the game. Scrabis came in and completed two straight passes, the second a four-yard touchdown toss to Powell, the only scoring pass of Scrabis's pro career.

The Patriots came back in the second half, and eventually tied the game at 30. The winning Titans score came on a pass from Dorow (whose neck responded to halftime heat treatments) to Maynard, a 13-yarder that gave New York a 37–30 victory. Maynard felt he had been roughed up by Patriots defensive back Fred Bruney all day, and after he wrestled the ball away from Bruney in the end zone, handed it to him. Bruney slammed the ball angrily to the ground.

The Patriots got the ball back on their own 35, with two minutes to go, for one final chance. Again, however, the New York defense rose to the occasion. On first down, Larry Grantham blitzed and batted down Songin's pass. On the next two plays, Tom Saidock and Sid Youngelman sacked Songin. On fourth and 22, Tom Yewcic tried to pass on a fake punt, but the ball wobbled and was intercepted by Lee Riley. The Titans offense then ran out the clock. In addition to timely defense and three touchdown passes, the game featured the first 100-yard rushing effort in Titans history, as Mathis picked up 109 yards on 19 carries.

After an off-week, the Titans met the San Diego Chargers, leaders of the Western Division, on October 15. The Chargers had swept all four pre-season games and their first five regular-season contests. Since moving to San Diego, they had assembled an awesome defensive line, consisting of rookies Earl Faison (6'5", 256) and Ernie Ladd (6'9", 310), CFL veteran Bill Hudson (6'4", 277), and second-year man Ron Nery (6'6", 244). Faison and Nery were the ends and Hudson and Ladd played tackle. Ladd, a product of Grambling, was the most flamboyant, the biggest (according to the *Herald Tribune*, the largest athlete ever to play at the Polo Grounds), and had the catchiest nicknames ("The Big Cat" and "Bigger than Big Daddy" to indicate that he was even bigger than Big Daddy Lipscomb of the Steelers). He was a massive man, with a 54-inch chest, 20-inch biceps, 22-inch thighs and size 17EEE shoes. During his visit to New York, Ladd broke a record at the Bear Mountain Inn by consuming 12 eggs for breakfast. This was a modest feat, as he once had eaten 124 small pancakes in a contest and, the previous year, in front of a number of writers who had doubted his gastronomic prowess, consumed a dinner consisting of three shrimp cocktails, two bowls of soup, four 16-ounce steaks, six potatoes, six rolls, and three servings of ice cream.

Jon Morris, longtime center of the Patriots, was asked what it was like to line up opposite Ladd. "It was dark," Morris replied. "I couldn't see the linebackers. I couldn't see the goalposts. It was like being in a closet." Ladd was not only big—he was quick as well. "You couldn't run over him," said Cotton Davidson, "and you didn't want to run away from him because he could run you down from behind. I was scrambling one time and he caught me from behind, clubbed me over the head and said, 'Don't you know you can't get away from the Big Cat?'"

In 1961 Ladd had not yet learned to use his immense physical ability to its best advantage. "I don't think he was a smart player then," said Bob Mischak, who played directly across from Ladd. "He came at you with his whole body and exposed himself for a trap, and you could get into his body. Because of our relative height [Mischak was six feet even], he'd rise up a little, and I could get a shot into his chest. He didn't know how to grab you like they teach today. You could cut him off, pin him against somebody, leverage him, or cut him down."

Ladd generally tried to fight the blocker rather than shed him, and had only a single bull rush move. "You could sucker Ladd," said Davidson, "because he'd always follow a pulling guard. You could run the sucker play behind him without even blocking him."

Hudock, outweighed by 65 pounds, admitted to having difficulty handling Ladd, but added, "He didn't know how to use his hands. He'd just try to overpower you. When a fellow tries to overpower you, that's what you want, because if you can get him tied up you can get him to the ground, or stay in contact with him. If he has to carry you seven yards to the quarterback, it's going to take a little while." Ladd's shortcomings did not make him an ineffective player, of course. He was simply not as awesome as his physical ability might have allowed.

Faison, however, was another matter altogether. "Faison was the best pass rusher I ever played against," said Buddy Cockrell, who, as the right offensive tackle, was responsible for handling the left defensive end. "He was real strong and had lots of speed. He'd get down in that sprinter's stance and he was hell to block."

"Earl Faison was the hardest person for me to control," agreed Dewey Bohling. "He was not only good, he was mean. Ladd was more easy-going. Faison had a mean streak in him. He'd go out of his way to try to hurt you. Ladd was a good ballplayer, but he wasn't half as mean as Faison."

Aided by the fearsome pass rush, the San Diego secondary had intercepted 18 passes in their first five games, and would eventually set a league record with 49. The Chargers' defense, coached by Chuck Noll, had limited its opponents to 72 points overall, by far the best total in the league. Fullback Keith Lincoln, a rookie from Washington State, a big back with breakaway speed in the mold of Billy Cannon, had joined Paul Lowe. Jack Kemp opened the season at quarterback, but was scheduled to report for six months of active military duty on the day of the game against the Titans. "If they take him," coach Gillman was reported to have said, "they might as well take me, too." A week earlier, however, Kemp had been given a reprieve pending a physical exam. He had previously been rejected by the Navy, and had applied for a medical deferment from the Army on similar grounds. Kemp's left shoulder was separated and had a torn deltoid muscle, while the right shoulder had been fractured and dislocated in 1960. Although healed, it had an unnatural bump in it. An exam was scheduled for October 23, leaving Kemp available to play against the Titans.

This was unfortunate for New York, since Kemp, even with a left shoulder that had to be strapped up in a sling and deadened with Novocain, riddled the Titans' defense with a flurry of short passes and draw plays. Overall, he threw for 302 yards. Paul Lowe added a spectacular 25-yard TD run. A former high hurdler at Oregon State, he leaped over Youngelman at the 10 on his way to the end zone.

The Chargers' defense put unrelenting pressure on Dorow and increased its league-leading interception total by picking off four of his passes. The Titans gained only 202 yards of total offense. The largest crowd to watch the Titans at the Polo Grounds, announced at more than 25,000, booed Dorow, the first time they had turned on him. After the game, Kemp returned to the locker room, had someone help him remove his jersey, and swallowed codeine to prepare himself for the moment the Novocain wore off. "The Army, as far as the Titans are concerned, is much too understanding," Howard Tuckner reported.

Following the game, the Titans made a number of roster changes, the most significant being the release of Bohling, the club's No. 2 rusher in 1960. Linebacker Pat Lamberti and rookie defensive back Dave Ames were also waived. Ames, who had played very little defense in college, had been badly beaten by Gino Cappelletti in the opening game. The defensive backfield, overhauled in training camp, was revamped again before the season was half over. Ames, Rechichar, and Wren were cut loose, leaving only Felt and Paulson from the group that had started the season. In his second year as a defender, Felt had made amazing progress. He compensated for a lack of blazing speed with excellent man-to-man coverage skills and an ability to read offenses and anticipate patterns. Like Grantham, Felt was a student of the game who watched film religiously.

The most valuable newcomer to the Titans was Lee Riley, older brother of current NBA coach Pat Riley. At 27, Riley was a six-year NFL veteran who had been released by the Giants. He was a strong defender who played nearly every minute at safety for the Titans in 1961 and led the AFL with 11 interceptions in 1962. "On every team you play on," said fellow defensive back Paul Hynes, "there's always one guy who carries the team flag. Lee was the one that everyone in the defensive backfield looked up to. I had a lot of respect for Lee. He had a great knowledge of the game."

Other additions included two running backs, Jim Apple and Mel West. Apple, from Upsala College, had been the surprise of training camp before separating his shoulder. He was now healed and ready to play. West was a speedster from Missouri, Most Valuable Player of the 1960 Orange Bowl and a *Sporting News* All-American, who had started the season with the Patriots. He was a talented runner and kick-returner, but limited as a blocker and receiver.

Yet another new Titans player was a redheaded defensive back from Louisiana Tech named Paul Hynes, who had been cut by Dallas at the end of training camp. Looking for a job, Hynes called Curley Johnson, who had played with Hynes's brother at the University of Houston. Johnson talked to Bones Taylor, who remembered that Hynes had had a spectacular game a couple of years earlier against an Arkansas State team coached by Taylor. The Titans signed Hynes and put him in the starting lineup at right cornerback.

Like Dick Christy, Hynes was believed to have a world of talent that had not yet come to the surface. He was fast, once clocked at 9.6 seconds for 100 yards, but had a predilection for parties and good times that prevented him from achieving his potential and gave Baugh fits. At this point, considering the problems he was having with the owner, Baugh needed another problem child like Wismer needed more pictures. One Saturday night, shortly after Hynes joined the club, the coach received a call informing him that his starting defensive back was in jail. Hynes had been drinking at the Peppermint Lounge and gotten into an argument over a cab. He punched the other man, sending him through the front window, and was arrested. "I can't even recall how that happened," Hynes said recently. "The way the papers wrote it up, I'd picked up a man and thrown him through the front window of the Peppermint Lounge. I don't know if it quite happened that way, but at least I got credit for it." Baugh and Grantham went down to the police station, bailed Hynes out and put him in the starting lineup the following day. "I had a good day," Hynes recalled.

For two years, the Titans gave Hynes every opportunity to prove himself. He was never able, or never cared, to put forth the effort necessary to succeed at the professional level. When Weeb Ewbank took over as coach of the Jets, he decided that he could not wait for Hynes to grow up. The cornerback reported grossly overweight following his recuperation from an offseason auto accident, claimed that the Jets owed him money, and had a bitter fight with Ewbank. When he failed to get in shape, Ewbank cut him. Hynes went up to the third floor of the dormitory at Peekskill and yelled down the stairs that anyone who wanted his playbook would have to come up and get it. He would beat the hell out of anyone who tried, he added. No one came. The coaching staff called the police. When Hynes learned that officers were on their way, he threw his playbook down the stairs, came down, jumped in his car, and took off. That was the last any of the Jets saw of him.

In October 1961, the Titans were willing to take a chance on a promising defensive back. After all, a number of Titans, including Powell, Maynard, and Christy, had come to New York with troubling reputations and had not only performed well, but proven to be good citizens. Unfortunately, Hynes would not join the group.

CHAPTER 15
7–7 AGAIN

As in 1960, the Titans had broken quickly from the gate, remaining in first place even after the loss to the Chargers. Although much had been written about the improved New York defense, the team had given up an average of 29 points per game, almost exactly the same as in 1960. However, a number of the points had come following turnovers, particularly in the most recent two games. Four fumbles against Boston and four interceptions versus San Diego had frequently pinned the defense deep in its own territory.

The AFL standings on October 16 were as follows:

EASTERN DIVISION		WESTERN DIVISION	
New York	3–2	San Diego	6–0
Buffalo	3–3	Dallas	3–2
Boston	2–3–1	Denver	2–4
Houston	1–3–1	Oakland	1–4

The defending champion Oilers had stumbled, winning only one of their first five games, and resided in the Eastern Division basement. Before playing the Patriots in the fifth game, owner Bud Adams, never known for his patience, told Lou Rymkus, the 1960 UPI Coach of the Year, he would be fired if Houston lost. With Adams' death sentence hanging over their coach's head, the Oilers trailed the Patriots 31–28 with six seconds left in the game. George Blanda, who had been benched for Jacky Lee, stood in the huddle preparing for a 25-yard field-goal attempt that could tie the game. One of his teammates suggested that he miss the kick intentionally. It would get Rymkus fired and serve him right for benching Blanda. George told his teammate what he thought of his idea and drilled the ball through the uprights, but it was not enough to save his coach. Even though the Oilers had not lost, Adams jettisoned Rymkus. The Houston coach was the third casualty in an unusually perilous season, joining Lou Saban of Boston and Eddie Erdelatz of Oakland among the ranks of the unemployed. By the end of the season, six of the eight AFL coaches had lost their jobs.

Rymkus had not been Adams' first choice in 1960. In December 1959, a "reliable source" told UPI that Tom Landry, 35-year-old assistant coach with the New York Giants, would accept the Oilers' head coaching position within a week. The following day, however, Landry contracted with Clint Murchison Jr. to be head coach of the Dallas Rangers. Landry could not actually begin coaching, for the Rangers were not really a team yet, as the NFL had not granted Murchison a franchise. Under the terms of Landry's contract, he would be released and receive a lump sum payment if the franchise never materialized. Of course, Dallas did receive a franchise, changed its nickname to the Cowboys, and Landry put on his hat and took to the sidelines. On January 2, 1960, Adams announced the signing of Rymkus, who had been an assistant with the Packers and Rams, to a three-year contract at $15,500 per season.

Rymkus had never been particularly popular with the players, who were on the whole happy to see him go. The product of an impoverished area of rural Illinois, Rymkus was an intense, driven man who had been determined to better his station in life. "He was as tough as they come," recalled Sid Gillman, who had hired Rymkus as an assistant in Los Angeles. Rymkus's father died when he was seven, and his mother moved to Chicago in the midst of the Depression to work in the stockyards. Her son found employment performing manual labor on the south side of the city. Rymkus eventually worked his way out of Chicago, and played at Notre Dame under Frank Leahy, which strengthened his internal discipline.

After a year with the Washington Redskins and two in the service during World War II, Rymkus joined the AAFC's Cleveland Browns in 1946. He hitchhiked 130 miles to training camp, made the club, and played on both offense and defense for two years. In his first year with the Browns, Rymkus suffered torn cartilage in his knee. Telling no one of his injury, he got the trainer to teach him how to pop the knee back into place when it locked. His main complaint about Cleveland coach Paul Brown was that the Browns' practices weren't tough enough.

When he took over as Houston's head coach, Rymkus was determined to remedy this deficiency. He was still a fit, well-conditioned man who felt that professional football was a serious affair. "He wants his athletes to know immediately," wrote Wells Twombly, "that they are doing more than just playing a football game. They are on a holy mission, a war to the death." Lou believed in scrimmaging, and that the best way to prepare his team was by grueling practice sessions and strict attention to business. "If you smiled, it was like you had committed a crime," said Jacky Lee. "If a guy laughed, Lou would stop practice and lecture us about being hard-nosed." In the Oilers' 1961 training camp, highly touted rookie line-backer Tom Goode and guard Walt Suggs walked out. Goode stated, "I would rather dig ditches than play pro football." Rymkus responded, "I'm disappointed in today's youth." Rymkus went out of his way to prove that Billy Cannon, the high-priced Heisman winner, was no better than the lowliest substitute. If anything, he was tougher on Cannon than on anyone else. "That guy would drive you nuts," Cannon complained. Given the Oilers' sizable investment in Cannon and the pains they had taken to acquire him, he was not a good person to drive nuts.

Antagonizing the players did not help Rymkus's cause, but upsetting the owner was the final straw. In Hawaii, where the Oilers spent a portion of their 1961 training camp, Rymkus, who had been drinking, made a number of uncomplimentary comments about the Houston owner, which were duly reported to Adams. "Our decision," said Adams when announcing Rymkus's dismissal, "is based upon the conclusion that the material on hand has not been used to its fullest potential."

Adams was a hands-on owner who fancied himself a pretty good judge of football talent. He had spent a great deal of money to bring professional football to Texas and felt he was entitled to his opinion on personnel matters. Rymkus insisted on having his own way, and often persisted in sticking with players he had chosen, even when their performances were clearly inadequate. He stubbornly kept utility player Charley Milstead at safety, rather than Adams' choice, Fred Glick. When Rymkus departed, Glick was inserted in the lineup and started for the next six years, leading the league with 12 interceptions in 1963 and earning all-pro honors that year and the next. Milstead went to the bench and, shortly thereafter, to retirement. Rymkus also wanted to cut former Bears receiver Willard Dewveall, one of the NFL's leading pass catchers in 1960. Spared through Adams' intervention, Dewveall became a regular in 1962 and caught 33 passes for 576 yards. Assistant coach Mac Speedie had to convince his boss not to cut Charley Hennigan, who became one of the AFL's all-time great receivers. Before his final game, Rymkus virtually dared Adams to fire him by announcing his intention to bench Cannon because of subpar performance.

In Rymkus's stead, Adams hired Wally Lemm, a former defensive assistant for the Chicago Cardinals who had coached the Oilers' secondary in 1960. A former college coach at Lake Forest and Montana State, Lemm was operating a sporting goods store in Libertyville, Illinois. He was the opposite of Rymkus, a players' coach who believed in positive rather than negative motivation. After the stifling discipline of his predecessor, Lemm was like a breath of fresh air. His first move was to restore Blanda to a starting position, despite the fact that Jacky Lee, in Rymkus's final game, passed for an AFL record 457 yards. With the team sitting in last place, however, it remained to be seen whether the new coach could reverse the Oilers' fortunes, or whether he would have enough time to do so.

The Titans helped the Oilers by going to Denver and losing to the Broncos. The game started out disastrously for New York. In training camp, Dorow had been so impressed with the plethora of talent at the receiving positions that he said, "I don't know what they're going to do with them all. They'll just have to trade some and cut some others."

Or send them out to block on screen passes. On the Titans' first series, Dorow threw a pass to Dick Christy in the flat. Christy caught the ball, broke free and ran 75 yards into the end zone, sprung by a downfield block by Don Maynard. The Titans' star receiver was not known for his blocking prowess. "I promise you he didn't get into the Hall of Fame for blocking," said Bill Mathis. "We didn't run too many sweeps to his side."

On this occasion, however, Maynard did throw a block, and it cost the Titans dearly. He suffered a separated shoulder that finished him for the afternoon and, it was thought at first, for the season. Worse yet, the play was called back due to a penalty.

At halftime, the Titans led 10–7. In the third quarter, Denver's Jack Hill kicked a 33-yard field goal to tie the score. The final quarter was all Denver, not an unusual occurrence in the Mile High City. Visiting teams always had difficulty coping with the thin air, and generally had their tongues hanging out by the time the final quarter arrived. "When we used to go to training camp," said Frank Tripucka, who played in Denver for four years, "it took a good two weeks of double sessions before you could get used to the air up there. It just left you breathless. It felt like somebody was standing on your chest. After you got used to it, the feeling disappeared. But for somebody coming in and playing one game...they just ran out of gas and we were still going strong."

In 1960 Boston led Denver 21–0 with three minutes left in the third quarter, only to lose 31–24. The same year, Buffalo led the Broncos 38–7 late in the third quarter, only to see Denver rally for 31 points in a swirling snowstorm to tie the game 38–38. LaVerne Torczon played for the Bills in that game. "The biggest problem teams had in the early years," he said, "was the lack of numbers." With a 33- or 35-man roster, it was difficult to rest players during the game. "You had to play on defense, kickoffs, run down on punts, extra points, so by the end of the third quarter and the fourth quarter, Denver was able to capitalize on their ability to overwhelm the opposition," Torczon said. "Even today, how often do you see Denver come back to win in the fourth quarter?"

A week before the game against the Titans, the Broncos took advantage of some late Oakland turnovers to erase a 24–14 deficit and win by a 27–24 score. Against New York, they scored 17 points in the final quarter, aided by a fumble by Powell and an interception of Dorow, to gain a 27–10 win.

Boston beat Buffalo to tie New York for first place, with the Bills a half game behind. The co-leaders had intersected while heading in opposite directions, Boston on its way up and the Titans slipping down. It was the year of the mellow coach in the AFL, as Patriots owner Billy Sullivan followed the lead of Bud Adams and replaced intense Lou Saban with the more relaxed Mike Holovak. In 1960, upon hiring Saban, Sullivan said, "Saban is Paul Brown with a heart." By the middle of the next season, Sullivan concluded that Saban was not Paul Brown, and the players decided that, if he had a heart, he concealed it well. "Saban was a very demanding coach," said Gino Cappelletti. "He almost put you through military drills. It seemed like he was always looking for that superman player, and there weren't that many around. But I liked his toughness and discipline. Mike was just a real nice, pleasant guy. He eased up on the practices, put us out in sweats. He did all the things we were looking to do." Following the installation of Holovak, Boston won its first game, and appeared to be headed in the right direction.

The Titans, on the other hand, were in rough shape. Maynard's injury was not as serious as first feared, but it still appeared that he would be unable to play against the Raiders the following week. Baugh moved Bob Renn from the defensive backfield to take Maynard's place at flanker and signed former Texan John Bookman, a UPI All-Star in 1960, to fill Renn's spot in the secondary. Powell, who caught 12 passes against Denver after Maynard's injury, had also been hurt. Baugh planned to shift Christy to split end and start Mel West at running back.

Powell prided himself on his ability to go to the post, even refusing to take Novocain to numb pain. "I want to feel what's happening to me," he said. He was able to play against Oakland, but caught only one pass for seven yards. With their top receivers hobbled, the Titans kept the ball on the ground, racking up 220 rushing yards. West had 99 and Mathis 76, including two short touchdown runs. The Oakland offense was the weakest in the league, the only one below the Titans, and New York was able to hold them without a touchdown, winning 14–6.

A high wind hampered the passing of both teams, and made the kicking game exciting. Curley Johnson and Wayne Crow each got off 70-yard punts and Johnson sent one kickoff 35 yards beyond the goal line. All points were scored with the wind. With a 14–6 lead, the Titans intercepted a pass and returned it to the Oakland 8 with only a minute and a half remaining in the game. Rather than kill the clock, Dorow elected to call timeouts and throw into the end zone, attempting to extend his record of having thrown touchdown passes in 20 consecutive games. He stopped the clock with 33 seconds to go. On fourth down, he was sacked and fumbled, but fortunately New York recovered and the clock ran out.

The Titans' win kept them in a first-place tie with the Patriots. Houston had won its first two games under Wally Lemm and was only a half game behind. Lemm's easygoing ways were working wonders with the talented Oilers team. Apparently, all they needed was to be left alone. Blanda was playing better than ever. In their nine regular-season games under the new coach, the Oilers' offense averaged 41 points per game. The defense, which had given up an average of 170 yards rushing per game under Rymkus, cut that figure in half in their first five games under Lemm.

The Titans' final West Coast stop was San Diego, where the Chargers were still unbeaten at 8–0, with a seemingly insurmountable lead over the second-place Texans, who were 3–4. Powell was back at full strength, but the Titans lost the heart of their defense, linebacker Larry Grantham, who fell into the clutches of the United States government.

The Cold War was in full swing, and virtually every physically fit male of draft age was under scrutiny by his local draft board. The best way to avoid a two-year military hitch was to join a National Guard or Army Reserve unit. This involved six months on active duty, followed by a two-week stint each summer. This would not interfere with the football season, presuming there was no crisis that would merit calling the reserves to active duty. Management generally provided whatever assistance they could to get their athletes into the coveted openings in the reserve.

There were other ways to avoid military service. Deferments were granted for a number of reasons, one of them being physical infirmity. Professional athletes found it very difficult to obtain a deferment on those grounds, since they were presumed to be in top condition. As seen in the case of Jack Kemp, however, this was not always the case. Four years of high school ball, four years in college, plus time in the professional ranks left many players with battered knees, shoulders, and other body parts. They had to be taped up, shot up, and strapped up to perform on Sundays. The general public was unaware of this, and had a difficult time understanding why the gridiron hero who had broken off a 60-yard run the previous Sunday was incapable of marching and drilling with the accountant next door who had been fingered by the Selective Service. Draft boards were extremely sensitive to charges of preferential treatment, generally subjected professional athletes to extensive scrutiny, and sometimes inducted those whose physical condition would have warranted a deferment had they been ordinary civilians.

Bob Reifsnyder was the victim in one such instance. Upon graduation from Annapolis, he was immediately granted a medical discharge from the Navy. When Reifsnyder was traded to the Titans in 1960, his Long Island draft board tried to induct him into the Army. "I think it was the publicity in the papers," he said. "Why is Bob Reifsnyder, a Naval Academy graduate, playing pro football? What kind of deal is this?" Reifsnyder was incensed. "I was definitely not a draft dodger," he said. "I had never attempted to avoid service, and I said that if I could go in as an officer, I'd go in immediately and drop football. They spent all that money to educate me at the Naval Academy to be an officer, not a private in the Army." Eventually the whole matter was dropped, and Reifsnyder, ruptured Achilles tendon and all, became neither an officer nor a private.

The most celebrated military case of 1961 involved Green Bay halfback Paul Hornung, the Heisman Trophy winner from Notre Dame who led the NFL in scoring in 1959 and 1960, setting a record with 176 points in the latter season. In mid-October 1961, with the Packers on their way to a second straight division title, Hornung, a reservist who had already served a six-month hitch, was ordered to report to the 896th Engineers Company at Fort Riley, Kansas. The same week, Uncle Sam also tabbed Packers middle linebacker Ray Nitschke and split end Boyd Dowler.

On October 24, Hornung underwent a physical exam in Milwaukee, during which the doctors discovered a chronic pinched nerve in his neck. The nerve had bothered Hornung for several years, and would eventually lead to his retirement in 1967. Pending a second exam, Hornung was given a two-week extension of his reporting date, affording him the opportunity to test his neck against the likes of Doug Atkins and Larry Morris of the Chicago Bears.

Republican Senator Jack Miller of Iowa seized upon the case as an example of special treatment. "Regardless of the merits of Hornung's case," Miller said, "it has been handled in such a way as to raise widespread suspicion. Favoritism in such matters has a highly detrimental effect on the morale of the armed forces." When Senator Wiley of Wisconsin supported a deferment, he was dismissed as a mere Packer shill. Wrote Milton Gross in the *New York Post*, "Lombardi should appoint Sen. Wiley an assistant coach and give him a permanent seat on the team's bench. The Senate could only be better for it." Not surprisingly in light of the charged atmosphere, Hornung passed his second physical and reported to Fort Riley on November 14 for duty as a light-truck driver and radio operator. He played the rest of the season on weekend passes and scored 19 points in the championship game against the Giants while on Christmas leave.

Even if a player went on active duty, it was possible, as Hornung had done, to obtain weekend passes for game day. Military regulations allowed soldiers to pursue other employment during their off-duty hours if the commanding officer granted permission. Soldiers could request a pass starting at 4:30 on Friday afternoon and ending at 6:00 a.m. Monday. For sports such as basketball or baseball, this was largely impractical, although in 1962, pitchers Steve Barber of the Orioles and Jim "Mudcat" Grant of the Indians performed exclusively on weekends for the entire season, starting once per week and wreaking havoc with their managers' pitching rotations. Football, with only one game each week, was much more adaptable to the weekday warrior. In mid-November, the AFL voided the league rule that had prohibited men on active military duty from playing in league games.

In order to play under weekend passes, the first key was to be assigned to a base within reasonable commuting distance. An Army demolition expert, Grantham was assigned to Fort Devens, Massachusetts, an easy drive to New York. All that remained was for him to obtain those precious passes. Grantham missed the San Diego, Denver, and Oakland games, while the Titans' linebacker corps became further depleted by an injury to Grantham's replacement, Jim Furey, who tore a ligament in his knee. Bobo, as always, was playing on one leg, and Baugh was reduced to using defensive back Don Flynn at linebacker. He also signed Jerry Fields, a former Ohio State player and a 12th-round draft choice of the Giants. The Titans, as in 1960, were hurting. The active roster was down to 30 and the taxi squad down to zero.

Baugh, with his team still in the race and bereft of linebacking talent, called Grantham's commanding officer and pleaded with him to allow Grantham to play on weekends. The commander agreed, but one more hurdle remained. Wismer had cut off Grantham's salary the moment he was inducted. If he returned to the team, Larry wanted to be paid not only for the games he played, but also for those he had missed. When Wismer reluctantly agreed, the deal was sealed.

Grantham played for the first time against Buffalo on November 23 and was interviewed on national television by ABC announcers Curt Gowdy and Paul Christman. During the interview, Grantham thanked, by name, his company commander, battalion commander, and, as he said, "every commander I could think of." Following this expression of appreciation before a national audience, he had no difficulty obtaining passes for future games.

It was unfortunate that Grantham could not have been sprung a few weeks earlier, for the Titans could have used him in the November 5 game at San Diego. New York scored the first 13 points of the game, only to watch as the Chargers scored the next 48, including 41 in the second half and 28 in the third quarter alone. As in New York, the Chargers' defense put tremendous pressure on Dorow, and the secondary picked off three more of his passes. In the absence of Maynard, Powell was double-teamed and held in check. Scrabis came on in relief and threw two more interceptions to his former teammates.

Paul Lowe again tormented the Titans, breaking off a 68-yard touchdown run and totaling 110 yards on only nine carries. The rest of the San Diego offense was unspectacular, but the six New York turnovers—the Titans also lost a fumble—were enough to turn the game into a rout. Special teams were also a problem, as the Chargers gained 165 yards on punt returns. The loss dropped the Titans to third place in the East, as Houston and Boston both won. The Chargers' win clinched a tie for the Western Division crown, a remarkable achievement with five games still remaining in the season.

The Titans returned home to face the Raiders, who at 2–6 resided in the Western Division basement. The Raiders were a beatable opponent, but unlikely to attract much of a crowd. Wismer therefore designated the game "Ladies' Night" and permitted all women to purchase a $3 seat for $1.25. He also staged a Pop Warner game before the regular match, figuring that two teams of 11 plus their parents would boost the crowd by 66, not counting siblings.

The promotions did nothing to increase attendance, as it was estimated that the announced crowd of 16,811 was approximately twice the number present. The game was sloppy, with the Titans struggling to a 23–12 victory. Dick Guesman kicked field goals from 22, 40, and 18 yards, and Mathis set a Titans mark with 127 yards rushing. A troubling note was Dorow's three interceptions, giving him 21 for the season and six games in which he had given up three or more.

Dorow could not afford to have an off day in the Titans' next game, which was a battle for the division lead in Houston against the Oilers. Wally Lemm was still undefeated, having led the team to four straight victories. The most recent win, a 27–15 conquest of Boston, put his team in first place.

In Boston's next game, on Friday night, November 17, the Patriots stayed in the race by defeating the Raiders 20–17 on a most unusual play. With Oakland clinging to a slender 17–13 lead in the fourth quarter, the Raiders' Wayne Crow dropped back to punt out of his own end zone. At that time, the goal posts were located on the goal line. Crow's punt hit an upright and bounced back into the end zone. Boston defensive end Leroy Moore fell on the ball for a touchdown that gave the Patriots the victory, putting them mere percentage points behind the Oilers.

EASTERN DIVISION

Houston	5–3–1
Boston	6-4-1
New York	5–4
Buffalo	4-6

Something always happened to the Titans when they played the Oilers. Not only had they lost both games in 1960; tragedy had struck in Houston, with the death of Howard Glenn. The rematch in New York featured a much more pedestrian mishap, the disabling of both Titans quarterbacks.

In the first 1961 meeting, there was no tragedy, other than a 49–13 stomping by the Oilers. George Blanda threw seven touchdown passes, shredding the Titans' secondary with three each to Bill Groman and Billy Cannon and tying the pro record held by Sid Luckman and Adrian Burk. Blanda's first touchdown pass came with only three minutes gone in the game, and before the first quarter was over he had thrown three. By halftime, he had already broken the AFL record of four. By the end of the game, he had completed 20 of 32 for 418 yards. Charley Hennigan caught eight for 123 yards, Cannon seven for 122, and Groman five for 152. "I just remember all those missiles flying over my head," said New York defensive tackle Proverb Jacobs. "They were running up and down the field on us all day long. It was just a helpless feeling. They gave us a good, old-fashioned thrashing." On the Titans' side of the ledger, Dorow threw for 278 yards on 47 attempts, but was again intercepted three times. Maynard returned for the first time since his injury in Denver. He caught four passes, but reinjured the shoulder. Once again, Youngelman was ejected for fighting, as were the Titans' other defensive tackle, Tom Saidock, and Houston's Al Jamison.

The second Mayor's Trophy Game, on Thanksgiving Day, pitted the Titans against the Buffalo Bills. This was the first meeting of the two clubs since Dorow's altercation with Buster Ramsey and Wismer wanted to be certain to generate maximum publicity. He sent a request to the New York police commissioner, Michael J. Murphy, for "strong police protection behind the Buffalo bench." It was not clear whether he wanted to protect Buster Ramsey and the Bills' players from revenge-minded fans, or protect the fans from Ramsey. Bills owner Ralph Wilson telegraphed Murphy, "The Buffalo Bills welcome New York City's finest on the field at the game with the Titans as long as none of them block, tackle, or catch passes." In addition to the police, there was another man who would not be doing any tackling on Thanksgiving Day. Richie McCabe, the Buffalo defender who had started the altercation with Dorow, had been forced to retire because of bad knees.

Before the game, Wismer also expressed extreme displeasure with his club's recent performances. He accused the Chargers and Oilers of running up the score against the Titans, and claimed to have a fund of $250,000 to acquire players good enough to compete with San Diego and Houston. He said he would trade anyone on the team except Maynard and Mathis. The summer of 1961 had witnessed the great home run duel between Roger Maris and Mickey Mantle, the M&M boys of the Yankees. Now Wismer had his own M&M boys, as Maynard referred to himself and Mathis. Wismer's threat to dismantle the roster, and the designation of two players as untouchables, might have caused dissension on some teams. The Titans, however, had become accustomed to Wismer's bluster. "That was just Wismer making his comments," said Maynard recently. "You read between the lines. You never know if he might have said it when he'd had a few." Mathis didn't even notice. "Maynard told me about it," he said. "I didn't read the papers much at that time." The rest of the players chalked it up to Wismer being Wismer and didn't give it a second thought. The failure to place Dorow in the same category as the M&M boys was an indication that the quarterback's favored status was eroding.

For the second year in a row, the Titans captured the Mayor's Trophy, getting sterling performances from some unexpected sources. Bob Renn, subbing for Maynard, who again re-injured his shoulder, hauled in a 67-yard scoring pass and had four receptions for 117 yards overall. Dick Felt returned an interception 55 yards for a touchdown.

Felt's touchdown had an interesting sidelight. The game was nationally televised, live in the East and on a delayed basis in the West. Felt's parents, watching in Utah, saw the latter version. Just seconds after Dick crossed the goal line on their television screen, the phone rang. It was their son, calling to tell them of the Titans' win and of his big moment. Felt's mother did not realize the game had ended hours ago, and thought her devoted son, not content to shout "Hi, mom!" into the cameras, had sprinted to the locker room and called her while the game was in progress.

The much-maligned Titans defense preserved the game in its final seconds. Leading 21–7, the Titans allowed the Bills to draw closer on a most unusual play. With the ball on his own 28, Dorow dropped back to pass. His throw was deflected and caught by New York lineman Huck O'Neil. Since the ball had been deflected, O'Neil could have run with it. Believing, however, that he was an ineligible receiver and would be penalized for touching the ball, he immediately dropped it. By letting go of it, O'Neil fumbled, and the Bills' Mack Yoho pounced on it at the 15. The Bills scored quickly, and then got the ball back. Behind quarterback M.C. Reynolds, they drove from their own 29 to the New York 9. A touchdown and two-point conversion would give them the game. With first and goal from the 9, and 30 seconds left, Reynolds attempted three straight passes. All three were batted away by defensive back John Bookman, the recent acquisition from Dallas. On fourth down, Tom Saidock and Ed Cooke dropped Reynolds for a loss, and the Titans' victory was sealed. Grantham, playing his first game on leave, was named Titan of the Week. General Motors awarded one month's use of a 1962 Buick convertible to each player so honored, allowing Grantham to drive around Fort Devens in style.

Ten days later, the club kept its title hopes alive with a surprisingly easy 28–7 win over Dallas, their third win over the talented Texans in as many tries. Bookman and Felt again played key roles, the former intercepting a pass and the latter recovering a fumble. The defense held dangerous Abner Haynes to 45 yards rushing, although he did catch six passes for 127 yards. Dick Christy was New York's main offensive weapon, catching six passes for 145 yards before leaving with a minor leg injury. Dorow threw for 272 yards and Mathis ran for 79 on only 10 carries. It was a rough game, as Haynes claimed that the Titans' defenders mauled him, and E.J. Holub of the Texans said that New York guard John McMullan spit in his face.

Unfortunately for the Titans, the Oilers kept winning. Their streak reached seven with a 33–13 win that dealt San Diego its first loss of the season after 11 wins. Boston was also hot, and the Titans remained in third place. In the West, the Chargers had it all their own way. Dallas had been a tremendous disappointment, having won only a third of their games despite Lamar Hunt's willingness to invest in talent. "I'm not sure what happened to us that year," said Cotton Davidson. "That year is a mystery. We had basically the same people as the year before with an extra year of maturity. That was the year we were expecting big things to happen. I really thought that would be the year we'd put it all together."

Denver and Oakland were patsies. The former had been outscored 383–230 and the latter 376–200. The dominance of the Chargers was disquieting, reminding many of the old AAFC, whose downfall had been hastened by its unbalanced nature. The Cleveland Browns ran roughshod over their opposition, winning all four championships and losing only four games, which diminished fan interest in the other, non-competitive teams. The Chargers' easy success gave rise to the fear that they, like the Browns, would destroy the competitive balance of the league. The standings of December 4 provided ample reason for concern:

EASTERN DIVISION		**WESTERN DIVISION**	
Houston	8-3-1	San Diego	11–1
Boston	7–4–1	Dallas	4–8
New York	7–5	Denver	3–10
Buffalo	6–7	Oakland	2–10

New York had a last chance to salvage its hopes for a division title when they faced the Oilers at the Polo Grounds on December 10. Having been burned by Blanda's seven touchdown passes just three weeks earlier, the Titans concentrated on stopping Houston's aerial game. All week long, Baugh worked with the Titans' defensive backs. Still, he had his doubts that they could win. "We'd have to play awfully, awfully damn good," he said the week before the game, "and they'd have to have troubles."

Despite the extra attention, the Titans did not stop Blanda, who passed for 287 yards and three touchdowns. They had even less success with Billy Cannon, who set an AFL record by rushing for 216 yards, easily breaking Haynes' old mark of 158. He also caught five of Blanda's passes for 114 more, accounting for 330 yards. Cannon scored five touchdowns, four rushing and one receiving. "It seemed like they were reading our defense," said Dick Guesman. "Every time we were there, Cannon went in the opposite direction." Blanda credited the Oilers' success to the fact that Houston deployed the offense in a spread formation. This caused the New York linebackers to spread wide to cover the receivers, leaving the middle open for Cannon. Baugh concurred, and added, "They just blocked the hell out of us. And our tackling stunk."

The pattern of the game was set on Houston's first play from scrimmage, when Blanda hit Cannon with a 67-yard scoring toss. The Titans countered quickly on a 21-yard scoring run by West, but after that it was all Oilers. They scored the first four times they had the ball and finished strong, with 21 points in the final quarter. The only satisfaction the Titans managed was the retaliation exacted by Youngelman and Saidock, both of whom had been ejected from the last Houston game and were enraged by what they considered the dirty play of Oilers offensive tackle Al Jamison. After the second game, Jamison sat in the locker room, blood pouring from his nose, and claimed that, on an extra point attempt, Youngelman had kicked him in the groin. "Then Saidock walked over and punched me in the nose," he added. In the New York locker room, neither Saidock nor Youngelman had any comment. The final score was 48–21, a defeat that eliminated the Titans from contention.

The only person able to thwart Cannon was a friend of Thurlow Cooper's from Augusta, Maine. The weather that day had been rainy and the field was sloppy. Although the conditions had not slowed Cannon a bit, the fog that accompanied the rain prevented the Oilers' plane from taking off. They were stranded in New York for the night. As chance would have it, Cooper and his roommates had planned a big party, and about half the Oilers attended. "Our best friends in the league were the Houston Oilers," Cooper said. "They were our buddies." Given the success the Oilers experienced against the Titans, their affection was understandable. After everyone had several drinks, Cooper's friend made off with Cannon's 10-gallon hat, part of the Houston club's traveling attire. "Billy was real nice about it," Cooper remembered. "My friend sent him a check for the cost of the hat."

Eliminated from contention, the Titans played poorly in their final game, which nearly did not take place. Scheduled to play in Dallas on Sunday, the Titans flew to Texas on Saturday night, but were unable to land due to a severe blanket of fog covering Dallas's Love Field. The Braniff Airlines jet was forced to turn around and return to New York. (The Titans had run a contest for their fans, with the winner entitled to fly to the Dallas game. The "lucky" fan spent more time on Braniff than anticipated.)

The club planned to try again Sunday morning, on a flight that was scheduled to land at 10:20 a.m., just four hours before the scheduled kickoff. Lamar Hunt stated that if there were further delays, the kickoff would be moved back one hour, rather than postpone the game until Monday. The Titans were not able to land until shortly before noon, and ran onto the field just before the game was scheduled to begin. One of the Dallas players asked Baugh about his team. "If we've got enough bennies to get us through this game," he replied, "we might win." The Titans' fatigue was apparent in their performance, as they fell behind 28–0. The club was suffering from a number of injuries, and Christy, Youngelman, Hudock, and Hynes were all below par. Play was sloppy, with a number of fights and personal foul penalties. After closing the gap, the Titans lost 35–24, giving them a 7–7 record for the second year in a row.

The battle between Wismer and Baugh had escalated and a new one had started between Wismer and Joe Foss. These incidents so dominated the news that *The New York Times* reported, "During a lull in the running battle between Coach Sammy Baugh and Harry Wismer, president of the Titans, news leaked out about the football team itself."

Early in the season, the coach and owner were communicating only through intermediaries. Finally, Baugh requested a meeting, and the two men went to the Essex House on September 26. Afterwards, both claimed that all was well and agreed to meet weekly thereafter. The relationship remained rocky all season, however, and by December Baugh was in limbo. Many were suspicious that Dorow, who was close to Wismer, and another player had gone to the owner and told him that Baugh was a poor coach and should be replaced. Dorow went to Baugh and denied it, but many of the players remained unconvinced.

Wismer urged Baugh to resign. "He's rapping me publicly all the time," the owner said. "He tells me he's unhappy about some of the things I've been doing. Well, if anybody is unhappy with his job, there's a simple way of taking care of that—quit." Baugh said he wouldn't quit, but hoped to be fired so that he could collect his salary for the final year of his contract. Said Wismer, "I'm paying him $28,000 [sic] to be disloyal. That's a fine situation, isn't it?"

"I've been loyal," Baugh responded. "I just don't like being treated like a dog by a man you can't trust around the corner. I wanted to trust this man. I just wanted him to be the kind of boss who acted in such a way that when someone said something about him I could stand up for him and back him all the way. Some owners don't talk and do help their team. Other owners talk all the time and don't do a bit of good. A month ago he promised to stop all this talk. Then he started again. Wismer doesn't actually know what goes on. He doesn't even watch us work out."

"I'm going to demote that man to assistant backfield coach," Wismer replied.

"I'd rather be a ticket taker," Baugh said. "It's a job that wouldn't keep me very busy."

And so the 1961 season came to an end, a second year of financial failure, a second year of abysmal attendance, and the coach and owner at each other's throats. Wismer was putting up a brave front, again challenging the Giants to a game for the city championship, with all the proceeds going to the United Catholic, Jewish, and Protestant charities. "I'm sorry the Giants lost so drastically to Green Bay (37–0) in their National Football League playoff game," Wismer said. "Coach Bulldog Turner thinks we can beat the Giants, too," he added.

There had been a number of noteworthy individual performances. Bill Mathis gained 846 yards on the ground, and led the league with 202 carries. Dick Christy led the AFL in punt returns with a 21.3-yard average. The pass defense, which Baugh and Sebo had valiantly attempted to improve, ranked fifth among the eight AFL teams, yielding 200 yards per game, compared to 209 in 1960. Mathis, Grantham, and Mischak made the UPI All-Star team, and all three, plus Dorow and Felt, played in the AFL's first All-Star Game. Dorow led a touchdown drive in a losing cause and, due to injuries, played some flanker. The five Titans each got a loser's share of $500.

Houston's Wally Lemm, who turned the Oilers' season around, was named coach of the year and Earl Faison of the Chargers was selected as the league's outstanding rookie. Cannon gained 145 yards rushing in Houston's final game to set a league record with 948 yards. Blanda threw for 3,330 yards and 36 touchdowns, and was named *Sporting News* and United Press Player of the Year. Jacky Lee passed for an additional 1,205 yards and 12 touchdowns, and the Oilers became the first professional football team to gain more than 6,000 yards. They captured their second consecutive AFL title with a 10–3 victory over the Chargers, a sloppy game marred by 10 interceptions and an unfortunate post-game incident. Chargers coach Sid Gillman, enraged by the calls of field judge John Morrow, went after Morrow following the final gun. "It was the worst officiating I've ever seen," said Gillman, "at least this season." Morrow allegedly grabbed Gillman's lapels, prompting San Diego safety Bob Zeman to plow into Morrow. "He was roughing up coach Gillman," Zeman said. "I just ran out to say good-bye," said Gillman. Following the Oilers' victory, Lemm resigned to take the head job with the St. Louis Cardinals and Blanda threatened to retire.

CHAPTER 16
HARRY, ERNIE, JOE, AND THE BULLDOG

By the end of the 1961 season, the management of the Titans was in a shambles. At Thanksgiving, Foss had visited New York to talk with Wismer, following which he publicly called for his removal. "It would be better for New York if the Titans got a new owner," he said, "Wismer gets only the worst kind of publicity. He feels any publicity is good publicity. He's unreasonable, he'll say anything, and he'll stick anyone in the mud. He thinks this kind of publicity will sell tickets. Well, look at this crowd."

During the Mayor's Trophy game with the Bills, Foss sat in the press box while Wismer roamed the sidelines. During the second half, the following announcement was made over the press box public address system: "Attention press: Harry Wismer, president of the Titans, will be available in his office for any reporters interested in contacting him." Wismer used the postgame interviews to heap abuse on Foss.

Foss's statement was the culmination of a long-standing feud, as there was bad blood between him and Wismer dating back to January 1960, when Foss agreed to refund H.P. Skogland's $25,000 good-faith deposit when he withdrew his Minneapolis franchise from the AFL. Wismer hinted that Foss's generosity was motivated by the fact that Skogland had been instrumental in bringing about Foss's appointment as commissioner.

Foss hadn't met Wismer prior to accepting the commissioner's post. "If I had," he said, "I'd never have taken the job."

"I think the major problem between us," Foss wrote in his autobiography, "was that Wismer always tried to crawl under the fence in any situation, while I insisted on enforcing the rules. . .Wismer could be a nice guy when he behaved himself, but he swigged too much, and you get goofy when you do that. . .You can't ride along down the trail with a burr like this under the saddle."

Following the commissioner's call for his removal, the burr replied that since Foss still owned stock in Skogland's Raven Industries, perhaps he was working for the benefit of the NFL and Skogland's Minnesota franchise. He claimed that Foss was doing such a good job for the other league that he should apply for a position as Pete Rozelle's assistant. Wismer said Foss had been his third choice as commissioner, and he had cast the only negative vote against him; he then called for Foss's ouster. "Who is this politician from Sioux Falls, South Dakota," Wismer said, "to think he can get out somebody who brought football back to New York after the Dodgers and Giants took baseball teams out of town? I want a new commissioner and I believe I have enough support." Wismer vowed to fight any attempt to force him to sell his Titans stock and said he would take Foss to court if necessary. All in all, his response confirmed Foss's criticisms.

"The time has come," Foss replied, "to decide whether Wismer's running the league or whether I'm the commissioner. It is pretty obvious this fellow is out to get my pelt. I have to do something or resign and I don't intend to resign." He said that Wismer could be removed by the affirmative vote of six owners, and, if necessary, he would take that route.

The late-season blowup between Wismer and Foss had been precipitated by the 1961 AFL draft, which proved a tremendous embarrassment to the league. The competition for top college players had escalated, and the NFL realized that the new league, entering its third year, was not about to fold quickly. In order to protect their athletes from overzealous general managers, the universities obtained an agreement that neither league would hold its draft prior to December 2, still a full month before the bowl games.

On November 19, *The Dallas Morning News* revealed that the AFL had already conducted a secret telephone draft of college seniors. Two days later, Pete Rozelle unleashed a blast of righteous indignation. He declared that the AFL "has brought discredit upon professional football as a whole in the eyes of the colleges and the public. The National Football League joins college leaders, who are shocked by the AFL sneak draft." Rozelle hinted that the AFL's action was precipitated by desperation, and speculated that they might soon begin drafting sophomores and juniors.

The concept of a clandestine draft was not unique. In July 1948, the AAFC held a secret, two-round draft, well before the college season had even *begun*, let alone ended. Fortunately for Rozelle, no one pointed out that just two years earlier, in 1959, the NFL had conducted a similar selection process. The timing was intended to give NFL teams a jump on their AFL and CFL counterparts and the secrecy was to prevent the AFL, which had no scouting system in place, from utilizing the NFL selections to judge talent.

Foss, greatly embarrassed, claimed not to have known of the entire AFL proceeding, which he said was organized and conducted by the owners without the participation of the league office. This statement is interesting in light of his later pronouncement that he, not Wismer, was running the league. The New York owner didn't miss the contradiction. "If he didn't know about it," Wismer said, "then he is a very poor commissioner. I told Milt [Woodward, the assistant commissioner] we were very happy about our draft selections, and he told me not to say it too loud because Foss doesn't want people to know what we're doing."

Foss, in a no-win position, said that the draft was not really a draft. He said the owners, "conducted a poll among themselves with respect to a limited number of players with whom they would have exclusive intraleague negotiating rights." That certainly sounded like a draft. Foss claimed, however, that these preliminary selections might be altered at the official draft, scheduled for December 2. He emphasized that eligibility would not be impaired by an early signing and promised to conduct a thorough investigation. "I was madder than hops," Foss wrote. "To think that grown men would pull something like this!"

Foss vowed to take the high road and attempted to minimize the damage, pledging not to recognize any contract signed prior to the official draft. The commissioner's pious stance was compromised, however, by his narrow definition of a contract. Foss said he would recognize conditional contracts signed before the draft, but contingent upon the player being selected in the "official" draft by the team that had signed him. Rozelle immediately pointed out the semantic differentiation, and vowed that he would recognize no NFL contract, conditional or unconditional, that was signed prior to the NFL draft.

Although the selections were ostensibly secret, Wismer wasted no time in revealing the Titans' choices. His first pick was halfback Ernie Davis, who wore Jim Brown's number 44 at Syracuse and had broken most of Brown's rushing records. He would soon become the first black player to win the Heisman Trophy, and was the star Wismer felt his team desperately needed to compete with the Giants and draw spectators to the Polo Grounds. He would stop at nothing to sign Davis.

On November 22, Foss announced that the results of his investigation convinced him that the selection process did indeed constitute a draft, and that he had voided the entire action. He also admitted that end Jim Cadile of San Jose State, one of the Chargers' selections, had already signed. Foss's action now put Cadile's status in limbo.

Wismer responded immediately to Foss's voiding of the selections. He charged that Houston owner Bud Adams had organized the draft, but that Foss had known all along what was happening. The commissioner had disavowed knowledge only when the proceedings became public. Wismer vowed to ignore Foss's ruling and negotiate with the six players on the Titans' draft list, including Davis.

Ralph Wilson, owner of the Bills, admitted that he, Hunt, and Adams had planned the draft without Foss's knowledge. He said there was nothing illegal about the process, since no player's eligibility had been impaired. Wilson expressed disappointment that Foss had voided the selections, and outrage that Wismer had called the commissioner a liar for denying knowledge of the draft.

Foss and Wismer prepared for a battle. The other owners, whose support was needed by each of the warring parties, expressed the hope that the dispute could be settled amicably. If it came to a showdown, however, most, including Lamar Hunt, indicated they would back the commissioner.

The official draft was held as scheduled on December 2. The Titans, selecting in the fifth position, still hoped to secure the rights to Davis, and Wismer said he was prepared to offer the Syracuse halfback $100,000 for three years plus a $15,000 bonus. "If anybody wants to top that," he added, "I'll top what they want to offer."

Oakland, with the worst record in the league, had the first choice and selected quarterback Roman Gabriel of North Carolina State. Denver, next in line, picked tackle Merlin Olsen of Utah State. Dallas selected halfback Ronnie Bull of Baylor, leaving only the Buffalo Bills between Wismer and Davis. Ralph Wilson thwarted Wismer's ambitions by selecting Davis with the fourth pick. The other teams then waited for 45 minutes while Sebo tried to contact Wismer for instructions. Finally, Wismer gave Sebo permission to draft quarterback Sandy Stephens of Minnesota.

It would have been out of character for Wismer to concede gracefully. He said he had spoken with Davis and that the youngster wanted to sign with the Titans. Wismer pledged to make a deal with Buffalo to acquire his draft rights.

On December 4, the Washington Redskins selected Davis with the first pick in the NFL draft. The *Washington Post* reported that owner George Marshall enlisted the aid of New York congressman Adam Clayton Powell, one of the country's most influential blacks, in his efforts to sign the Syracuse halfback. Davis, an economics major, said he was just looking for the best deal, including an offseason job to prepare him for a career after football. He had no particular preference for any team, and indicated that Marshall's well-known racial attitudes would not prevent him from signing with the Redskins. Davis also said he did not intend to make any decisions until after the first of the year.

Davis was not only an outstanding athlete, he was an admirable human being. "Ernie would have been somebody even if he wasn't good at sports," said Marty Horrigan, Davis's high school coach and surrogate father. "He'd have been a leader." Davis was very religious and a good student, earning his undergraduate degree in four years. He was modest and highly respected by his classmates, teachers, and teammates.

During the next few weeks, Wismer continued to speak bravely of striking a deal with Buffalo and signing Davis. It all proved for naught, however, as, prior to the draft, Washington had agreed to trade the rights to the Heisman winner to the Cleveland Browns for halfback Bobby Mitchell and the Browns' first draft choice, Leroy Jackson of Western

Illinois. The Browns quickly signed Davis to a three-year contract valued at $65,000 plus a $15,000 bonus, substantially less than Wismer's hypothetical offer. There would be no Heisman Trophy winner in the Polo Grounds in 1962.

Sadly, Davis, the object of such a bitter struggle, never played a game for the Browns, or any other pro team. On June 29, 1962, he took part in the Coaches All-America Game in Buffalo, but was sluggish and did not play well. He thought the extreme heat had affected him. Prior to the game, however, Ernie's gums had been bleeding and sores had formed in his mouth. In early July, he went to his hometown of Elmira to see Horrigan. Mrs. Horrigan became worried when Davis refused all offers of food and drink, for he generally consumed vast quantities of food and soda whenever he visited the Horrigans.

The Browns' physician diagnosed Davis's ailment as trench mouth and removed two wisdom teeth. Ernie then went to Evanston, Illinois, to begin practice for the College All-Star Game against the Green Bay Packers. He was the leading rusher in a scrimmage against the Bears, but two days later, on July 31, awoke with a swollen neck and was hospitalized with what was believed to be a case of mononucleosis. The following day, tests revealed that the young athlete was suffering from acute monocytic leukemia. Davis was not told of the seriousness of his condition, but immediately began treatment. He responded favorably to the drug 6-MP, and by early October the disease was in complete remission. At that time, Davis was told he had leukemia. His only response was, "Darn."

Davis was given clearance to begin practicing with the Browns, and said he felt as good as ever. He often sat on the bench during games, but was never placed on the active roster. After the season, he played on a basketball team with a number of Cleveland players, and worked as a salesman for Pepsi Cola. In early March, however, the disease became active again, and in mid-May, Davis informed Browns owner Art Modell that he had to re-enter the hospital. He apologized for all of the expenses he had caused the Browns to incur. Davis entered Cleveland's Lakeside Hospital on May 16, went into a coma the next day, and died on May 18 at the age of 23. Davis's funeral was held in Elmira; 1,600 people attended, while 3,000 more waited outside. He was buried in Woodlawn Cemetary, also the resting place of Mark Twain.

Meanwhile, back in New York, the Wismer–Foss battle had long since cooled off. After the New York–Dallas game on December 3, Wismer said, "We think the commissioner is doing a great job." In early January 1962, however, Wismer insisted that Foss move the league office from Dallas to New York, where the AFL could get greater exposure. Foss said he would quit rather than move his family. Later that month, at the annual league meeting, the AFL owners showed their support of the commissioner by giving him a new five-year contract and an increase in pay. Wismer voted in favor of the extension, and was uncharacteristically quiet throughout the session. He even asked Foss to serve as best man at his upcoming July wedding.

The battle with Baugh was resolved in Wismer-like fashion. Baugh reiterated his desire to be fired, but vowed that he would not quit and give up the final year of his contract. He continued his criticism of Wismer's lack of success in signing top players. "There's no way you can win," Baugh said, "by using people who aren't good enough to make the teams you're trying to beat." In 1961 the Titans had signed only three of 27 draft picks, the top signee being 18th-round choice Bobby Brooks, who played sparingly. When asked about the chances of signing Davis, Baugh said, "I've heard so much about Davis I'd like to spit. Why doesn't [Wismer] go get some of the guys he's drafted instead of getting some guy we ain't never going to get. I'll make you a bet now he doesn't sign five percent of the players drafted. He puts out publicity about the big money he's going to pay them and while we're fooling around with the big names, the NFL is picking off the other top players which we would have a chance of signing. Big names are not always the best football players." When asked about the attempt to force Wismer out of the league, Baugh retorted, "I wish I had a vote."

If Baugh did, as he claimed, want to be fired, he was doing a very good job of it. Continued public criticism of the owner was a brand of publicity that even Wismer did not find appealing. If Baugh kept up his attacks, Wismer would have no choice but to fire him. That would have been the logical step, but Wismer was not a logical man. On December 17, nearly two years to the day he had named Baugh coach, Wismer announced that he had signed Clyde "Bulldog" Turner to a two-year contract at $20,000 per year as head coach. Baugh would remain with the club as a consultant. To rub salt in Baugh's wounds, Wismer declared that, in 1960, Turner had been his first choice for head coach. Otto Graham, Wismer said, had been second, Frank Leahy third, and Baugh fourth.

Turner was 42, five years younger than Baugh, and also had a Hardin-Simmons connection, having played there from 1936 to 1939. In 1940 the center-linebacker was the first draft choice of the Chicago Bears. For the next 13 years, he was a star for the Bears, winning all-pro honors six times, and was eventually elected to the Hall of Fame. In his rookie year, Chicago defeated the Washington Redskins, quarterbacked by Baugh, 73–0 for the NFL championship. Turner scored one of the Bears' many touchdowns on a 24-yard interception return. Known principally for his toughness, he was agile enough to lead the NFL with eight interceptions in 1942.

After his retirement as an active player, Turner served as an assistant coach for the Bears from 1953 through 1958. He had been out of football for three years and had ballooned to 280 pounds, 43 above his playing weight. Like Baugh, he was a rancher, having earned enough money trading cattle as a teenager to finance his education at Hardin-Simmons. Following his retirement from football, Turner worked a 1,200-acre ranch in Gatesville. Also, like Baugh, he was greatly lacking in organizational ability.

Despite their similarities, Turner was unlike his predecessor in two important respects. First, he had no previous experience as a head coach. Second, he lacked Baugh's personal charm, humor, and skill in relating to the players. Turner had a personality one would expect of a man nicknamed "Bulldog": a gruff, hard-nosed temperament, with little concern for pomp and circumstance. Karl Kaimer remembered meeting him for the first time. "I liked Bulldog," he said. "He was kind of a tough old guy. When I met him, I said, 'Hello, Coach Turner, it's nice to meet you.' He said, 'Just call me Dawg.'"

In terms of personality, Turner could be compared to Buddy Ryan, former coach of the Philadelphia Eagles and Arizona Cardinals. Turner, however, lacked Ryan's strategic genius. He had been a reasonably intelligent player, but his main attribute on the field had been great physical strength and an aggressive nature. "I don't think he made the transition from playing to coaching," said Kaimer. "He'd rather get out there and whup on somebody."

Ted Daffer, who played for the Bears when Turner served as line coach, agreed. "He was a hard charger. Bulldog's whole life had involved contact," he said. "Even when he was coaching, he'd haul off and knock the hell out of you. He'd get frustrated, and would have to get rid of it that way."

Turner was a heavy smoker and drinker. While Baugh had carried a soda bottle with him at all times to use as a spittoon, Bulldog carried a six-pack. Like Wismer, Turner drank every day and was often unpredictable.

Turner was not a great coach. Many of the players thought he knew very little about strategy, and showed him little respect. "He had no class and no ability to communicate with the players," said one Titans player. Others were more kindly in their assessment. "Bulldog was a nice guy," said Roger Ellis. "We all kind of felt sorry for him because Bulldog was in over his head."

"Bulldog was real old school," said another former Titans player. "He knew the game but couldn't explain it. Bulldog tried to force regimentation on the players, but he didn't have a lot of self-discipline in his own life."

At training camp in Stroudsburg, Turner attempted to instill the discipline that had been absent under Baugh. He initiated a number of rules, which the players almost uniformly ignored. Larry Grantham reported late, having just been discharged from the service. "Bulldog said," Grantham remembered, "'You've only been here a week and you've already violated every one of my damn rules.'"

Turner was operating under very adverse circumstances. First, the Titans job was his initial opportunity as a head coach. Further, he was succeeding a man who was probably one of the most popular coaches of all time. The players had tremendous loyalty to Baugh and felt Wismer had treated him shabbily. In particular, there was a Texas contingent that had been brought to New York by Baugh and who, to a man, considered him a personal friend and hero. Whoever succeeded Baugh would have a difficult time being accepted by the holdovers and Turner, although decent, honest and a hard worker, was no charmer. "When I got there," recalled Lee Grosscup, "Bulldog had just replaced Sammy Baugh. Sammy was a legend and all the players loved him. I think Bulldog had a bit of a complex about that and felt uncomfortable."

Bulldog knew that, for the most part, he didn't have the players' respect and, one night, after a few beers, shouted out pathetically to a number of them, "You liked Sammy better than you like me." He was right. They did, there was nothing he could do about it, and all of his efforts to win them over backfired.

"I remember when we were at Stroudsburg," said one veteran. "Bulldog had gotten pretty well looped and called a bunch of us in and said, 'Let's cut some goddamn rookies!'" He asked the veterans which of the first-year men he should let go.

"Coaches don't do that," said a second player who was present.

"I thought, 'Jesus, what a way to run an organization!'" added a third.

Two of Baugh's assistants, Bones Taylor and John Dell Isola, remained on Turner's staff. The third aide provided an even more perplexing situation for the new coach. George Sauer, former Packers player and head coach at Kansas, Navy, and Baylor, was signed as an assistant in early January. He, like Turner, had been out of football for the past three years, operating an insurance agency in Waco, Texas. Sauer had an excellent football mind, was probably the most knowledgeable of the New York assistants, and, given Turner's limited coaching experience, would seem to have been an excellent person to have on the sidelines. The situation was complicated, however, for during the offseason the Titans' front office had come tumbling down along with the coaching staff. Sebo resigned after two chaotic seasons to become athletic director at the University of Virginia. Bill Tackmann, hired with such fanfare a year earlier, left two weeks after Sebo. His efforts had resulted in only 3,000 season-ticket sales in 1961, and Tackmann had found it difficult to work for Wismer, as had all of the others. Sauer was named general manager, and was now Turner's assistant as well as his boss.

A further complication was the continuing presence of Wismer, who had proven incapable of working with Baugh, and would have been incompatible with most coaches. Surveying the Titans' lack of talent prior to the 1962 season, Dick Clemente wrote in *Newsday*, "The impression is that Bulldog will make a rebuilding season out of this one. That means plenty of losses along the way. Harry doesn't like to lose."

"I think I'm going into this thing with my eyes open," Turner said at his signing. "I've known Harry although I've never been related to him in a business way. There may be some things I don't know." Were there ever! The combination of Turner's lack of experience; the popularity of Baugh, who was still on his staff; the presence of Taylor, one of Baugh's cronies, as an assistant; the dual role of Sauer; the financial difficulties of Wismer; and the owner's volatile nature was a formula for disaster. Alex Kroll said of Turner, "He was in a very difficult situation with so few financial resources and difficult management. He was caught between management, which wasn't paying anybody, and a team that was increasingly restive. Bulldog was seriously under-supported. I liked him. He was a decent enough fellow. I don't know how good a coach he would have been under normal circumstances." Even Vince Lombardi would have had difficulty succeeding in Turner's situation, and Turner was certainly no Lombardi.

It was customary to permit a new head coach to bring in his own people. The only crony Turner brought along was trainer Buddy Leininger, who provided him with a drinking companion and confidante, a friend in hostile territory. Leininger was short, with a protruding beer belly, physically almost Turner in miniature. The players sarcastically referred to them as "Bulldog" and "Puppy Dog."

Unfortunately, Leininger had virtually no skill as a trainer. His predecessor in the Titans' first two years had been Jackie Copeland. Copeland, yet another Hardin-Simmons grad, had prior experience at his alma mater, at Ohio State, and also in minor league baseball. He was youthful (25), enthusiastic, competent, and liked by the players. Leininger, on the other hand, was seen as Bulldog's informer and a threat to the players' well-being. His taping was dangerous, tight enough to cut off circulation. "It's a good thing you don't have to breathe through your leg," observed Art Powell to Lee Grosscup after examining the tape job Leininger had done on the quarterback. Most of the Titans were so leery of approaching Leininger when he had a roll of tape in his hands that they enlisted Thurlow Cooper to act as unofficial assistant trainer. Cooper had been a physical education major at Maine and taken a course in training technique. If the team played on Sunday, Leininger would give Cooper a basket filled with tape and gauze when he left practice on Friday. Cooper then taped many of the players in his room.

Turner had his work cut out when he arrived in Stroudsburg. He had spent much of the winter and spring studying films and vowed to take a more structured approach than Baugh. Starting February 1, Turner and his assistants were reported to be at the Polo Grounds from 8:30 until 6:00 every day. Having learned his lesson, Wismer drafted a contract for Turner that required him to spend at least 10 months per year in New York and to participate in public relations events during the offseason.

Turner arrived in Stroudsburg ready to translate his offseason film study into victories. Baugh showed up to collect his pay for the final season of his contract. Dorow appeared expecting to start his third year as the Titans' regular quarterback. Baugh was the only one who would fulfill his ambition.

CHAPTER 17

THE QUARTERBACKS

When the Titans assembled in Stroudsburg, they had an old quarterback, Sammy Baugh, an incumbent quarterback, Al Dorow, and a new quarterback, Butch Songin. In terms of football age, however, the Titans had three old quarterbacks. Dorow was 30, or so he said. That age was based upon the premise that he had been but 16 when a freshman at Michigan State. He may therefore have been as old as 33. In addition, his hell-bent-for-leather style of play had caused his body to take a beating, and the iron-man performances of the past two years had taken their toll. Early in his career, Dorow had a strong arm, but, after eight professional seasons, he relied increasingly on accuracy and timing to compensate for a lack of zip on his passes. It took him an inordinately long time to loosen up before a game, and it is almost certain that his arm was hurting more than he let on. His performance in 1961 was erratic, as he threw 30 interceptions, most in the league.

To back up Dorow, Wismer acquired Songin from the Boston Patriots. Songin did not come cheaply, as the Titans had to part with all-star defensive back Dick Felt. At the time of the trade, Wismer said that the new quarterback would get a significant amount of playing time and made a hopeful comparison between the 38-year-old Songin and Y.A. Tittle, whom the Giants had acquired the previous year to share time with Charlie Conerly. Turner indicated that he planned to alternate Songin and Dorow.

Songin was no Tittle, but he was a remarkable athlete in his own right. He played quarterback at Boston College with future all-pro linemen Artie Donovan and Ernie Stautner, and was also an All-American hockey player who showed enough ability to draw the interest of the NHL. "He was a great hockey player at BC," recalled Mike Holovak. "They never took him out of the game, which was very rare in hockey. Butch went in and just stayed there. He played the whole game." Songin continued to play competitive hockey, and, at the time he was acquired by the Titans, was trying out for the US team that was to compete for the world amateur championship in Colorado Springs.

Upon graduating from college in 1949, however, Songin opted for a career in football, intending to join the New York Yankees of the All-America Football Conference. He planned to sign with the Yankees on the Thursday following his final game at Boston College. For some reason, however, he decided to wait a week, a fateful delay, as it turned out. On December 10, the AAFC announced that it was merging with the National Football League and the Yankees ceased to exist.

Weeb Ewbank, then a Cleveland assistant coach, signed Songin to a contract with the Browns, one of the three AAFC teams that had been assimilated into the NFL. Otto Graham was the Browns' starter, and Paul Brown told Songin he did not intend to keep a second quarterback. He had two defensive backs capable of stepping in in an emergency. Songin spent four weeks in the Browns' camp and acquired a wealth of knowledge in addition to his eventual release. "Paul Brown was head and shoulders above anyone else I'd ever known as a coach," he said later. "For my money, no one can measure up to him."

Following his release, Songin became a football gypsy. He had trials with the Eagles and Colts, then had a few good years in Canada. In 1953 he led Hamilton to the Grey Cup final. Returning home, however, he found that Hamilton wanted to cut his salary for the 1954 season. Songin balked, and wound up with his unconditional release and a reputation as a troublemaker. "I found out later," he said, "that Carl Voyles, the coach and general manager at Hamilton, had put the knock on me, telling people that I wanted to hold him up for big money. If there was such a thing as blacklisting, I was blacklisted."

Songin was outspoken and opinionated. "Butch was a little cocky at times," said Roger Ellis, a close friend for the last 20 years of Songin's life. "He rubbed some people the wrong way. He would just say what was on his mind. He meant well, but sometimes Butch would say things when he probably should have kept his mouth shut."

For the next six years, Songin played semi-pro ball all over New England, sometimes with as many as three teams at the same time. His first venture into the semi-pro ranks was as player-coach of the Canton, Massachusetts, town team for $15 a game. He was the highest-paid, in fact the only paid, player on the Canton team. On Wednesday nights, he made $50 throwing passes for the North Attleboro Jewelers. Playing with so many pickup teams, Songin had little opportunity to employ the organizational skills he learned from Paul Brown. "We'd use a pro-type offense, and I'd put in some passes, draws, traps, and screens. We never practiced. I'd just tell them what to do in the huddle and that was that."

When the AFL was organized in 1960, Songin, 36, saw an opportunity to end his semi-pro wanderings. Mike Holovak approached him about a tryout with the Patriots. Songin agreed, filling out a questionnaire in which he stated that he was 34 years old. "I guess I lost a couple of years in Canada," he joked later.

In preparation for what he knew was his last chance, Songin worked out every day with Ellis, who was preparing to go to camp with the Titans. By the time he reported to the Boston camp, Songin was in the best shape of his life. Not wanting to show his age, he discarded the back and knee braces he normally wore and plunged into the routine of two-a-day drills.

One by one, the younger quarterback aspirants, nearly a dozen in total, fell by the wayside. "The training camp looked like Dunkirk," Songin said later. "People were coming and going every day. I think there were more than three hundred players who went through that first camp."

No one questioned Butch's head, or his heart, but many had doubts about the strength of his arm. Songin claimed that he threw short passes because they were more effective. "When I got to that first Patriots training camp," he said, "we had a bunch of green defensive backs, so I threw quick-outs all day long. I never missed and everyone was impressed. I knew the backs were scared of being beaten deep, so I kept throwing in front of them." Could he have thrown deep if he wanted to? At age 36, it was unlikely.

Songin had a good exhibition season, throwing the first touchdown pass in AFL history on July 30 against Buffalo. When the Patriots took the field against Denver in the AFL's first game, their top two playcallers were Tommy Greene of Holy Cross and Songin, getting his first major league chance 11 years after the end of his college career. Although Greene received most of the early playing time, Songin soon took over regular duties when Greene was hobbled by a lingering ankle injury. His head and what was left of his arm were enough to place him fourth among AFL passers in 1960, with nearly 2,500 yards and 22 touchdowns. During the offseason, Boston traded for Babe Parilli, and Saban announced that the veteran from Kentucky would be the No. 1 signal caller. Parilli was a good runner, much quicker than the immobile Songin, and Saban wanted a quarterback who could roll out and put pressure on the defense. Gino Cappelletti said, "Songin was your pro set, drop back, sit in the pocket type of quarterback. He'd throw the ball with a nice, soft touch. He had very, very little mobility. Babe, on the other hand, had the bouncy feet. He would get out of the pocket. He could run a little and he threw the ball with just a little more zip on it."

In training camp, Songin was in danger of losing his spot on the roster. In addition to Parilli, the Patriots brought in former Michigan State player Tom Yewcic and highly touted rookie Paul Terhes, a Little All-American from Bucknell. Songin survived, as he again played well in exhibition games. Terhes left camp to pursue a teaching career, and Saban elected to keep three quarterbacks. When the season started, the coach announced that Parilli would be his No. 1 quarterback, but soon he began alternating Songin and Parilli. "When we are in a passing situation," he said, "I use Songin; when we want to run, it's Parilli."

When Saban was fired and replaced by Holovak, Songin and Parilli continued alternating, sometimes on every play. Under this disjointed arrangement, Songin passed for 1,400 yards and 14 touchdowns in only 212 attempts. After the season, the Patriots decided that their future rested with the 32-year-old Parilli and the 29-year-old Yewcic, and traded Songin to the Titans in January 1962.

The incumbent New York quarterback, Dorow, was disappointed by the change in coaches. Although he had not been particularly close to Baugh, and some suspected him of undermining the coach in the feud with Wismer, Dorow loved Baugh's wide-open offense. He was not the

least bit happy with Turner, who he thought would impose a more conservative scheme. "We had all this passing talent," he said, "but he was
going to run it down everybody's throat." Some of the players believed
that Dorow suggested odd plays to Turner just to test him and see if he
would accept them. Turner usually went along.

During his long football career, Turner had never been actively involved
in offensive strategy. His major innovation to the Titans' offense was to
reverse Baugh's numbering system. In football jargon, a number frequently
indicates the direction of a running play. For example, the hole between
the center and the left guard might be two, that between the left guard
and tackle four, and on down the line. The holes on the right side would
be indicated by odd numbers, one for the center–guard hole, three for
guard–tackle. The backs were also numbered. A play that called for the
halfback, or two-back, to run between the right guard and tackle would
therefore be called 23, plus a descriptive word, such as cross-buck. When
Turner became the Titans' head coach, he reversed the numbering system, putting the even- and odd-numbered holes on opposite sides from
those in Baugh's system. That was the extent of his changes.

For the first time, however, the Titans had playbooks. Unlike the
books used by most teams, loose-leaf notebooks filled with mimeographed
copies of pre-printed plays, the Titans' playbook was a small spiral note-
book filled with blank sheets. The players were to copy plays into their
books during sessions in which the coaches wrote them on a blackboard.
Drawing the plays sometimes caused Turner embarrassment. One classic moment occurred when Turner was sketching a pass play called 51
Banana, so named because the route run by the receiver was the approx-
imate shape of a banana. Turner drew the play, but had difficulty labeling
it. After several failed attempts, he turned in frustration to Bones Taylor
and said, "Bones, how the hell do you spell banana?"

Turner was forced to rely on Taylor for more than spelling, for the
head coach had little knowledge of offensive strategy. Karl Kaimer remembered breaking from the huddle in training camp to Turner's instructions,
"X fly, Z post, and Y just fuck around." Kaimer, the Y receiver, started
toward the line of scrimmage, and realized he hadn't the slightest idea
what he was supposed to do. "Coach," he said, "I'm not sure I know what
that fuck-around pattern is."

Kaimer liked Turner and found his foibles humorous, but some of the players were openly contemptuous. On a few occasions during the exhibition season, Dorow disregarded plays Turner sent into the game and called his own instead. Dorow's relationship with Wismer was not as close as it had been, and Wismer tried to stir up discord by stating that the other players were jealous of Dorow's salary. In early August, he told the press that Dorow "could be washed up. Sometimes last year he couldn't throw the ball fifteen yards."

In an exhibition game against the Bills in New Haven, Connecticut, New York quarterbacks threw five interceptions, putting Wismer in the mood to make a change. On August 16, four days after the game, Dorow was traded to Buffalo for safety and punter Billy Atkins and quarterback Johnny Green. Dorow, in the doghouse of both Wismer and Turner, was happy to depart and left Stroudsburg immediately. "I guess I wasn't Bulldog Turner's type of man," he said later.

"Al will be a lot better off in Buffalo," said one teammate. Another added, "I wish I was in Dorow's shoes." Atkins, a five-year pro who had previously played with the 49ers, led the AFL with 10 interceptions in 1961 and also paced the circuit in punting with a 45-yard average. Unfortunately, he arrived with a dislocated left shoulder. The Bills agreed to send another player if he was not ready for the season opener.

Green, a 25-year-old Tennessee native who played college football at Tennessee-Chattanooga, was Songin with a stronger arm. He rarely left the pocket, but could throw the long ball well. *Sports Illustrated*, in its 1961 season preview, gave the following scouting report on Green: "Although he throws the long pass well and accurately much of the time, he is erratic with shorter tosses and tends to overlook secondary receivers up close."

A member of the Steelers' taxi squad in 1959, Green had been with the Bills for two years. Buffalo had not truly had a regular quarterback, but, despite a separated shoulder in 1961, Green saw enough playing time during his Buffalo career to pass for a total of 2,170 yards and 16 touchdowns. He was elected a co-captain just a week before the trade, and scored the winning touchdown against the Titans in New Haven. A Titans spokesman said the new quarterback would get a shot at the starting position. His competition was Songin, Bob Scrabis, back for a third season, and Dean Look, acquired from Buffalo on July 31 in a trade that sent Sid Youngelman to the Bills. Like Dorow, Youngelman found himself in Wismer's doghouse, and was fortunate enough to get himself traded.

Look was an All-Big Ten selection at Michigan State in 1959, a roll-out, running quarterback, like Dorow, a Spartans player of an earlier vintage. After receiving a number of Heisman votes, Look was drafted by the Detroit Lions and Denver Broncos, but did not negotiate with either team. He had grown up near Lansing and, when he was in high school, often went to watch the Spartans' spring practice sessions. "They'd just hammer on each other for twenty days," he remembered. "I thought, at my size (5'11", 185 pounds) it didn't make sense for me to get beat on for twenty days." In order to avoid the punishment he associated with spring football, Look tried out for the Michigan State baseball team. He had not played baseball in high school, but talent ran in his family. His father had been a skilled local player and his younger brother Bruce was good enough to play with the Minnesota Twins in 1968.

Baseball proved much more than a way to avoid spring football practice. In his three years, Look hit .298, .343, and .357. After a strong sophomore season, major league scouts began to take notice. Chicago White Sox owner Bill Veeck was a friend of Michigan State football coach Duffy Daugherty, giving the Sox the inside track. At that time, baseball did not conduct a draft of amateur players; it was open season on all of them. When Look completed his football eligibility, he signed with the White Sox, who had just won their first pennant in 40 years, for a $50,000 bonus. There was no point in talking to pro football scouts, for football was not offering bonuses in that range. The Rams had offered Billy Cannon only a $10,000 signing bonus.

Look played in the Chicago farm system for two years, getting into three games with the parent club in 1961. At the end of that season, Veeck sold the club, and Look decided that his prospects in pro baseball were not very promising. He had no desire to be a career minor leaguer, and called Daugherty, who had another friend named Ralph Wilson. Wilson acquired Look's draft rights from Denver and signed him to a contract. In Buffalo's camp, he played mostly flanker, but also filled in at quarterback and defensive back.

After about two weeks in the Bills' camp, Look found himself headed for Stroudsburg, where Wismer was still collecting Michigan State alums. The shift from the Bills to the Titans proved a shock. From the intense, disciplined approach of Buffalo taskmaster Lou Saban, Look entered the disorganized, laid-back world of Bulldog Turner. "At the Titans' camp," Look said later, "I don't think anybody knew what anybody was doing. I don't know if anybody knew what the first team, the second team, or the scout team was."

All of the training camp battles were for naught, as the No. 1 Titans quarterback did not appear until the week before New York's opening game at Oakland. The acquisition of Lee Grosscup represented a potential coup for Wismer. The Giants had projected Grosscup as a star, although it was a prophecy that had not come to pass. Wismer was always looking to outshine his cross-river rivals, and felt that, if he could mine Grosscup's great potential, he would upstage the Maras in their own city.

The new quarterback was a complex individual who often felt out of place in the world of pro football. Sensitive, artistic, and prone to brooding, introspective moods, Grosscup had experienced some rough moments with the Giants and Allie Sherman. Grosscup wrote, "Sherman told me once I did not look or act like an athlete. I certainly was not an intellectual either." He was lost in no-man's land. Grosscup possessed Don Maynard's uniqueness, but not the latter's thick skin and self-assurance. Maynard didn't give a tinker's damn what anyone thought of him. Grosscup, on the other hand, was always questioning. Did he belong in football? Should he become a writer? What if...?

Although his hair was short and conservatively styled by today's standards, it was long enough to require the use of a comb, which set the boyish-looking Grosscup apart from most of his crew-cut brethren. He also had literary aspirations, which he made known to writer Murray Olderman during his college days. The result was a series of diary entries that appeared in *Sports Illustrated* in August 1959, under the title "Private Life of a Forward Passer." The article covered the period from January 1958 through June 1959, the end of his career at the University of Utah and the beginning of his career as the No. 1 draft choice of the Giants.

Grosscup's rookie year was an unpleasant experience. Sensitive men were not in vogue in pro football, and many of the Giants' veterans found the rookie's diary entries silly and full of girlish emotion. Among other observations was the author's declaration that he was determined to write a novel. "I feel I must," he wrote. "Something is alive inside me and I'm burning to release it."

"That really hurt me," Grosscup said recently of the article. "I wish it had never appeared. I had no idea of the impact it would have on me. There were some things in there that were extremely immature, extremely arrogant, and also extremely naive. They [the Giants' veterans] really resented it. I got started on the wrong foot because of that article."

Unfortunately, things got worse. Reporting late to the Giants' camp after playing in the College All-Star Game, Grosscup made the mistake of telling reporter Howard Tuckner that he felt lonely and isolated. When the veterans read the ensuing story, entitled "The Lonely Life of a Rookie Quarterback," they made him feel even more lonely and isolated. "The Giants were a veteran-oriented team," Grosscup said, "and they worried about rookies. They were very protective of their jobs and their teammates. Maybe I deserved it, but I was not treated well in my initial season."

Many Washington politicians saw Tuckner's article and sent letters of encouragement to the youngster, releasing copies of their correspondence for public consumption. Sam Huff told the rookie he would make all-pro by an act of Congress. Another player told him he had a letter at mail call ... from President Eisenhower. Life on the playing field was no better. During his rookie season, Grosscup was on the taxi squad, manning the sideline phones while Charlie Conerly and George Shaw led the Giants to the Eastern Division title.

For the next two years, Grosscup was on the active roster but played in only four games, throwing a total of 47 passes. In August 1960, he appeared in an exhibition game against the Bears, but was sacked six times during his brief appearance. He did manage to complete a 65-yard touchdown pass, only to see it called back because of a penalty. The Giants' fans adopted him, as fans have a tendency to do with backup quarterbacks, chanting his name in the late stages of blowout games. Dick Young, the caustic writer for *New York's Daily News*, was hard on him, comparing the fans' call for Grosscup to the call of the Romans for another Christian. "Funny thing," he wrote, "but I never hear the good Giant fans yell, 'We want Grosscup' when the score is 7–0." In November 1961, Grosscup got into a game in which the Giants were trouncing the Washington Redskins. His first pass was wild and incomplete. His second was intercepted, as was his third. Young wrote, "He appeared what he was, raw and petrified. Grosscup has a good arm. He also has a fine mind, academically. Whether it's applicable to the job of quarterbacking a pro football team still hasn't been proved."

Grosscup's arm was better than good. Dick Clemente of *Newsday* felt that the only quarterback with a stronger arm was Johnny Unitas. Yet, Grosscup continued his knack for the unfortunate episode. In training camp one year, rather than call a play on the count of two, he called it "on the deuce." The call became a cause celebre of sorts, an almost beatnik-like expression. The players made a big joke of it and further branded Grosscup as an eccentric.

In 1961 Shaw went to the Vikings in the expansion draft, and it appeared that Grosscup would move to the backup spot behind the aging Conerly. In fact Sherman, now head coach, said he would use Grosscup extensively during the exhibition season and give him a shot at the start-ing job. Following his best performance ever in an exhibition game against San Francisco, where he completed 12 of 17 pass attempts, Sherman was effusive in his praise. Yet, he said shortly afterward, "Quarterback is our number-one problem." Within days, New York acquired Y.A. Tittle from the 49ers and Grosscup dropped to third-string once again. Disheart-ened, he played poorly against the Rams the following week. After another difficult day against the Colts in New Haven, he went to Sherman's office and, in an emotional session, told the coach of his frustration and disap-pointment at his inability to play better. Sherman, a former second-string quarterback himself, was sympathetic, but sympathy would not get Gross-cup playing time as long as Conerly and Tittle were around. As Grosscup joked at banquets, "Tittle's the bald eagle, Conerly's the grey eagle, and I'm the clay pigeon."

Early in 1962, Conerly retired, and Grosscup again thought he had moved up to the No. 2 position. In May, however, the Giants acquired veteran Ralph Guglielmi—the quarterback who had been coveted by Wis-mer the previous year—and Sherman informed Grosscup that he was likely to be traded.

The Giants' attempt to move the young man fell through, however, and Grosscup reported to camp at Fairfield University, feeling useless and not knowing what would happen to him. One of his tasks was to stand on the field faking passes so the defensive backs could practice backpedaling. As time went by, he fretted, knowing that every day that passed would make it more difficult for him to catch on with another team. Rosters were being solidified and it would take practice time to learn another club's offensive system. Finally, on August 2, he was claimed on waivers by the Minnesota Vikings and headed for their camp in Bemidji, Minnesota. Grosscup departed with mixed emotions. He was glad to have a chance to get some playing time, but disappointed to leave New York. "It's an unresolved time," he said recently of his Giants experience. "It's kind of a disappointing time. I really wanted to make it. I think I was trying too hard, and I think I stayed too long." Bill Gallo, renowned cartoonist of *New York's Daily News*, sent him off with best wishes in a cartoon with the following text:

> There was a young fella named Lee-
> Who played for the Giants, QB-
> Well, not really played;
> Advice he relayed-
> From Mara for Sherman to see-
>
> Oh, he'd get in the game now and then-
> When the score was a hundred to ten.
> But it never seemed fittin'
> To keep a man sittin'-
> Just sittin' and sittin' and sittin'.

At the bottom, Gallo added, "Good luck, Lee Grosscup!"

Grosscup needed the luck Gallo wished him, for Vikings coach Norm Van Brocklin, who had been Grosscup's boyhood idol, was even less tolerant of intellectual non-conformists than Sherman. Fran Tarkenton was the Minnesota starter, following an excellent rookie year, and Grosscup was put in competition with Shaw and John McCormick, a 26-year-old rookie from the University of Massachusetts, for the backup spot. Grosscup received a good deal of playing time during the exhibition season, and performed fairly well. On August 28, Shaw was cut, and Grosscup thought he had made the team. Van Brocklin, however, decided to keep

McCormick, and once again, Grosscup found his name on the waiver wire. He was shocked, for he had been almost certain he would make the Vikings.

Grosscup waited out the 48-hour waiver period in Minneapolis, hoping to be claimed by another team. He was approached by the Toronto Argonauts and Saskatchewan Roughriders, but deferred, still hoping for a job in the States. By the second day of his vigil, he still had not heard from any NFL teams.

In late May, while attending a high school awards banquet in Oradell, New Jersey, Grosscup had met Turner, who was there with Dorow and Titans publicist Murray Goodman. They got to talking and Turner told Grosscup, out of Dorow's earshot, that if things didn't work out with the Giants, Grosscup should give him a call, for he would love to have him with the Titans.

The AFL teams had maintained their agreement that each would have exclusive rights to all players released by the NFL teams assigned to them. Denver held the rights to all players cut loose by the Vikings, and thus to Grosscup. When Grosscup contacted Turner, who was in Oakland preparing his team for the opener, the quarterback was put in touch with Sauer, who called Wismer in New York. Sauer and Wismer obtained Denver's blessing in return for a draft choice, and the next morning Grosscup was on a plane for San Francisco, to be introduced at a noon press conference as the Titans' new quarterback.

With the signing of Grosscup, the New York quarterbacks were Songin, Green, and the new man. The three had very different styles and made a good combination, if the Bulldog wanted to alternate signal callers. Grosscup recently compared the abilities of the triumvirate. "Songin had his limitations with arm strength. He wanted to go in and establish the run and get some play-action going. Green and I were bigger and had more arm strength. Johnny wanted to get the ball into the intermediate zones and I had a tendency to always want to go deep."

The other quarterbacks had departed. Dean Look was released, but not signed by another team and was still available. Bob Scrabis was cut for the third year in a row. He had run afoul of Turner in the same manner as Dorow, by refusing to run a play that Turner had sent into the game. Scrabis went back to Pittsburgh to start a new career in accounting.

Johnny Green would soon be gone as well. With the arrival of Gross-cup and with Songin's guaranteed contract, Green knew that his opportunities would be limited. After playing briefly in the Titans' opener, he attempted to contact the Patriots and make a deal for himself. When he was unable to do so, the Titans cut him loose after the second game of the season, and he returned to his home in Tennessee. With two quarterbacks ahead of Green, and Look waiting in the wings, Sauer figured he was expendable. But, like Dorow contemplating the wealth of receivers in the Bear Mountain training camp a year earlier, Sauer soon discovered that discarding surplus quarterbacks would cease to be a problem.

CHAPTER 18

STROUDSBURG

In the spring of 1962, Harry Wismer was searching for a training-camp site. Many thought the reason he could not return to Durham or Bear Mountain was that he had left a trail of unpaid bills behind him. As Wismer pondered his limited choices, athletic director John Eiler and coach Jack Gregory of East Stroudsburg State Teachers College appeared in his office and made a proposal to hold camp at their school. There was not much activity at East Stroudsburg during the summer, and the school administration felt that the presence of a pro football team would generate some revenue and, more importantly, bring publicity to the small college. They were right on the second count, for, during the summer months, numerous articles from the major wire services appeared with the dateline "East Stroudsburg, PA." Tony Cesare, sports editor of the *Daily Record*, wrote on July 11, "This is a first for the Poconos. An important first ... already the names 'Poconos,' 'East Stroudsburg,' and 'Stroudsburg' are beginning to appear in the top news media."

For Eiler, the decision to invite the Titans had been a wrenching one. He was serving on an NCAA committee, the purpose of which was to oppose the use of college facilities by professional teams. Eiler had not supported the decision to approach the Titans, but was overruled by the college president. "When the boss says that's it," he recounted recently, "that's it." Eiler apprehensively accompanied Gregory to New York for the meeting with Wismer.

When the Titans arrived in Stroudsburg, they found a field that was hard as a rock. The practice field had no sprinkler system, and had recently been leveled off by moving large amounts of soil, which further disrupted the topography. The college attempted to alleviate the arid conditions by installing a watering system, but the turf remained stubbornly firm, for there was precious little rain in Stroudsburg that summer. Nearly every player had shin splints by the time the club left town, and Don Maynard's injured hamstrings did not heal until mid-season.

Eiler, who had been hesitant to invite the Titans to Stroudsburg, found his fears justified. "I thought we were operating a harem," he said recently. "When you have a lot of adults on a college campus, their standards are different. I felt we had a responsibility to the students and had to be very careful. Sometimes what [the players] did didn't meet what I thought was a proper model for the students." Those who were at the camp remember one player getting drunk in town, swimming the river naked to get back to camp before curfew, and falling asleep on the shore in an unclothed condition, where he was discovered the following morning.

Such incidents were in the future, and, when the Titans arrived in town, the residents greeted them warmly, with a parade and a dinner at the Penn Stroud Hotel, which was attended by 250 people. Gregory was the master of ceremonies and Turner gave a short talk during which he said, "I hope we will be here for many years. We will live up to our end of the bargain and you can be as proud of us as we are of you." On the evening of July 23, the entire team was invited to watch comedienne Nancy Walker in *Everybody Loves Opal* at the Pocono Playhouse.

By the time the Titans left, the citizens were much less enthused. Not only did they leave without paying the college, they ran up a number of bills with local businesses, which likewise remained unsatisfied. Apparently, Eiler's instincts had been correct. In addition to providing a poor example for the students, and wreaking financial havoc upon the business community, the Titans wore out the limited facilities, leaving them in rough shape for Gregory's East Stroudsburg squad when it began fall practice.

The 1962 training camp saw the arrival of Alex Kroll, the Titans' first highly touted draft choice. Kroll had taken a circuitous route to the New York club. After starring in high school at Leechburg, Pennsylvania, he received scholarship offers from schools such as Brown, Cornell, Penn

State, and Indiana. Kroll did not, however, hear from Yale, the school he felt was the best in the country and the one he really wanted to attend. Not only did Yale have a tremendous academic reputation, the quality of Ivy League football in the 1950s was quite good. Kroll therefore wrote to New Haven, pointing out that the Bulldogs' scouting network had not extended far enough to the west. Yale came through with a scholarship and Kroll repaid their faith by earning All-Ivy honors at center on an excellent 1956 club that won the Ivy League championship with an overall record of 8–1.

In the spring of 1957, at the end of his sophomore year, Kroll found himself in trouble. He was riding around New Haven with some of his fraternity brothers, when the car in which he was a passenger was involved in a minor accident. His friends got out of the car, while Kroll stayed inside. On the street, tempers grew short and a fight appeared to be brewing. When someone snapped off the car's antenna, Kroll jumped out. Out of the corner of his eye, he saw someone running at him. "I thought for sure he was going to attack me," Kroll said. "I turned around and threw, unfortunately, what was probably the best right cross I ever threw in my life, hit him, and broke his jaw."

The following day, Kroll discovered, to his great chagrin, that the recipient of his right cross was a young assistant professor of zoology. "It took them about forty-eight hours to send me to the exit ramp," he said. For Kroll, it was a regrettable end to his career at a school he had been so eager to attend.

Out of college, Alex realized that he would have to serve a hitch in the military at some point, and decided to enlist in the Army. He played football at Fort Campbell, where one of his teammates was Art Robinson, former Rutgers captain. At that time, Kroll had very nebulous plans for his future. Since his class at Yale had completed its eligibility, he was entered in the NFL draft pool, and had been selected by the Los Angeles Rams. Robinson, however, talked to Kroll about Rutgers and eastern football and, when he was discharged in August 1959, Kroll enrolled at the New Brunswick, New Jersey, school. After sitting out a year, as required of all transfers, Kroll played well in 1960 and was elected captain for the 1961 season.

At a banquet following the 1960 campaign, when Kroll was officially installed as captain, he stood up and, in Joe Namath fashion, guaranteed an undefeated season. Although Rutgers had played in the first intercollegiate football game in 1869, the school had never finished a season without a defeat or a tie. They had come close in 1960, their only loss a 14–12 shocker to Villanova, a team that had been beaten 51–0 by Army the week before. In 1961 the Scarlet Knights won the first eight games of their nine-game schedule and met Columbia, co-champion of the Ivy League, in the finale. Kroll had a fine season individually. The combination of his ability and the herculean efforts of young Rutgers sports information director Les Unger made him an All-American.

During the week before the Columbia game, Kroll purchased an engagement ring and planned to propose to his girlfriend, Phyllis Benford, after the game. In the wake of Rutgers' first perfect season, he would take her to the top of Rutgers Stadium and pop the question. "I figured she would be at such a psychological disadvantage," said Kroll, "that she could never say no." (Kroll may have needed a psychological advantage, for he was sporting a broken nose incurred against Colgate two weeks earlier.) He gave the ring to the trainer to stuff into a sock and hold in his pocket during the game. Everything was perfectly planned. The day was sunny and beautiful. Phyllis Benford and Kroll's parents, celebrating their 25th anniversary, were among the overflow crowd of 25,500, as Rutgers stood poised on the verge of a perfect season.

For the first three quarters, however, Columbia refused to play its assigned role in Kroll's drama. Rutgers outplayed the Lions, but a series of unfortunate bounces stopped the Scarlet Knights time after time. At the end of the third quarter, Columbia held a 19–7 lead and Kroll was near tears on the bench. Rutgers scored on the first play of the fourth quarter, but failed on a two-point conversion attempt, leaving the score 19–13. The Knights got the ball back and drove to Columbia's one-yard line. Kroll obliterated the center of the Lions' defense and quarterback Bill Speranza followed him into the end zone for the tying touchdown. Another extra point try was botched, but Rutgers' momentum could not be stopped. The Knights scored twice more for a 32–19 win, a perfect season, and the ideal setting for Kroll to propose.

With the season completed and his engagement finalized, Kroll began to think about his future and his wedding. The latter presented a minor problem. Miss Benford came from Kroll's hometown of Leechburg, and both sets of parents knew each other. "No one objected to our being married," said Kroll, "but how we got married was a real problem. Phyllis' parents were Episcopalian. My parents are Roman Catholic. Phyllis' father had only one daughter and he had a long-standing vision of walking his only daughter down the aisle of that Episcopal church. My mother promised to have a major aneurysm if that ever happened, so we were stuck."

During the weeks following his engagement, Kroll received a number of invitations to college all-star games. The players received a stipend and traveling expenses for themselves and, if they were married, for their wives. The mention of wives set Kroll to thinking. Indeed, he could have a wife. He asked Phyllis to meet him in Miami, where he would be playing in the North–South Game at the Orange Bowl. They planned to have a quiet civil ceremony to break the denominational standoff in Leechburg.

Thanks to Kroll's roommate, Rutgers fullback Steve Simms, the quiet little ceremony escalated to the dimensions of a royal wedding. Simms and Kroll were in a bar having a celebratory beer, when they encountered the entertainment editor of *The Miami Herald*. Kroll said, "Simms started to sell the wedding. He said, 'Gee, here's this guy Kroll, he's an All-American and he's getting married tomorrow. Nobody's paying any attention to him.'"

Between Simms and the entertainment editor, they sold segments of the bachelor party to various hotels on Collins Avenue, and convinced the mayor of Miami Beach, Kenneth Oks, to perform the marriage ceremony. By this time, both sets of parents had discovered that their children were about to be married, getting the news from the sports section of *The Pittsburgh Post-Gazette*. They telegraphed to Miami urging the couple to wait.

"But it was too late," Kroll said. "Momentum had taken over." At six o'clock a parade of white Chevrolet convertibles carried football players, coaches, scouts, and hangers-on to the traveling stag party. "Phyllis was alone," remembered Kroll, "except for Duffy Daugherty [coach of the North squad], who was giving her a pre-wedding pep talk at the bar when I left." The bachelor party went from one location to another, finally ending at the Playboy Club.

The revel broke up at 6 a.m., three hours before the scheduled start of practice. Mercifully, Daugherty cut the session short, and the players left for the wedding, scheduled to take place at the Shelbourne Hotel at 11:00. Racing through a shower, Kroll dashed downstairs to find a crowd awaiting him. The players and coaches were there, of course, as was Mayor Oks. There was a mock set of goal posts and a buff-colored wedding cake in the shape of a football. There were television crews and some congressmen from New Jersey, along with a number of hotel guests gathered around the pool in their swimsuits. Everyone who was anyone in Miami Beach was there.

Well, not quite everyone. Phyllis was nowhere to be found. "Forty-five minutes later," Kroll remembered, "I'm still standing there, smoking my seventh L&M, and it's starting to rain." It turned out that Anita Bateman, wife of the Rutgers coach, realized at the last minute that Phyllis didn't have a veil, and the two women set out down Collins Avenue to find one.

Finally, Mrs. Bateman arrived with the bride in tow, the sun came out, and Oks prepared to perform the ceremony. One obstacle remained. The marriage certificate had been misplaced. When finally located, it was missing the signature of both bride and groom. All of the loose ends were eventually buttoned up, and, finally, Alex Kroll and Phyllis Benford became husband and wife.

The South team, better rested, beat the North, 35–10, the following day. Kroll thereafter continued with his bowl appearances, traveling to Tucson and then to Mobile, Alabama, for the Senior Bowl. "It was a great honeymoon," he said, "just me and Phyllis and forty-one football players."

Kroll had been selected by the Titans in the voided secret draft, and picked again in the second round of the legitimate draft, the most prominent signee in the club's brief history. Thus, he was much heralded when he arrived in Stroudsburg in July. In the early 1960s, rookies were expected to tread lightly, especially in training camp. They were asked to stand on tables during meals and sing their school song and perform menial tasks for the veterans. Usually, mild embarrassment and some off-key vocalizing were the only results. In 1961, however, linebacker Edward "Wahoo" McDaniel of the Broncos was told to stand on his chair and sing the Oklahoma fight song. While he was in the midst of a rousing rendition of "Boomer Sooner," someone threw a roll and hit him in the head. McDaniel, who was Chief Wahoo, a well-known professional wrestler, in the offseason, leaped down from the table and ran up to his room, saying he was going to get his gun and shoot the player who had thrown the roll. Bud McFadin ran after him, calmed him down, and convinced him to put the gun away.

The Titans had a similar incident, sans firearms. Bob Florini, a tough kid from Indiana, when told to sing, replied, "I'll see you on the field," and sat down. The next day, the veterans did see him on the field, stretched out after being flattened during a drill. "After that," said fellow rookie Larry McHugh, "we all got up and sang pretty quick."

"Back then," added McHugh, "we were told where to sit, to go out and get food, stand on the table, sing, make my bed. If a veteran said, 'Get me juice' or 'Bring me a beer', you did it. If you went out at night, the veterans sat together, the rookies sat together, and you didn't mix. If you did go over, you'd hear about it the next day." A rookie who showed promise in early drills might find that those on the opposite side of the line seemed to know his assignments. The veterans looked after their friends.

As a highly touted All-American with a guaranteed contract, Kroll was a particular target of the veteran players. Due to the Titans' lack of success in the draft, the hazing that was generally spread among 15 or 20 players was concentrated on Kroll, the only draft choice of note that Wismer had managed to sign.

Kroll was not a typical football player. At Rutgers, he majored in English literature, was elected Phi Beta Kappa, chosen a Henry Rutgers scholar, and won an Earl Blaik fellowship for graduate study. His thesis topic was "A Critical Study of Lawrence Durrell's Application to the Einsteinian Space-Time Continuum in the Modern Novel." Durrell was an Irish novelist whose works were probably not familiar to the Bulldog.

An articulate, charismatic young man, Kroll refused to assume a deferential posture and almost went out of his way to attract attention, irritating many veterans in the process. Just before the start of the exhibition season, he told sportswriter Maury Allen of his confidence he would do well in professional football. "All I need is experience," he said. A teammate said to Allen, "All he needs is a smaller head."

"In my inimitable fashion," Kroll said, "I attracted more attention, because I bought a car that was different than anybody else's." Kroll had purchased a Mercedes 190 SL, then little known in the US. The Cadillac and Lincoln were the status vehicles of choice, and foreign autos were merely exotic. Kroll drove his Mercedes ostentatiously around Leechburg, but, much to his chagrin, no one seemed to notice. Finally, he asked a friend what he thought of his new car. "It's nice," the friend said, "a couple of guys down at the Westinghouse plant have them."

"What do they pay at the Westinghouse plant?" Kroll wondered.

"It's a Volkswagen, right?" his friend asked.

At Stroudsburg, Kroll's hazing culminated when his hand was broken during a drill. "I had the unusual experience," he recalled, "of seeing both sides of the line collapse on me. All the offensive players and all the defensive players fell on me and grabbed my arm. Dick Guesman, who actually broke my hand, was a little ticked off. He said he meant to break my arm."

In total, 63 players, plus two head coaches, reported to the Titans' camp. Turner, the "real" head coach, said, "It's just great to be out on the field hollering again." His film study had convinced him that the greatest shortcoming of the Titans was a lack of speed. His quest in the Poconos was to discover which of the prospective Titans were able to move with alacrity. Turner was also, like Baugh the previous summer, looking for linebackers and seeking to improve the pass rush, which had proven woefully inadequate against the likes of Kemp and Blanda.

Although Turner appeared tougher than Baugh, he brought no structure to the Titans organization. John Drebinger reported in the *Times*, "Discipline, slick organization and perfect co-ordination have taken over," but he was mistaken. Practices were as loosely organized and haphazard as ever, and Turner was once discovered asleep in a pole vault pit adjacent to the field. Drebinger's colleague at the *Times*, Robert Teague, was more cautious. He described the enthusiasm in the Titans' camp, and commented, "Such spirit, plus ten yards, will be worth a first down when the Titans play their first exhibition game."

The Titans had another poor exhibition season. Hampered by injuries, they lost their first game to Houston 33–27. Several players did not make the trip, and Tiller was the only halfback available for action. The club struggled through the remaining games without a single win. They lost to the Patriots in Lowell, Massachusetts, in a game that was originally to have been played in Atlanta's newly built America Field. This was the second of two AFL exhibitions planned for the Georgia capital, and the first, between Denver and Houston, had drawn only 11,500. Bill McCane, chairman of the Greater Atlanta Athletic Association, contacted the Titans and Patriots and asked if the game could be played elsewhere. Based upon the financial guarantees he had promised the two clubs, it was apparent that the game would be a losing proposition. Atlanta, which had fought hard to get an AFL franchise, had perhaps learned a cheap lesson.

On the way to Lowell, fueled by several drinks, Wismer announced to the press that he had traded, or was about to trade, Maynard to Boston. In return, Wismer expected to get either Gino Cappelletti or Tom Yewcic, although he had not consulted the Patriots. The owner was offended by Maynard's slow recovery from his hamstring injury and said, "He hasn't worked up a sweat yet in camp. I think he'd be happier in Boston than in New York." The Titans' public relations men assured the reporters that Wismer was just looking for attention and that there was no trade. The Patriots expressed surprise and disavowed any knowledge. "I don't know what Mr. Wismer has in mind, but I am sure that he's not making deals for us," Holovak said. Maynard said later in the season, "I tried not to let what he said bother me. You know how people get ulcers? They let things like that bother them. Not me. You know all this trouble with Cuba? I didn't let that worry me one bit. There was nothing I could do about it."

Throughout the evening, Wismer roamed up and down the sidelines, hectoring the referees. Late in the game, he appeared in the press box to condemn the officiating loudly and publicly. "Where's Willie Sutton?" he asked. "I now know how the Brink's and mail truck robberies could have happened in this section. The Titans will never play an exhibition game in Lowell because the officials are from Lowell and are robbers." The officials, of course, were on the AFL staff and were not from Lowell, but the truth was never sufficient to blow Harry off course. "They were under Lowell pressure and under Boston pressure," he explained.

Turner was also working the sidelines with great vigor, for on that evening he had become probably the first coach to use performance-enhancing drugs. Noticing a player taking a pre-game bennie, he asked for a couple for himself. During the game, Turner coached like a man possessed. "He was really wired," remembered one player, "running up and down like crazy—he was crazy—his eyes were dilated and never closed. He was yelling at players and officials, running down to the goal line, getting all sweaty."

The Titans lost, 17-10, with Songin playing most of the game at quarterback. Bill Shockley misfired on three of four field-goal attempts. New York also dropped its final exhibition in San Diego, despite the absence of any Lowell-influenced officials.

When the season began, Kroll's hand had healed and he was riding the bench, backing up Hudock. Grosscup was trying to cram the offensive system into his head, and Turner was preparing for his first game as a head coach.

CHAPTER 19

VICTORY, DEFEAT IN SAN DIEGO, AND WHERE IS SAMUEL GOMPERS WHEN YOU REALLY NEED HIM?

In the days before the Oakland game, Grosscup doggedly tried to soak up the essence of the Titans' offense. Being released twice in a 30-day period had made him eager to get on the field as soon as possible and show that the Giants and Vikings had been wrong. In a car with Turner, and in his hotel room, he rattled off formations, patterns, play-numbering. After his first practice with the Titans, he stayed for an extra hour throwing passes to Maynard.

In the NFL, Grosscup had been an isolated non-conformist. In the AFL, and with the Titans, it was a different story. He was among friends. "I felt like I was home when I got to the AFL," he said. Grosscup had learned a lesson from his early days with the Giants. He had adjusted to the world of pro football, learned to get along, and claimed that he was no longer an idealist. "I can socialize with the players," he said, "and go out for a drink with them. I feel I belong here." With the Titans, Grosscup was popular with his teammates, while his fellow intellectual, Alex Kroll, was never really accepted by the veterans.

When he arrived in Oakland, Grosscup walked into his room at the Merritt Hotel and introduced himself to his new roommate. "Jack Klotz," the man replied, sticking out his hand. "I hope you don't mind rooming with me. I'm a little eccentric." That was putting it mildly. Klotz was the left offensive tackle, 6'5" and 255 pounds of toned muscle. He had been with the Titans since the first camp in Durham, and had been a starter since early in the 1960 season. Although he was known as Jack when he joined the club, Klotz soon acquired the nickname "Petey," thanks to teammate Eddie Bell. At that time, there was a product known as Pennsylvania Dutch Noodles, whose primary television advertisement featured a man in full Amish regalia announcing in a heavily accented voice, "Hello lady, my name is Petey Klotz, the Pennsylvania Dutch Noodle Man." Bell saw the ad, and Jack became Petey, a nickname that stuck throughout his tenure with the Titans.

Klotz played his college ball at the Pennsylvania Military Institute (now Widener College) and was drafted by the Los Angeles Rams in 1956. Before the start of the season, however, he was conscripted into military service. Klotz played service ball for the San Diego Marines with Ted Karras (a pro lineman and brother of Alex), Mike Connelly (later the starting center for the Dallas Cowboys), and Daryl Rogers (coach of Arizona State and the Detroit Lions). After leaving the Marines, he worked for the Sun Oil Company and played the 1959 season in a Canadian minor league with the Sarnia Golden Bears. Klotz earned roughly $100 a game playing alongside a number of former NFL performers, including player-coach Fran Rogel, Len Ford, and John Kissell. (Rogel, who played eight years for the Steelers, went to training camp with the Titans in 1960, but was injured during the exhibition season and did not make the club.) When the Titans began looking for players, Klotz was contacted by Sebo and signed before the start of camp.

In an age where most players stopped working out the day after the season ended and didn't resume until the first day of training camp, Klotz was an anomaly. He was what was referred to at the time as a "physical fitness nut" and was an avid weightlifter. He began lifting in the Marines, where he was cleaning and pressing 315 pounds, and cleaning and jerking 355. He continued to lift throughout his professional career, and still does so faithfully. At the age of 63, he was only 10 pounds over his playing weight, and was lifting three days per week. He could press 230 pounds and was doing repetitions with 215 pounds.

Klotz is one of very few men who actually enjoyed Marine boot camp. "I loved the physical [activity]," he said. "That's one thing I loved about the Marine Corps. They busted our humps but I loved it." His Titans teammates dreaded the days on which Klotz was selected to lead calisthenics, for he prided himself in seeing how hard he could push them. He even loved the Polo Grounds, a stadium made for a man who enjoyed hardship, a man who would have made the All-Madden Team had it existed in 1962. "I liked the Polo Grounds," he said. "You could get down in the dirt and get sweaty and kick up a cloud of dust."

Part of his commitment to physical culture was a total abstention from alcohol and tobacco. Klotz had a number of heavy drinkers in his family, and promised his mother as an adolescent that he would never touch a drop of alcohol. He has kept that promise his entire life.

As the straight arrow of the team, Klotz presented a natural target for jokes. In 1963, after a few days of training camp, coach Weeb Ewbank asked Klotz to identify himself. "You're a hell of a man," Ewbank said. "I've had three stewardesses call this week looking for Petey Klotz."

"The guys were rolling on the floor," Klotz recalled. "They were all using my name. They'd meet a girl and when she'd ask their name, they'd say 'Petey Klotz'."

"My hat's off to you," Ewbank said.

While avoiding tobacco and alcohol, Klotz consumed prodigious quantities of vitamins, to the degree that he did an advertisement for Hudson Vitamins (Pennsylvania Dutch Noodles missed a tremendous opportunity by failing to hire him as a spokesman). Perhaps his most unusual trait was a habit of standing on his head for a few minutes almost every day. "Everybody has some idiosyncrasies," he said. "I just like to concentrate on my football assignments while I'm upside down like that."

"I thought it was good for my neck," he added recently. "I thought it was good for my circulation."

Klotz's unusual habit aroused suspicion among his conservative Catholic neighbors in Chester, Pennsylvania. "Some of the people complained to my mother about my head-standing," he related. "They said how could a good Catholic boy like me read those books on yoga and do all that stuff. They told my mother if she didn't watch out, the next thing she'd know I'd be a Buddhist."

Klotz did not add that he also had a penchant for walking around naked. To enter a room and see a man standing on his head is disconcerting, but to enter a room drunk and see a 255-pound man standing on his head naked was downright frightening. "I remember Lee Grosscup coming in one night in Oakland," he said. "I was standing on my head. He christened me with a Coke... I'm not sure how I was attired, but it found its mark."

As the Titans' certified eccentric, Klotz was the perfect roommate for Grosscup. "Lee was considered kind of a Bohemian. He was different than what I was used to," Klotz said. "He got such a kick out of me," said Grosscup, "because I had tried to convince Turner I only needed forty-eight hours to get ready. I was talking to myself in the room. Klotz was doing his headstands, eating his wheat germ and reading whatever he was reading, and I was mumbling to myself." By the time Sunday morning in Oakland rolled around, Klotz was heartily sick of hearing the new quarterback repeating play calls over and over. Despite his continuous mental exercise, however, Grosscup had been told by Turner that he would probably not see any action against the Raiders. Songin would start.

On paper, the game did not appear to be a great matchup. The Titans had lost all four of their exhibitions, while the Raiders had won only once, by a single point. In addition, New York was without their principal running threat, for Bill Mathis had been injured during the exhibition season. On July 27, the *Herald Tribune* ran a story about Mathis entitled, "No Tape for T-Bird—He's a Healthy Titan." (Mathis had been nicknamed T-Bird by Maynard, due to his yearning for a new Thunderbird.) The fullback was quoted as saying, "I've played in every game the Titans have been in, and I've never been hurt, not the least little bit." Such a remark tempted fate a bit too much. On New York's first offensive play in the August 22 game against the Patriots, Mathis, carrying the ball on a sweep, stumbled without being hit and fell, his elbow hitting the ground first. The force of the landing snapped Mathis's collarbone. The medical staff cut his jersey off right on the field, bound up his shoulder, and took him straight to the hospital. That night Patriots owner Billy Sullivan visited the Titans running back and shared a bottle of scotch to ease the pain. Mathis was expected to miss two months.

To take his place, the Titans acquired Charley Flowers from the Chargers in exchange for a draft choice. Had the trade been consummated two years earlier, it would have been a major coup, for Flowers had been a highly sought after fullback from the University of Mississippi. In December 1959, he signed with the Giants, who had made him a future pick the previous year, for $11,000 per year plus a $3,500 bonus. He said he was told by Wellington Mara, "Son, if you don't want to play with the Giants, just say so. We don't want any player who doesn't want to be a Giant."

On January 1, 1960, upon receiving an offer for $17,500 per year and a $10,000 bonus from the Chargers, Flowers took Mara at his word, returned the Giants' bonus and signed with Los Angeles. The Maras decided that they now wanted Flowers, whether he wanted them or not. They wrote a letter to Joe Foss asking him to void the Los Angeles pact.

Flowers, Foss, and the Chargers refused to budge, and the Giants were forced to look to the courts for help. They obtained a temporary restraining order preventing Flowers from playing in the AFL. The case, very similar to that of Billy Cannon, went to trial in June. The NFL contract was signed prior to Mississippi's appearance in the Sugar Bowl, and therefore prior to the expiration of Flowers' collegiate eligibility. Like Cannon, Flowers was told that the contract would not be filed with the league office until after the Sugar Bowl.

The trial produced some interesting testimony. Flowers declared on the stand that Giants coach Jim Lee Howell had come to Oxford in February and told him that the NFL would spend "every cent we've got" to run the AFL out of business. Under cross-examination, Howell completely lost his temper. He shouted, jumped up, and pounded the railing of the witness box. It took two U.S. marshals to restrain him.

As in the case of Cannon, the judge ruled in favor of the AFL, stating that Flowers was a "naive" youngster who didn't understand the document he had signed. While Cannon might be characterized as such, Flowers was an honor student in law school. Nonetheless, he was free to join the Chargers.

It was a Pyrrhic victory, for Flowers gained just 161 yards rushing in 1960 and 177 in 1961, when he lost his starting job to Keith Lincoln. "The Chargers should sue the Giants," wrote one pundit, "and make them take Flowers back." Perhaps Flowers' greatest contribution to the Chargers was bestowing the nickname "Bambi" upon Hall of Fame receiver Lance Alworth. In September 1962, San Diego was happy to unload Flowers for anything the Titans were willing to offer.

With Flowers at fullback and Songin at the helm, the offense started sluggishly against Oakland, as Songin threw two early interceptions. The Raiders opened the scoring midway through the second quarter on a 28-yard field goal by Jackie Simpson. Simpson then kicked off and the ball was touched down in the end zone by Dick Christy and spotted at the 20. Grosscup, who had been warming up on the sidelines, entered the game for the first time. The Oakland fans might have wondered who he was, for the Titans had not even had time to get his name on the program. The public address announcer, who heralded him as "Grasscup," was little help. The night before, Grosscup had decided that he would go for broke on his first play, to demonstrate the boldness many thought he was lacking. If this were to be his last chance, he would make the most of it. He called an up pattern to Powell, with whom he had played previously in a high school all-star game. Powell took off and Grosscup lofted a long pass into the wind. The breeze held the ball up and Powell had to come back for it. With his height and leaping ability, he was able to out-jump 5'10" Oakland defender Bob Garner. Coming down with the ball at the Raider 35, Powell broke Garner's attempted tackle and sprinted to the end zone. On his first pass with the Titans, Grosscup had thrown for an 80-yard touchdown.

The Raiders took the kickoff back to their own 22. On the first play from scrimmage, the blitzing Grantham dropped Oakland quarterback Don Heinrich for a nine-yard loss. On second down, Heinrich's pass was intercepted by Billy Atkins, recovered from his separated shoulder, and returned to the Raiders' 19. The Oakland quarterback was in the midst of a difficult day. A Giant from 1954 through 1959, he came out of retirement when Tom Flores suffered a respiratory ailment that sidelined him for the entire season. After the Titans game, Heinrich went back into retirement.

Grosscup re-entered the game following Atkins' interception and, on the first play, rolled out to his left and hit a wide-open Christy at the 9. The halfback could have walked into the end zone. After Shockley's extra point, the Titans held a 14–3 lead. On two passes, Grosscup had gained 99 yards and accounted for two touchdowns, equaling the total of his three-year career with the Giants. On the bench, responding to congratulations from Kroll, he said, "I just hope Sherman got the message." If Sherman didn't, the Maras certainly did, for the last thing they wanted was a highly touted Giants castoff making it big in their own city.

Songin started the second half and seemed to have caught the fever as well. On the second play from scrimmage, from the Titans' 36, he hit Maynard on the sideline at the Oakland 45. Maynard broke Fred Williamson's tackle and went all the way for the score.

The two quarterbacks alternated on each series, and, after Oakland scored to close to 21–10, Grosscup came in. On first down from his 22, he barely missed on a long pass to Powell. He completed a 17-yard pass to Christy for a first down, after which Curley Johnson lost three yards on a draw play. On second and 13, Grosscup called a comeback pattern to Powell. As he entered the Raiders' secondary, Art recognized a rollup zone, broke off his pattern, and ran a post toward the open area. When Grosscup looked downfield, he saw his receiver running free, waving his left hand to call for the ball. The pass was perfect, hitting Powell in full stride at the 20, with no one between him and the end zone. The score was 28–10, and remained that way until the end of the quarter.

Oakland tallied a minute and a half into the final period on a two-yard run by Alan Miller, but for the remaining 13-and-a-half minutes there was no further scoring. Dick Christy broke off a couple of long runs, finishing with 106 yards on just 10 carries. Ninety-four of those yards came in the second half. Cornerback Wayne Fontes (who then pronounced his surname Fon-tez) intercepted a pass deep in New York territory, and Dainard Paulson batted down a key, fourth-down pass to preserve the Titans' third straight opening-game win. The game ball went to Turner for his first victory as a head coach. "Thanks," he said, "I don't know what I did to deserve this."

Sounding like Wismer, Turner proclaimed that Grosscup "is going to be one of the greatest pro quarterbacks of all time." On only eight passing attempts, he had five completions for 186 yards and three touchdowns. After experiencing his first taste of success in pro ball, Grosscup was so excited he could not eat the post-game buffet. He called his wife, who had seen the game on television. Susan Grosscup told her husband how happy she was about his performance and about the fact that he had started getting paid, for their checking account was down to $74.

Although the opening win was exhilarating, the Raiders were a much softer touch than the Titans' next opponent: the Chargers. "I think we had a false sense of security," said Grosscup recently, "because of the fact we had fired up against the worst team in the league. We'd gotten a lot of ink that week and the game had been on national TV. We just went down to San Diego thinking we'd play the same kind of game we'd played before."

That was unlikely. The Chargers had, along with Houston, one of the most potent offenses in the league. Jack Kemp and Keith Lincoln had returned, but, fortunately for the Titans, their long-time nemesis—Paul Lowe—was sidelined with a broken arm. Yet, there was a new offensive weapon in the Chargers' arsenal even more potent than Lowe. Lance Alworth, a rookie flanker from the University of Arkansas, was a thin, whippet-like speedster with good moves who was a threat to score every time he got the ball. "Lance Alworth is probably the finest end who ever played the game," Sid Gillman said recently.

Dean Look remembered the first time New York faced Alworth, in an exhibition game at San Diego two weeks earlier, during which the rookie caught two scoring passes. Alworth, with his blinding speed, was defended by Wayne Fontes, whose running ability was quite average. On the first play, Alworth split out wide, looked across the line of scrimmage and said, "So you're Wayne Fontes."

"You've got that right," Fontes replied. Alworth went into his pattern and Fontes tackled him as he sped by, drawing a penalty for interference.

"He saved a touchdown," said Look. "I told him it was one of the greatest plays of his career."

The Titans remained in California and practiced at San Diego State all week. Wismer hired a bus to transport the players from their base at the Stardust Hotel to the practice field and back. On Friday, practice ended, but the bus did not appear, for Wismer had not paid its owner. When the bus failed to materialize, some players managed to get rides from the high school girls who had been watching practice. Turner hopped into a sports-writer's car and rode back to the Stardust. After about an hour of waiting, the 25 or so remaining Titans took off on foot. Still dressed in their prac-tice gear, they trudged across a golf course and through several back yards until they found their way back to the Stardust. "Big time football sort of lost its luster that day," said Klotz. It was a bad omen.

The weather in San Diego on September 16 could not have been bet-ter for football. It was 71 degrees and sunny, with a 12-mile-per-hour breeze blowing down from the northwest. It was a beautiful day, but it would not be a happy day for Grosscup, nor for his roommate, Petey Klotz.

On New York's first series, Grosscup threw an interception, but the defense held. The second time the Titans had possession Grosscup attempted a shovel pass to the inside. San Diego defensive end Ron Nery hit him as he let go, shaking the ball loose. The officials ruled a fumble—the first of three for Grosscup—and Ernie Ladd recovered on the New York 8. The Chargers scored in three plays.

In the second quarter, Keith Lincoln took a hand-off and started to sweep to the right side. Suddenly, Lincoln, a high school quarterback, pulled up and lofted a pass to Alworth, who had gotten free in the Titans' secondary. The result was a 23-yard touchdown, making the score 14-0 San Diego.

Meanwhile, the Chargers' front four was doing a job on Grosscup. Nery, in particular, was having a field day against Klotz. The big defensive end had only one move, a feint to the inside, where he grabbed the offensive tackle's shoulder pads, followed by a break to the outside and an attempt to throw the blocker aside. With his one move, Nery beat Klotz and punished Grosscup repeatedly, once incurring a penalty for a personal foul. Grosscup still has a picture of the Chargers' end grabbing him by the facemask and swinging him around. "Every time I looked around," he said, "Nery was there." Even Nery was surprised by his success, for Klotz was probably New York's best pass blocker. Grosscup spent much of the first two periods on the seat of his pants and by halftime the Titans trailed 21-0.

In the second half, when Nery continued to run by Klotz, Turner replaced him with Roger Ellis, the Titans' only other tackle. After two plays, Ellis suffered a leg injury and had to leave. Turner told Kroll to go in. "Me?" asked Kroll, "I never played tackle in my life."

"Christ," replied Turner, "the score's thirty-one to nothing. What difference can it make?"

Finally, in the fourth quarter, Grosscup hit Powell with a 10-yard scoring pass to end the shutout. Within seconds, however, the game was effectively over, as Lincoln took the ensuing kickoff back 103 yards for a touchdown. The final score was 40-14, as Grosscup hit Powell with a second scoring pass with two minutes left. Fortunately for the Titans, Kemp played the second half with a broken middle finger on his throwing hand. He completed only two passes, or the Chargers might have scored more than 40 points. In contrast to his exultant mood of the previous week, Grosscup limped off the plane in New York. He had a twisted left knee and a multitude of bruises, enough of them, he wrote, "for a technicolor extravaganza in black and blue."

On Tuesday, Wismer, embarrassed by the lopsided loss to the Chargers, ordered practice in full pads, or full boards, as the players called it. This was an unusual occurrence during the season. Wismer's timing was bad, for Tuesday was usually payday, but on this Tuesday, after ordering the heavy practice, Wismer did not produce any paychecks. During the prior two years, the checks had been sporadic and many had bounced, but this was the first time checks had not appeared at all.

On previous paydays, the challenge had been to get to the bank before the money ran out. "Don't cash it with anyone you like," Grantham had warned Kroll about his paychecks. The only bank branch in the city that would accept Titans checks was the Irving Trust office at 39th Street and Madison Avenue, where Wismer had his account. Anyone with a check drawn on the Titans was directed to a single teller, who would honor the checks until the account balance reached zero, at which time the rest of the players would tender their checks and wait for the call indicating that the money was in the bank.

At the close of practice, the coaches usually gathered the players at the foot of the clubhouse stairs, and then ordered them to take a lap, while they went inside. "The lap was to give them a head start to the bank," said Karl Kaimer. "Everybody knew only half the dough was there." Once in 1961 the coaches went even further. "We're running plays," said one player, "and we turn around and the coaching staff is already out of there. The coaching staff walked out in the middle of practice and we can't figure out what's going on. They got word that Wismer didn't have enough money in the bank to cover the whole payroll, so the coaches took off so they could get their checks cashed first."

When the players finally got to the clubhouse, the race was on. "Players would jump into cars in cleats," said Kaimer, "trying to get a toehold in the marble."

"Maynard was faster than me," complained Grantham. "He would sprint to the bank and his check would clear first. I was mad that I couldn't run fast enough to get there." All the players, in fact, marveled at the blinding speed of Maynard with an uncashed check in his hand. His vaunted ability to shift gears was nowhere in evidence, for Maynard was in high gear all the way from the Polo Grounds to the Irving Trust lobby.

On Tuesday, September 18, there was no race to the bank, for there were no paychecks, and the players' patience ran out. "Wismer's flaunting of payroll negligence was too much for the Titans' veterans who'd been putting up with this same tardiness for three years," Grosscup wrote. "Some players were still hunting for places to live in New York and needed money right away to make deposits on apartments or to send money to their wives to pay transportation expenses in moving families to New York for the season." The players decided that they were going on strike unless the money was forthcoming by noon on Wednesday. When none appeared, the work stoppage was on.

"We were kind of rebellious people for 1962," said Nick Mumley.

Wismer's response was to tell Turner to put the entire squad on waivers. Turner told his team, "I don't think this is a good thing you fellas have done. I hope we have things back to normal tomorrow." Turner was soon out of the picture, for Wismer decreed that if the players were on strike, the coaches would not be allowed to coach them.

"We had a meeting," said Proverb Jacobs, "and said, 'We're not going to practice.' They said, 'We're not going to pay you anyway.' We all sat around for about an hour and then went home."

The Titans were striking against Wismer and the lack of paychecks, not against football, and they fully intended to prepare for the game with the Buffalo Bills. None of them, paid or not, had any intention of going home. "Hell, no," said Thurlow Cooper, "that was the furthest thing from our minds. We'd have had to go out and look for jobs."

"The truth is," wrote Kroll, "a football player feels orphaned without his coach, and not practicing is a little like missing mass on Sunday."

"We came back the next day," said Jacobs, "and said, 'We've got to play a game. We can't not practice and not play.' So we got ready to play."

Mischak improvised an offensive plan and Grantham did the same for the defense. "All the guys had been around," said Jacobs, "They were old pros, so we knew how to practice."

"Everyone was submitting ideas," said Mischak. "Maynard was suggesting patterns." As captain and one of the team leaders, Mischak found himself in an awkward position. "I was trying to support both sides," he said recently. "I had visions of this league getting better and I wanted to be a part of it as it grew. It wouldn't grow if the players didn't play or coaches didn't coach properly or ownership didn't see the big picture."

On Friday, the players and coaches reunited on the flight to Buffalo for the Saturday night encounter. The game had an added attraction, for the starting Buffalo quarterback was Al Dorow. A crowd of 24,000, large for the Titans, but the smallest in three home games in Buffalo, watched in the rain as the visitors methodically put away the home team. Grosscup played the entire game despite his sprained knee, and performed well, completing 17 of 26 passes for 169 yards. There were no spectacular bombs, as in Oakland, but a series of short, effective, ball-control passes. Perry Richards had his finest game of the season against his former mates, hauling in five Grosscup passes (he caught only six all season). The Titans managed two touchdowns, one on a short run by Christy and the other on a six-yard pass from Grosscup to Cooper, on the famous 51 Y banana pattern. In the huddle during the second touchdown drive, on a third-and-short situation, Grosscup suddenly realized that the team had not prepared any short-yardage plays. In the dirt of War Memorial, he drew a play with his finger and said, "Fake 49 (a sweep to Christy) X up." That was a long pass to Powell, the X receiver. Powell got behind cornerback Booker Edgerson and the 43-yard completion to the 9 set up the scoring pass to Cooper.

The New York defense, drilled by Grantham, was outstanding. Midway through the second quarter, Dorow departed with an arm injury. His replacement, Warren Rabb, managed to throw a touchdown pass to Elbert Dubenion, but also contributed to seven Buffalo turnovers. When the game ended, the Titans had a 17–6 victory, even though they were outgained 327 yards to 235. By the fourth quarter, the Buffalo fans turned ugly. The tribulations of the Titans had been heavily publicized, and the thought of losing to a team that hadn't even practiced was too much. Wells Twombly wrote of old War Memorial, "It has the worst dressing rooms since the Roman Coliseum and the surliest crowds since Caligula was emperor." The disgusted fans started to rain hundreds of beer cans down on the players. On the asphalt track that surrounded the gridiron, the cans landed like artillery shells. The players kept their helmets on as they left the field. "Just think how good we'd be if we practiced," said Songin in the locker room. "That game set coaching back ten or fifteen years," Grosscup said recently.

With a 2–1 record, New York was tied for first place with the Oilers and Patriots. No one should have been overly excited about the lofty position in the standings, however. In its annual pro football pre-season issue, *Sports Illustrated* had predicted a difficult season for the New York club. "Titans begin to look more like the Mets (who would finish 40–120 in their first National League season)—a fall to last place seems inevitable." The fast start was deceiving, for the Titans' victories had been achieved at the expense of Buffalo and Oakland, two clubs that had failed to win a game in five combined attempts. In their only game against a capable team, the Chargers, they had been soundly beaten. New York had shown that they could beat the bad teams and lose to the good ones, just as they had done in their first two years. What would they do the following Sunday against Denver?

CHAPTER 20
OUT OF QUARTERBACKS AGAIN

Perhaps concerned that the Titans had won without him and his coaching staff, Wismer sprung into action during the week between the Buffalo and Denver games. He activated Jim "the Thriller" Tiller, who had been released at the end of camp, and released Mel West, who had averaged 43.6 yards on kickoff returns, but fumbled three times in only three games. Klotz, who had such a difficult time with Ron Nery in San Diego, was waived and claimed by the Chargers. Kroll, listed at only 230 pounds, and who, by the end of the season, actually weighed less than 220, was inserted into the lineup at left tackle. Kroll weighed 25 pounds less than Klotz and was, even by the standards of the time, too small to play tackle.

Grosscup aggravated his knee injury in practice; therefore the Titans brought back Dean Look and signed Hayseed Stephens, giving New York four quarterbacks. With a 33-man roster, this left the club perilously thin at other positions.

Stephens, after three years under Baugh at Hardin-Simmons, was not drafted by either the NFL or AFL, and had been playing with Louisville of the United Football League. In Louisville, he had a lucrative job selling insurance, and claimed he made more money in insurance than he did with the Titans. At 5'10", he was short for a professional quarterback, but shifty and elusive, in the mold of Fran Tarkenton, and much more effective throwing on the run than from the pocket.

As if overhauling the roster weren't enough, Wismer decided to change the coaching staff as well. He added assistant Ed Sprinkle, who made the Pro Bowl four times as a defensive end for the Bears in the 1940s and 1950s, playing in front of linebacker Bulldog Turner.

During his playing days, Sprinkle was known as "The Meanest Man in Pro Football," the result of an article by that name published in *Collier's Magazine*. "I never considered myself mean," Sprinkle said later. "I loved football, loved to play. I did anything I could to get to the passer. I'm not a mean guy. I never was." At the time of the interview, Sprinkle was 72 years old, friendly and gracious, sounding like anything but a man who at one time wished only to sever quarterbacks' heads from their bodies.

When informed of Sprinkle's protestations of innocence, Ted Daffer, his backup in 1954, laughed. "He absolutely deserved his reputation," Daffer said. "I'd go into the game and they'd punch me and kick me, and then say, 'Oh, I'm sorry, I thought you were Ed.' He'd lull you to sleep and then kick you in the back. You just never knew what he was going to do. He was so quick and had all those little moves he could put on you."

Rushing the passer was Sprinkle's forte. "I loved that weak side defensive end spot," he said. "There weren't many teams that ran predominately to the left. I didn't have to worry about the run, and I would get into the backfield in a hurry."

Bob Waterfield, quarterback of the Los Angeles Rams, and the husband of Hollywood starlet Jane Russell, was a particular target. Sprinkle recalled, as a guard in 1945, pulling on a sweep and getting ready to block Waterfield who, playing both ways, was coming up from his safety position. "He threw an elbow and broke my jaw," Sprinkle said. From that moment on, Waterfield was a marked man, spending much of his time in games against the Bears on the seat of his pants. Sprinkle's battles with Charley Trippi, star running back of the Chicago Cardinals, were also legendary.

At the beginning of the 1962 season, Sprinkle, yet another Hardin-Simmons grad, was head coach of the Chicago Bulls of the United Football League. In late September, he was contacted by the Titans and offered a job as a defensive assistant. "I think that Bulldog needed somebody to confide in—a friend," said Sprinkle. He signed on September 25, joined the club immediately and, like Baugh, soon regretted his decision. "It was just a team that was in complete chaos," he said. "They wouldn't listen to Bulldog. I was sorry I ever went up there, because I couldn't help. They already had Johnny Dell Isola as defensive coach. Maybe they didn't know who I was and what kind of player I'd been. There weren't too many guys who knew who I was or cared."

With their new cast of characters and a full week of formal practice under their belts, the Titans took on the Broncos (2–1) at the Polo Grounds on September 30. The home opener had been delayed until the fourth week of the season, as the Titans had to wait for their co-tenants, the Mets, to finish their first season in the National League. It was worth the inconvenience, for upon occupying the old park, the Mets spent $300,000 on much-needed improvements, including resodding the entire playing surface and renovating the dilapidated locker rooms. The stadium was in the best shape it had been in since the Titans began playing there, yet the real attendance was estimated at less than 5,000.

The Broncos were a much-improved team. They had a new owner and president, Cal Kunz, who had purchased Bob Howsam's interest in the club; a new coach, Jack Faulkner; and new uniforms, having changed their brown, gold, and white outfits to orange, blue, and white. They even discarded the hideous vertical-striped socks, which were burned at a public bonfire. More importantly, the team was playing much better, and would stay in the Western Division race almost until the end. Faulkner was the antithesis of the laid back Filchock, organized to the point of overload. "I told Jack," said Frank Tripucka, "that if we had the ball for two straight hours inside the ten-yard line, we still couldn't run all his goal line plays." The Broncos featured an exciting offense, which attempted an average of 54 passes in their first three games, completing an average of 28. The fans came out to watch, as attendance increased from 11,000 per home game in 1961 to 27,000 in 1962.

On New York's first offensive series against the Broncos, the Titans found themselves in a third-and-seven situation from their own 33. Grosscup called a pass to Powell, but when he saw the split end blanketed by double coverage, broke out of the pocket and started to run up the middle. Three yards beyond the line of scrimmage, 260-pound Don Joyce brought him down with such force that his helmet popped off when it hit the ground. More importantly, his injured left knee was twisted by the impact, and he limped off the field.

"The tape saved you," said Dr. Nicholas as he examined Grosscup's knee on the sideline. "Get up and start walking around." Grosscup tried to jog, but couldn't put any weight on the injured leg. Songin went in at quarterback the next time the Titans got the ball. He hit Maynard with a 45-yard touchdown pass that gave New York a 7–3 lead late in the first quarter.

With eight seconds left in the half, Gene Mingo kicked a 17-yard field goal that gave the Broncos a 13–10 advantage. Grosscup had re-entered the game for one play, a hand-off to Christy, but was in such pain and was so immobile that he had to leave immediately. In his place, Songin played well, passing for 153 yards in the first half. On the Denver side of the ledger, Tripucka had done even better, hitting 17 of 22 for 196 yards, including a touchdown to Lionel Taylor.

The Titans could easily have led at halftime. In the second quarter, with New York ahead, Songin threw long to Christy, who had broken free down the left sideline. Christy reached for the ball but, as he stretched out, stepped in one of the infamous Polo Grounds potholes, lost his balance, and the ball fell harmlessly to the ground. Had Christy not stepped in a hole, he could have put the Broncos in one, and possibly changed the complexion of the game.

At the start of the second half, the two quarterbacks traded interceptions, followed by an exchange of punts. The rest of the third quarter was scoreless, as Bill Shockley and Dick Guesman of the Titans each misfired on a field goal attempt. Early in the fourth quarter, Tripucka completed a pass to Bo Dickinson, who was tackled on the 1-yard line. After releasing the ball, the Broncos' quarterback hit his hand on a Titans helmet and dislocated his thumb. Tripucka gamely popped it back into place, went up to the line of scrimmage, called his own number, and scored on a quarterback sneak.

With the Titans now trailing 19–10, Wismer became impatient. "You can't stay with a loser, Bulldog," he shouted on the sideline. "Put Dean Look in there." Wismer had been pressuring Turner to play Look all season. Obediently, Turner sent the former Michigan State quarterback into his first professional game. Look took the ball around left end on a rollout and gained eight yards. On third and one, he ran for two yards and a first down. "See that, Bulldog," Wismer yelled happily, "now we've got a quarterback."

A few seconds later, Wismer no longer had a quarterback, at least not Dean Look. On the next play, Look rolled out and threw a pass over the middle. As he released the ball, 280-pound Bud McFadin hit him in the jaw with his forearm, lifting him completely off the ground. Landing on his head, Look suffered a concussion and a fractured vertebra, effectively ending his football career.

Look, who has been an NFL official for more than 25 years, joked recently that he has been trying for the entire quarter century to find the identity of the official who failed to throw a flag on McFadin for the vicious hit. No penalty was called, and the ball floated into the hands of Denver's Bob Zeman, who ran it back 30 yards for a touchdown that sealed the Titans' fate. Mingo added two more field goals for a final margin of 32–10. Songin, bothered by the Denver blitz, passed for only 38 yards in the second half. At least he remained healthy, for, in addition to losing the game, the Titans had lost two quarterbacks. Look went to the hospital and Grosscup finished the afternoon the same way he spent so many Giant games, operating the field telephone.

Wismer was not one to take adversity lying down. As Jim Bouton wrote in *Ball Four* about Seattle Pilots general manager Marvin Milkes, Wismer was not a man to remain calm in a situation that clearly called for panic. He told Grosscup he planned to sue the Broncos for a million dollars for intentionally injuring his quarterback, claiming that Cal Kunz told him after the game that Denver's strategy had been to get Grosscup out of the game. Wismer planned to watch the game film with the FBI to see if the injury had been inflicted intentionally.

The Titans suffered a number of other injuries against the Broncos. Three defensive backs, Paulson, Atkins, and Fontes, suffered a separated shoulder, injured knee, and chipped ankle, respectively. End Perry Richards and guard Sid Fournet had also been hurt. Charley Flowers, suffering from an internal injury, was cut, as was Look. On Tuesday, Turner could muster only 15 able-bodied players for practice. Sauer brought in a number of replacements, the most valuable of whom was defensive end LaVerne Torczon, an All-AFL performer in 1961 and 1962 who was available after a falling out with Bills coach Lou Saban.

The injured Titans would have an extra day to rest, for Wismer changed the date of the Boston game from Friday to Saturday. The Yankees were playing the Giants in the World Series, with Game 2 taking place in San Francisco on Friday and Game 3 at Yankee Stadium on Sunday. Wismer figured that sports fans coming to New York for Sunday's game might like to attend a football game on Saturday night at the Polo Grounds.

Like most of Wismer's schemes, this one backfired. In 1960, when he moved the ill-fated Patriots game from Friday to Saturday, many fans stayed home. Now, they did more than stay home. Several ticket holders protested to New York Attorney General Louis Lefkowitz, claiming they could not attend on Saturday. Lefkowitz ordered the Titans to offer refunds to anyone who asked. The great influx of World Series fans failed to materialize, and attendance at the Polo Grounds was announced at only 14,000. As the *Times* observed sarcastically, "that figure undoubtedly included the 64 musicians and 14 drum majorettes in the Midland Park marching band, as well as about 8,000 empty seats."

In contrast to the Patriots, who fielded the same 33-man roster that left training camp, the Titans produced a makeshift lineup. Jerry Fields, a linebacker, started at cornerback and Ed Kovac, a 1960 draft choice who had been cut several times by New York, started at safety. On offense, Bill Mathis returned to action for the first time since his shoulder injury. In order to protect Grosscup's gimpy knee, the Titans operated from the shotgun formation whenever he was in the game.

Songin and Grosscup alternated at quarterback, and the club switched between the T-formation and the shotgun. Neither proved effective, and Boston methodically built a 17–0 lead midway through the second period. At that point the Bulldog inserted Hayseed Stephens for the first time as a pro quarterback. Although he had recently joined the club, Stephens had been staying with Sprinkle and getting a crash course in the Titans' offense. As Stephens recalled, "Bulldog said, 'Man, do you think you can go in there? Do you think you know enough?' I said, 'I believe I do.'" In he went.

Stephens had a much better debut than that of Dean Look the previous week. On his first play, he hit a quick slant to Art Powell for seven yards. The next play was another completion to Maynard for a first down. By the end of the day, Stephens had completed 10 of 15 for 90 yards and was the club's leading rusher, picking up 34 yards on five scrambles.

None of Stephens' success led to points, however, as the only Titans scores came on two long passes by Grosscup, a 73-yarder to Powell and an 86-yarder to Maynard. The final score was 43–14. The New York rushing attack was pathetic, the top two ground gainers being Stephens and the lead-footed Songin. Despite the return of Mathis, no Titans running back gained more than four yards. Mathis, who had boasted of his durability prior to the season, was bothered by physical ailments all year. When his shoulder healed, he developed knee problems. His rushing yardage dropped from 846 to 245, but he was still the No. 2 ground gainer for the Titans, who ended up with the lowest rushing total of any team in the league. Christy, Mathis, and Curley Johnson were the only New Yorkers to amass more than 100 yards on the ground for the entire season. The lack of a viable running attack made the crippled Titans quarterbacks even more vulnerable, for, by the end of the season, they were passing on almost every play.

After the Boston game the Titans were in a bad situation. The club was decimated by injuries. They had lost two games in a row by lopsided scores, dropping them to 2–3, and were going to Houston to play the first place Oilers. Even the two New York wins were suspect, for their two victims, Oakland and Buffalo, were now a combined 0–9.

Wismer again leapt into action. He told Turner that, if Grosscup's knee was serviceable, he should release Songin, who had been largely ineffective and plagued by interceptions. Songin's contract was guaranteed for seven games, and he had but two more to go. In order to find out about any other problems that might be lurking in Titandom, Wismer summoned Mischak, Grantham, Mathis, Atkins, Grosscup, and Stephens to his office. The first five players were veteran leaders, but the inclusion of Stephens was inexplicable. "What in the hell was Hayseed doing here?" Grosscup wondered.

"I was as surprised as Grosscup was," said Stephens later. "I'd just gotten there and I barely knew who Grosscup was. I bummed a ride to the meeting with him and we talked about it. I said, 'Man, I just showed up, how would I know what's wrong?' As a short-timer, the best thing I did was just keep my mouth shut."

"What's wrong with the Titans?" Wismer asked, but received no response. "How do you like Bulldog?" The players said that Bulldog was okay. "How's the squad morale?" Mischak said that it was good.

"Have we got any drinkers or lovers on the squad?" was Wismer's next question.

"Not that I know of," replied Mathis diplomatically.

"Are the guys putting out?"

"I think they are," said Grosscup. "I don't think anybody was willing to say everything that was on their minds," he added recently. After an hour of questions, and non-committal answers, the meeting broke up.

When the Titans flew to Houston, quarterback Johnny Green was on the plane. He had been called back from Tennessee to join the squad in anticipation of Songin's release. Another Wismer dictate was that Turner make extensive use of Tiller, particularly on screen passes. The owner, like his wife, was certain the little scatback could break loose in the open field.

The opening series did not bear out Wismer's confidence. On second and 10, Tiller was stopped for no gain on a sweep around the left side. On the next play, he caught a pass from Grosscup, but was tackled for a three-yard loss. Late in the first quarter, with Houston leading 7–3, Grosscup dropped back to pass from his own 20. The Oilers were blitzing, and one of the Houston linemen threw Tiller aside and hit Grosscup solidly on the left knee, just as he released the ball. The quarterback could hear the ligament pop on impact and lay writhing on the ground. "That injury was so painful," he said recently, "hearing the noise, feeling the pain, rolling over and screaming, tears involuntarily coming into my eyes. To this day, when people come up on my blind side, I instinctively protect myself." Grosscup was carried off the field and laid on the ground next to the Titans' bench. Since Dr. Nicholas had not made the trip to Texas, the Titans' signal-caller was examined by the Houston team physician.

After Grosscup's departure, the roof caved in. Songin and Stephens were ineffective, Songin throwing three interceptions and Stephens fumbling twice. George Blanda threw six touchdown passes, as the Oilers set a single-game scoring record with 56 points. The Titans managed just 17. Their only highlight was Christy's 58-yard punt return for a touchdown. Tiller carried eight times for 14 yards and caught three passes for 28. By the end of the game, both he and Stephens were playing defensive back.

The Oilers' doctor estimated that Grosscup, who had severely strained ligaments on both sides above and below his left knee, would be out for six weeks. The Titans were not scheduled to return to New York until after the Dallas game, and, rather than fly ahead for treatment, Grosscup stayed with the team and visited the Texans' physician. Since that doctor's specialty was proctology, he was of little help with cruciate ligaments. Finally, Grosscup was sent back to New York to have his knee examined by Nicholas. "Today," said Nicholas, "it would have been put in a brace and he could have played." In October 1962, that was not possible. The treatment for a serious knee injury was surgery, followed by two months of immobility. A less serious case was treated with rest, plus immobilizing the joint, which caused it to become inflexible, and the muscles surrounding it to atrophy. For Grosscup, Dr. Nicholas prescribed rest and placed him in a heavy cast that stretched from hip to ankle. After clearing waivers, Grosscup was placed on the reserve injury list. Sauer said he was expected to return for the Oakland game in three weeks. Wismer, prior to any x-rays or orthopedic examination, declared, "He will be lost for the season and may be all through as a player."

Johnny Green was activated to take Grosscup's place on the roster. He would start against Dallas on Sunday, backed up by Songin, who was to be released after the game, the last of his guaranteed contract. It didn't seem as if it would matter who started at quarterback. After suffering consecutive losses by a total of 68 points, the Titans appeared to be cannon fodder for the Texans, 4–1 and headed for the AFL championship. Yet, contrary to expectations, the overmatched Titans fought their talented opponents tooth and nail, not succumbing until the final minute.

The action was so spirited that two fights broke out in the fourth quarter, the first of which stopped the game for nearly 10 minutes. The battle started when Titans linebacker Jerry Fields hit Abner Haynes out of bounds after a pass reception. As Fields started to get up, Haynes kicked him. Fields grabbed Haynes' leg, picked him up, and dropped him. Unlike Al Dorow at Buffalo the previous year, Haynes had selected a site directly in front of his own bench, and had plenty of assistance when he went after Fields. The latter's New York teammates came sprinting across the field to join the fray, which featured linebacker E.J. Holub of the Texans at the center of the action. "Someone was trying to pull my helmet off and beat me to death with it," said Grantham. "I think it was E.J. Holub."

"E.J. Holub had a couple of helmets and was cracking heads," added Hayseed Stephens. Stephens was standing on the sideline when the battle started, ran on the field to get a better look, and took part in some minor skirmishing. Titans linebacker Hubert Bobo, on the other hand, was an enthusiastic participant in the brawl, grabbing one of the Texans in a headlock with his left arm and pummeling him with his right, despite being hit with a helmet at the same time.

When the smoke cleared, Bobo made his greatest contribution of the day, convincing the officials that Stephens, the third-string quarterback who was not going to see any action anyway, had started the entire episode. Bobo explained after the game, "We only had three linebackers left and didn't want to lose Fields, so I told the officials Fields didn't have anything to do with it. I accused them of not knowing who to throw out. Hayseed was standing there, so I told them he did it. So they threw him out of the game."

A second skirmish broke out with less than a minute to go when Buddy Cockrell of the Titans, a former Golden Gloves boxer, earned an ejection following an interception by Dallas's Dave Grayson. The New York tackle, along with Duane Wood and Haynes, was fined $50. Cockrell's fine was paid by Wismer.

The game itself was a credit to the spirit of the Titans. At halftime, the score was tied 10–10. The crippled New York defense played ferociously, sacking Dallas quarterback Len Dawson for 71 yards in losses overall. After Haynes put Dallas ahead with a one-yard run in the third quarter, New York came right back and tied the score on a two-yard run by Green. Shockley missed a long field goal attempt on the Titans' next possession, and Dallas took the ball on its own 37 with just over four minutes left in the game. The third play of the drive was the one on which Haynes and Fields had their altercation. After Haynes and the martyred Stephens left the field, two short passes to Chris Burford brought the ball to the New York 29 with 2:03 left. The Titans' defense broke through and tackled Dawson on consecutive plays for losses totaling 25 yards, resulting in third down and 35 from the Dallas 46 with 1:07 left. Dawson threw a screen pass to fullback Curtis McClinton over the middle. The rookie thundered to the Titans'

35, well short of the first down, but within the range of kicker Tommy Brooker. With 51 seconds remaining, Brooker kicked a 42-yard field goal to give Dallas a 20–17 victory. The Titans, with the season half over, were 2–5, tied with Buffalo for third place, two-and-a-half games behind the Oilers and Patriots.

CHAPTER 21

CRASH OF THE TITANS

The wave of injuries had continued in the Dallas game. During a failed New York goal-line stand, Abner Haynes hurtled over the Titans' line. Dick Guesman reached up to catch him, but Haynes' helmet hit Guesman's arm and snapped it, putting the defensive tackle on the sidelines for the remainder of the year. All teams suffer from injuries, but the Titans, unlike other clubs, had no one to replace the missing players. The revolving door continued to spin, with Guesman and Songin departing and defensive linemen John Kenerson and Bob Watters and tight end Karl Kaimer arriving. Songin did not leave quietly, delivering a series of broadsides against Wismer, Turner, and the entire Titans organization. "I'm happy to be the hell out of here," he said. "I can say that I have never seen an outfit as fouled up as this one. Harry calls all the shots."

"[Wismer] stands on the sidelines during the game and makes substitutions," he added. "He is ruining the Titans and he is bad for the whole league."

Turner, Songin continued, was "nothing more than Wismer's puppet," an opinion Turner later confirmed when, discussing Songin's release, he said, "Wismer didn't want me to play him, so I couldn't."

Hayseed Stephens remained on the roster, but not with the team. His wife, driving to see him play in Dallas, was involved in a horrible auto accident near Weatherford, Texas. Mrs. Stephens, who was nursing a one-month-old infant, was seriously injured, and her 12-year-old brother, a passenger in the vehicle, was placed in an intensive care unit, with little hope of surviving. Stephens left the team to be with his family, leaving Dick Christy as the emergency quarterback.

As insurance against the possibility that Stephens would not return, the Titans re-signed old reliable Bob Scrabis for his third tour of duty. In training camp, Turner hinted that Scrabis might pass both Songin and Dorow and assume the first string position. "He's my number one," Turner had said, "and I am giving Scrabis every chance." A Catholic, Scrabis was in church when he found out about the Dorow trade.

"Hey," Dick Guesman told him, "it looks like you're number one." It was not to be, for he was cut at the end of the exhibition season, and went back to Pittsburgh to look for an accounting position. "Football was out of my mind," he said. When Scrabis got the call from the Titans, however, he returned to New York to back up Green.

Fortunately for Turner, the San Diego Chargers, the Titans' next opponent, were even more decimated by injuries than his own team. Faison, Lincoln, and Lowe were sidelined. Alworth was bothered by a pulled leg muscle. Kemp was no longer with the team, having been claimed on waivers by Buffalo, who he would lead to consecutive AFL championships. The Chargers' starting backfield consisted of rookie quarterback John Hadl, halfback Jacque MacKinnon, a converted lineman, and a fullback with the ponderous handle of Hezekiah Ezekial Braxton III. The injuries had taken their toll, and the two-time Western Division champions were just 3–4.

The parking lot at the Polo Grounds was full on Sunday afternoon. Unfortunately for Wismer, however, most of the cars contained Giants fans, who paid their dollar, then took the subway under the Harlem River to watch the Giants play the Redskins. This was the first time the Titans had challenged the Giants at home, the first time there had been two pro football games in New York on the same day since 1949. The head-to-head confrontation was not Wismer's doing. The AFL needed a Sunday game to telecast to the west, and the Titans–Chargers contest was selected. The crowd at the Polo Grounds was announced as 21,467, but estimated by the Associated Press at 12,000 and by the *Times* at 7,500. Wismer did not share in Polo Grounds parking revenue, and thus did not even benefit from the Giants fans using his parking lot.

Those who went to Yankee Stadium saw Y.A. Tittle tie an NFL record by throwing for seven touchdowns. Those who went to the Polo Grounds saw the Titans beat the Chargers for the first time in six regular-season tries. Early in the third quarter, Johnny Green broke a 3–3 tie with a 63-yard touchdown pass to Maynard, who gained 157 yards receiving on the day. With his hamstrings finally recovered from the hard turf at Strouds-burg, Maynard had put in a full week of practice for the first time all season. Powell added 105 receiving yards, as Green threw for 313 overall. Mischak had a tremendous game against Ernie Ladd, and Green burned the Chargers repeatedly down the middle when they tried the safety blitz. Christy returned a punt 73 yards for his fourth scoring return with the Titans, picking up a bouncing punt near the sideline, cutting back to the middle of the field, and going all the way. Christy had a fine day, rushing for 71 yards, catching four passes for 45, and returning kicks for 114. Tiller was again ineffective, netting negative yardage on 10 carries. Paulson, Ed Cooke, and Ed Kovac had interceptions, as the crippled Titans defense held the crippled Chargers offense without a touchdown. It was a case of the resistible object versus the movable force. Hezekiah Ezekial Braxton III carried four times for -8 yards as San Diego gained only 28 yards on the ground.

The final quarter was played in semi-darkness. It was a gloomy afternoon and, from the Polo Grounds press box, reporters could see that, across the river at Yankee Stadium, the lights had been shining brightly since practically the opening kickoff. "They got brighter and brighter as the sun went down," recalled Gordon White, "but no lights went on at the Polo Grounds. No lights ever went on at the Polo Grounds."

As visibility began to recede, Chargers coach Sid Gillman complained to the officials, who came over to the Titans' bench to ask Turner to have the lights turned on. Turner called upstairs to Wismer, who said to finish in the dark. He wasn't about to pay the $250 fee that kicked in when the lights went on. The final score was New York 23, San Diego 3. Wismer, who had promised each player $100 for every touchdown by which his team beat the Chargers, again failed to deliver. Perhaps he kept the lights off to make his escape before the players could find him.

The following week, the Titans captured their second consecutive win, rallying from a 14–3 deficit to beat the Raiders 31–21. Oakland was in the midst of a dreadful season, which would see them lose their first

13 games. A young girl told a joke on a local children's show: What has 22 legs and lives in the cellar? Answer: The Oakland Raiders. Starting quarterback Cotton Davidson, obtained from the Texans when Don Heinrich retired, was playing with a separated throwing shoulder that required him to get pain-killing injections every Thursday. Coach Marty Feldman, hired in 1961, was fired and replaced by Red Conkright, who installed an offense he called the "running gun," a variation of the shotgun.

The Titans contributed to the Raiders' misery, inflicting loss number eight. Mathis, who had carried the ball only four times all season, had his best game of the year, rushing for 89 yards. Powell, playing on a hemorrhaging and heavily bandaged right leg, caught five passes for 102 yards. Green played almost the entire game at quarterback for the third week in a row, surviving four first-half interceptions to come on strong after halftime. In the third quarter, he put the Titans ahead, 17–14, with a touchdown pass to Maynard, who was guarded by Fred "the Hammer" Williamson. Williamson, a talented cornerback, was also a boastful, flamboyant character, a future actor, and briefly a member of ABC's Monday Night Football broadcasting team.

The Titans put Maynard and Powell wide to Williamson's side of the field and sent them on crossing patterns. As Maynard crossed paths with Powell, he yelled "switch" causing his man, thinking it was Williamson's voice, to leave him for Powell. As Maynard sped past him, the Hammer got caught in traffic, and was left standing in the middle of the field with his hands raised helplessly in the air. Maynard was so wide open in the end zone he had to come back to catch Green's pass. "I saw Don open," said Turner after the game, "and waited for Green to throw. I was afraid he'd never throw. All I could see was him freezing and throwing the ball to the ground."

After the Raiders took a 21–17 lead, the Titans were the beneficiaries of a pass-interference penalty against Oakland's Bob Garner on the goal line. Two plays later, Green snuck across for the winning touchdown. The game, played in competition with the Giants, who beat the St. Louis Cardinals at Yankee Stadium, drew a crowd announced at 18,247, but estimated by both *The New York Times* and the *New York Herald Tribune* at 6,000 and by the *New York Post* at 3,000. New York's second straight win boosted the Titans' record to 4–5.

The Titans' win over Oakland was overshadowed, for it came on the day following Wismer's announcement that the team was for sale, at least 49 percent of it. He designated Clark Clifford as his negotiator.

It was remarkable that the Titans had reached the season's halfway point before running out of money. Before training camp even began, Wismer was scrambling to raise enough cash to start the season. He hoped either Lamar Hunt or Bud Adams would lend him enough to get through what he believed would be his final season in the Polo Grounds. In return for the much-needed funds, Harry offered a percentage of the team to anyone who would pay a like share of the bills, but found no takers. Finally, Wismer managed to get a $200,000 loan from Howard McCullough, sales manager of Brunswick Corporation, who received an assignment of the Titans' share of proceeds from the ABC contract.

The money from McCullough's loan was long gone, and Harry's only viable alternative was to sell the club. Wismer, who owned 80 percent of the stock, was asking $1.25 million for half ownership, and needed to get it in a hurry. Checks were bouncing higher than ever and the players, while not planning another strike, were becoming uneasy. They had fallen into a routine, racing to the bank, handing over their check, and waiting for word that the money had arrived. It was not the best way to do business, but there was some security in the fact that the money always got there eventually. Now, the routine had been disrupted. Checks were bouncing not once, but twice, and Wismer had moved his account from Irving Trust to Chase Manhattan, meaning that the payday route had to be changed. Some checks from the game against the Chargers remained unpaid more than a week later.

When it became apparent that Wismer would also be unable to cover the checks for the Oakland game, the league decided to take action. Milt Woodward, assistant commissioner of the AFL, met with the Titans' players on Thursday, November 8. He told them the league would be involved in facilitating the sale of the Titans and, in the meantime, would guarantee the players' paychecks. This announcement proved a tremendous relief to most of the players, but Maynard had one more concern. "What about the $1.50 charge our banks hit us with on these bad checks?" he asked Woodward. The latter told Maynard to submit the charge as an expense to the new owner.

The league raised $40,000 by assessing the other seven clubs and loaned it to the Titans. The advance covered outstanding checks and the payroll for the next game against Dallas. "It was felt that the attitude of the New York players wouldn't be proper if they hadn't been paid for their last game," said Woodward. The league was also concerned about its image and the reaction of television sponsors. Woodward hoped that the club would be sold before the $40,000 ran out. "We trust the affair will be completely settled by another week," he said. On November 9, the league gave Wismer an ultimatum. If he did not sell the team in one week, he would be required to forfeit the franchise to the league.

Woodward's optimism for a quick sale appeared to be well founded. An AFL owner was quoted in *Sports Illustrated*, "For anyone who wants out, there are at least six who will take any franchise available."

"We have three very substantial groups ready to step in and take over the franchise if Wismer goes down the drain," added Bud Adams. In its third season, the league was beginning to prosper. ABC estimated that the number of viewers had increased by 44%. In 1961 two teams (Buffalo and Boston) had come close to breaking even. Adams' Oilers, who lost $420,000 in 1960 and $200,000 in 1961, anticipated a $50,000 profit in 1962. Joe Foss declared confidently that he expected that four of the other seven clubs would also realize a profit. The level of talent on the field had also improved. Billy Sullivan of the Patriots pointed out that AFL clubs no longer drooled over NFL rejects, as they had in 1960. Ralph Wilson of the Bills claimed that, of the top 200 rookies drafted in 1961, 76 had signed with the NFL and 73 with the AFL. But, Wilson pointed out, the NFL signees were spread among 14 teams, while the AFL had only eight clubs and thus signed more rookies per club.

Despite all the signs of increasing prosperity, Wismer and Foss had great difficulty finding anyone willing to take over the floundering Titans. Part of the problem, not surprisingly, was Wismer himself. "[Wismer's] passion," wrote Maury Allen in the *New York Post*, "is stubbornness." Allen quoted a friend of Wismer's as saying, "Harry would sooner die than sell the ball club. He wants to make it to Flushing Meadows." Despite the Titans' difficulties, Wismer gave himself a promotion to chairman of the board, appointing his wife president.

Many prominent names were mentioned as prospective purchasers, including those of Joan Shipman Payson, owner of the Mets; Alicia Patterson, publisher of *Newsday*; Richard Whitney, ambassador to the Court of St. James; Tom King Jr., an executive with Merchandise Mart in Chicago; and Frank Leahy, the renowned former Notre Dame coach. On November 11, Wismer said, "I'm negotiating with two separate people. On one side is a woman and on the other a man. Both are wonderful people from New York." He denied that Mrs. Payson was the woman, saying that he had refused to deal with her, for she wanted to steal the team from him. He claimed she offered only $200,000. Foss and Wismer had, in fact, met with Mrs. Payson and Donald Grant, a Mets executive, but Wismer made some statements to the press following the meeting that irritated Mrs. Payson. She immediately terminated the negotiations.

Leahy, who in 1960 had served as the color commentator for Titans games on WMGM radio, was part of a syndicate led by Dick Flanagan, a 48-year-old vice president of Webb and Knapp. The group was the only suitor to pursue serious discussions, and came close enough to have Wismer declare on November 20, "Leahy's got the team, unless one of the other groups makes me a better offer." Under Leahy's proposal, Wismer would retain 25 percent of the club and remain active as a minority partner. Leahy, who had resigned as general manager of the Chargers due to ill health prior to the start of the 1960 season, would be coach and general manager. Upon moving to Flushing Meadows, he planned to rename the club the Long Island Titans. Leahy's group was unsuccessful in raising financing, however, and had to abandon the effort. That did not stop Wismer from spreading the rumor that he and Leahy had reached a handshake agreement to sell the team for $1.7 million. When he heard the story, Leahy said that would have been impossible, since he had not been in New York in two weeks. "I'm highly flattered," he added, "that anyone thinks I have one point seven million dollars."

One difficulty in securing a buyer was the fact that the club's debts, which would become the obligation of the purchaser, were mounting. In mid-November, the outstanding bills were estimated at more than $400,000. The actual number was much higher. When the Titans finally filed for bankruptcy in February 1963, the obligations of the club were just over $2 million. Of that amount, however, $739,000 was claimed as owed to Wismer for salary and repayment of money he had advanced to the Titans from his personal funds. Of the remaining $1.3 million, the largest creditors were Irving Trust, owed more than $400,000, and the AFL, which by then had advanced $255,000 to subsidize the club's operations. East Stroudsburg State Teachers' College had not been paid approximately $20,000 for training camp expenses. Some debts dated back to 1960.

In November 1962, the amount owed represented more than mere statistics in a bankruptcy petition. They were a threat to the team's continuing existence. Wismer was behind on his payments to virtually everyone who supplied services to the club, some of whom were threatening to stop providing those services. In addition, some creditors had obtained judgments and engaged sheriffs to attach the Titans' assets. One officer appeared prior to the Dallas game at the Polo Grounds and threatened to place an attachment on all proceeds to settle an unpaid bill of about $900. A fast-talking Titans official convinced the sheriff that the team would be sold within a week and all debts would be paid. The sheriff left without placing his attachment.

As the season wound down, negotiations continued without success. On November 22, Wismer indicated that a sale would be announced the following day, but nothing happened. Then, in a complete about face from his previous position, in which Foss gave Wismer a week to sell the team, the commissioner said that Wismer could retain ownership if he were properly financed. Foss spent a great deal of time in New York, attempting to broker a sale. The consensus was that, no matter what happened, the team would remain in the city.

That did not stop rumors from flying about. One held that Barron Hilton would sell the Chargers to a local group, and then buy the Titans. A similar story said that the Chargers, whose support was eroding along with their record, would move to New York and the Titans would relocate to New Orleans. The Chargers, a stronger club, might have a better chance of competing with the Giants. Billy Cannon announced that the Raiders, who could not draw in Oakland, were moving to New Orleans. Another rumor had the Raiders moving to Kansas City.

When the Titans' financial difficulties became public, New York writers put the blame squarely on Wismer. "A man's ego can be a laughable thing," wrote Dick Young. "It can also be quite sad—and terribly self-destructive. Such is the case of Harry Wismer, who made the gargantuan mistake of trying to sell Harry Wismer for three years. From the inception of the Titans, the star of the show has been Harry Wismer. The blue-and-gold posters advertising the full schedule for the first season featured a king-sized unfiltered portrait of Harry Wismer. That sold a lot of tickets. Wismer would arise and talk about what he was going to do to the Maras. That sold a lot of tickets. He was feuding with his coach, Sammy Baugh. He was feuding with the AFL commissioner, Joe Foss. He was feuding with, and firing, his publicity man—who had the bad manners to attempt publicizing the ballplayers rather than Harry Wismer. That sold a lot of tickets. He came up with a big name, Sammy Baugh—and proceeded to make an anonymity of him."

Wismer had indeed worked his way through an astounding number of publicity men. One of the first was Robert Fulton Kelly, a Yale graduate who had for many years been a well-respected reporter for *The New York Times*. After leaving the *Times*, Kelly worked in public relations for the local racetracks. He was well connected with the New York papers, and Wismer hired him on the presumption that he could use those connections to get publicity for the Titans. Unfortunately, many of his connections were outdated, and there was one other problem. Kelly had never been particularly well acquainted with football, and his long absence from the reporter's beat had done nothing to improve his knowledge. At an early season press luncheon in 1960, Kelly informed the writers that the Titans' Al Dorow had better passing statistics than Baltimore's John Unitas. Unfortunately, Kelly butchered the latter's name, accenting the first syllable and calling him U-ne-tus.

The following year, Kelly again experienced press luncheon difficulties. During the meal, there was a knock on the door of the suite, which Kelly went to answer. Instead of opening the door inward, he attempted to push it open, and stood there struggling. Wismer shouted in his booming voice, "You don't have to attend Yale, Kelly, to know how to open a door."

In 1960 Wismer also employed Arthur Susskind Jr. and Ted Emery, a former Dartmouth public relations man. "Ted did the best he could," said one of the writers who covered the Titans, "but he was overwhelmed because there was no way to cover Harry." When Emery left the Titans, he had to ask the league office to help him recover unpaid wages.

In the wake of Kelly, Susskind, and Emery came Murray Goodman, former PR man for Yonkers Raceway and Madison Square Garden. Goodman was fired early in the 1962 season. Wismer's last public relations man was Al Busse, of the firm Rader and Finn. Busse left because his firm was not being paid. By that time, not even P.T. Barnum and Norman Vincent Peale could have put a positive spin on Wismer's situation. Barnum's presence, however, would have been appropriate.

"They were frustrated," Gordon White said of the Titans' many publicity men. "The men who worked for Harry Wismer knew our business, so they were good to deal with. They were as ticked off at him as anybody. They did more placating of the players and of Wismer than anything else."

In 1961 the legendary Red Smith took a shot at Wismer, while discussing the anemic attendance of the Titans. "Although he is too modest to admit it," Smith wrote, "Harry Wismer is entitled to a major share of the credit." The column was written after the Thanksgiving Day grudge match with Buster Ramsey and the Bills had attracted a modest assemblage. Two attendance figures (8,114 and 12,023) were announced as official. The lower figure was given first, and later the higher number was announced as a "corrected turnstile count." "To be sure," wrote Smith, "neither crowd would be considered great in Green Bay, Wisconsin, but it must be remembered that the Polo Grounds is accessible to only 15 million or so dedicated football fans, and there were competing attractions such as the Coney Island Walk and the Hofstra–C.W. Post game."

The same year, Joe Trimble wrote in the *Daily News*, "Speaking of Christmas, the best Christmas present to give Howling Harry Wismer would be a dead 'mike.' Wismer represents the end of an era in sportscasting types. That is, the screaming egotists of the Thirties through Fifties, as exemplified by Bill Stern, Ted Husing, and, finally, Wismer. Wismer's attack on commissioner Joe Foss was strictly in the gutter-fighting motif of Madison Ave., where they chop a man to bits in order to steal an account or knock him out of a job."

As the Titans' difficulties multiplied, *Sports Illustrated* discussed the plight of the league's two weak sisters. "Oakland has a weak team and a horrible attendance. New York has the same, plus Harry Wismer. . . . Wismer can antagonize anyone within shrieking distance." Added John Ahern in *The Boston Globe*, "The market is the world's best, but still the Titans do not draw...The world's largest market must be able to support more football than the Giants and Columbia can supply. But as a National Football League official stated it: 'Does logic dictate to Harry Wismer?'"

Some of the players resented the continual negative press. "I couldn't understand," Maynard said, "why the media couldn't write nice things about new jobs for coaches, new jobs for front office personnel, new jobs for thirty-three players, new jobs for trainers. There was a new team in town and the people who couldn't get in to see the Yankees or the Giants could go to see this new ballclub."

"I always thought that the press was very supportive of the team," Eddie Bell said, "but they didn't like Wismer. I think they made a conscious effort to separate any criticism between the team and the players on one hand and the owner on the other hand."

Meanwhile, as Wismer sought a buyer, his Titans had five more games to play. With all the distractions surrounding them, it was difficult to concentrate on the field, although, after Woodward's visit, most players had confidence that they would be paid. The game against Dallas, the first under league stewardship, was an offensive battle, as the Texans, led by quarterback Len Dawson, defeated the Titans 52–31. Dawson was a late bloomer who played under Dallas coach Hank Stram when the latter was an assistant at Purdue. After languishing on the Steelers' bench behind Bobby Layne, and sitting behind Milt Plum with the Browns, Dawson was rescued by Stram prior to the 1962 season. He beat out incumbent Cotton Davidson and highly touted rookie Eddie Wilson and was in the process of leading the Texans to the AFL championship.

The game with the Texans was not artistic. Turner said afterwards that he had difficulty motivating his distracted club. Each team fumbled four times, and the officiating was erratic. One call in particular might have cost the Titans the game. With New York trailing 38–31, Green overthrew an open Cooper in the end zone. Dallas got the ball back, and with four minutes left in the game, Haynes dropped the ball at the Titans' 35. George Strugar recovered, but the officials blew the play dead, ruling that Haynes was down before the fumble. Turner protested so vigorously that he received a 15-yard penalty for unsportsmanlike conduct. Haynes scored shortly thereafter to salt away the Dallas victory.

Dawson completed only five passes in the entire game, but passing was unnecessary, as Haynes and rookie of the year Curtis McClinton, a bruising 227-pounder from Kansas, each gained more than 100 yards rushing. One of Dawson's passes went to Haynes for a 75-yard touchdown. Three of the five Dallas completions, in fact, resulted in scores. Perry Richards, a tight end playing defensive back, had difficulty staying with Chris Burford, one of the AFL's best receivers. Although not exceptionally fast, Burford was a lanky, long-striding runner with very quick moves. Three times he was the beneficiary of pass-interference penalties. Finally, in the third quarter, he caught a 25-yard touchdown pass from Dawson, with Richards and Lee Riley riding him into the end zone. Burford got up, slapped the ball into Richards' stomach and laughed as he walked away.

For the Titans, Johnny Green completed 21 passes, but many were short screens to Christy, who caught 11 for 83 yards. Wismer stood on the Titans' sideline and joked with photographers as if his financial difficulties and the impending sale of the team did not exist. After the game, the players received checks drawn on the league account at First National Bank of Dallas.

Following that game, the Titans had a week off, which was good in two respects. First, it gave New York's many injured players an extra week to heal. Second, it gave the league a week in which it did not have to meet a Titans payroll, which was roughly $25,000 per game (Wismer, with his penchant for exaggeration, claimed it was $45,000 per week). The team returned to action on Thanksgiving Day at Denver, in a game that was one of only three 1962 AFL contests to be telecast nationally. In addition to covering salaries, the league put up $12,000 for airfare, but pocketed the $20,000 payment guaranteed each visiting team.

Under nationwide exposure, the Titans provided what some thought to be their finest hour. The crippled, nearly bankrupt club faced a vastly improved Bronco team that stood 7–4 and lurked just a game and a half behind the Texans in the Western Division standings. Denver was a 10-point favorite.

Prior to the game the Titans players had to endure the heckling of the Broncos' fans. "You son of a bitches been paid this week?" one of them shouted at the players as they warmed up. They had, in fact, been paid in the locker room before the game by Sauer, and took the field with renewed spirit. Aided by two key pass-interference penalties, they scored the first 17 points of the game on touchdowns by Mathis and Christy and a field goal by Shockley. The defense knocked Tripucka out of the game early, rendering the potent Denver offense less potent for most of the first half.

With 12 seconds left in the half, the Titans had the ball deep in their own territory, guarding a 24–10 lead. Green threw an ill-advised pass that was intercepted on the New York 15 and returned to the 1. After an incomplete pass, time ran out, but the Broncos coaches and players stormed onto the field, insisting that the clock had not been stopped promptly following the incompletion. The officials agreed, putting enough time back on the clock to allow Gene Mingo to kick an eight-yard field goal that narrowed the margin to 24–13. The kick, Mingo's 24th successful field goal of the season, broke Lou Groza's professional record set in 1953.

Another turnover by Green, this time deep in Denver territory, allowed the Broncos to pull even closer. Hit hard by Denver lineman Ike Lassiter, the Titans' quarterback coughed up the ball. Bud McFadin picked it up and rumbled 69 yards for a touchdown. Three minutes later, former Giants and Vikings signal caller George Shaw, replacing Tripucka, connected with Bob Scarpitto for a score that gave the Broncos a 27–24 lead. Following a safety, Green hurled a 35-yard pass to Maynard to put the Titans back in front 32–27.

Early in the final period, it appeared that Denver was staging one of its patented mile-high comebacks. Facing fourth down and one from their own 24, Broncos coach Jack Faulkner decided to gamble. Fullback Bo Dickinson got much more than the first down, racing 41 yards to the New York 35. Two plays later, Shaw hit Lionel Taylor for the go-ahead touchdown. With 9:30 to play, Green threw his third interception of the day. Linebacker Wahoo McDaniel, who later became one of the most popular Jets, picked off the pass at his own 41. At the New York 48, he lateraled to defensive back Jim McMillan, who took it all the way. Later, when Mingo booted a 49-yard field goal to give Denver a 45–32 advantage with only 5:57 left, it looked as though Denver had done it again.

This time, however, the visitors had something left in their tank. After the kickoff, Green huddled his team up and said, "With two we've got a winner." He then proceeded to lead them to two scores. For the first, Green capped a 65-yard drive with a six-yard scoring pass to Christy. Shortly thereafter, Lee Riley recovered a fumble on the Denver 20. The winning touchdown came on a three-yard pass to Powell. Denver had one last chance, but incurred a holding penalty that forced Mingo to attempt a field goal from 52 yards. His kick was low and wide and the Titans had an emotional 46–45 victory. Green was the hero, having thrown five touchdown passes, the best performance in Titans history.

Dr. Nicholas, who accompanied the team, felt the win was the key to the survival of the New York franchise. A loss, he thought, and a spiritless game, would have destroyed the team. The fact that they overcame the injuries, the altitude, the cold weather, and a two-touchdown deficit gave the team enough momentum to struggle through the rest of the season. *Newsday* said, "The Titans kept bouncing back yesterday, just like one of Harry's . . . aw, Harry has enough troubles." Wismer, who stayed in New York and watched the game on television, was so excited that he raised his asking price from $1.75 million to $2 million.

The final three weeks of the Titans' schedule were an endurance contest. From the 33 players on the roster, there were probably not more than 40 or 45 serviceable knees. Green and Grosscup had but one between them. Bobo had none. Linemen George Strugar and Buddy Cockrell had knee problems of long standing that prevented them from practicing on a regular basis. Both had already endured two operations, and the cold weather of November and December only made it more difficult for them to get loose. Mathis and Billy Atkins were also hobbling. Many of the good knees belonged to players such as running backs Bobby Fowler and Ed Kovac, emergency pickups who disappeared from pro football after the season. The club was just trying to accumulate enough bodies to get through the year. Of the seven players released on the final pre-season cut, five (Tiller, Look, Kovacs, Bob Watters, and Fran Morelli) found their way back on the squad before the season ended. Depth was non-existent. Any further injuries would require desperate measures for replacements; defensive players would have to play offense and vice versa. Roger Ellis, the Titans' utility lineman and spare linebacker, started several games, nearly every one at a different position. The team was not only thin, but also young and inexperienced. Following the release of Songin, there was not a single player over 30 on the roster.

The biggest problem was at quarterback, where Green had been playing in pain for several weeks. Not only did he have a bad knee; he was suffering from a severely sprained ankle as well. Green's knee problems began in 1959 in Pittsburgh, when, in a freak accident, he tripped and tore cartilage in his right knee. He re-injured the same knee in 1962, but kept playing. The coaches never ordered him to play, but kept asking if he thought he could, hoping the answer would be yes, since there was no one to take his place but the untested Scrabis. With his job on the line, there was no way Turner was going to play Scrabis unless he absolutely had to.

Green, a gritty Southern boy, kept assuring the coaches he could play, although he was limping badly. "Boy, he could really stand in there and take a shot," said Grosscup. "I don't know why the hell I did it," said Green. "I ruined the knee. Grosscup was smart enough to lay off his knee for most of the season. I played the last three games with the knee locked. I just wore the joint out. That was the one good season I had and I wanted to play as much as I could, but looking back, it was stupid." Ironically, Green still has his original right knee, but had the left one replaced a few years ago.

Grosscup felt guilty about the fact that he was on the sidelines while Green dragged himself around the field. "I felt embarrassed watching Green," he wrote, " because his knee was now worse than mine, but apparently he had a way of concealing fright and pain better than I did. I was suddenly appalled by my inadequacies as a professional football player. I don't fit the mold. Green's more the type. He's got a big, strong body, a rugged face, and the quiet courage that makes his teammates and coaches alike respect him."

Grosscup listened to the November 30 Titans–Patriots game on the radio, while Green started at quarterback. During the week before the game, Turner told the press that his team's morale was "the worst I've ever seen in football." Turner's spirits were down as well. "Boston plays too solid a game for us to do too much hoping," he said before the game. "We look for a victory, but I don't know how we'll get it."

Morale was no better after Wismer delivered his final pep talk to the club on the bus. "Fellas," he said, "this has been a rotten season. It's been a rotten season. But it's not over yet. But today is my wife's birthday. And I want you to win this one for her." Harry sat down, but the bus did not move. Finally, after Sauer paid him in cash, the driver pulled away from the curb.

The boys nearly came through, for the Patriots were almost as injury-riddled as the Titans. Babe Parilli was out with a broken collarbone, and in his place at quarterback was Tom Yewcic, a Michigan Stater and former Detroit Tiger farmhand, who, like Dean Look, had a brief trial in the major leagues. Prior to signing with the Patriots, he had been out of football for five years. To replace injured halfback Larry Garron, the Patriots activated Tom Stephens, a former Syracuse player who had been serving as assistant publicist for the Boston club.

Yewcic was unable to move the offense in the first half, and the Titans held a 10–3 advantage at intermission. The teams exchanged touchdowns in the third quarter, and, as the fourth period began, the New York lead was 17–10. In the first Titans–Patriots game, in September 1960, New York had been undone by Sapienza's botched punt. Now, in the final Titans–Patriots encounter, the punting game again proved New York's downfall. On the first play of the final quarter, Curley Johnson took an ill-advised gamble, attempting to run from punt formation out of his own end zone. He was swarmed under on the 10-yard line, well short of the first down, and the Patriots took possession of the ball. Shortly thereafter, Yewcic, who ran from scrimmage nine times for 90 yards, scored his second touchdown, tying the score at 17. With just over a minute left and the score still tied, the Patriots had the ball and faced a third down and 11 from their own 21. Yewcic called timeout and went to the sideline for a conference with Holovak, Parilli, and assistant coach Fred Bruney. Yewcic wanted to call a flare pattern to Ron Burton, but Holovak overruled him and called for a pass to Jimmy Colclough, the Patriots' best receiver.

Colclough didn't look like a professional football player. He was only 5'11" and 180 pounds, and his boyish looks had earned him the nickname "Peter Prep School." Colclough had been drafted in the 30th round of the 1959 draft by the Redskins, the 353rd player selected, and signed by Boston as a free agent. "By height, weight, and speed," said Holovak, who also coached Colclough at Boston College, "Jimmy shouldn't be playing in this league." Yet, hard work, desire, and good hands enabled Colclough to lead the Patriots with 49 catches in 1960. He had 42 in 1961, and 40 the following year. Colclough had been getting open all night against the Titans, but Yewcic had been unable to get the ball to him. Just two plays earlier, he had been five yards behind the New York secondary, only to see Yewcic's pass skitter off his fingertips.

Yewcic took the snap from center and faded back. Pursued by the Titans' line, he scrambled until he saw Colclough breaking free behind Perry Richards, the tight end pressed into duty at safety. Colclough pulled in Yewcic's pass at the New York 35 and headed for the goal line. Richards kept up a desperate pursuit and managed, with a dive, to trip Colclough at the 20, but Jimmy stumbled into the end zone with the winning touchdown. Yewcic completed only six passes in the game, but they accounted for 195 yards and the winning score. As the game ended, the Boston fans poured onto the field, mobbed the players and officials, and tore down the goal posts. The Internal Revenue Service also rushed onto the field, placing a lien on $18,000 of the proceeds in partial satisfaction of more than $25,000 in taxes owed by the Titans.

Wismer's financial difficulties caused more immediate problems for the players. Mischak said it had been suggested to him that the team try borrowing from Household Finance, and that his father-in-law jokingly offered to extend a loan to the Titans. For two days during the week preceding the Boston game, there was no hot water in the locker room, sparking a controversy as to whether it was simply a mechanical problem or the fact that Wismer had neglected another bill. "Our locker room became the Tobacco Road of pro football," wrote Kroll. "It was like living under siege." He reported that with the financial outlook bleak, the price of bennies in the locker room had risen to 50¢ per capsule. Clubhouse man Nick Torman stopped supplying shaving gear, and left dirty clothes on the floor, unwashed. The supply of tape ran low. The players tried to disregard the sideshow, although it was difficult to ignore the lack of hot water. "Pride is the most important thing about this game," said Bill Shockley, who had been re-acquired in a trade with Buffalo, "pride in yourself. I think all the fellows here have pride."

"We figure the franchise situation is not our problem," added Powell. "All we have to worry about is playing ball." It would not be Powell's problem for long, since he was playing out his option and would be free to leave the team at the end of the season. In October Wismer had announced that, since Powell was leaving anyway, he was then available to the highest bidder.

With Grosscup and Green both doubtful due to injury, it appeared that Scrabis might start against the Bills December 8 at the Polo Grounds. He was all that was left from the wealth of quarterback talent the Titans had gazed upon since the beginning of training camp. Dorow had been traded, Songin cut, Stephens was back in Texas to care for his injured wife, Green and Grosscup were hurt, and Dean Look was finished for the season. The last quarterback remaining was Scrabis, who worked with the first unit all week in practice. When game time came, however, both Grosscup and Green were suited up and available, and Scrabis remained on the sideline. "I didn't even practice the whole week," said Green, "but Bulldog said, 'You're starting.' I hadn't even picked up a ball all week. I don't know what the hell his thinking was. I think everybody'd just kind of given up, from the coaching staff on down."

This was the first action Grosscup had seen since his injury in Houston, and he was rusty, gimpy, and less than eager. When Turner asked if he wanted to go into the game during the third quarter, Grosscup shrugged and responded, "That's up to you, you're the coach." Turner decided to put him in, despite his lack of enthusiasm. Grosscup threw four passes, all of them incomplete, before departing in favor of Green. Playing on one leg, Green stuck mainly to short pass patterns. He had no mobility, could not avoid the rush, and had to get rid of the ball quickly. Although he completed 20 passes, they gained only 206 yards, and no touchdowns.

The Buffalo offense, which had been so anemic in the league's first two years, had suddenly become potent. In late September, San Diego placed quarterback Jack Kemp, who had led them to two division championships, on waivers. Under the rules, an injured player remained on waivers for 16 days. If unclaimed, he stayed the property of the team that had asked the waivers. Chargers coach Sid Gillman knew he was taking a gamble, but thought that no one would claim Kemp, who had a broken finger and would be unable to play for some time. "The doctor told us he was through for the season," Gillman said recently. Rarely did a team claim another club's injured players. If Kemp cleared waivers, the Chargers could clear a roster spot and activate a healthy player. Also, the Chargers had a rookie from Kansas, John Hadl, who they thought was their quarterback of the future. "Hadl was going to be our number-one guy," said Gillman, "and that was another thing that caused the decision. We needed somebody healthy to take Kemp's place." Gillman's gamble backfired, as Buffalo put in a claim for the waiver price of $100. The Chargers tried to withdraw the waivers, but it was too late. Kemp pondered retirement, but decided to report to Buffalo, giving the Bills a top-quality quarterback for the first time.

The Bills also had a running back, 243-pound Carlton "Cookie" Gilchrist, a load capable of running right over defenders. Said Dorow, who played with him briefly in 1962, "When Cookie Gilchrist came out of the blocks, you just heard this rumbling, like an earthquake. The quarterback handed off to him and got the hell out of the way. We were in as much danger as a defensive lineman."

"The only bad thing about blocking for Cookie," Buffalo guard Billy Shaw told an interviewer, "was that if my man held me to a stalemate, Cookie would run up my back, and that hurt."

Like so many early AFL players, Cookie had a checkered past. He starred at Har-Breck High School in Breckinridge, Pennsylvania, then attended Cheshire Academy in Connecticut to try to improve his grades sufficiently to gain acceptance to Michigan State. The Cleveland Browns derailed the Michigan State plan by offering Gilchrist a $5,500 bonus, which he eagerly accepted. Cut by the Browns, he went to the Canadian League, where he spent eight years. At the age of 27, Cookie was released by Toronto in August 1962, and signed by the Bills, who paid the Argonauts a $300 waiver fee. The fee made up only a small part of the $5,700 in salary advances Gilchrist had taken from Toronto.

Money had always been a problem for the big fullback. He perpetually claimed to be underpaid, and did everything he could to increase his salary. "I'm selling my body for X number of dollars," Gilchrist once said, "and when I negotiate a contract I'm negotiating for my future. I have no education. I've got nothing to fall back on after football."

Cookie was unable to hold onto the money he did earn. A series of bad investments, including a restaurant and a lighting fixture company,

coupled with general financial irresponsibility, left Gilchrist in a state of
perpetual insolvency. His financial problems, along with a violent temper,
earned him a reputation as a troublemaker.

Harvey Johnson was a Buffalo scout and one of Gilchrist's many
former coaches. He told the Bills, "We have to take a chance with this
guy. If he stays out of trouble he can help us." Thus far, Cookie had stayed
out of trouble and gained nearly 1,000 yards rushing, something no AFL
player had done in the league's first two seasons. He also blocked, kicked
off, and handled field goals and extra points.

Ralph Wilson was in the process of building a strong organization,
one that would win AFL championships in 1964 and 1965. It was generally acknowledged that Buffalo had lost the least amount of money of any
team during the league's first two years. Wilson stated that his break-even
crowd was 24,000. The Bills averaged 18,500 in 1961 and would draw
28,000 per game in 1962. Unlike Wismer, Wilson had drafted wisely,
and signed 12 of his 18 picks in 1961. Tired of Buster Ramsey's erratic
behavior, Wilson brought in Lou Saban, dismissed by Billy Sullivan the
previous fall, to install discipline. As the 1962 season wore on, Saban's
approach brought results. With Kemp and Gilchrist in the backfield, the
Bills came on strong after their slow start. Going into the game with
the Titans, they were 6–6–1, having gone 6–1–1 in their last eight games.

Against the Titans, Kemp was relatively ineffective, throwing for only
151 yards while being intercepted four times. The Bills dominated the
ground game, however, rushing for 284 yards while holding the Titans
to 27. Gilchrist gained 143 yards, becoming the first AFL player to gain
more than 1,000 yards in a season. He did all of the Bills' scoring, with
two touchdowns, two field goals, and two extra points. The Titans could
muster only a single field goal by Bill Shockley and went down to their
eighth defeat by the score of 20–3.

The final week of the Titans was a depressing one. Most of the
players were struggling with injuries. To make matters worse, the miserable, biting cold of December set in. On Monday, it snowed, blanketing
the Polo Grounds in white. The temperature hovered in the teens all
week. On game day, the mercury poked its nose just above 20 degrees,
but it remained windy and uncomfortably cold. Unfortunately, with the
Titans' precarious financial condition, there was precious little equipment

to protect the players from the elements. Karl Kaimer jokingly estimated the value of pads and sponges at $100 per square inch. "Anything that could absorb a blow," he said, "was found and taped on."

The Polo Grounds turf was frozen solid, and the Oilers appeared in sneakers, for better traction. The only Titans player similarly clad was Grosscup, who had purchased a pair at a Manhattan department store. There was little enthusiasm in the New York locker room, as most of the players were only concerned with leaving for their homes after the game. Turner gave an unusual pep talk, as quoted by Kroll. "This is the final game of the season," he said. "There probably won't even be any New York Titans next year. So most of you are playing in your last pro game. Most of you aren't good enough to play anywhere else." Buoyed by those inspirational words, the Titans trotted, jogged, and limped onto the playing field for the final time.

The players had to be there in order to get paid. The fans did not and only a few thousand saw fit to brave the cold to witness the Titans' last stand. The official attendance was announced as 8,167, and only 3,828 paid. Kroll estimated the crowd at 2,000, and even the announced paid attendance was the lowest in AFL history. Although New York (5–8) had nothing at stake, the game had great significance for the Oilers. A Titans win, coupled with a Patriots victory over Buffalo, would give Boston the Eastern Division title. Houston could clinch with either a win or a Patriots loss.

The Oilers got the ball first, and George Blanda drove his club methodically to the New York 23. Wayne Fontes, playing for the first time since his early-season ankle injury, intercepted the Houston quarterback on first down. Fontes picked off the ball at the 16, and chugged down the sideline the entire length of the field for a touchdown. Larry Grantham claimed that the Titans had to knock every member of the Oilers down twice in order to give the slow-footed Fontes enough time to cover 84 yards. "I got in front of him and knocked somebody down," said Grantham, "got up, got in front of him again and knocked somebody else down."

That was the high point of the afternoon. Blanda, unfazed, put together a 15-play drive that consumed nearly seven minutes and tied the score. After Houston went ahead 14–7, Fontes intercepted another pass and returned it to the Houston 28. Shockley kicked a 29-yard field goal to narrow the margin to 14–10 with 11 minutes left in the second quarter.

The Titans got no closer. Green and Grosscup, both limping badly, alternated at quarterback and were equally ineffective. Grosscup completed just four of 20 passes and Green two of eight. For the day, New York connected on only six of 31.

At halftime, the sideline heaters mysteriously disappeared. The final 30 minutes were a battle for survival. Billy Cannon scored twice, on a 64-yard run and a 33-yard pass from Blanda. Kroll was knocked unconscious trying to tackle Freddie Glick, who was returning an interception of a pass by Green. Glick's knee hit Kroll in the head and drove it back into his shoulder pads. He was carried off the field on a stretcher, into immortality, he hoped. "I would be the last man ever carried out of the Polo Grounds on a stretcher," Kroll wrote. Even this vision of dimly reflected glory was dashed, as construction delays at Shea Stadium relegated the Jets to the Polo Grounds for another year. Another season of professional football meant more stretcher cases. Kroll, who retired after the season, was not one of them.

When the score reached 44–10, the players simply wanted the game and the season to end. Only a handful of fans remained. Finally, with the game long gone, Turner put in Scrabis, his only healthy quarterback. He called a sweep. The New York tackle manning the side to which the play was to go growled, "Run it the other way, Scrabis." The quarterback dutifully changed the play to go in the opposite direction.

Ironically, Scrabis, who had taken the first snap in the first Titans practice at Durham more than two years earlier, and precious few since, took the final snap in Titans history. He dropped back to pass, was hit, and fumbled. The ball was recovered by Houston's Bill Wegener as the final gun sounded. The New York Titans were history.

EPILOGUE

THE PLAYERS

Don Allard   Allard had to sue the Titans to get the remainder of his salary. In 1962, when Babe Parilli was hurt, he was signed by the Patriots, played in four games, and was released at the end of the season. Allard played for several years in the Atlantic Coast League, where he enjoyed working with the younger players and earning a little extra money. He never viewed playing in the minors as an opportunity to return to the AFL or NFL. He found full-time employment in the Massachusetts court system, where he works as a probation officer

Sammy Baugh   In August 1962, just weeks after his departure from the Titans' camp in Stroudsburg, Baugh took a job as assistant coach at Oklahoma State University. One of his conditions for accepting the position was that he would be on campus only during the football season. Two years later, in 1964, Baugh was named head coach of the Houston Oilers. He clashed with Oilers star Billy Cannon, first fining him for violating curfew and then trading him to Oakland. Despite Baugh's offensive genius and the passing arm of George Blanda, Houston finished 4–10, placing them last in the AFL's Eastern Division. As with the Titans, Baugh had no playbook, and, as in New York, his club filled the air with footballs. Blanda threw 505 passes, including 68 in one game, but the Oilers' defense gave up more points than any other Eastern Division club. Baugh stepped aside after the season in favor of his old friend Bones Taylor, and finished his football career as an assistant with the Detroit Lions. Ironically, the head coach of the Lions was Harry Gilmer, who, as a young quarterback, understudied Baugh with the Redskins in the late 1940s and early 1950s.

After the 1966 season, Baugh returned for good to his 7,600-acre spread in Rotan and became a full-time rancher. In 1990 Edmonia, his wife of 52 years, died. Baugh continues to live on the ranch, playing golf and reading, activities he has pursued voraciously throughout his life. He still weighs 175 pounds, the same as when he played, and remains an American original. His son David, a high school football coach, was quoted as saying, "Basically, he's always been a person who is going to do what he wants to do, no matter what anyone else says. Pretty much he has lived his life exactly the way he wanted." In 1963 Baugh was inducted into the Pro Football Hall of Fame, a member of the first class.

Ed Bell   Bell retired after the 1960 season, and took a job with the Atlantic Refining Company in California. He stayed in the west until 1977, when his 16-year-old son died of a congenital heart problem. He returned to his home in Philadelphia and commuted to New York, where he worked in a fund-raising capacity for the United Negro College Fund. Bell then formed a marketing company that handled the advertising for the Pennsylvania Lottery. He is currently retired and living in Philadelphia.

Dick Christy   Christy played for the Jets in 1963, backing up Bill Mathis and Mark Smolinski at running back. He rushed for 88 yards, caught eight passes, and averaged five yards per punt return and 24 yards per kickoff return. That was his final season as a professional football player, as he was released during training camp in 1964. He died in an automobile accident in 1966.

Buddy Cockrell   Cockrell began trading cattle for profit as a teenager. He parlayed his bartering skills into real estate holdings and acquired a number of large ranches, including a 750,000-acre parcel in the northwest corner of Australia. Cockrell continues to ride every day and competes on the senior rodeo circuit. He was recently victorious in the national finals of the steer-roping competition.

Thurlow Cooper   Cooper was signed by the Jets for the 1963 season, but released at the end of training camp in favor of former Colts player Dee Mackey. Cooper began working for Balfour, a marketer of high school rings, and has been employed by Taylor Publishing, a major producer of high school yearbooks, since 1969. These jobs kept Cooper in contact with high school sports, where his renown as a professional athlete and local collegiate star gave him an entree. "They remembered me," he said. "It's all worked out. I've had a very enjoyable life."

Roger Donahoo   Donahoo suffered a serious shoulder injury in training camp in 1961 and was released. He taught and coached at Melvindale High School in Michigan for six years, served as defensive coordinator at Northwest Missouri State, then went to Riverview High School in 1969. He has coached and taught science and physical education at Riverview ever since. He also owns a landscaping business that he has operated for more than 20 years.

Al Dorow   Dorow's arm injury suffered against the Titans ended his football career. "My arm just gave out," he said. "They wouldn't send me to a doctor, and it just wouldn't come around." He was released by the Bills in October 1962, and became the offensive coordinator at his alma mater, Michigan State, where he remained for several years. A friend who operated a company called Champion Motor Homes convinced Dorow that he had the talent to make a lot more money selling motor homes than he could coaching the Spartans' offense. He worked for Champion for 19 years, the last nine as national sales manager, before retiring in 1992. Dorow lives in Sierra Vista, Arizona, which he claims has the best climate he has ever seen, excepting San Diego. "And you can't live there," he said of the latter city, "it's overrun with people." Dorow spent enough of his life being overrun by people from San Diego, particularly large ones with lightning bolts on their helmets.

Roger Ellis   Ellis made the opening day roster of the 1963 Jets as a backup lineman. After the first game of the season, however, Ewbank cut him and offered him a spot on the taxi squad. Having been on the team for more than three seasons, Ellis said that if he could not be on the active roster, he was going home. A day later, after a conversation with George Sauer, Ellis changed his mind and went back to see the head coach. In the intervening 24 hours, however, Ewbank had contacted Pete Perreault, a guard cut in training camp, and Perreault had accepted the taxi-squad position. Ellis's major league career was over. He went to Canada and played with the Saskatchewan Roughriders in 1964, then embarked upon parallel careers in minor league football and law enforcement. Ellis played for a number of teams, sometimes more than one at a time, and teamed up with Butch Songin on the 1966 Hartford Charter Oaks of the Continental Football League.

Through a friend, Ellis got an interview in 1968 with the United States Secret Service, an interview that, fatefully, took place on the day after Bobby Kennedy was murdered. In the wake of Kennedy's assassination, President Johnson ordered Secret Service protection for all presidential candidates. This opened up a number of jobs, and Ellis landed one of them. He spent more than 20 years in the Service, serving at one time on the detail that guarded Vice President Spiro Agnew. He remained close to Agnew, corresponding with him until the latter's death in 1996. Ellis retired in 1989 at the age of 51, and lives in Holden, Maine, with his black Lab, Shadow.

Dick Felt   Felt was traded to Boston for Butch Songin following the 1961 season. He played five seasons for the Patriots, retiring in 1966. Since that time, he has been employed by his alma mater, Brigham Young University. Felt was an assistant coach for 27 years, before moving to an administrative role due to health reasons.

Larry Grantham   Grantham was the last person to score a touchdown as a Titans player, when, during the AFL All-Star Game played in January 1963, he ran an interception back for a score. Grantham played 10 seasons with the Jets, and then joined Orlando of the World Football League as a player-coach under Jack Pardee. He was a full-time coach when the league folded the following year. Since 1980 he has operated his own marketing and sales company, acting as a manufacturers' rep for premium and specialty businesses. He is in excellent health, has eight grandchildren, and is a five handicapper who plays golf nearly every day.

Lee Grosscup   In one of the last game programs of the 1962 season, a Titans publicist lamented the injuries to Grosscup and Johnny Green and prophesied, "Put them together in one piece in 1963 and the Titans have the winning combination." Both were healthy in 1963, but played poorly during the exhibition season. In a surprising move, Grosscup was released just before the regular season started. He signed with the Saskatchewan Roughriders, but played only one game in Canada before returning to the US. In 1964 he went to training camp with the 49ers, but was released during the exhibition schedule. Grosscup joined the Oakland Raiders, and spent the season on the taxi squad, where it was hoped that he would be one of the first of Al Davis's reclamation projects. Grosscup was cut again in 1965 and was asked to be on the taxi squad, but declined in order to take the position of player-coach with the Hartford Charter Oaks of the Atlantic Coast Football League. One of his first moves as coach was signing Ron Nery, the former Chargers defensive end who had tormented him in the second game of the 1962 season. "I don't like you at all because of what you did to me," he told Nery, "but I want you on my side." Unfortunately, Grosscup and Nery couldn't salvage a team that ended up 2–12. "I knew my career was over," Grosscup said, "when people were booing me in practice."

During his college days, the articulate Grosscup had hosted a five-minute sports show on KSL-TV. In the summer of 1966, he signed with NBC as a color commentator for AFL games. During the next few years, he announced football games, obtained some small acting parts, and did some freelance writing. His book about the 1962 season, *Fourth and One*, sold out one edition of 10,000 copies, and had been scheduled for abridged serialized publication in *The Saturday Evening Post*. The *Post*, however, had recently been sued for libel by University of Georgia coach Wally Butts over a story involving the fixing of college games, and was skittish about publishing Grosscup's diary. It was quite tame by today's standards, but contained descriptions of behind the scenes events that might have been considered offensive by some. The *Post* paid Grosscup, but did not publish the material, costing him valuable publicity.

Meanwhile, Grosscup's personal life was coming apart at the seams. He had been through a difficult divorce in 1963, and became addicted to both pills and alcohol. (Ironically, his *Sports Illustrated* article, written during his college days, described his intense reaction to caffeine: "Some nights, after I drink coffee," he wrote, "I lay awake for hours and can remember things that happened to me when I was 2 years old. It's amazing how a non-powerful drug like caffeine can have such an effect on me.") In 1971 he hit bottom, attempted to commit suicide by walking into San Francisco Bay, then began a recovery that has continued until the present. Grosscup has not taken a drink since 1971 and, in addition to his broadcasting career, works for the National Council on Alcoholism. For the past 24 years, he has gone, twice a year, to Laney Junior College in Oakland, site of Frank Youell Field, where he had his greatest day as a professional. At Laney, he speaks to a health education class on the subject of alcoholism. "Today I say, 'boring is beautiful.' I had a lot of excitement early in life. My favorite days today are days when nothing happens."

Dick Guesman   Guesman recovered fully from his broken arm and played with the Jets in 1963. He was the regular kicker, scoring 57 points on nine of 24 field goal attempts and 30 of 30 extra points. In March 1964, he was traded to the Denver Broncos in a transaction that brought to New York one of the early Jets crowd favorites, linebacker Wahoo McDaniel. After one season with the Broncos, Guesman retired at the age of 27 to work for the Shell Oil Company. He left Shell in 1974 to become an independent real estate developer in the Atlanta area. His company, C.I.R. Realty, does commercial sales and develops small shopping centers and office buildings.

Pete Hart   Hart left the Titans following his back injury in mid-1960. After working in the oil fields for a year, he coached football until 1973. Oil was in his blood, however, for he had begun working in the fields as a teenager in 1952. More than 20 years later, he returned and began drilling wells, prospering through the boom times and hanging on during the price collapse of the mid-1980s. In 1986 he began teaching high school physics and chemistry. After four years, he discovered he had difficulty relating to the new generation of students, and left teaching. He taught briefly at a prison, and now lives in semi-retirement. "I just do odd jobs and enjoy life," he said. "I'll always work."

Mike Hudock   Hudock played with the Jets through 1965, feeling rookie Joe Namath's hands on his backside during his final season. He went to the expansion Miami Dolphins in 1966, but had some differences with the coaching staff. He asked to be traded and got his wish, finishing his career with Kansas City in 1967. The end came when he tore his knee and arch at the same time, an injury so severe that he was told he might never walk again. Hudock went into teaching briefly, then worked in construction until 1979. He became a policeman, serving until he retired in 1992 due to severe arthritis. He had one knee replaced in 1995, and was scheduled to have the other replaced in 1997.

Paul Hynes   "It probably took me a couple of years to realize it," said Hynes of his eventful departure from the Jets, "but Weeb Ewbank did me a big favor by cutting me. I went into business, which was a lot easier than playing pro football." Hynes worked for large construction companies, installing offshore drilling platforms in the North Sea, off South America, in the Middle East, and in Southeast Asia. He eventually formed his own company and acts as a consultant for offshore construction projects. In the early 1980s, he lived in London and operated a company in Libya, and has lived and worked in Indonesia since 1986.

Proverb Jacobs   After leaving the Titans in 1962, Jacobs returned to the University of California and finished his degree requirements in 1963. He was working as a probation counselor when Al Davis of the Raiders called and asked if he was interested in making a comeback. Although he was lukewarm about the prospect of returning to pro football, Jacobs used his vacation time to attend the Raiders' camp. He made the team and wound up playing a year and a half with Oakland. Following his eventual release, Jacobs earned a doctorate in education, while still working in the probation department. He then learned that the Berkeley school district was looking to replace a departing teacher named Dale Brown, who eventually found his way to LSU and became a legendary basketball coach. Jacobs took the job and stayed until 1968, when he became a junior college coach. He was also the defensive coach for the San Jose Apaches of the Continental Football League under Apaches head coach Bill Walsh. For several years, Jacobs taught math and sociology at Laney Community College, and also coached track. Laney was somewhat of a football factory among junior colleges, producing four players who eventually became NFL first-round draft choices. Jacobs is currently teaching and writing his autobiography.

Dick Jamieson   Jamieson's 1961 back injury essentially ended his football career. He went into radio broadcasting, but in 1965 Bones Taylor became head coach of the Houston Oilers, and asked Jamieson to join the club as player-coach. He played during the exhibition season, and then served as an inactive assistant coach and insurance in the event that either George Blanda or backup Don Trull was injured. That was the start of a lengthy coaching career, which continued at the high school level from 1966 through 1972, then at the University of Missouri as offensive coordinator in 1973. In 1978–79, Jamieson was head coach at Indiana State, where his club played second fiddle to a basketball team led by Larry Bird. In 1980 he went to the NFL as an assistant with the St Louis Cardinals, where he remained until 1985. Following two years with the Oilers, he returned to college coaching for five years. In 1995–96, he assisted Ray Rhodes with the Eagles and, in 1997, became the offensive coordinator of the Arizona Cardinals.

Fred Julian   Julian was cut in August 1961, in the confusion surrounding his draft status. He played for Grand Rapids in the newly organized World Football League, with former Titans halfback Leon Burton, while holding down a full-time job as a high school coach. Julian later operated an insurance agency in Detroit before getting back into coaching in 1969. For 16 years, he compiled an outstanding record at a Grand Rapids high school, achieving such success that he was named head coach at Grand Rapids Junior College. Since assuming the head job in 1985, he has led the Raiders to a record of 111–36–1.

Karl Kaimer   Kaimer's football career ended in Peekskill, New York, in 1963, after being cut by the Jets in training camp. During the previous offseason, he had been employed in the petro-chemical industry, manufacturing parts used in instrumentation. Eventually, Kaimer bought the company and expanded it. He now owns three companies, one domestic and two international, that market instrumentation equipment for high-tech semi-conductors. He lives in New Jersey.

Jack Klotz   Placed on waivers by the Titans early in the 1962 season, Klotz was signed by the Chargers. Like Bob Scrabis, he did not take to life in California. "I'm an East Coast boy," he said. He asked Sid Gillman for his release, got it, contacted Weeb Ewbank and got a contract with the Jets. Klotz played with New York in 1963 and with the Oilers in 1964. Early in his final season, he suffered a severe injury, ripping the muscles in his right leg. He limped through the year, the final season he needed to qualify for his pension. It took two years for the muscle to heal completely.

Klotz then coached briefly in the Atlantic Coast Football League. "It was like the Titans," he remembered. "Checks were bouncing; federal marshals came looking for the guy who ran the team." He was an assistant coach in the minor leagues for several years, while holding down full-time sales jobs. Jack also served as assistant basketball coach at Widener College from 1967 to 1990.

In the mid-1970s, Klotz owned and operated a company that manufactured various types of energy conservation devices. Unfortunately, the CBS news show *60 Minutes* aired a segment claiming that such devices were worthless. The business failed and Klotz bottomed out financially. He did some substitute teaching, scraped and hustled, and managed to hold on. In the early 1980s, he began working with troubled teenagers. City Team Ministries hired him in 1989. "It's more of a calling than a job," says Klotz, a devout Roman Catholic. During the past 20 years, he has helped many young men turn their lives toward a better road.

Alex Kroll   During his All-America season at Rutgers, Kroll was the subject of a profile article in a national magazine. The author asked him what he planned to do after his football career was over. "I didn't know," Kroll said recently. "My horizon was football. But I was standing in a square donated by a guy named Charley Brower, a Rutgers grad who'd made a lot of money at BBD&O [Batten, Barton, Durstine and

Osborne, a top New York advertising firm]. I knew Charley. He was a
great guy. So I said, 'Well, I might go to law school or I might go into the
advertising business.'" The article appeared in print, and shortly thereafter Kroll received a call from Harry Carpenter, another Rutgers grad
who worked at an ad agency called Young and Rubicam. Kroll accepted
Carpenter's invitation to visit the agency, liked the management
immensely, and agreed to take a job as a trainee in the research department in the spring of 1962. He hated it. In June, when the company denied
his request for a leave of absence to play in an all-star game, he quit.

Following the 1962 football season, Kroll returned to Young and Rubicam and asked them to let him try another position. He had become dis-
illusioned with pro football during his one turbulent season with the
Titans. "For me, that was distressing," he said, "because football was really
my great love and passion. Playing in those demeaning circumstances
bothered me." Young and Rubicam, much to Kroll's surprise, welcomed
him back, this time as an apprentice copywriter. He took to the new
assignment with the same passion he had felt for football. When Jets
coach Weeb Ewbank called about a contract for the 1963 season, Kroll
decided to retire.

Progress at Young and Rubicam was rapid. Kroll became a full-fledged
copywriter, a supervisor, and in 1970 creative director. In 1975 he was
named president of the entity that handled all US operations. In 1982
he became chief operating officer and president of the entire company,
and in 1985 chairman and CEO. At the end of 1994, Kroll retired and
became chairman of the Advertising Council, a non-profit enterprise that
produces most public-service advertising.

Dean Look   After recovering from the severe neck injury suffered
in the 1962 game against Denver, Look sued the Titans to get the salary
due him, and then attempted a comeback with the Detroit Lions in 1963.
He abandoned his efforts after two weeks, convinced that his physical
ability would not return. Look returned to the Lansing area and entered
the insurance business, where he remained until 1979. He then began manufacturing and marketing instruments used for arthroscopic surgery, and
still markets medical products, developing dealer relationships in Europe.
Look has also been an NFL game official since 1972.

Bob Marques   Marques tried to come back in 1961 from a serious injury suffered the year before but was released in training camp. He went into teaching and is currently vice principal at a high school in Everett, Massachusetts.

Blanche Martin   Martin finished the 1960 season with the Los Angeles Chargers, playing in the first AFL Championship Game. He left football after that game to resume his education and graduated from the University of Detroit Dental School in 1967. He is currently practicing dentistry in Michigan, where he lives with his wife and five young children, although he is also a great grandfather. "I can't retire now," Martin said in 1996, "because I've got five babies under nine. I'm going to be working the rest of my natural born days. Maybe I'll play some more football. With the money these guys make now, all I'd have to do is get one year in."

Bill Mathis   Mathis remained with the Jets through the 1969 season, serving principally as a backup to Matt Snell and Emerson Boozer in his later years. He finished his 10-year career with a total of 3,589 rushing yards and 149 pass receptions and played in the Super Bowl III victory against the Baltimore Colts. During his last several years as an active player, Mathis worked as a broker for Bear, Stearns and Company during the offseason. When he retired from football, he became a full-time broker, and in 1972 he moved to Atlanta to help the company open its first office in that city. After spending 20 years with Bear, Stearns and Company, Mathis moved to the investment firm of Sterne, Agee and Leach, where he is still employed. He lives in Atlanta and enjoys attending his son's high school football games.

Don Maynard   Maynard played with the Jets through 1972, finishing his career with 633 catches for 11,834 yards. The latter total was an all-time record at the time of his retirement. Maynard caught the winning touchdown pass in the 1968 AFL Championship Game against the Raiders, and finished his career in 1973 with the St. Louis Cardinals. He coached briefly in the World Football League with Shreveport and employed a four-wide-receiver offense years before it was used in the

NFL. "I didn't have a choice," Maynard said, "because I didn't have a tight end." In the offseason during his playing career, he was employed at various times as a carpenter, a licensed plumber, and a teacher. Maynard now sells annuities and pension plans to individuals and small businesses. He was elected to the Pro Football Hall of Fame in 1987.

Larry McHugh   McHugh suffered a broken foot during training camp in 1962, tried to return too soon, and was cut. He was offered a contract with the Jets in 1963, but had gotten married and opted for the security of a head coaching job at Xavier High School, a new institution just opening in Middletown, Connecticut. McHugh led the Falcons to a 160–38–6 record during the next 21 years. He was elected to the Connecticut Coaches Hall of Fame in 1984 and the National Coaches Hall of Fame in 1986. In 1983 McHugh became president of the Middlesex County Chamber of Commerce, a position he retains today. He also serves as chairman of the Connecticut State University System and as a director of Liberty Bank, one of the largest banks in Connecticut.

John McMullan   McMullan was cut by the Jets during 1963 training camp, and took a job with Navajo Trucking. When his wife died a few years later, he got into the restaurant business, with its flexible hours, so that he could spend more time at home with his young family. He died of cancer in 1994.

Bob Mischak   Mischak was traded to the Oakland Raiders during the summer of 1963, commencing a lengthy association with that club and its rookie coach, Al Davis. Mischak played through 1965, when he retired due to a severe knee injury. He spent 1966 through 1973 at West Point, his alma mater, as a member of the coaching staff. In 1974 he returned to Al Davis and Oakland, serving as tight ends coach and scout. Under John Madden and Tom Flores, he accumulated three Super Bowl rings (XI, XV, XVIII), a feat he scarcely could have imagined during the dark days of the 1962 Titans.

From 1988 through 1996, Mischak was semi-retired, coaching occasionally in Arena Football, and in Europe for the World League. He worked briefly in Munich for Lamar Hunt's brother Bunker, and in 1994, returned to the Raiders.

In 1996 Mischak retired completely from football and is currently absorbed in tending to his investments and traveling the world. He and his wife Doris have toured extensively, including a trip across the Himalayas to Siberia and Mongolia on the Silk Road made famous by Marco Polo.

Nick Mumley   Mumley played sporadically in the Canadian League after leaving the Titans following the 1962 season. He retired just before the start of the 1966 season and took a sales job with a foundry in Wheeling, West Virginia. In 1974 he left his native West Virginia for Columbus, Indiana, when an old fraternity brother convinced him to join his company and sell industrial equipment. Nick is now director of the Structural Steel Division of Krot Corporation in Columbus, where he lives with his wife of more than 40 years. He is an exceptionally proud two-time grandfather.

Joe Pagliei   Pagliei has had one of the more interesting post-football careers of any of the former Titans. A fast-talking hustler from Philadelphia, he was always attracted to life in the fast lane. After reporting to training camp overweight in 1961, he was cut and returned to Philadelphia, where he managed a bowling alley owned by Bones Taylor. For several years he bounced around, making contacts and selling automobiles. When the Middle East oil crisis hit in 1979, the auto business suffered and Pagliei found himself out of work. He survived by playing gin at a country club (making $400–500 per week, he claimed) and acting as a jockey agent. "I always liked hustling," he said, "I'd go to the race track. That was my true love."

It may have been his true love, but in 1979, it was not supporting his family. From his stint with the Eagles, Pagliei knew Philadelphia owner Leonard Tose, who was a close friend of former Cleveland Indians baseball star Al Rosen. Rosen had recently been named vice president of Bally's. Tose made the introduction, and Pagliei found himself in the casino business, where he proved a natural. A lover of celebrity, he worked with Willie Mays, met Donald Trump, and found himself in charge of authorizing credit for the casino's high rollers. After 14 years in the casino business, Pagliei is now selling automobiles again. "Unfortunately," he said, "all the high rollers ended up broke or dead."

Dainard Paulson   Paulson played with the Jets through 1966, intercepting a total of 29 passes, which at the time was a New York record.
He played in the AFL All-Star Game two times and led the league with
12 interceptions in 1964. Paulson currently owns a recreational vehicle
dealership in Yakima, Washington, and operates a nearby farm.

Art Powell   After playing out his option during the 1962 season, Powell signed with the Oakland Raiders, where he had four outstanding seasons, leading the league in 1963 with 1,304 receiving yards and 16
touchdowns. Powell finished up with Minnesota in 1968, ending his career
with 479 catches for 8,046 yards and 81 touchdowns, averaging almost 17
yards per catch.

Following his retirement from pro football, Powell went to Toronto,
where he managed construction and renovation projects for 15 years. He
then returned to California, where he is involved with international
finance, packaging and structuring investments.

Bob Reifsnyder   After his release by the Titans in 1961, Reifsnyder,
who has an engineering degree from the Naval Academy, went to work
for the New York Telephone Company as a sales representative, while
playing semi-pro ball with the Long Island Giants. After nine months of
commuting on the Long Island Railroad, he had had enough and decided,
like so many of his old teammates, to get into coaching. He coached at
Massapequa High School for 18 years and finished his career in Patchogue.
In January 1997, Reifsnyder was elected to the College Football Hall of
Fame. He is retired and lives in Ocean Pines, Maryland.

Perry Richards   The 1962 season with the Titans was Richards' last
as a professional football player. He returned to Detroit, where he had
played with the Lions, and became a teacher, while simultaneously operating two businesses. One manufactured a graphite-based oil additive and
the other owned a patent for a type of material used in signs. Neither
business achieved great success, and Richards concentrated on teaching.
During his 1968 summer vacation, he worked at St. Peter's Home for Boys,
a facility that works with abused and neglected children. He found a home
at St. Peter's, and has been there ever since.

Joe Ryan   Ryan was claimed on waivers by the Patriots midway through the 1960 season, but decided not to report. His wife was pregnant in New York and Ryan, a backup with the Titans, didn't foresee a long-term future in professional football. He played in the Atlantic Coast League, and was an assistant coach at Jersey City in 1963 under John Dell Isola. In 1964 he began a career of teaching and coaching, starting a football program at Susan Wagner High School. He eventually left Susan Wagner to start another program at St. Joseph's by the Sea, located in his hometown of Staten Island. He is presently head coach at St. Joseph's.

Rick Sapienza   Released the week following his disastrous abortive punt against the Patriots, Sapienza went on to a lengthy career in New England minor league football. He played until the age of 36, while pursuing a full-time career as a high school teacher.

Bob Scrabis   Scrabis was not offered a 1963 contract by the Jets. In 1962, attending classes during the offseason, he completed a Master's degree in business administration. The following year, after leaving football, he earned a Ph.D in accounting. As a youngster in New Jersey, Scrabis's goal had been to become the youngest chairman of the board in the history of US Steel Corporation. When he got a job in the accounting field, however, he found he didn't like it, and the childhood dream vanished. At that point, fate stepped in. Scrabis married a young lady whose father owned a Buick dealership. He began working there and, when his father-in-law passed away unexpectedly in 1969, Scrabis assumed management of the dealership. He has operated it ever since.

Ed Sprinkle   When Bulldog Turner was released from his coaching duties following the 1962 season, Sprinkle was let go as well. He received only about a quarter of the salary due him, and got that only because of the intervention of Joe Foss. Sprinkle returned to his business interests in Chicago, which included a bowling alley and a retail carpet and tile business. He considered an offer from George Halas to become an assistant coach with the Bears, but decided that coaching would require too much time away from his growing family. Now 75 years old, he works for the Department of Senior Community Services in Chicago, issuing

ID cards to senior citizens. A rarity among old football linemen, he does not have bad knees, and is a regular on the golf course.

Hayseed Stephens   Raised as a devout Christian, Stephens was introduced to alcohol and nightlife at Hardin-Simmons. He took to both with enthusiasm and, following his departure from the Titans, embarked on a roller coaster life of glitz, money, and glamour. Achieving great success in the oil business, he made and gambled away millions of dollars. Finally, in 1978, in Las Vegas, Stephens had what he refers to as his "personal Super Bowl." In his hotel room, he re-discovered the religion he lost in college. He now operates the Hayseed Stephens Evangelical Association, and has done missionary work around the world, particularly in South Africa and the Middle East. There are 200 affiliated churches in South Africa, and Stephens is a covenant brother with the King of the Zulus.

The former quarterback remains very active in the oil business, and is currently preparing to drill in Israel where, based upon biblical prophecies and geological testing, he believes he has discovered one of the largest oil deposits in the world. "The big joke," Stephens said, "is that when Moses came to the Promised Land, he made a wrong turn." Hayseed intends to prove that Moses' decision was not wrong, only premature. "You'll turn on the TV," he said, "and see oil—a gusher—blowing out in Israel, and you'll say, 'That's an old Titan.'"

George Strugar   Strugar played for the Jets in their first season, then retired. While with the Rams in the 1950s, he founded a trucking company called Rams Express, with fellow players Don Burroughs and Will Sherman. Upon leaving football, Strugar devoted his full energy to the business. He died in 1997.

LaVerne Torczon   Torczon played with the Jets through 1965, and then went to the Miami Dolphins in the expansion draft. After a year in Miami, he fell victim to a youth movement and was released. During his year with the Dolphins, Torczon began selling real estate. He is now in his 35th year in the real-estate profession, having specialized in appraisals since 1982.

Mel West   West was cut in October 1962 to make room for Jim Tiller. He had a tryout with the Patriots, but was not signed because of torn cartilage in his knee. West played briefly for a semi-pro team in Florida, then signed with the Toronto Argonauts of the Canadian League, but his knee was shot and he played very little. His athletic career over, West returned to school and earned a Master's degree in secondary administration. He spent 23 years as a principal in the Minneapolis school system, retiring in 1996 due to health problems.

Harry Wismer   After Sonny Werblin acquired the New York franchise, Wismer faded into oblivion, the worst possible fate for a man with his insatiable thirst for recognition. In April 1963, he was ordered to appear in court to answer charges that he had failed to register the Titans as a business and neglected to pay $36,000 in business and amusement taxes to the City of New York. When Wismer did not appear, a warrant was issued for his arrest. Wismer's attorney obtained a postponement on the basis of poor health, for Harry was suffering from a severe episode of arthritis and gout. In 1964 Wismer filed suit to recover his Lions stock from his father-in-law, who had acted on his behalf in 1947. Wismer prevailed and collected $100,000. During the next few years, he continued to frequent mid-town restaurants and hotels, but was not the ebullient, effusive Wismer of old. "He just sort of faded out of the scene," recalled Gordon White. "Once Leon Hess took over the team, I never ran across Harry Wismer again."

In 1965 Wismer published his autobiography, *The Public Calls It Sport*. The book is a mixture of braggadocio and bitterness. Wismer claimed credit for virtually every development in the relationship between professional football and broadcasting, and listed Bert Bell, J. Edgar Hoover, and Ed Sullivan among his close friends, confiding that he "made" Sullivan by getting him his first major television sponsor.

Lamar Hunt and Sonny Werblin were not Wismer's close friends. "I made a fundamental mistake when I agreed to help start the American Football League," he wrote. "I aligned myself with amateurs, and I assumed that we were one for all and all for one...I hadn't learned, though I should have known, that amateurs and dilettantes in any field are unpredictable, uncertain qualities."

He also wrote: "My co-owners needed me to start the New York franchise, otherwise there would have been no AFL, no grand stadium in Flushing Meadows ...Yet, when I needed help, they turned their backs; and in the wings, ready to administer the *coup de grace*, stood one of my own ilk, a hustler like myself, the guy down the block, who bruised my own toes and picked up my team."

Wismer proved remarkably inaccurate as a prophet. "I am not sure that the AFL is going to survive," he wrote, along with: "I doubt if there is much to be said for the possibilities of a merger between the AFL and the NFL. The NFL has nothing to gain." In his book, Wismer vowed that he would return to professional sports. He did not, and died December 4, 1967, at the age of 54, of a fractured skull suffered in a fall.

THE TEAM

Despite a bevy of rumors and a few premature announcements, the 1962 season ended with Wismer as the nominal owner of the Titans and the league footing the bills, to the tune of $255,000. On December 23, the AFL's executive committee met in Houston prior to the league's championship game. They discussed the Titans' situation for more than four hours without reaching any decisions. Wismer, who claimed to be delayed by bad weather, arrived just as the meeting broke up and did not participate in the discussions. During the first week of January 1963, with no buyer in sight, Foss announced his intention to revoke the New York franchise. Under the league constitution, Foss could do so, with the approval of at least six owners, if he felt a club had engaged in activity detrimental to the AFL. On January 4, the day the owners were scheduled to vote on Foss's proposal, Wismer negotiated a compromise with the commissioner. He would have until the end of March to peddle the team and, if unsuccessful, the league would buy the Titans for $1 million.

In mid-January, the league office announced that 15 proposals for the purchase of the Titans had been considered, but none had been accepted. About the same time, Ted Barron, a 42-year-old Boston businessman, said that he and three partners were in the final stages of negotiating the acquisition of the New York club. Barron would rue his decision to pursue the Titans, for not only was he unsuccessful, he and an associate were sued by Wismer for alleged fraud and misrepresentation. Wismer asked for $2.5 million. The same day, Wismer charged Wayne Valley, the Raiders' owner, of tampering with Art Powell. Knowing he was going to the Raiders, Wismer claimed, Powell didn't give him a full effort in 1962. If so, Powell put on quite a performance at half speed, leading the league with 1,130 receiving yards and placing second with 64 receptions.

The peace between Wismer and Foss did not last, and soon the perpetual antagonists found themselves at odds once more. Foss accused Wismer of violating his agreement to actively market the team and called a meeting on February 6 to again propose the revocation of the New York franchise. This time, rather than compromise, Wismer chose a legal solution. Just prior to the scheduled meeting, Wismer's attorneys filed a petition in United States District Court in Manhattan requesting protection under Chapter XI of the Bankruptcy Act for Titans of New York, Inc., the Wismer-controlled corporation that owned the franchise. A Chapter XI filing is intended to provide a company time to restructure and reorganize a business and emerge with a plan to recover and carry on profitably. Creditors are prevented from taking any action to collect debts or enforce contracts while the company is under the court's protection. Thus, Wismer's action froze Foss's attempt to revoke the franchise. Wismer did not, however, declare personal bankruptcy. One can assume he retained sufficient assets to maintain a relatively comfortable lifestyle.

In order to receive the court's protection, the debtor must show that there is a reasonable possibility that its plan will be successful. This safeguard is intended to prevent a filing from being used simply to dodge creditors. Although the Titans' debts far exceeded their assets, Wismer's plan depended heavily upon the benefits of moving to Shea Stadium, which was expected to be ready in time for the 1963 season.

The AFL's attorneys immediately appeared in court with a request that the league be allowed to proceed with its action despite the bankruptcy filing. They would attempt to show that Wismer's plan had little chance of success and thus should not be accepted by the court. On February 27, just two days after Wismer mailed a letter to season ticket holders asking for their support, the court granted the AFL permission to proceed with the revocation of the franchise.

On March 1, Foss received a letter from David "Sonny" Werblin, president of Music Corporation of America, television agent for the AFL, and well known to both Foss and Wismer. In November 1962, when Foss was looking for a buyer for the beleaguered franchise, Sullivan Barnes, an attorney for the league, reminded Foss of a birthday dinner Werblin had given for Foss at the 21 Club. Wismer had been drinking, got into an argument with Werblin, and called him a "kike." Werblin threatened Wismer, and Foss had to keep them apart. While being restrained by the commissioner, Werblin yelled to Wismer that he would eventually own the New York franchise. (Not surprisingly, in his autobiography, Wismer recalled the event differently: Werblin had insulted him, and Foss tried to attack him physically. Given that Foss was sober and generally a more reliable source, his version seems more likely.)

In late December, Foss flew to New York to have lunch with Werblin. The two quickly agreed upon the price of $1,350,000 and Werblin wrote out a check for $100,000 on the spot. When Foss called Wismer with the good news, Wismer decided that he did not want to sell the team to Werblin and managed to scuttle the deal. By March, as a result of the bankruptcy court's ruling, Foss was free to deal directly with Werblin who, in early February, along with Leon Hess, Phil Iselin, Donald Lillis, and Townsend Martin, had formed an entity known as Gotham Football Club, Inc. Werblin's letter of March 1 to Foss stated that his new company was willing to purchase the Titans for $1 million, the same as the AFL guarantee, $350,000 less than what he had offered in December, and well short of Wismer's $2.5 million asking price of the previous fall. Foss accepted Werblin's offer on March 8, the bankruptcy court approved the transaction March 14, and the sale was consummated on March 28.

At the closing, Wismer was handed a check for $1 million, which he promptly endorsed and handed over to the bankruptcy trustee. In his autobiography, Wismer recalled the event in his typical dramatic fashion:

> I stumbled out of the office into a bar. It was empty; the smell of whiskey gagged me. Was this all I had left? I had been wounded before, but the cut had never been so deep. Out on the street again, I walked...Everything I can recall now seemed touched with ugliness—women in the streets with uncombed hair, dirty children, finally a battered cab, its driver dropping me off at the apartment. I sat in the darkened room, beset alternately by waves

of indignation, humiliation, self-pity, unable to think clearly, unable to gather my forces. I felt that I had run a long distance and was tired and lonely.

While Wismer wallowed in self-pity, Werblin had a franchise, but little else. He had a lame-duck coach and only the remnants of the talent that had staggered through the 1962 campaign. Preoccupied with their financial difficulties, and absent any funds with which to pay bonuses, the Titans had made little attempt to sign any of their draft choices, who included future stars such as John Mackey of Syracuse, Jerry Stovall of LSU, and Willie Richardson of Jackson State. Even had the Titans made an effort, it is unlikely that any collegiate stars would have been willing to hitch their star to the wagon of Wismer as he teetered on the verge of bankruptcy. Werblin would have to build his team practically from scratch, just as Sebo and Baugh had done in the summer of 1960.

The new owner's first move was to hire 55-year-old Wilbur "Weeb" Ewbank as head coach. A disciple of Paul Brown, Ewbank was an NFL veteran who led the Baltimore Colts to NFL championships in 1958 and 1959. However, when the team slumped to a 7–7 record in 1962, he was fired and replaced by a youngster named Don Shula, starting his first head coaching assignment at the age of 33.

Ewbank brought many of Brown's organizational skills to a franchise badly in need of order. In place of the honest, well-meaning cronies who had formed the Titans' staff, Ewbank imported bright young assistants like Chuck Knox and Walt Michaels. Sauer, assistant coach and general manager during the final year of the Wismer regime, was appointed director of player personnel. In order to distance themselves from the specter of the Titans, the club changed its name to the Jets and its colors from blue and gold to green and white.

For the second year, the AFL held an "equalization" draft, in which the league's two weakest organizations, New York and Oakland (which had won only one game in 1962 and traded away its first five draft choices) had the opportunity to choose players from the other six clubs in what amounted to an expansion draft for existing teams. The two bottom teams were also given first crack at any player released by another professional club.

In late June, attempting to add more bodies to the training camp roster, the Jets held a tryout camp in New York's Van Cortland Park. The new coach had found Johnny Unitas at such a camp in 1955, and perhaps hoped that lightning would strike twice. Ewbank and his staff looked over 96 invitees, including Bob Brodhead, a quarterback who had played for the Buffalo Bills against the Titans in their first regular-season game in 1960. Ewbank came away without a second Unitas, but with seven men whom he invited to camp, one of whom—defensive back Marshall Starks—made the team.

In mid-July, when the club started training camp at the Peekskill Military Academy, it was finally admitted that Shea Stadium would not be ready until at least the end of the year, sentencing the New York franchise to a fourth consecutive season in the decaying Polo Grounds. At least Wismer was spared the tortuous thought that he had come, oh so close, to the promised land. There is no way he could have survived another season in the Polo Grounds.

In Peekskill, Ewbank set to the task of assembling a team from the free agents and Titans holdovers that walked out onto the practice field. As camp wore on, many of the old Titans disappeared. Bob Mischak was traded to Oakland for guard Dan Ficca. Al Davis conveniently forgot to tell the Jets that Ficca was in the service and not scheduled to be released for six weeks. Buddy Cockrell and Nick Mumley went to Denver. Paul Hynes was cut and barricaded himself in the dormitory. Ed Kovac, Hubert Bobo, Karl Kaimer, and Fran Morelli went quietly. On the final cut, Ewbank dropped Thurlow Cooper, Lee Riley, Perry Richards, John McMullan, and Bill Shockley. In a surprising move, the Jets also cut Grosscup, who had been expected to be the starting quarterback. Neither Grosscup nor Johnny Green had been able to move the club in exhibition games, so Ewbank signed Dick Wood and named him the starter. Wood, 6'5" and 27 years old, was an Auburn graduate who taxied with the Colts for two seasons before playing briefly with Denver and San Diego in 1962. Often injured, Wood had bad knees and was virtually immobile in the pocket. He had a strong arm, however, and was familiar with Ewbank's system.

Many of the other players on the opening-day roster were also familiar with Ewbank's system, for nine were former Colts. Two, fullback Mark Smolinski and flanker Bake Turner, picked up just before the start of the season, would lead the club in rushing and receiving, respectively. Only

17 former Titans made the squad. The number was 15 after Green and Roger Ellis were cut following the first game, a 38–14 loss to the Patriots in Boston. A week later, the Jets achieved their first victory, a 24–17 win over the Oilers, a team the Titans had been unable to beat in six regular-season and three exhibition games.

Hampered by injuries and lack of depth, the Jets struggled, but so did most of the Eastern Division. In mid-October, New York was in first place with a 3–1 record, the only club above .500. On December 1, after beating Kansas City, to where Lamar Hunt's club had fled from Dallas, they were 5–5–1. This placed the Jets just a half game behind first-place Boston, which had played one additional game and stood 6–5–1.

The following week, the Jets played Buffalo, with the opportunity to gain first place. The Bills were in the midst of a mediocre season. Jack Kemp had played poorly and was alternating with rookie Daryle Lamonica. Perhaps the biggest reason for the Bills' lack of success, however, was the decline of thundering fullback Cookie Gilchrist, about whom Deane McGowan wrote in *The New York Times* on the eve of the Jet game: "Thus far this season Gilchrist has been just another Buffalo back."

The next day at War Memorial Stadium, Cookie was anything but just another back. He carried the ball 36 times for 243 yards and five touchdowns. His rushing yardage eclipsed the league record and his scoring binge tied the mark set by Billy Cannon against the Titans two years earlier. The day was a complete disaster for the New York club. They lost the game 45–14, essentially putting an end to their title hopes, and also lost their starting quarterback. On the first play from scrimmage, Wood was sacked by Tom Sestak and old Titan Sid Youngelman and suffered ligament damage in his knee. He missed the rest of the season.

Under the leadership of backup quarterback Galen Hall, New York lost its final two games to finish in last place with a 5–8–1 record. Individual standouts were Bake Turner, who had 71 receptions for 1,007 yards, and Maynard, with 38 for 790 and nine touchdowns. Mark Smolinski was the leading rusher with 561 yards. Turner, Mathis, and Grantham played in the AFL All-Star Game. Mathis scored a touchdown, but the star of the afternoon was Art Powell, who caught the winning touchdown pass with 48 seconds left in the game.

On the financial side, home attendance was only 103,550, and the Jets' loss was estimated at $1.5 million, even more than Wismer had dropped. During the month of December, however, a month so lacking in success on the playing field, the Jets scored some off-the-field triumphs of greater magnitude. They outbid the rival Giants for the services of their first-round draft choice, fullback Matt Snell from Ohio State. Snell, who played his high school ball on Long Island and had worked as a laborer during the construction of Shea Stadium, was the Giants' third pick. He was the first of a number of Jets draft choices who would enter the fold, many of whom formed the nucleus for New York's Super Bowl III champions. Werblin also outbid the Giants for Michigan State guard Dave Herman and Illinois quarterback Mike Taliaferro. By June 1964, only nine former Titans remained on the New York roster.

In January 1964, the American Football League ensured its long-term survival by signing a $36 million, five-year contract with NBC to televise its games beginning in 1965. This increased the revenue per team from $261,000 per year to $900,000 and paved the way for signing wars that eventually led to the merger with the NFL. Unlike the 1960 ABC contract, which was renewable on an annual basis, the NBC pact was fully guaranteed.

Prior to the start of the 1964 season, the Jets sold 17,500 season tickets for their debut at Shea Stadium. Joe Foss, relieved of the burden of Wismer, was delighted with Werblin. "I wish you folks could see the change in the New York picture made by the new owner, Sonny Werblin," he said in April 1964. While Wismer promoted Wismer, Werblin promoted the New York Jets. In place of the pictures of Wismer were radio commercials featuring Jet Set Janie. For the opening game at Shea, Jets' kelly green and white replaced the Mets' blue and orange. The ticket takers, ushers, and grounds crew were suitably attired in the Jets' colors and Jets souvenirs were everywhere. The Jetliners, a 110-piece band, entertained the fans.

Despite the improved finances, Werblin was troubled by the lack of a charismatic star. Quarterback was the glamour position in pro football, but the Jets' Dick Wood was steady, not exciting. "This is show business," Werblin said. "Personalities mean everything." He tried to obtain Abner Haynes from Kansas City, but was unsuccessful.

On September 12, 1964, the Jets defeated Denver 30–6 in their first game in Shea Stadium, before 52,663 fans. The attendance broke the AFL record by almost 20,000. "It was the greatest experience of my life," said Grantham. "I just wish Harry Wismer had been there to see it. Shea was his dream. I still take my hat off to Wismer. Without Harry having the guts, or chutzpah, nobody would have gotten it done in New York. He gambled everything he had. H.L. Hunt said after [Lamar's] one million dollar loss that at that pace he could only last a hundred and fifty years. Harry couldn't."

The old Polo Grounds at one time seemed as if it might have more lives than the proverbial cat. Left for dead by the Giants in 1957, it sprung back to life when the Titans were born in 1960. Its death sentence was commuted in 1962, then again in 1963 when the new stadium in Flushing was not ready. Finally, throughout the spring and summer of 1964, a 30-man demolition crew hacked away at the remains of the grand old park. Seats were sold to souvenir hunters for $3 each and finally the scoreboard clock, forever stuck at 10:24, came tumbling down. Flagpoles were sold for $50 each, and many old Giants fans rummaged through the debris for a chunk of turf, or a brick. Dick Sisler, former Phillies first baseman, asked for a piece of a right-field seat. When all the memorabilia had been removed, apartment buildings were erected on the site.

The first season at Shea brought no miracles, as the Jets again finished 5–8–1, good for third place in the Eastern Division. While the club was 5–1–1 at home, New York lost all seven road games. Matt Snell gained 948 yards rushing and was named rookie of the year. The Jets led the AFL in attendance. The following season brought a third consecutive 5–8–1 mark, but also witnessed the appearance of quarterback Joe Namath, who, with his reported $400,000 contract, arrived from Alabama and became the marquee star needed to compete in New York. He was the Ernie Davis that Wismer had never gotten.

The Namath years and the dramatic Super Bowl III upset victory over the Colts belong to another story. Yet without Al Dorow of the Titans, there would have been no Joe Namath of the Jets. Without Sammy Baugh, Bob Mischak, Dewey Bohling, Roger Ellis, and the hundred others who gathered in Durham, New Hampshire, in July 1960, that magical afternoon in Miami would never have taken place. If only a stocky, middle-aged man could have rushed up to Namath as he left the field that day and shouted "Congratulations!"

INDEX

ABC 26-29, 125, 134, 146, 168, 191, 213, 284-286, 326

Adams, Kenneth "Bud" 7-10, 12, 13, 15-18, 21, 28, 77, 102, 124, 137, 139, 204-208, 225, 285, 286

Agajanian, Ben 164, 182

All-America Football Conference 12, 15-17, 26, 28, 106, 119, 206, 217, 224, 235

Allard, Don 55, 56, 196, 197, 303

Allen, Maury 171, 253, 286

Alworth, Lance 161, 261, 264, 265, 282

Ames, Dave 179, 201

Atkins, Billy 122, 145, 239, 262, 274, 276, 294

Atlantic Coast League 65, 303, 317

Baldwin, Jim 94, 95

Baltimore Colts 4, 12, 29, 52, 57, 69, 84, 90, 95, 111, 135, 153, 235, 243, 305, 313, 323, 324, 327

Barber, Steve 212

Baugh, Sammy 1, 2, 6, 14, 32, 36-50, 58, 59, 62, 66-68, 70, 81, 84, 89, 90, 92-94, 96, 97, 99-103, 108, 109, 111, 113, 114, 116, 117, 120, 121, 126-129, 131, 132, 134, 140, 142, 146, 150-152, 154, 156-161, 163, 165, 170, 178, 184-186, 188, 191-193, 195-197, 202, 209, 212, 218-221, 228-234, 237, 238, 254, 270, 271, 289, 303, 304, 323, 327

Bell, Bert 2, 17, 18, 21, 22, 51, 53, 81, 103, 135, 137, 319

Bell, Eddie 101, 107, 108, 111, 114, 148, 186, 258, 291, 304

Benzedrine ("bennies") 143, 144, 219, 297

Blanda, George 47, 74, 94, 135, 136, 138-140, 150, 151, 161, 166, 205, 207, 210, 214, 218, 221, 254, 277, 301-303, 310

Bobo, Hubert 48, 179-181, 212, 279, 294, 324

Bohling, Dewey 30, 40, 43-45, 79-81, 90, 100, 101, 109, 113, 114, 117, 134, 150, 151, 163, 165, 190, 191, 194, 200, 201, 327

Bookman, John 209, 216, 217

Boston Patriots 16, 24, 75, 90, 112, 113, 122-127, 129, 156-158, 167, 168, 183, 184, 187, 188, 196-198, 204, 205, 208, 209, 213, 214, 217, 218, 234, 236, 237, 255, 275, 276, 280, 286, 295-297, 301, 306, 325

Breen, John 20, 135

Brown, Jim 76, 77, 225

Brown, Paul 22, 26, 41, 54, 55, 70, 92, 97, 106, 206, 209, 235, 236, 323

Brown, Willie 73

Bruney, Fred 198, 296

Buffalo Bills 15, 27, 36, 54, 62, 69, 71, 73, 74, 80, 96, 103, 110, 117, 121-123, 145, 150, 167, 177, 188-192, 204, 208, 213-215, 218, 226, 237, 239, 240, 267-269, 270, 276, 278, 280, 282, 286, 297-301, 324, 325

Burford, Chris 160, 279, 292

Burton, Leon 130, 133, 154, 155, 164, 187, 310

Canadian Football League 54-57, 65, 73, 101, 124, 139, 140, 199, 224

Cannon, Billy 43, 44, 74, 102, 131, 136-141, 150, 167, 189, 200, 206, 207, 214, 215, 218, 219, 221, 240, 261, 288, 302, 303, 325

Cappelletti, Gino 28, 52, 68, 91, 128, 188, 189, 201, 209, 237, 255

CBS 9, 26, 28, 29, 191, 311

Chicago Bears 1, 9, 17, 22, 26, 39, 46, 130, 131, 135, 136, 176, 186, 207, 211, 227, 229, 230, 242, 271, 317

Chicago Cardinals 9, 10, 16, 40, 94, 121, 207, 271

Christy, Dick 148, 156, 183, 184, 188, 194, 202, 203, 207, 209, 217, 219, 221, 262, 263,

268, 273, 276, 277, 282, 283, 292-294, 304

Clemente, Dick 231, 243

Cleveland Browns 26, 36, 54, 55, 62, 69, 84, 86, 88, 92, 97, 116, 152, 153, 179, 186, 206, 217, 226, 227, 235, 291, 299

Clifford, Clark 23, 33, 285

Cockrell, Buddy 41, 76, 114-116, 200, 279, 294, 304, 324

Colclough, Jim 126, 156, 296, 297

Conerly, Charley 53, 71, 148, 149, 234, 242, 243

Cooke, Ed 111, 186, 216, 283

Cooper, Thurlow 6, 43, 46, 54-56, 59, 61, 66, 67, 80, 86, 87, 93, 101, 114, 126, 130, 157-159, 164, 219, 232, 267, 268, 291, 305, 324

Copeland, Jackie 192, 232

Crow, Wayne 209, 214

Daffer, Ted 46, 230, 271

Dallas Cowboys 24, 32, 76, 205, 258

Dallas Texans 3, 9, 17-19, 71, 75, 91, 94, 95, 97, 100, 106, 108, 111, 131-134, 141, 143, 159-161, 167, 177, 187, 202, 204, 216-219, 226, 228, 278-281, 286, 288, 291, 292, 325

Davidson, Cotton 41, 68, 72, 85, 91, 108, 132, 133, 159, 160, 199, 200, 217, 284, 291

Davis, Al 25, 41, 42, 62, 63, 79, 97, 307, 309, 314, 324

Davis, Ernie 225-228, 327

Dawson, Len 75, 279, 291, 292

Dell Isola, John 46, 58, 59, 66, 84, 116, 231, 272, 317

Denver Broncos 15, 20, 24, 27, 31, 48, 52, 70, 73, 74, 101, 102, 120, 124, 125, 129-132, 162, 167, 184, 188, 192-194, 204, 207-209, 212, 215, 217, 218, 226, 237, 240, 245, 255, 269, 270, 273, 274, 292-294, 308, 312, 324, 326

Dewveall, Willard 137, 207

Dickinson, Bo 273, 293

Ditka, Mike 158

Donahoo, Roger 91, 92, 99, 114, 131, 159, 160, 178, 305

Dorow, Al 30, 32, 45, 51, 57, 70, 71, 74, 76, 93,

95, 96, 99, 101, 109, 110, 111, 115, 121-123, 130, 131, 133, 140, 145, 146, 148, 150-152, 154-156, 158-160, 162-165, 176-178, 186-195, 197, 198, 201, 207-209, 213-217, 220, 221, 233, 234, 237-240, 245, 246, 268, 278, 282, 289, 298, 299, 305, 327

Dubenion, Elbert "Golden Wheels" 189, 268

Durham, New Hampshire 67, 88-90, 94, 96, 97, 100, 111, 153, 186, 247, 257, 302, 327

Eiler, John 247, 248

Eisenhower, Dwight D. 32, 33, 242

Ellis, Roger 6, 42, 43, 46, 59, 64, 66, 67, 79, 80, 84, 90, 98, 99, 101, 110, 118, 130, 158, 161, 170, 191, 198, 230, 236, 265, 294, 305, 306, 325, 327

Emery, Ted 289, 290

Erdelatz, Eddie 155, 205

Ewbank, Weeb 41, 52, 61, 203, 235, 259, 306, 309, 311, 312, 323, 324

Faison, Earl 199, 200, 221, 282

Faulkner, Jack 41, 73, 97, 272, 293

Felt, Dick 62-64, 67, 74, 92, 114, 139, 156, 164, 178-180, 191, 193, 201, 216, 217, 221, 234, 306

Fields, Jerry 57, 161, 212, 275, 278, 279

Filchock, Frank 40, 41, 129, 130, 193, 272

Flowers, Charlie 23, 74, 137, 260-262, 274

Fontes, Wayne 77, 176, 263, 264, 274, 301

Foss, Joe 20-24, 27, 29, 128, 129, 137, 138, 159, 166-169, 171, 187, 191, 220, 222-225, 228, 261, 286-290, 317, 320-322, 326

Fowler, Bobby 77, 294

Furey, Jim 186, 212

Gabriel, Roman 226

Gallo, Bill 244

Garner, Bob 90, 262, 284

Gifford, Frank 53, 57, 148, 149, 183

Gillman, Sid 53, 70, 90, 97, 106, 182, 196, 200, 205, 221, 264, 283, 298, 299, 311

Glenn, Howard 141-145, 178, 214

Glick, Fred 207, 302

Gogolak, Pete 69, 70

Goodman, Murray 2, 31, 245, 290

Gowdy, Curt 213

Graham, Otto 36, 166, 229, 235

Grange, Red 4, 16

Grant, Jim "Mudcat" 212

Grantham, Larry 4, 6, 41, 52, 57, 60, 77, 82,
   101, 111, 114, 116, 117, 152, 155, 162, 164, 185,
   186, 191, 194, 198, 201, 202, 210, 212, 213,
   216, 217, 221, 230, 262, 266-268, 276, 279,
   301, 306, 325, 327

Gray, Moses 176, 182

Green Bay Packers 54, 58, 62, 69, 72, 211,
   221, 227

Green, Johnny 121, 239, 245, 246, 277-279,
   282-284, 291-295, 298, 302, 307, 324, 325

Gregory, Jack 94, 247, 248

Grey Cup 235

Grier, Rosey 66, 182

Griffing, Dean 20, 124, 129

Groman, Bill 138, 139, 150, 214, 215

Grosscup, Lee 5, 33, 53, 71, 75, 77, 109, 144,
   180, 230, 232, 241-246, 256, 257, 259, 260,
   262, 263, 265-270, 272-278, 294, 295, 298,
   301, 302, 307, 308, 324

Groza, Lou 55, 69, 293

Guesman, Dick 81, 101, 111, 157, 214, 218,
   254, 273, 281, 282, 308

Guglielmi, Ralph 196, 243

Halas, George 9, 16-18, 22, 26, 36, 135, 136,
   317

Hardin-Simmons 36, 40, 43-45, 62, 94, 101,
   103, 113, 115, 116, 138, 229, 232, 270, 271,
   318

Hart, Pete 43, 44, 62, 99, 109, 113, 114, 126,
   138, 143, 308

Haynes, Abner 131-134, 160, 217, 218, 278,
   279, 281, 291, 292, 326

Heinrich, Don 53, 71, 262, 284

Heisman Trophy 43, 102, 136-138, 181, 189,
   195, 206, 211, 225-227, 240

Hennigan, Charley 75, 136, 138-140, 151, 161,
   207, 215

Herring, George 131, 194

Hess, Leon 61, 174, 319, 322

Hilton, Barron 15, 16, 18, 21, 24, 25, 28, 98,
   167, 288

Hirsch, Elroy "Crazylegs" 78

Holovak, Mike 73, 75, 76, 90, 91, 125-127,
   184, 197, 209, 235-237, 255, 296

Holub, E.J. 217, 278, 279

Hornung, Paul 69, 77, 211, 212

Houston Oilers 6, 20, 43, 48, 49, 74, 77, 102,
   106, 108, 134-143, 149, 150, 156, 161, 162,
   164, 166, 167, 184, 193, 197, 204-206, 210,
   213-215, 218, 219, 221, 225, 254, 255, 264,
   276, 277, 301-303, 310

Huarte, John 166

Hudock, Mike 114, 115, 127, 180, 194, 198,
   200, 219, 256, 309

Huff, Sam 148, 242

Hunt, Lamar 7-10, 12-24, 28, 54, 74, 100,
   124, 131, 133, 137, 168, 177, 217, 219, 225, 285,
   314, 319, 325, 327

Hynes, Paul 5, 132, 201-203, 219, 309, 324

Izo, George 20, 94

Jacobs, Proverb 79, 106, 108, 182, 183,
   215, 267, 309, 310

Jamieson, Dick 41, 42, 72, 75, 94, 95, 99-101,
   110, 111, 114, 121, 122, 140, 150-152, 162,
   164, 185, 187, 192-194, 310

Jamison, Al 215, 218

Johnson, Curley 3, 4, 42, 48, 94, 187, 198,
   202, 209, 263, 276, 296

Jones, Deacon 75

Jones, Jerry 32

Jones, K.C. 72, 73

Julian, Fred 41, 67, 75, 96, 99, 114, 141, 150,
   151, 160, 178, 179, 310

Kaimer, Karl 33, 77, 87, 229, 238, 266, 281,
   301, 310, 311, 324

Katcavage, Jim 148, 182

Kemp, Jack 52-54, 74, 98, 99, 121, 164, 200, 201, 210, 254, 264, 265, 282, 298-300, 325

Kennedy, John F. 14, 29, 32, 143

Klotz, Jack 48, 49, 69, 77, 86, 108, 114, 115, 148, 183, 257-260, 264, 265, 270, 311

Kroll, Alex 5, 62, 63, 75, 78, 179, 181, 232, 248-254, 256, 257, 262, 265-267, 270, 297, 301, 302, 311, 312

Kunz, Cal 272, 274

Ladd, Ernie 199, 200, 265, 283

Lamberti, Pat 188, 201

Landry, Tom 205

Layne, Bobby 53, 140, 184, 291

Leahy, Frank 15, 16, 19, 205, 229, 287

Lee, Jacky 136, 205-207, 221

Leininger, Buddy 181, 232

Lemm, Wally 207, 210, 214, 221

Lincoln, Keith 200, 261, 264, 265, 282

Lipscomb, Gene "Big Daddy" 199

Lombardi, Vince 42, 58, 85, 115, 211, 232

Look, Dean 239-241, 245, 246, 264, 270, 273-275, 294, 296, 298, 312

Los Angeles (San Diego) Chargers 15, 19, 23-25, 53, 54, 74, 90, 95, 97-99, 101, 106, 107, 124, 146, 147, 156, 157, 163-165, 167, 171, 179, 182, 193, 196, 199-201, 204, 205, 210, 213, 215, 217, 221, 225, 260, 261, 263-266, 269, 270, 282, 283, 285, 287, 288, 298, 299, 307, 311, 313

Los Angeles Rams 22, 26, 72, 78, 102, 105, 136, 137, 193, 240, 243, 249, 258, 271, 318

Louisiana State 37, 43, 44, 102, 131, 136, 137, 309, 323

Lowe, Paul 98, 156, 163, 200, 201, 213, 264, 282

Lucas, Richie 121, 123, 152, 189, 190

Mackey, John 158, 323

Mantle, Mickey 76, 171, 215

Mara, John 23 146, 147

Mara, Wellington 22, 182, 183, 261

Maris, Roger 76, 171, 215

Marques, Bob 34, 58, 59, 92, 98, 101, 114, 125-127, 140, 142, 143, 186, 313

Marshall, George Preston 10, 14, 16, 17, 38, 56, 195, 196, 226

Martin, Blanche 43, 81, 106-108, 111, 112, 143, 164, 313

Mathis, Bill 4, 6, 52, 59-61, 74, 77, 102, 114, 127, 160, 184, 187, 191, 199, 207, 209, 214-217, 221, 260, 275-277, 284, 293, 294, 304, 313, 325

Maynard, Don 6, 46, 57-61, 67, 74, 77, 82, 96, 99, 102, 108, 109, 113, 114, 116, 120, 122, 133, 141, 142, 150, 151, 154, 158-161, 164, 173, 178, 182, 183, 188, 189, 191, 194, 198, 203, 207-209, 213, 215, 216, 241, 248, 255, 257, 260, 263, 266-268, 273, 275, 276, 283-285, 291, 293, 313, 314, 325

Mayor's Trophy Game 159, 215, 216, 222

McCabe, Richie 190, 191, 215

McCormick, John 244, 245

McDaniel, Edward "Wahoo" 252, 253, 293, 308

McFadin, Bud 193, 253, 274, 293

McHugh, Larry 3, 85, 253, 314

McMullan, John 46, 114, 115, 134, 142, 217, 314, 324

Michigan State 13, 35, 36, 43, 57, 64, 71, 92, 95, 112, 152, 176, 186, 234, 237, 240, 273, 296, 299, 305, 326

Mingo, Gene 125, 130, 273, 274, 293, 294

Minnesota Vikings 18, 19, 53, 223, 244, 245, 316

Mischak, Bob 5, 46, 77, 82, 84-86, 88, 96, 114, 115, 141, 164, 165, 199, 221, 267, 268, 276, 277, 283, 297, 314, 315, 324, 327

Morelli, Fran 183, 294, 324

Motley, Marion 106

Mumley, Nick 77, 101, 111, 114, 122, 131, 162, 267, 315, 324

Murchison, Clint Jr. 22, 205

Namath, Joe 38, 249, 309, 327

NBC 9, 13, 26, 134, 191, 196, 307, 326

NCAA 29, 70, 247

Nery, Ron 199, 265, 270, 307

New York Daily News 88, 89, 95, 168, 242,
    244, 290

New York (football) Giants 6, 12, 22, 23, 28,
    36, 39, 46, 53, 55, 57-59, 66, 71, 76, 78, 81,
    82, 84, 85, 94, 104, 115, 117-119, 120, 123,
    141, 146-149, 151, 181-183, 201, 205, 212,
    221, 225, 234, 241-245, 257, 260-263, 282,
    284, 288, 291, 293, 326

New York Herald Tribune 53, 86, 87, 151,
    170, 194, 199, 260, 284

New York Mets 171-175, 269, 272, 286, 287,
    326

New York Post 74, 131, 157, 171, 211, 284, 286

New York Times 22, 35, 39, 77, 122, 132,
    147-149, 161, 167, 168, 170, 187, 220, 254,
    275, 282, 284, 289, 325

Newsday 151, 231, 243, 287, 294

Nicholas, Dr. James 142, 143, 173, 180, 192,
    273, 277, 278, 294

Nitschke, Ray 211

Noll, Chuck 64, 97, 200

Notre Dame 13, 15, 16, 18, 20, 35, 36, 92,
    94, 95, 97, 115, 205, 211, 287

O'Brien, Terry 94, 97

O'Malley, Walter 11, 171

Oakland Raiders 24, 25, 73, 79, 85, 91, 97, 99,
    151, 154, 155, 163, 167-169, 183, 204, 205,
    208, 209, 212, 214, 217, 218, 226, 241, 245,
    257, 260, 262, 263, 268, 269, 276, 278, 283-
    285, 288, 290, 303, 307, 309, 314, 316, 323,
    324

Ohio State 11, 176, 179, 195, 212, 232, 326

Olsen, Merlin 75, 226

Pagliei, Joe 33, 48, 49, 79, 94, 124, 132, 133,
    142, 145, 146, 148, 163, 186, 315

Paige, Satchel 186

Parilli, Babe 94, 155, 183, 187, 197, 237, 296,
    303

Paterno, Joe 152, 153

Paulson, Dainard 5, 32, 73, 177-179, 186, 189,
    201, 263, 274, 283, 316

Penn State 92, 93, 152, 153, 189, 248, 249

Philadelphia Eagles 18, 26, 28, 74, 86, 94, 95,
    101, 103-105, 113, 126, 128, 132, 166, 176,
    182, 196, 229, 235, 310, 315

Pittsburgh Steelers 18, 51, 53, 113, 139, 140,
    179, 184, 199, 239, 258, 291

Polo Grounds 6, 31, 39, 47, 67, 93, 111, 117-
    120, 122, 123, 125, 145-147, 149, 154, 157,
    159, 171, 173-175, 185, 192, 194, 197, 199,
    201, 218, 225, 227, 233, 259, 267, 272, 273,
    275, 282, 283, 285, 288, 290, 298, 300-302,
    324, 327

Pop Warner 213

Powell, Art 6, 33, 74, 77-79, 92, 103-105, 107-
    111, 113, 114, 121, 129, 133, 140, 150, 151, 155,
    156, 158, 160-164, 183, 188, 191, 194, 198,
    203, 208-210, 213, 232, 262, 263, 265, 268,
    272, 275, 276, 283, 284, 294, 297, 298, 316,
    321, 325

Powell, Charley 155

Pyle, Charles C. 16

Ramsey, Buster 41, 121, 122, 177, 189-192, 215,
    290, 300

Rechichar, Bert 69, 179, 201

Reifsnyder, Bob 57, 98, 111, 114, 181, 182, 211,
    316

Renn, Bob 193, 194, 209, 216

Richards, George 13, 14

Richards, Perry 108, 178, 268, 274, 292, 297,
    316, 324

Rickey, Branch 10, 11

Riley, Lee 198, 201, 292, 294, 324

Roach, Jim 147, 148

Robinson, Jackie 10, 65, 106

Robinson, Johnny 131, 133, 159

Robustelli, Andy 46, 182

Rosenthal, Harold 104, 120, 194

Ross, Dave 111, 133, 145, 183

Rote, Kyle 55, 57, 58, 71

Rozelle, Pete 22, 28, 29, 112, 137, 138, 149,

166, 169, 176, 223-225

Rutgers 36, 62, 78, 249-253, 311, 312

Ryan, Joe 62, 80, 82, 85, 101, 111, 140, 141, 317

Rychlec, Tom 73, 80, 96, 117

Rymkus, Lou 102, 139, 204-207, 210

Saban, Lou 68, 196, 197, 205, 208, 209, 237, 240, 274, 300

Saidock, Tom 114, 155, 156, 198, 215, 216, 218, 219

San Francisco 49ers 24, 52, 98, 243

Sapienza, Rick 101, 120, 126-132, 296, 317

Saskatchewan Roughriders 56, 116, 245, 306, 307

Sauer, George 3, 231, 232, 245, 246, 274, 278, 293, 296, 306, 323

Scrabis, Bob 79, 93, 94, 101, 102, 152-154, 156, 180, 190, 193, 196-198, 213, 239, 245, 282, 295, 298, 302, 311, 317

Sebo, Steve 35, 36, 85, 89, 90, 99, 111, 112, 129, 142, 151, 157, 175, 177, 185, 186, 192, 221, 226, 231, 258, 323

Shaw, George 53, 242-244, 293

Shea Stadium 33, 49, 174, 302, 321, 324, 326, 327

Shea, William Alfred 11, 12, 15, 27, 172

Sherman, Allie 58, 59, 182, 183, 241, 243, 244, 262

Shockley, Bill 69, 98, 107, 108, 122, 133, 134, 140, 150, 154, 155, 164, 256, 262, 273, 279, 293, 297, 300, 302, 324

Skogland, H.P. 16, 19, 21, 222, 223

Soar, Hank 82, 93

Soda, Chet 25, 169

Songin, Ed "Butch" 66, 126, 156, 197, 198, 234-237, 239, 245, 246, 256, 260, 262, 263, 269, 273-278, 281, 282, 295, 298, 306

Southern Methodist University 7, 8, 37, 168

Speedie, Mac 139, 207

Spikes, Jack 131, 159

Sports Illustrated 31, 82, 124, 239, 241, 269, 286, 290, 308

Sprinkle, Ed 180, 271, 275, 317

St. Louis Cardinals 221, 284, 310, 313

Steber, John 45, 46, 49, 58

Steinbrenner, George 11, 32

Stengel, Casey 148

Stephens, Harold "Hayseed" 40, 41, 44, 59, 71, 118, 161, 270, 275-277, 279, 281, 282, 298, 318

Stram, Hank 3, 291

Stroudsburg 1-3, 5, 85, 94, 230, 231, 233, 234, 239, 240, 247, 248, 252, 254, 283, 288, 303

Strugar, George 82, 291, 294, 318

Sugar Bowl 37, 136-138, 261

Susskind, Arthur Jr. 157, 289, 290

Tackmann, Bill 175, 231

Tarkenton, Fran 244, 270

Taylor, Hugh "Bones" 45, 93, 202, 231, 232, 238, 304, 310, 315

Taylor, Lionel 130, 131, 194, 273, 293

Texas Christian University 37, 38, 42, 62, 102, 131

Texas, University of 37, 77, 112, 137, 168, 193

T-formation 38, 40, 151, 275

Thanksgiving 148, 157-159, 171, 192, 215, 222, 290, 292

Tharp, Corky 114, 157, 179

Thorpe, Jim 118

Tiller, Jim 4, 5, 254, 270, 277, 283, 294, 319

Tittle, Y.A. 53, 77, 95, 147, 234, 235, 243, 283

Todd, Dick 45, 46

Tolar, Charley 139-141, 150

Torczon, LaVerne 54, 208, 274, 318

Toronto Argonauts 95, 245, 299, 319

Tripucka, Frank 31, 41, 55, 56, 70, 72-74, 91, 94, 124, 125, 129-131, 162, 194, 208, 272, 273, 293

Tuckner, Howard 22, 42, 122, 149, 187, 188, 194, 195, 201, 242

Turner, Clyde "Bulldog" 1, 2, 4, 5, 221, 228-234, 238, 239, 241, 245, 248, 254-257, 260, 263-265, 267, 271, 273, 274, 276, 277, 281-284, 291, 295, 298, 301, 302, 317

Twombly, Wells 20, 206, 268

Unitas, Johnny 65, 77, 92, 95, 146, 153, 243, 289, 324

United Football League 5, 65, 270, 271

Valley, Wayne 25, 169, 321

Van Brocklin, Norm 70, 94, 182, 244

Vermeil, Dick 103

Wagner, Robert 11, 147, 159, 172, 173

Walsh, Bill 103, 310

Washington Redskins 10, 12, 13, 17, 38, 40, 45, 46, 56, 95, 195, 196, 205, 226, 229, 242

Watters, Bob 281, 294

Werblin, Sonny 61, 166, 319, 322, 323, 326

West, Mel 202, 209, 218, 270, 319

White, Gordon 147, 148, 170, 283, 290, 319

Wilkinson, Bud 44, 115

Wilson, Ralph 15, 18, 215, 225, 226, 240, 286, 300

Winter, Max 16, 18, 19

Wismer, Harry 1-6, 8, 12-16, 18-21, 23, 26, 27, 29-37, 45-50, 60, 61, 64, 80, 95, 97, 99, 111-113, 119-121, 123, 125, 128, 129, 132, 142, 146-150, 152, 154, 157, 159, 161-171, 173, 175, 191-193, 195-197, 202, 212, 213, 215, 216, 220-234, 237, 239-241, 243, 245, 247, 253, 255, 263, 264, 266, 267, 270, 273-279, 281-283, 285-292, 294, 295, 297, 298, 300, 319-324, 326, 327

Wolfner, Walter 9, 10

Woodward, Milt 224, 285, 286, 291

Wren, Junior 179, 186, 201

Yankee Stadium 118, 119, 148, 149, 186, 275, 283, 284

Yewcic, Tom 198, 237, 255, 296, 297

Young, Dick 88, 94, 95, 122, 150, 171, 173, 187, 242, 288, 289

Youngelman, Sid 30, 86-88, 92, 96, 114, 156, 165, 178, 198, 201, 215, 218, 219, 239, 325

Zeman, Bob 221, 274